IN THE "COUNTRY LIFE" SERIES OF MILITARY HISTORIES

THE
42nd (East Lancashire) DIVISION
1914–1918

MAJOR-GENERAL SIR WM. DOUGLAS, K.C.M.G., C.B., D.S.O.

By permission of Lyddell Sawyer.

The
42ⁿᵈ (East Lancashire) Division
1914–1918

BY
FREDERICK P. GIBBON
Author of "The Lawrences of the Punjab"

To the

Officers, Warrant Officers, Non-Commissioned Officers, and Men

of the

42nd (East Lancashire) Division

As their late Commander, I dedicate this history of their achievements, conspicuous even in days of great deeds, in the hope that the record of their unchanging spirit of courage, loyalty, and comradeship may give gratification to survivors and solace to relatives of the fallen.

A. Solly-Flood.

Major General.

11th November, 1920.

MAJOR-GENERAL A. SOLLY-FLOOD, C.B., C.M.G., D.S.O.

By permission of Keturah Collings.

FOREWORD

THE 42nd (East Lancashire) Division was only a comparatively short time under my command, but during that period officers, N.C.O.s and men showed themselves to be possessed of a magnificent fighting spirit.

The 42nd Division came to France at a time of crisis, and shared in the glory of breaking the most desperate and most dangerous German offensive made since the early days of the war. In my Despatches I have drawn attention to some of the outstanding actions of the Division. I am glad now to express to all ranks my personal gratitude for their splendid service.

D. Haig.

FIELD-MARSHAL.

G.H.Q. The Forces in Great Britain,
　Horse Guards,
　　London, S.W.1.
　　　14*th July,* 1919.

PREFACE

"Sir WILLIAM DOUGLAS asks me 'to write a few lines' to be embodied in the preface to a history of the 42nd Division.

"In the regions of time and space the Dardanelles enterprise forms only a trifling part of the record of this famous Division; but, in the sphere of the imagination, that part will be reckoned by Lancastrians yet unborn as the most precious heirloom bequeathed to them by the generation who fought the great war.

"Why? I will give the reasons in the words of a gallant young Australian killed shortly after he wrote me as follows from the front in France: 'I often compare the two situations: out here and on those wild romantic shores of the Ægean; I compare them and I find that the Peninsula war stands quite alone and apart, an ineffaceable memory.'

"Bearing in mind that I am limited to a few lines I propose to think out nothing new, but to repeat now what was jotted down about a sample of the 42nd Division at the time (the 4th June, 1915), in my post of command, shared that day with two enormous tarantulas—

"On the right the French rushed the 'Haricot'—so long a thorn in their flesh; next to them the Anson lads stormed another big Turkish redoubt in a slap-dash style reminding me of the best work of the old Regular Army; but the boldest and most brilliant exploit of the lot was the charge made by the Manchester Brigade in the centre who wrested two lines of trenches from the Turks; and then, carrying right on to the lower slopes of Achi Baba, had *nothing* between them and its summit but the clear, unentrenched hillside. They lay there—the line of our brave lads, plainly visible to a pair of good glasses—there they actually lay! We wanted, so it seemed, but a reserve to advance in their support and carry them right up to the top. We said—and yet could hardly believe our own words—'We are through!'

"Alas, too previous that remark. Everything began to go wrong. First the French were shelled and bombed out of the 'Haricot'; next the right of the Naval Division became uncovered and they had to give way, losing many times more men in the yielding than in the capture of their ground. Then came the turn of the Manchesters, left in the lurch, with their right flank hanging in the air. By all the laws of war they ought to have tumbled back anyhow, but by the laws of the Manchesters they hung on and declared they could do so for ever. . . .

GENERAL,
" LIEUTENANT OF THE TOWER OF LONDON."

1st *September,* 1919.

THE foregoing words were written by the Commander-in-Chief under whom the 42nd (East Lancashire) Division went into action for the first time of its existence. It is nearly a year now since Sir Ian Hamilton wrote them; this will give the reader some idea of the gigantic task those who have collected the material for, and the writer of, this book have had.

The work is an attempt to record the doings and follow the fortunes of the 42nd (East Lancashire) Division in the Great War, but nothing that can be written can adequately disclose the noble manner in which these lads preserved throughout that dogged courage and insistent resolution from which it was impossible, for those who were present, to withhold their admiration. My own four years' experience of them has left me with the deepest feelings of pride and affection. From first to last they proved themselves to be gallant, loyal and self-sacrificing soldiers, warm-hearted, responsive and lovable men.

The thanks of the Committee responsible for the publication of this book are due to Captain E. R. Streat and Mr. George Bigwood, who collected much of the data, but more especially to Mr. F. P. Gibbon, who so kindly consented to write the History. The labour of collecting information from War Diaries and comparing the various accounts which so many old members of the Division have been kind enough to send him, has been very great, and we owe Mr. Gibbon a debt of deep gratitude.

7th *August,* 1920.

THE Committee and the Author wish to record their warm appreciation of the assistance given in the compiling of this History by many Officers, Non-commissioned Officers and Men of the Division.

As the final proofs of the book were being passed, there came the sad news of the death of the first Divisional Commander, Major-General Sir William Douglas, K.C.M.G., C.B., D.S.O., at Cultz, near Aberdeen, on November 2nd, 1920. He had come to be regarded as the Father of the Division. It was under him that it earned the distinction of being the first Territorial Division to leave these shores, and under him it received its baptism of fire. Even when he had passed from command—both during the war and after hostilities had ceased—his interest in the welfare of all ranks remained unabated, and the affection he felt towards them was warmly reciprocated.

In expressing their deep sorrow and their sympathy with Lady Douglas, the Committee feel that they may speak for all ranks and all services of the Division.

CONTENTS

CHAP.		PAGE
I.	LANCASHIRE AND EGYPT (AUGUST 1914–MAY 1915)	1
II.	GALLIPOLI (MAY 1915)	19
III.	GALLIPOLI (JUNE 1915–JANUARY 1916)	34
IV.	THE SUEZ CANAL AND SINAI (JANUARY 1916–MARCH 1917)	63
V.	FRANCE (MARCH–AUGUST 1917)	86
VI.	YPRES (SEPTEMBER 1917)	97
VII.	NIEUPORT (OCTOBER–NOVEMBER 1917)	106
VIII.	LA BASSÉE (DECEMBER 1917–MARCH 1918)	114
IX.	OPENING OF THE GERMAN OFFENSIVE (MARCH 21–APRIL 8, 1918)	128
X.	ENTR'ACTE (APRIL 9–AUGUST 20, 1918)	142
XI.	THE BEGINNING OF THE END (AUGUST 21–SEPTEMBER 6, 1918)	155
XII.	THROUGH THE HINDENBURG LINE (SEPTEMBER 7–30, 1918)	171
XIII.	ACROSS THE RIVER SELLE (OCTOBER 9–23, 1918)	179
XIV.	FORÊT DE MORMAL AND HAUTMONT (NOVEMBER 3–11, 1918)	191
	ROLL OF HONOUR	200
	HONOURS AND AWARDS	232
	HEADQUARTERS STAFF AND OFFICERS COMMANDING UNITS	242

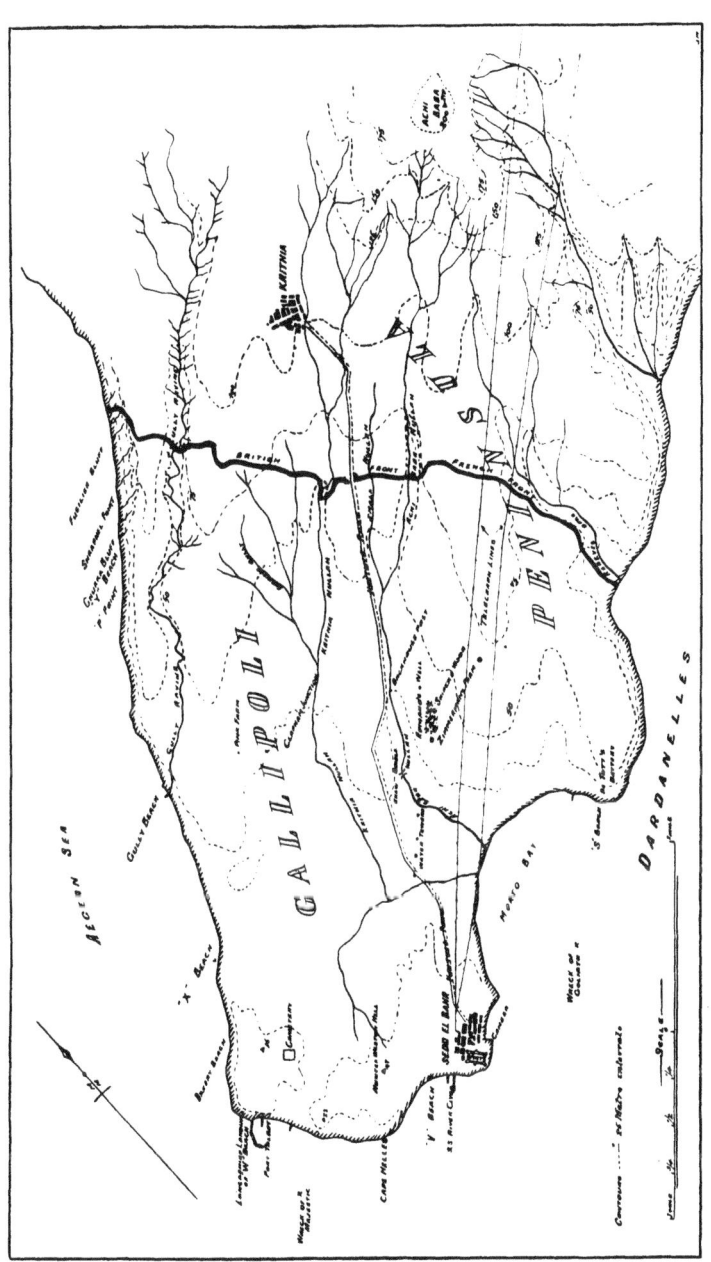

Lc.-Corp. J. Mort, R.E. (T.)

MOVEMENTS FROM OUTBREAK OF WAR UNTIL ARMISTICE

1914–1915		
Sept.–May		British Army of Occupation in Egypt, and on Suez Canal Defences.
1915–1916		
May–Jan.	M.E.F.	At Cape Helles, Gallipoli Peninsula.
1916–1917	E.E.F.	Suez Canal Defences and Sinai Peninsula.
Jan.–Feb.		Advance through Romani to El Arish.
1917		
Feb. and March	B.E.F.	Arrived at Marseilles and proceeded to neighbourhood of Abbéville.
May		In the line at Epéhy and Lempire.
June		,, ,, Havrincourt Wood and Trescault.
Aug. and Sept.		,, ,, Ypres.
Sept.		,, ,, Coast Sector, Nieuport Bains.
Oct., Nov.		,, ,, Nieuport and St. Georges.
Nov., Dec., Jan., Feb., 1918	}	,, ,, Opposite La Bassée.
1918		
Mar., April		,, ,, Ervillers, Bucquoy.
May, June, July		,, ,, Bucquoy, Gommecourt, Hebuterne.
Aug.		Advanced through Miraumont, Riencourt, Villers au Flos.
Sept.		,, ,, Havrincourt Wood to Welsh Ridge.
Oct.		,, ,, Esnes, Beauvois, across R. Selle.
Nov.		,, ,, Le Quesnoy, Mormal Forest to Hautmont.
Nov. 11		Stood fast on line of Maubeuge–Avesnes Road.

ILLUSTRATIONS

Facing page

MAJOR-GENERAL SIR WM. DOUGLAS, K.C.M.G., C.B., D.S.O. *Frontispiece*	
MAJOR-GENERAL A. SOLLY-FLOOD, C.B., C.M.G., D.S.O.	iv
CAPT. W. T. FORSHAW, V.C., 1/9TH BN. MANCHESTER REGT.	46
LIEUT. A. V. SMITH, V.C., 1/5TH BN. EAST LANCS. REGT.	57
PTE. W. MILLS, V.C., 1/10TH BN. MANCHESTER REGT.	116
SGT. E. SMITH, V.C., D.C.M., 1/5TH LANCS. FUS.	157
LC.-CORP. A. WILKINSON, V.C., 1/5TH BN. MANCHESTER REGT.	187
LIEUT.-COL. P. V. HOLBERTON	131
THE DIVISIONAL COMMANDER AND BRIGADIERS	242
EGYPT AND SUEZ CANAL	18
GALLIPOLI: C. HELLES AND KRITHIA NULLAH SECTOR	19–29
C. HELLES AND GULLY RAVINE SECTOR	48–60
SINAI PENINSULA	76–83
COLOURED PLATE: DIVISIONAL FLASHES	84
BELGIUM: YPRES SECTOR	98–104
NIEUPORT SECTOR	105–108
FRANCE: LA BASSÉE SECTOR	114–118
THE GERMAN OFFENSIVE, MARCH 1918	130–131
GOMMECOURT–HEBUTERNE SECTOR, APRIL–AUGUST 1918	142
THE BRITISH ADVANCE: MIRAUMONT–TRESCAULT	148–166
,, ,, THE HINDENBURG LINE	172
,, ,, ACROSS THE R. SELLE	182–186
,, ,, FORÊT DE MORMAL AND HAUTMONT	192

MAPS

KEY MAP
GALLIPOLI: CAPE HELLES
    TRENCH MAP
FRANCE: THE GERMAN OFFENSIVE, 1918
    THE BRITISH ADVANCE, 1918, FIRST STAGE
    ,,   ,,   ,, FINAL STAGE

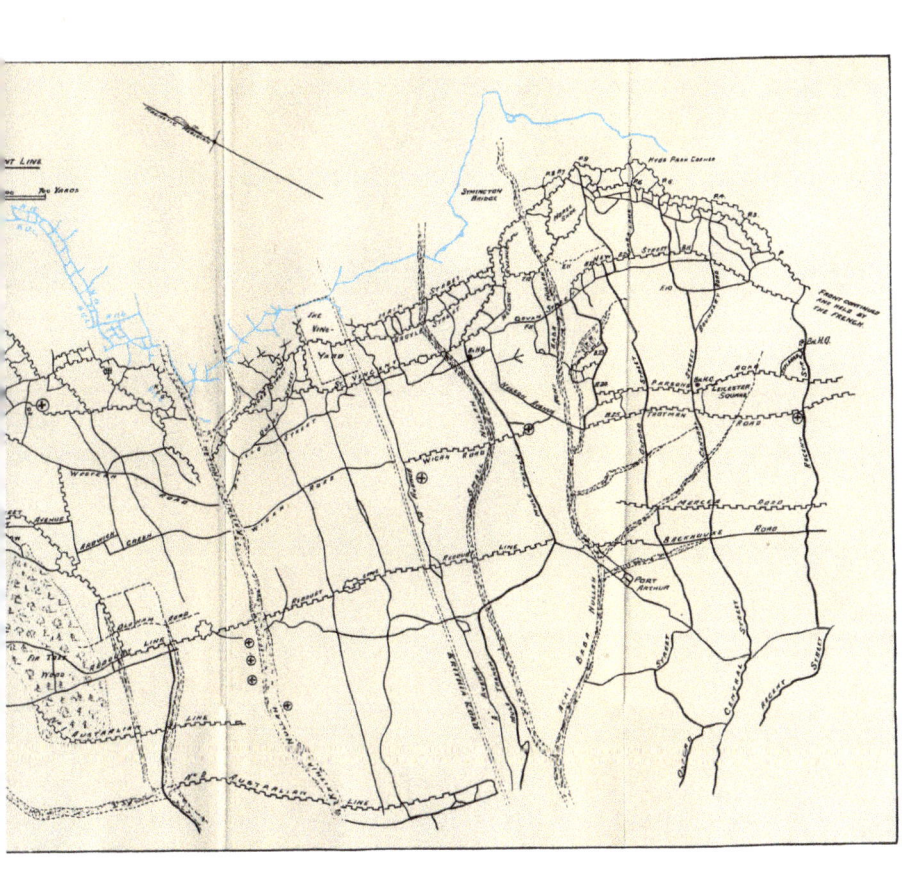

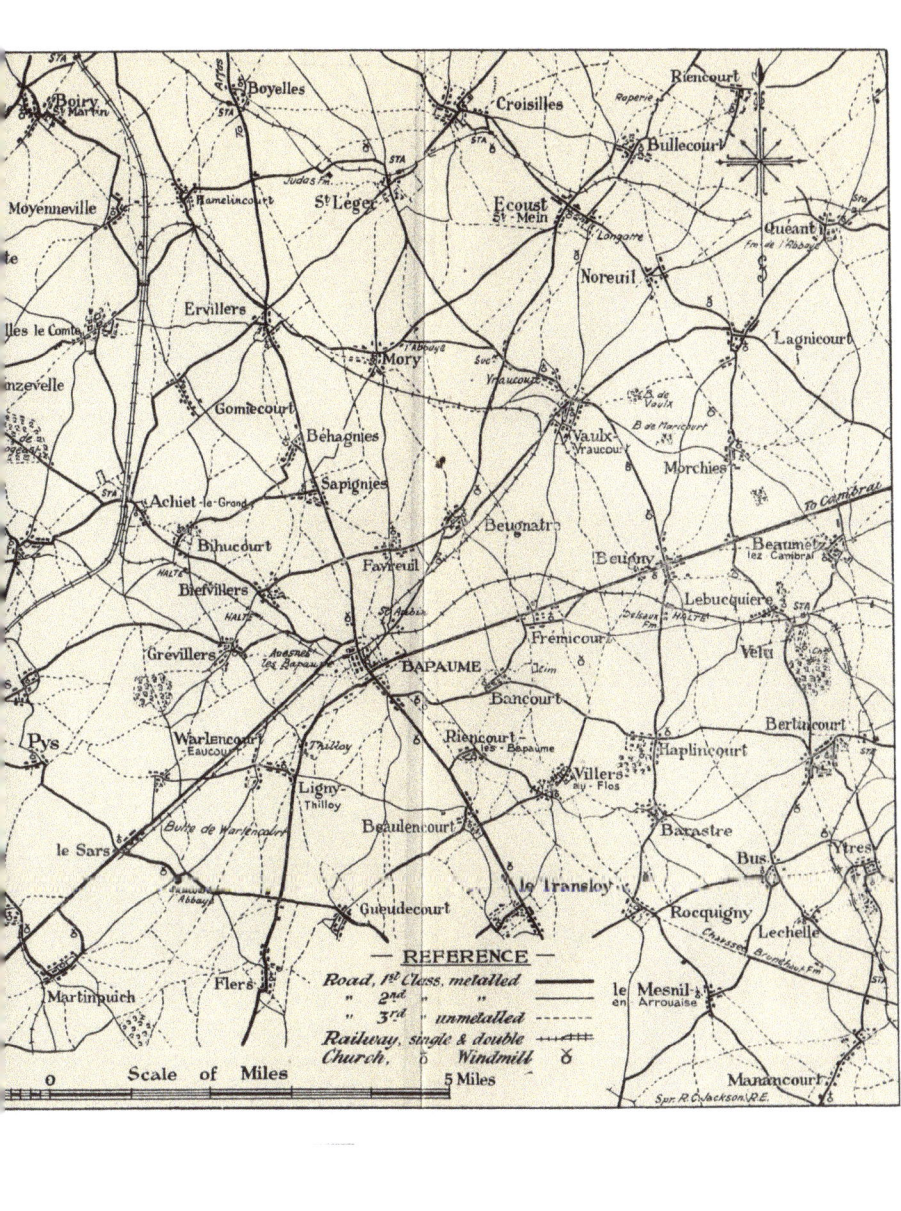

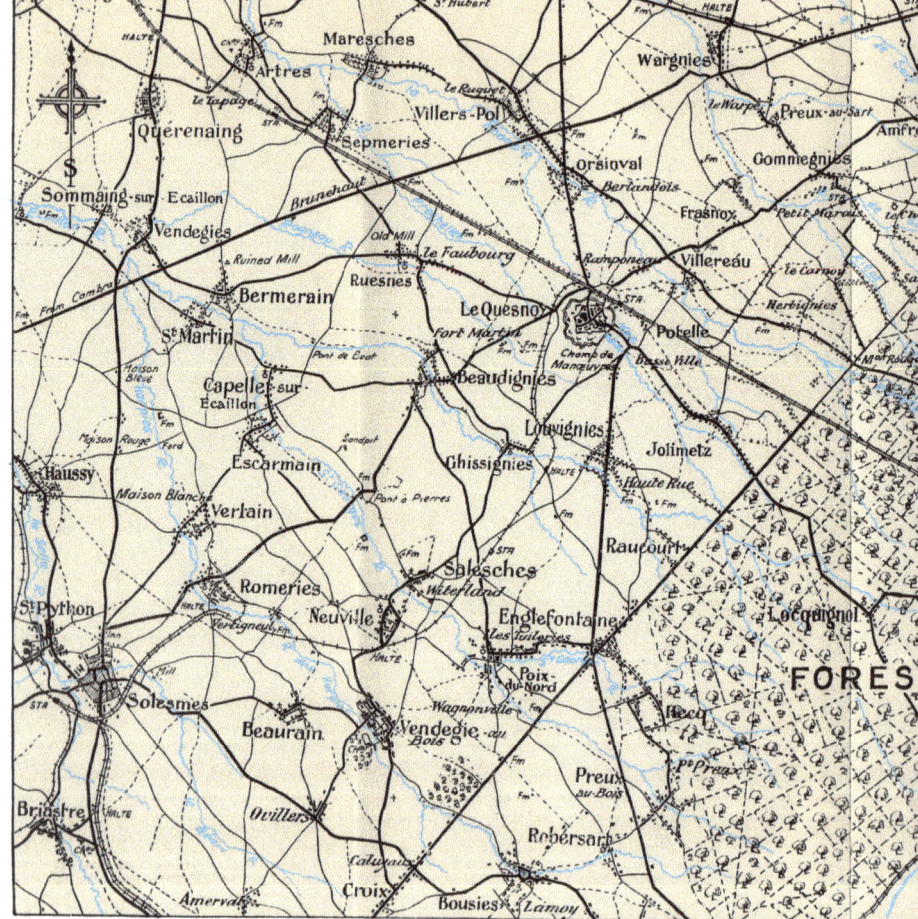

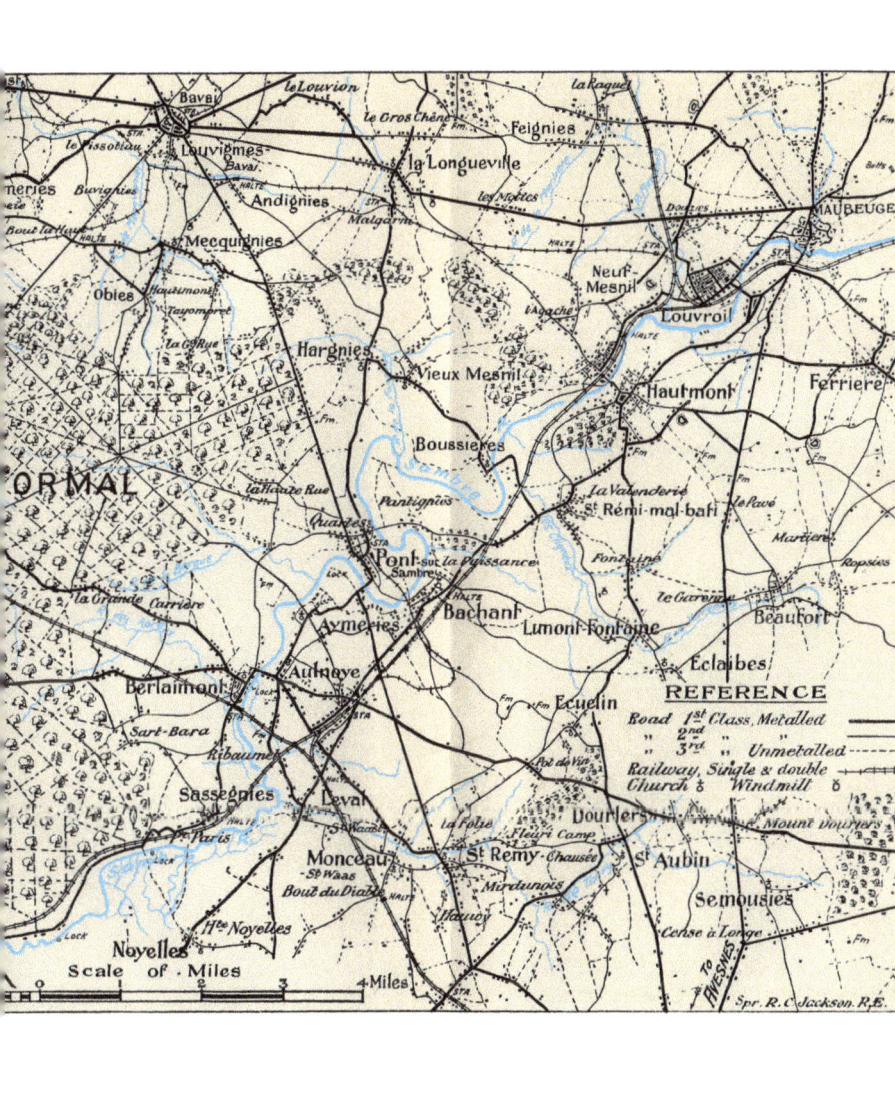

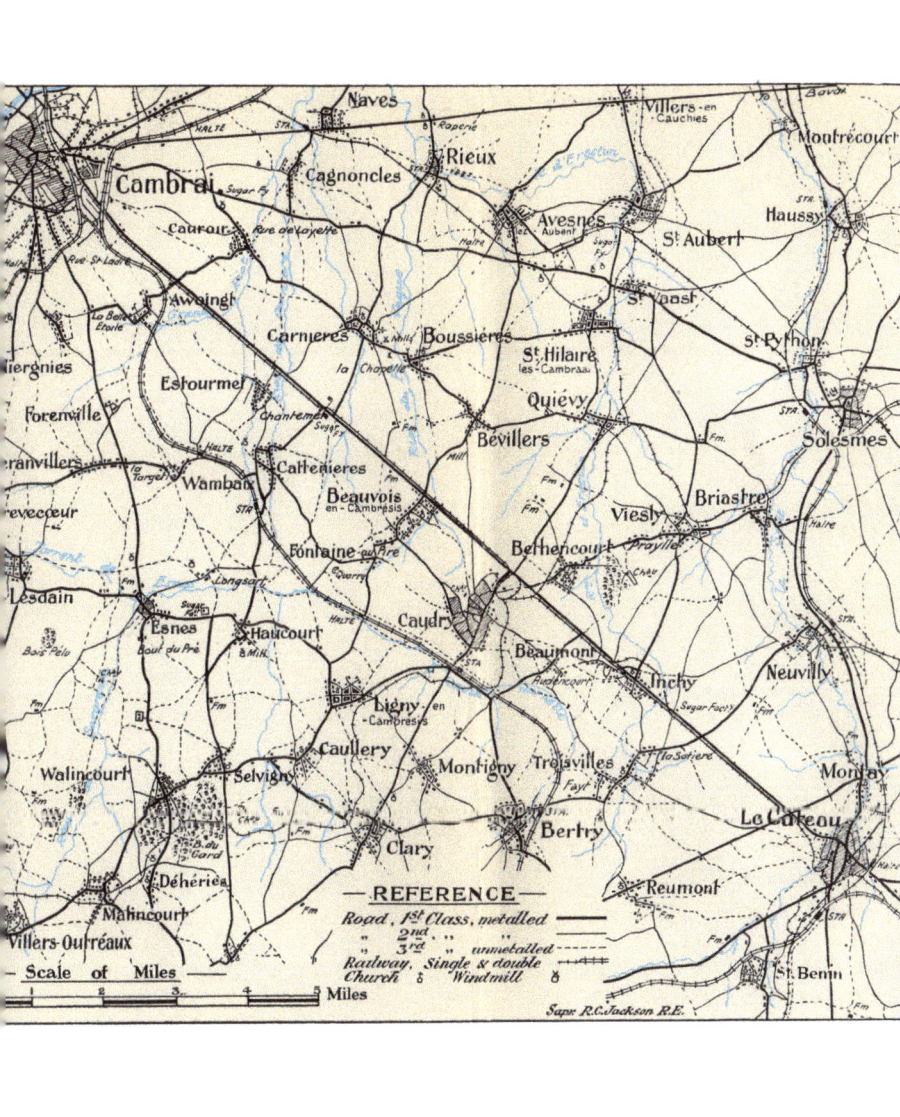

THE 42ND (EAST LANCASHIRE) DIVISION

CHAPTER I

LANCASHIRE AND EGYPT

(*August* 1914—*May* 1915)

For a week or two there had been talk of war and of the likelihood of England being involved. The prospects and possibilities formed an interesting topic of conversation and speculation. We leant over the sheer side of the precipice and caught glimpses of the black chasm below, but few really doubted the soundness of the fence over which we peered.

Warnings of disaster had been frequent—but disaster had always been averted, and fair words had prevailed. For years we had been living on the verge of national ruin through strikes of railway-men, transport-workers, miners, or the spinners and weavers of Lancashire, but at the last moment conciliation always won; there was always room for compromise. Though civil war in Ireland seemed imminent, it was comforting to reflect how much common sense there was in the world. Besides, had it not been proved to every one's satisfaction that under modern conditions war between great nations could not possibly last for more than a month or two, as in that short period victor and vanquished would alike be reduced to bankruptcy and impotence? Knowing this no Great Power would be likely to commit suicide. We were living in the twentieth century, and a great European war was an abstract conception, not something that could actually occur.

In the closing days of July 1914 this complacency was giving way to a very real dread. War might mean suicide even for the victor, might be " unthinkable," but it was in sight—plain, stark, menacing. War such as other nations had known; not a war in which those who had a taste for soldiering might take part while the rest of us could read about it in the papers, feel proud of a success and depressed by a disaster, and wonder whether sixpence would be added to the income tax. The fantastic image that had thrilled us not altogether unpleasantly—as children experience ecstatic shudders when listening to tales of ogres and hobgoblins—was taking on an appearance of grim reality. Could it after all be a grisly spectre and not a mere bogey of turnip and white sheet? England began to regret that the warnings of her greatest soldier had passed unheeded.

A day or two later Germany flung down her challenge to Christianity and Civilization, stripped herself of the cloak of decency and stood revealed in stark brutishness; and on Tuesday, August 4, 1914, England took up the challenge and declared war. The decision was apparently not expected by the German Staff. To them it was rather a matter for exasperation than for apprehension. England had her hands full at home, and her vast possessions would prove a source of weakness. She had a small regular army, a force with high traditions, well trained and well equipped for service on the frontiers of India and other outposts of the Empire, containing a larger proportion of officers and men with experience of actual fighting than any other army of the Great Powers, yet so small in numbers and so scattered over the face of the globe, that one can almost sympathize with the German belief that the few thousand men who could be spared from the duty of policing India, Egypt, South Africa, and other possessions, might safely be regarded as negligible. She had, too, a small, indifferently trained and equipped, unprofessional, home-defence force, but even the British themselves did not take the Territorials seriously.

As to the rest of the potential fighting material of the British Isles, had it not been proved to the satisfaction of the Germans (who had made a special study of such matters with the typical Teutonic thoroughness which works so efficiently when applied to material facts, and fails so lamentably when the human factor enters) that the young manhood of the nation was mainly decadent, of poor physique, weak-chested, half-educated, lacking in patriotic purpose, with no thought of the morrow and no ideals? With the exception of the few hundred thousands who had received some training in physical drill and discipline in the Boys' Brigade and its daughter-organizations which teach discipline, self-respect, and *esprit de corps*, or in the School Cadet Corps, all were utterly untrained, and they hated discipline. England had clearly shown that she was too selfish to submit to any form of compulsory service; too wrapped up in the love of comfort, ease and luxury to do more than bribe fools to die for her. It was a nation that had lost its soul. The military aid she could give to France could be contemptuously brushed aside. When France had been paralysed and the Channel ports secured, the British mercantile marine could be sunk or scared off the seas, and the British Empire brought to its knees.

Teutonic reasoning was wrong. The British character is too simple or too complex for the Hun. It may be that no other nation brings so much froth to the top as ours; that none extends such tolerance to cranks, nor gives so much rope to little cliques of shrieking egoists, nor shows such stolid indifference when the few,

Composition of the Division

claiming to speak on behalf of the nation, so egregiously misrepresent her. On August 5, 1914, it was seen that practically every man, woman and child approved what the Government had done, and felt instinctively that their country would have been shamed had there been a day's hesitation. England had found her soul, not lost it. A nation supposed to consist largely of pleasure seekers, of lovers of compromise, conciliation and tolerance, of comfort and luxury, had decided that all it held most dear would be as dust and ashes if it stood aside, a passive spectator of the agony of France and Belgium. Practically without a dissentient voice the nation prepared to sacrifice its all. Unhappily, the politicians, unaccustomed to realities, were not ready to make the most of this spirit of sacrifice. Unable to leave their grooves of finesse, intrigue, and opportunism, they knew not how to appeal simply to the noblest instincts; so they talked of " business as usual," and attempted to cajole the nation into giving a part when the whole was ready to be offered.

. . . . . .

This is the story of the part played in the most appalling of human tragedies by the East Lancashire Territorial Division, which, on leaving England, was composed of the following units—

Cavalry : " A " Squadron, Duke of Lancaster's Own Yeomanry—6 officers, 132 men.
R.F.A. : The 1st (Blackburn) and the 3rd (Bolton) East Lancashire Brigades—55 officers, 1289 men.
R.E. : 1st and 2nd Field Companies and Signal Company—19 officers, 568 men.
Infantry : The 5th, 6th, 7th and 8th Battalions, the Lancashire Fusiliers—120 officers, 3962 men.
The 4th and 5th Battalions, the East Lancashire Regiment—60 officers, 1990 men.
The 5th, 6th, 7th, 8th, 9th, and 10th Battalions, the Manchester Regiment—180 officers, 5966 men.
A.S.C. : Three Companies and the Transport and Supply Column—16 officers, 276 men.
R.A.M.C. : Three Field Ambulances—30 officers, 665 men.
Total (including Divisional and Brigade Headquarters) : 511 officers, 14,966 men.

The twelve battalions of infantry were brigaded as follows—
The Lancashire Fusiliers Brigade—the 5th, 6th, 7th, and 8th Battalions, Lancashire Fusiliers.
The East Lancashire Brigade—the 4th and 5th Battalions, East Lancs Regiment, and the 9th and 10th Battalions, Manchester Regiment.
The Manchester Brigade—the 5th, 6th, 7th, and 8th Battalions, Manchester Regiment.

The 5th L.F. was mainly composed of men from the Bury district, the 6th from Rochdale, the 7th and 8th from Salford, the 4th E. Lancs from Blackburn, the 5th from Burnley, the 5th Manchesters from Wigan, the 6th and 7th from Manchester and its suburbs (including a good proportion from the Cheshire suburbs), the 8th from Ardwick and East Manchester, the 9th from Ashton-under-Lyne, the 10th from Oldham.

The 1st R.F.A. Brigade (Blackburn) was composed of the following batteries: the 4th (Blackburn), the 5th (Church), the 6th (Burnley). The 3rd R.F.A. Brigade (Bolton) of the following: the 18th, 19th and 20th, all from Bolton and district.

Many of these units date back to 1859, when the Volunteer movement came into being. For forty-one years the Volunteers were an untried force, but in the year 1900 their offers of service in the South African War were accepted, the infantry battalions providing detachments which served with credit in that campaign. It was not until 1907 that serious thought was given to the equipment and organization of this fine body of patriotic men. Lord Haldane's Territorial Scheme, based on the model of the Regular Army, did more than change the name from Volunteers to Territorials. Major-General Douglas Haig, Director of Military Training at the War Office, had charge of the scheme, and in bringing about this great change, he gave evidence of the foresight and grasp of essentials which in 1918 enabled him to lead the armed strength of the Empire to victory. The various batteries, battalions and corps, no longer scattered and independent units, were organized and trained as divisions, and the force was actually treated as a valuable and even essential element in the system of national defence, with the result that the Territorial Force soon reached a higher state of efficiency than the Volunteers had ever been permitted to approach. The East Lancashire Division had the reputation of being one of the smartest and most efficient of the whole force.

On August 3 units in camp for their annual peace training were recalled, and the order to mobilize the Division was received at 5.30 p.m. on the following day. Probably few members of the Territorial Force had realized that their " calling-up " notices had been ready from the day they joined; that month by month the addresses on the envelopes were checked and altered when necessary; that enough ball ammunition was stored at the various headquarters to enable every man to march out with the full complement of a fighting soldier, and that field dressings were available for issue. It must be remembered that never before had the Force been embodied, and that officers and men were civilians, few of whom had ever regarded mobilization as other than a remote possibility quite outside the range of practical politics. Yet the absence of confusion was remarkable, as all ranks threw themselves into their new parts with zest, making the best of unusual conditions and treating discomfort as a jest. The men were quartered in drill-halls or schools within easy reach of their Headquarters. Major-General Douglas, commanding the Division, with his General Staff Officer, Lieut.-Colonel A. W. Tufnell, was daily at the Divisional Headquarters in

Mobilization

Manchester, or at the Headquarters of units, supervising the mobilization and arrangements. These have been described as " hectic days." Improved though the organization was as compared with that of the Volunteers, it was anything but complete. Animals and vehicles for transport, harness, and an infinite variety of requisites had to be procured by free purchase or by commandeering in great haste. This was the weakest part of the scheme, and though much ingenuity was displayed by officers unaccustomed to this sort of thing, the waste was great. To such shifts were they reduced that street watering-carts were bought from Urban District Councils, and actually taken to Egypt. Among the weird varieties of carts thus acquired one of the best remembered is the " Black and Green " van which did duty as a Medical Officer's vehicle, and was last seen bleached by the sun, but with the original lettering still traceable under the service grey, at Gabari Docks, Alexandria in February 1917. Nothing could better illustrate the inability of a large and patriotic section of the public to grasp the significance of events than the expectation freely expressed by vendors that their horses or carts would be returned to them in the course of a few weeks. In some cases the drivers of requisitioned animals joined the Territorial unit in order to remain with their horses.

On August 10 Lord Kitchener invited the Territorial Force to volunteer for foreign service. By August 12 the three Infantry Brigades had accepted the invitation, and within a few days ninety per cent. of the East Lancashires eagerly seized the opportunity. England saw with pride the keenness of the Territorials to meet the enemy, and knew that her sons were true to the breed. For more than fifty years she had treated her citizen-army as something that must not be taken too seriously, but that is England's way. The response was magnificent, but it was expected, for the nation never doubted that they would answer the call. It was no small gift they offered. The most powerful army the world had ever seen was moving forward victoriously towards Paris, remorseless and apparently irresistible; and the Territorials offered their bodies for death and mutilation, and gave up parents, wives, children, homes, prospects, and all they held most dear. At a later period such sacrifice was demanded as the nation's right, but in August 1914 a lead had to be given, an example set. Old volunteers were not content to look on while the younger generation fought and suffered. Daily a stream of old members, N.C.O.s and men, many in the autumn of their lives, besieged the Headquarters of their old corps and clamoured to be allowed to join up, lying cheerfully and brazenly in respect of their age. Many gained their object; more were almost broken-hearted by their rejection. The example set in those dark days was a stimulus and incentive to recruiting all over the country, and especially so in the great towns of Lancashire, where the " Pals " battalions were soon to be raised. It was the vindication of the Volunteer. " Defence, not Defiance," had been their motto, but who among the prescient founders and bulwarks of the movement could ever have conceived the idea of the glorious rôle to be filled by the corps they had helped to raise—of the old Volunteer units from every county and city, at full strength, fighting and laying down their lives in Belgium, France, Egypt, Gallipoli, Palestine and Greece, and taking an inspiring part in the greatest of all crusades against the Turk?

Until August 20 officers and men remained within easy reach of their Headquarters. The Division was then moved into camps in the neighbourhoods of Bolton, Bury and Rochdale, and anxiously it awaited the summons. Another fortnight passed, and the rumour that Egypt was to be the destination began to gain ground. Rumour was, however, at this time a discredited jade, fit subject for scorn, for was she not responsible for the passage through England and Scotland of myriads of Russian soldiers, the ice and snow of Archangel still clinging to their boots and beards, who had been seen by thousands of British optimists at every railway junction in the land? But in the training camps of East Lancashire she was restored to public favour when a telegram, dated September 5, was received by the Divisional Commander from Lord Kitchener—

"Inform the Division from me that I hope that they will push on hard with their training in Egypt, as, before they are ready, there will be plenty of troops from India to garrison Egypt, and I hope they will be one of the first of the Territorial Forces to join our Army on the Continent. All will depend on their fitness for service against the enemy in the Field.—KITCHENER."

General Douglas spoke for every man in the Division when he replied: "All ranks much gratified to receive your message. They are animated with keen desire to fit themselves to join our forces on the Continent."

On the 9th September the Division entrained for Southampton, about forty trains being required to convey men, horses, guns, and all the material of war; and on the 10th 15,500 Lancashire men, with about a thousand officers and men of the Hertfordshire and City of Westminster Yeomanry, embarked upon the great adventure, the first Territorial Division to volunteer for foreign service, and the first to leave England's shores. It was a record of which the Lancashire men were justly proud, and which secured to them from the start the prestige and *esprit de corps* that are usually the outcome of long and honourable tradition. The details that were not going out with the Division became the nucleus of the Second Line, which sent drafts to the First Line until about the end of August 1915, when the Second Line East Lancashire (66th) Division was formed. After that date the drafts came from the Third Line units. The Duke of Lancaster's Own Yeomanry had been accepted for voluntary service overseas, and it had been hoped that the whole regiment would accompany the Division, but finally only "A" Squadron, was ordered to embark.

Departure for Egypt

It was midnight when the troopships steamed out of the harbour, a dark night, all lights doused, no coastwise lights to guide, the blackness stabbed by scores of searchlights. The troops on board one of the ships began to sing and the whole convoy took up the strains. In the morning the first arrivals lay-to off the Eddystone, until, by late afternoon, a great fleet had assembled. At sundown the convoy sailed in three lines ahead, escorted by the battleship *Ocean* and the cruiser *Minerva*. It is said that this was the first actual convoy that had left England since the Napoleonic wars.

The rough weather of the first three days and much unavoidable discomfort aboard ship were borne with cheerfulness. The men had the impression that they were sadly overcrowded, but subsequent experience of life in " cubby-holes " and " dug-outs " modified their ideas of what lack of space really means. It was noticed that even the worst sufferers from seasickness never lost hope, as, although whole messes did not eat a meal during those three days, the daily indent for one bottle of beer per man was always drawn, to be saved for happier days. Rumours of the presence of enemy craft off Portugal gave rise to a pleasing sense of excitement and risk, but nothing happened. Early on September 17 the mighty rock of Gibraltar loomed suddenly out of the mist, and soon the mystical, sun-scorched, tawny hills of Northern Africa were sighted.

From Gibraltar the convoy was escorted by the *Minerva* only. As the weather improved it was found that, in spite of the crowded life aboard the troopships, quite a lot of theoretical training, and even a certain amount of physical, could be given, and there was little time for leisure in the Mediterranean. One brilliant day, after Malta had been passed, the sight of a great fleet sailing towards the West caused much excitement. Soon the news spread that this was the Lahore Division bound for Marseilles — war-hardened Sikhs, Gurkhas, Dogras, Punjabis, Pathans, and Rajputs, all eagerly looking forward to the day when they should cross steel with the famous soldiers of Germany, and confident of the result of such meeting. After exchange of greetings and of escorts, the *Weymouth* taking the *Minerva's* place, flags were dipped and adieux waved. It was a wondrous sight, this great gathering of mighty ships, carrying tens of thousands of men and all their material of war from East to West and from West to East—an object lesson of the strength and resources of the Empire.

On the 25th September, a misty, languorous morning, the low, sandy coast of Egypt, fringed with surf, with here and there a clump of palm trees, was sighted. It was the Egypt of anticipation, curiously familiar even to men whose travels had rarely taken them beyond the confines of Lancashire. As the troopships slowly entered Alexandria Harbour they passed a battle-cruiser of the U.S. Navy. Though a strict neutrality had to be maintained in respect of action, there was no attempt to observe it in sentiment. To the delight of the Lancashire men the Americans manned ship; their band played " God save the King," and generally " they did us proud." The

Division was keen to show its appreciation. The band of the 8th Manchesters, uncertain whether "Yankee Doodle," "The Starspangled Banner," or "My Country, 'tis of Thee," is considered the national anthem of the United States, and doubting their ability to render either of the first two airs pleasingly—the third tune being that of our own national anthem, and therefore open to misconstruction—struck up "Marching through Georgia." All too late came the reflection that possibly the cruiser's complement had been drawn from States which might not appreciate this air. However, every one seemed delighted by the display of cousinly emotion, and felt the better for the incident.

The disembarkation, which began the same day, was watched critically by regular officers who were waiting to embark for France, and who expressed their delight at the fine appearance and soldierly bearing of the Territorials. The first troops to land went on by train to Cairo, where the Yeomanry, the Lancashire Fusiliers Brigade, the Signal Company, and the Transport and Supply Column took over Abbasia Barracks. The East Lancashire Brigade were partly in the Citadel and Kasr-el-Nil Barracks in Cairo and partly in camp on the Heliopolis Racecourse. The Artillery also encamped on the racecourse, and the Engineers occupied the Kasr-el-Nil Barracks. The 5th, 6th and 8th Battalions of the Manchester Brigade and one company of the 7th Manchesters remained in Alexandria as garrison, the greater part being quartered in the Mustapha Barracks and Camp, while detachments were accommodated in the forts of Ras-el-Tin and Kom-el-Dik. Later, half of this company of the 7th was sent to Cyprus. The other three companies of the battalion had been sent to Khartoum via Port Sudan. Detachments of the R.A.M.C. accompanied the 7th Manchesters to Cyprus and Khartoum, but the Field Ambulances as units remained with their affiliated Brigades, the 1st at Alexandria, the 2nd at Heliopolis, and the 3rd at Abbasia. Detachments of the T. and S. Column took over A.S.C. duties from the Regulars at Alexandria, Khartoum and Cyprus. Abbasia was chosen for Divisional Headquarters.

"Khaki" helmets were quickly issued, but as the Embarkation Staff had put the tropical clothing in bulk in one ship, some time elapsed before the heavy serge could be discarded in favour of light drill, and it was astonishing how well the younger lads endured the excessive heat. They showed their grit from the start. The usual conditions of issue were experienced. When only the smaller sizes in headgear, boots, and clothing are available, how is it that so large a proportion of big-footed, big-headed, big-framed men turns up? The sun-helmets were approved. "Bill, will they let us tak' these whoam wi' us?" one man was heard to ask. Bill was not one of the many optimists who took for granted that they would be home for Christmas. "Tha'll be lucky if tha tak's thi yed whoam, never mind thi —— 'emlet!" he replied.

Many of the horses had died on the voyage, for not only were the ships ill-fitted for horse transport, but orders had been received from the War Office, in spite of the Divisional Commander's expostulations, not to exceed one man to every six horses. It was not possible for so small a proportion of men, most of whom were inexperienced, to cope with so many animals. On one boat alone, the *Norseman* (an Australian emigrant boat), there were more than 700 horses in charge of ninety-five men, and forty-six animals died during the voyage. The horses at first suffered greatly from climatic conditions, and especially from sand-colic. One apparently decided to lay a protest before the highest quarter, so, evading the picket, it made its way through a narrow gate into the garden of the C.R.A. and lay down to die almost on the General's doorstep. The veterinary officers had a busy time, and a story concerning one of these was told with much enjoyment by General Maxwell himself. The " vet " was working at the highest pressure, when a gentleman in civil garb came along and, proceeding to ask him sundry questions, was curtly requested to seek the nether regions and mind his own business there. His horror on discovering later that his abuse had been levelled at the head of the Commander-in-Chief may be imagined.

Lord Kitchener had asked the Territorials to push on with their training, and General Douglas had assured him that all ranks were animated by a keen desire to fit themselves for whatever service might be required of them. Training had now begun in earnest, and before long a new stimulus, a fresh incentive, to efficiency appeared, and the prospect of the Division's participation in actual warfare became less remote. During October the suspicion that Turkey might take the plunge and declare herself on the side of the enemy had become a probability. An attempt to incite Egypt to revolt, and, indeed, to persuade Mohammedans throughout the world that the day had dawned when a swift blow should destroy British supremacy for ever, might confidently be looked for; and an attack upon the Suez Canal would surely follow. To Mohammedans—with the exception of the comparatively feeble Shiah sect—the Sultan of Turkey was the Defender of the Faith, the representative of the Prophet. Who could say what religious fanaticism might not accomplish if he should proclaim *Jehad* against the infidels? The situation was grave; it might become critical, for the Khedive's good faith was distrusted, and with reason.

The Regular Army of Occupation had left Egypt for France and Flanders, and Lancashire civilians—clerks, warehousemen, artisans, mill-hands, merchants, professional men—were responsible for law and order in the ancient land of the Pharaohs, for its defence and for the safe-guarding of the Suez Canal and the communications between West and East. They kept their charge inviolate, and during eight months, amid strange surroundings and under trying conditions of climate, the East Lancashire Division gained the confidence of the Administration and the respect and esteem of British colony and native population alike, by their efficiency, their grit, and their exemplary conduct. As soldiers under fire they had yet to be tested; as men they were proved and approved. Lancashire, and, indeed, the whole Territorial Force, have reason to be proud of the first civilian army that was placed in a position of grave responsibility.

On the 22nd of October intelligence was received of considerable Turkish activity in the Sinai Peninsula. We were still at peace with Turkey, but it was highly probable that a surprise attack upon the Suez Canal might precede a formal declaration of war. The Canal had been patrolled by a battalion of Highland Light Infantry until early in October, when its duties had been taken over by Indian troops. To strengthen the Canal defences the 1st and 2nd Field Companies, R.E., were sent to Ismailia on October 26 and 27, and a few days later a detachment of the Signal Company and the machine-gun sections of the 5th Battalion, East Lancashires, and 10th Battalion, Manchesters, also left Cairo for the Canal zone. The Sappers bridged the Canal in three places, manned the searchlights, supplied crews for steam-tugs—it was in consequence of an explosion on one of these boats that the first casualties of the Division occurred, Lieutenant Woods and six non-commissioned officers and men being killed—supervised the water supply, destroyed the native village of Kantara, and built fortifications. The Signal Company laid a cable between Kantara, Ismailia, and Suez, and the motor-cycle despatch riders of this company were the first ever employed on active service outside Europe. The work of the Engineers received much-valued commendation from the Commander-in-Chief.

A section each of the 2nd and 3rd Field Ambulances had been sent to Ismailia and Kantara respectively to be attached to the Canal defences, and these gave what assistance was needed to Indian troops as well as to the men of their own Division.* Another section of the 2nd Field Ambulance took charge of the Australian hospital at Mena, at which place, and also at Meadi and Zeitoun, the East Lancashire Transport and Supply Column had formed depots and undertaken transport duties for the Anzacs until their own A.S.C. units arrived.

On October 31 a force of nearly 9000 Yeomanry and Territorials marched through the streets of Cairo. Such a display of troops had never before been seen by the natives, and they were much impressed at a critical time. The Commander-in-Chief, Sir John Maxwell, expressed his appreciation of the splendid appearance of the men and of the salutary effect of the parade on the Egyptians. Native agitators and German and Turkish agents had for some time been active in Egypt and the Sudan, seeking to discredit the allies, and one of these did his best to convince spectators that what they took to be a powerful force was in reality but a stage army—the same unit marching in a circle. On November 1 Martial Law was proclaimed throughout Egypt and the Sudan. On the 5th of November war was declared against Turkey. The island of Cyprus was formally annexed on the 7th. Two companies of the 8th Manchesters had relieved the half-company of the 7th Manchesters as garrison on

---

* The first Indian troops to reach Egypt arrived on October 30, the New Zealanders on November 30, and the Australians on December 2.

Work and Play

October 20, and detachments were sent to the various towns of the island to prevent disturbances between Greeks and Turks when the proclamation was made. On December 20 Prince Hussein was declared Sultan of Egypt under British Protectorate, and the 5th Lancashire Fusiliers provided a guard of honour on the occasion of the formal entry of the new Sultan into his capital. In Alexandria and Khartoum the Manchesters had ceremonial marches through the towns.

For some months the Division was occupied in strenuous training. The men suffered from the heat, the glare of the sun, the dust, sand-storms, flies, and other plagues of Egypt, the remarkable drop in temperature at night, the long, shadeless, desert marches; but they took it all cheerfully as part of the day's work, and by the end of the year 1914 they were fairly well acclimatized and thoroughly fit. There was play as well as work; cricket, rugger, soccer, lacrosse, and hockey teams were soon hard at it; concert parties and pierrot troupes discovered unsuspected talent. There were also boxing contests, and the race meetings on Gezireh Island provided many dinners at the Continental and Shepheard's for the winners. Full advantage was taken of the opportunities given at week-ends to visit the marvels of Egypt. The hospitality of the British colonies at Cairo, Alexandria, and elsewhere was warmly appreciated, and many friendships were formed between the residents and the men from Lancashire.

The good feeling and comradeship that prevailed throughout the Division may be illustrated by an incident, slight but typical. On the occasion of some special parade the 5th Manchesters had to cross the very sandy parade ground before reaching the asphalt road that led out of barracks. Noticing the dusty state of their boots the men of D Company of the 6th Manchesters darted into their quarters, which were close at hand, and, producing brushes and rags, they quickly polished the boots of the Wigan men. It was a trifling incident, but still a perfect expression of the spirit of good comrade-ship, and it had a wonderful and lasting effect. The two battalions were knit more closely together, and later, in Gallipoli, there was a sense of absolute security in either battalion in the knowledge that the other was in support.

The first Christmas on active service was celebrated in traditional style, plum-puddings and other Christmas fare being sent out by friends at home. The old hymns and carols at the Morning Service stirred the emotions deeply, and thoughts of home and memories of bygone Christmas gatherings became poignant. Dining huts and messes, rooms and verandahs, were garlanded with palm branches, flowers, lanterns, and chains of coloured paper. Nothing was omitted to make the day a memorable and happy one, and one to look back upon. Still, there were some decidedly novel features, chief of which, perhaps, was the after-dinner swim in the sea, indulged in by a number of Manchester men in Alexandria. On Boxing Day a great sports meeting was held at the Gezireh Sporting Club, Cairo, and many Lancashire men were successful competitors. They were, however, outshone by the men of the Ceylon Planters Rifle Corps, whose prowess was hailed with enthusiasm by their Territorial and Yeomanry rivals.

Casual mention only has been made of the 7th Manchesters. As the greater part of this battalion occupied a position of splendid isolation its very interesting experiences must be referred to separately and all too briefly. B Company had been dropped at Alexandria to take over the duties of a company of the Suffolk Regiment in that town and in Cyprus, and the other three companies remained on board the troopship. Port Sudan was reached on September 30 after a five days' voyage, and the warm reception given them by the Suffolks and the British officials was very welcome after four weeks at sea. Half of C Company was left to garrison Port Sudan and, later, among other duties, to patrol the Red Sea in H.M.S. *Enterprise*, and to run an armoured train. The rest of the battalion entrained for Khartoum, a journey of 600 kilometres, where, on October 2, they were welcomed by the Sirdar, Sir F. R. Wingate, and his Staff.

Khartoum and the Sudan furnished a succession of novel experiences to the men from Burlington Street, but no surprise quite equalled that conveyed to them by the intimation that they were at once, without preliminary coaching, to supply a half-company to form the British Camel Corps. The two platoons of C Company were detailed for this duty. The departing O.C. Camel Corps had little time in which to impart information to his successor, and there were many documents to sign, some of these being in Arabic. He seemed grieved that Manchester men should be ignorant of Arabic and of the customs, habits, and requirements of camels, but volunteered as much information as could be crammed into five minutes. Captain C. Norbury and his subalterns gazed upon their new pets, seventy in number, without affection, and sat down the better to enjoy the humour of their predicament before sampling its difficulties. In despair and not in hope, expecting rather to provoke merriment than to elicit information, the new O.C. Camels asked his half-company if any man among them had had experience of camels. Forth stepped the former camel-keeper of Bostock's menagerie. The Hour had brought forth the Man. The 7th Manchesters now felt that they were equal to any emergency, and soon they provided piano-tuners for the Sirdar's palace, trained gardeners for the barracks gardens, and skilled artisans for every variety of job for which an expert was demanded.

The Camel Corps was soon proficient enough to be sent by the Sirdar on a two-weeks' trek through villages where white men had rarely been seen, and their presence gave the lie to reports circulated by Turco-German emissaries that all white troops had been recalled from Egypt and the Sudan to defend their home country from the enemy at its gates. Incidentally they had the opportunity of seeing the wonderful results of Manchester enterprise in the great cotton-growing areas through which they passed. Not only had Khartoum been transformed from a collection of mud huts into a town of imposing buildings, shops, and public works, but the savage Sudan of a few years ago was in process of transformation into a land of peace and prosperity.

Training proceeded under the same trying conditions of climate experienced by their comrades in Egypt; the same games and sports were enjoyed with similar zest; and fitness and efficiency prevailed. The conduct of the men received and merited high praise from the Sirdar—who paid the battalion the distinction of becoming its honorary Colonel—and from all with whom they came in contact. Relations with the natives were excellent, and a firm friendship was formed with the Egyptian regiment in Khartoum. The first of all active service periodicals, *The Manchester Sentry*, was published in Khartoum, the Sirdar and Lady Wingate contributing. The three companies rejoined their comrades of the Manchester Brigade in Cairo on April 23, 1915.

On January 19, 1915, the Manchester Brigade was transferred from Alexandria and Cyprus to Cairo, and the 5th and 8th Lancashire Fusiliers were sent to Alexandria. Reports of renewed activity on the part of the Turks pointed to an attempt to seize the Suez Canal and invade Egypt. On January 20 the 1st and 3rd Brigades, R.F.A., were despatched to the Canal zone, to be followed a few days later by the 1st Field Company, R.E., which had recently been brought back to Cairo in order to take part in divisional training. The artillery was posted on the west bank of the Canal at El Kubri, Serapeum West, Ferry Post (Ismailia), El Ferdan, and Kantara, most of the guns being concealed among the pines that grow within a hundred yards of the bank. The Field Companies assisted the garrisons of Indian troops in the strong points of the east bank to improve their defences.

The expectations of hostile attack were realized in the early hours of February 3, when a force of 12,000 Turks and Germans attacked, and made an attempt to cross the Canal midway between the east bank strong points of Serapeum and Toussoum. Heavy rifle and machine-gun fire developed between those places about 3 a.m. The guns of the Egyptian Mountain Battery had, by happy chance or remarkable intuition, been mounted on the west bank within 400 yards of the main crossing-place selected by the Turks. The chanty of the enemy, as, unaware of the battery's proximity, he attempted to launch the heavy steel pontoons, was much appreciated by the gunners, who opened fire in the dark at point-blank range. When daylight came the Battery Commander was able to congratulate himself on some accurate " spotting," several holed pontoons and many dead Turks being found at the water's edge. One of these pontoons is now in possession of the Manchester Corporation.

Two sections of the 1st Field Company had been detailed to

hold the west bank at this point, and in the course of the fighting on February 3 they lost one man killed and two wounded. The 19th Battery, under Major B. P. Dobson (which had already been in action on the previous day against the Turkish Camel Corps), played a conspicuous part in the enemy's defeat. They had hauled one 15-pounder through a wood to the bank of the Canal and had fired point blank into the Turks as they vainly attempted to launch their iron boats. Another gun was man-hauled to a hill behind the wood, and this found good targets as the enemy approached the Canal. Captain P. K. Clapham did some good spotting for the battery from a precarious and exposed position in a tall fir tree. The 18th Battery, at Ismailia, fired on the enemy positions with good effect from 2000 to 3000 yards, and every battery of the two brigades shared in the victory. The 20th Battery, at El Ferdan, had the distinction of being the first Battery of the Division—and probably the first of any Territorial unit—to open fire upon an enemy. The total casualties of the East Lancashire Artillery were five men wounded, four of these belonging to the 19th Battery. The men of the Signal Company, who had done good work in this sector, also received their baptism of fire.

The attempt to invade Egypt had failed. The Punjabis (upon whom fell the brunt of the fighting), the Rajputs and Gurkhas on the east bank were fully prepared both to meet the attack and to assume the offensive, inflicting a serious defeat and making important captures. The Divisional Yeomanry arrived at Ismailia on the 4th of February in time to co-operate with Indians, Anzacs, and the 5th Battery in following up the enemy's retirement. More than 1600 prisoners were taken. On the 10th General Douglas visited the posts on the Canal, held by units of his Division, to congratulate his men on their good work. The 2nd Field Company reached Ismailia on the 6th, and for the greater part of the month the sappers were kept busy strengthening the Canal defences, making entanglements, trenches and bomb-proof shelters, and laying mines. Another attack upon the Canal was made on the 22nd of March, when the 5th Battery was again in action, and the next day the Battery accompanied a column which attacked the Turks in the Sinai Desert about nine miles N.E. of El Kubri. While the East Lancashire Batteries remained in the Canal zone Brigadier-General A. D'A. King, Divisional C.R.A., assumed command of the artillery of the Canal defences.

From the beginning of the year 1915 the training had become more and more strenuous. There were long marches in the desert— occasionally very long ones—in full marching order, through native villages in which the many odours were only excelled in numbers, variety, and offensiveness by the yelping curs that were stirred into noisy activity by the tramp of the battalions. The Khamsin wind was sickly in its heat, the atmosphere heavy and laden with sand, the glare of the sun pitiless, the only shade available while resting being the very inadequate shelter provided by a blanket stretched on rifles. But the men were physically fit—they had to be, for only fit men were needed. The amateurs had become *soldiers*. The days were past when the colour-sergeant's whispered order to the right-flank man of a company in extended order for " two scouts " would reach the left-flank man in the form of " the colour-bloke wants a couple of stouts." In spite, however, of good physical condition and a fine spirit, it could not truthfully be stated that the Suez road, with its five-mile towers, and the Virgin's Breast had endeared themselves to Lancastrians. Familiarity had bred not contempt but a whole-hearted loathing for that accursed highway and that distant mound. The Third Tower was the usual goal, the advance ceasing just beyond it. How the troops hated the sight of this detestable pile which, in the dust and glare, seemed to recede mockingly as they tramped towards it! On the homeward march one very hot day, while the men were cursing the dust and sand, a party of natives passed, all being mounted on asses. A bulky and perspiring Salford Fusilier regarded them enviously, and growled : " They say those blighters ain't civilized. But *they* don't —— well walk!" There were night operations and marches, during one of which, after a battalion had been wandering for hours in pitch darkness along the numerous roads in and around Helouan, the company humorist suggested to his Captain that they had lost their way. On being asked why, he replied, " Well, we've just passed a road that we haven't been down."

Brigade " shows " and Divisional " stunts," in conjunction with Australian and New Zealand troops and English Yeomanry, now began to play an important part in the training. The sounding of the *Cease Fire* was the signal for importunate orange-sellers to spring up on all sides, holding out the refreshing fruit with shrill cries of " Two for half " (piastre). Under the alleged cover of imaginary battle ships " landing-schemes " were rehearsed. These, like so many less provocative events, gave rise to highly coloured rumours which, in spite of the hard fate of earlier rumours, were entertained with much satisfaction, for Hope is a cheery soul, always quick to reply that he is not downhearted. The men looked forward eagerly to an exodus from the captivity of Egypt and longed for the promised land, where an opportunity to test their soldierly qualities might be found. Rehearsals, training, and all duties were carried out with alacrity and unfailing cheerfulness, but they were becoming monotonous; and the feeling undoubtedly existed that the Division had—quite unintentionally—been penalized through being the first Territorial Division to be complete for service. Had they been a little less efficient another Territorial Division might have been chosen for useful but inglorious garrison duty in Egypt, and the East Lancashires might by now have been in France or Flanders. It seemed to be a case of the first being last.

On Palm Sunday, March 28, a brilliant day, the Division was reviewed in Cairo by General Sir Ian Hamilton, who had lately arrived to command the Mediterranean Expeditionary Force, and Major-General Douglas had good reason for his pride in the troops under his command. The critical eye of the Commander-in-Chief seemed to take stock of every individual that passed before him, and he was obviously impressed by their soldierly bearing and fitness.* Here was a Division whose outward appearance equalled that of Regulars, and, as a judge of men, he was convinced that their martial spirit would not belie the outward appearance. He never had reason to alter his opinion or regret the judgment then passed. From that day the East Lancashires were " in the ring," and were destined to play a part in one of the war's greatest tragedies. In a Special Order of the Day the Divisional Commander published the following letter—

> " General Sir Ian Hamilton, having been accorded the privilege of reviewing the East Lancashire Division, wishes to congratulate the General Officer Commanding in Egypt, as well as Major-General Douglas, on the turn-out and soldierly bearing of that force.
> " He was able to observe to-day that the East Lancashire Division has made full use of the advantages which continuous fine weather and the absence of billeting have given them over their comrades now bearing arms, whether at home or on the continent of Europe.
> " Ever since the siege of Ladysmith, General Sir Ian Hamilton has interested himself specially in the military output of Manchester, and it is a real pleasure to him now to be able to bear witness to the fact that this great city is being so finely represented in the East."

Early in April there were signs that a fresh attack on the Canal was contemplated by the Turks, and orders were received that an Infantry Brigade of the Division must be ready to occupy a position covering Kantara at short notice. Major-General Douglas selected the East Lancashire Brigade for this important task. The move was not begun, however, until the 16th, when two battalions left for Kantara and Port Said, the others following on the 19th and 20th.

On April 28 verbal orders were received by the Divisional Commander that the Division must be prepared to move to the Dardanelles at short notice. The news soon spread; it was no rumour this time, but the real thing, and on April 30 excitement was at fever heat. At last the Territorials were to be given the opportunity to which all ranks had looked forward so eagerly, and towards which recent training had been directed. Little time was given for

---

* It is a striking testimony to the fitness of the Lancashire Territorials— mainly recruited from large manufacturing towns—that, though the men had undergone no more than a hurried medical examination to ascertain their fitness for home service, very few broke down under the rigorous training in Egypt.

preparation, but no more was needed, as the Division was ready to take the field. On May 1, 1915, the embarkation of the East Lancashire Division began, the Lancashire Fusilier Brigade, the Brigade Signal Section and No. 2 Company, A.S.C. leaving Alexandria for the Dardanelles on the 2nd May. The Manchester Brigade, the Brigade Section Signal Company, No. 4 Company, A.S.C., and the 1st Artillery Brigade sailed on the night of the 3rd. Some of the transports had just brought many hundreds of wounded men from Gallipoli. The *Derflinger*, a captured German vessel, had landed 550 casualties a few hours before she was boarded by the 5th and 6th Manchesters, and the gory clothing and stretchers which littered her decks were sufficient evidence of war's brutality to sober the most irresponsible and banish all idea of a " picnic " expedition. The embarkation of the remainder of the Division was delayed by the lack of trains, but on the 4th all units, with the exception of the Yeomanry, left their stations for the ports of embarkation, and on the 6th of May were at sea. The men carried with them grateful memories of the ladies of Alexandria, from whom much kindness had already been received, and who now opened a buffet on the quay, and from dawn until dusk supplied tea, coffee, and other refreshments to troops awaiting their turn to embark.

While the troops were embarking Major-General Douglas received the following telegram from Sir John Maxwell—

" When you have an opportunity will you let the East Lancashire Division know that during the time they have been under my command I have been filled with admiration of their conduct, keenness, capacity for hard work, cheerfulness and soldierlike spirit. Now they are going on hard active service I am sure they will fight gallantly and uphold the great traditions of Lancashire and the Empire, and prove, if proof be needed, that the trained Territorial soldier is second to none. Good luck and God speed to you all."

On May 1 the Embarkation State of the Division was as follows—

	Officers.	Other Ranks.
Headquarters and Signal Service	21	242
Artillery (with twenty-four 15-pr. guns)	57	1,273
Engineers	15	410
Infantry (two machine-guns to each battalion)	369	11,189
R.A.M.C.	34	653
A.S.C.	24	313
Total	520	14,080

The 42nd Division

Officers commanding units—

C.R.A.	Brig.-General A. D'A. King, D.S.O.
1st Brigade R.F.A.	Lieut.-Colonel A. Birtwistle.
3rd Brigade R.F.A.	Lieut.-Colonel C. E. Walker.
C.R.E.	Lieut.-Colonel S. L. Tennant.
Div. Signal Company	Major A. N. Lawford.
1st Field Company .	Major J. H. Mousley.
2nd Field Company	Major L. F. Wells.
Lancashire Fusiliers Brigade .	Brig.-General H. C. Frith.
5th Batt. L.F. . .	Lieut.-Colonel J. Isherwood.
6th Batt. L.F. . .	Lieut.-Colonel Lord Rochdale.
7th Batt. L.F. . .	Lieut.-Colonel A. F. Maclure.
8th Batt. L.F. . .	Lieut.-Colonel J. A. Fallows.
East Lancashire Brigade	Brig.-General D. G. Prendergast.
4th Batt. E.L. . .	Lieut.-Colonel F. D. Robinson.
5th Batt. E.L. . .	Lieut.-Colonel W. E. Sharples.
9th Batt. Manchester	Lieut.-Colonel D. H. Wade.
10th Batt. Manchester	Lieut.-Colonel J. B. Rye.
Manchester Brigade .	Brig.-General Noel Lee.
5th Batt. Manchester	Lieut.-Colonel H. C. Darlington.
6th Batt. Manchester	Major C. R. Pilkington.
7th Batt. Manchester	Lieut.-Colonel H. E. Gresham.
8th Batt. Manchester	Lieut.-Colonel W. G. Heys.
E.L. Divisional Train .	Major A. England.
1st E.L. Field Ambulance	Lieut.-Colonel H. G. Parker.
3rd E.L. Field Ambulance	Lieut.-Colonel W. M. Steinthal.

With one or two exceptions these officers were in command when the units left England. Lieut.-Colonel Heywood (6th Manchesters) had been pronounced unfit for active service by reason of defective eyesight, and Lieut.-Colonel Needham (A.S.C.) was left at Alexandria sick.

1/2ND GĤURKA RIFLES CROSSING 1ST FIELD COMPANY'S BRIDGE OVER SUEZ CANAL AT FERRY POST.

TURKISH PONTOONS CAPTURED AT TOUSSOUM, SUEZ CANAL.

6TH BN. MANCHESTER REGT. EMBARKING AT ALEXANDRIA FOR GALLIPOLI.

UNLOADING HORSES AT C. HELLES.

SHIPPING OFF C. HELLES, MAY 1915.

BIVOUACS IN THE "REST AREA," C. HELLES.

CHAPTER II

GALLIPOLI

(*May* 1915)

GALLIPOLI ! Who in Lancashire, in England, before the year 1915, knew where or what it was, or had even heard the name? Bitter was the dispelling of ignorance; hard indeed the road that led to knowledge ! A name of death, of affliction, of suffering almost too heavy to be borne; but also a name of heroism and endurance and of high endeavour. A name of Failure, but no less of Glory.

More than 14,000 Lancashire Territorials—bronzed, clear-eyed, *trained* men now—put forth from Egypt in the first days of May 1915, upon the second stage of the Great Adventure, bound for the Ægean Sea, the very source and well-spring of adventure, whose shores and islands were the playgrounds of heroes. As the transports steamed northward into the Ægean, some, perhaps, had visions of a parade across the peninsula, an astonished enemy falling back before them in disorder, and a triumphant procession into Constantinople. The glamour of that romantic city laid hold of the imagination of others, who pictured a victorious entry after some weeks or months of hard fighting, and the loss of good comrades. The majority, however, had a better, if still rather vague, idea of the difficulties of the task that confronted them, for most had heard by now of the enemy's preparedness and of the reception that had been given to the 29th Division, the Anzacs, and the French, and of the awful losses sustained before a precarious footing had been gained.

So, while the Division is at sea, let us review very briefly the position on the peninsula of Gallipoli. After a naval bombardment on February 15, which only served as a threat and warning to the enemy, a naval attempt on March 18 to force the Straits failed disastrously, though it certainly attained one of its objects—that of relieving the pressure upon the Russians. But as the large Turkish forces withdrawn from the Caucasus were employed upon the defence of Gallipoli and the Straits, the result was that the hitherto undefended peninsula was converted into an impregnable position against the now expected attack. Artillery was mounted to cover every approach, and barbed wire entanglements were concealed in the shallows and placed on shore—wire compared with which the British article was as thread.

On April 25 General Sir Ian Hamilton's army landed, the 29th Division at various beaches of the southern extremity of the peninsula, around Cape Tekke, Cape Helles, and the village of Sedd-el-Bahr, and the Anzacs on the western shore a dozen miles to the north, just beyond the headland of Gaba Tepe. The loss incurred had been appalling. The marvel was that the feat had been accomplished. History records no grander achievement, no more inspiring example of heroism. Surely men who could achieve the impossible as these had done could go anywhere or do anything! They could indeed do what men can do, but there were no reserves to fill the huge gaps, and the important gains made so gallantly and at so terrible a cost had to be abandoned by the fragments of what had once been battalions and companies. The story of Gallipoli might have been very different had General Hamilton been granted the support of the East Lancashire Division a week earlier. On April 30 the 86th Brigade (the four Fusilier battalions) of the 29th Division could only muster 36 officers and 1830 men out of a normal strength of 104 officers and 4000 men, the 1st Lancashire Fusiliers being reduced to 11 officers and 399 men.

The finest troops of Turkey made desperate efforts, with a courage and enthusiasm that won the admiration of the British, to complete the destruction of the invading force or to drive it into the sea. With equal determination British, Anzacs, and French held on to their dearly-won foothold, and made desperate counter-attacks to improve their position. On May 1 the Indian Brigade under Brig.-General Cox arrived from Egypt.

On May 5–6 the Lancashire Fusilier Brigade, with No. 2 Section Signal Company and the 2nd Transport and Supply Company, disembarked at " W " and " V " Beaches, across the blood-drenched hulk of the River Clyde, and were temporarily attached to the 29th Division. Vehicles and animals were slung into the lighters, and though it was their first experience the men did their job well. The A.S.C. mules had been supplied from the 49th Reserve Park a few hours before embarking at Alexandria, and were therefore unknown to their drivers, who deserve credit for bringing them safely ashore. As the cable-wagons could not be landed each man of the Signal Section took as much equipment as he could carry.

Had stimulus been needed to inspire the men from Bury, Rochdale and Salford, here was their inspiration. They had set foot ashore close to the spot made world-famous as " Lancashire Landing " a few days earlier by the 1st Battalion of their own Regiment, with whom they were now privileged to act. " So strong," wrote Sir Ian Hamilton, in his first despatch on the Gallipoli landing, " were the defences of ' W ' Beach that the Turks may well have considered them impregnable; and it is my firm conviction that no finer feat of arms has ever been achieved by the British soldier—or any other soldier—than the storming of these trenches from open boats, by the 1st Lancashire Fusiliers." Within a few hours of landing the Territorial Brigade was in action, and at the close of two days'

ACHI BABA FROM HIGH GROUND ABOVE "LANCASHIRE LANDING."

MORTO BAY AND ENTRANCE TO THE NARROWS.

The First Battle—May 6, 1915

severe fighting it had a casualty list of 673. The first battalion to disembark, the 6th Lancashire Fusiliers, took over trenches from the K.O.S.B. at dusk, on the extreme left of the British line, between Gully Ravine and the Ægean Sea. The remainder of the Brigade marched during the night, reaching a point above Gully Beach at daybreak on May 6.

A general advance of the whole line, stretching right across the peninsula, from a point about three miles north of Tekke Burnu on the left to a point about one mile north of De Tott's Battery on the right, was ordered for 10 a.m. that morning. The 6th L.F. gained more than 400 yards before being held up by heavy fire from rifles and machine guns. This was the greatest advance made by any unit that day, and the ground won was held. The 7th were in support of the 6th. One company of the 8th reinforced the extreme left; another company supported the left of the 88th Brigade on the right of the Gully Ravine. This ravine, about fifty yards wide, with steep cliffs forty to sixty feet high, formed a dangerous gap in the line, and during the night its bed was occupied by another company of the 8th. Under cover of night the trenches, having been cleared of dead and dying, were deepened and improved.

The attempt to continue the advance next morning was not successful. The 5th L.F. deployed and passed through the 6th in the front line, the rest of the Brigade being in support, to press home the attack. The Brigade's objective was a point about a mile to the north of the furthest point reached by British troops throughout the campaign. Some parties of the 5th gained a little ground, but they were enfiladed, the intensity of the fire drove them back, and the line remained unaltered. A renewal of the attack in the afternoon, when the Brigade was reinforced by two battalions of the 87th Brigade, also failed. At sundown the Brigade was relieved, and the Lancashire Fusiliers rested on the cliffs until the following evening, when they were moved to a less exposed bivouac further inland, among the trees near Morto Bay. The Territorials had been severely tested and had stood it well. They had been thrust at once into the fighting line because they were badly needed. When they landed the position of the depleted 29th Division was precarious. The men were exhausted, for there is a limit to human endurance, and that limit had almost been reached. It was vital, if they were not to be driven into the sea by force of numbers, that an advance should be made and less exposed positions secured; and the arrival of the Territorial Brigade had enabled the worn-out Regulars to attain this object. No. 2 Section Signal Company had done good work. For two days their tasks had been done in the open, under continuous fire, all lines having been laid on the surface by hand.

By some blunder or misunderstanding on the part of the Naval Authorities most of the transports conveying the remainder of the Division were sent northwards up the coast to Gaba Tepe, instead of to Cape Helles. The first to arrive, the *Derflinger* with the 5th and 6th Manchesters on board, was chased by a destroyer and brought back with all speed to Helles, where these two battalions disembarked on the evening of May 6 at " W " and " V " beaches. The 7th and 8th Manchesters landed on the same beaches on the following day under shell fire, which caused several casualties. The Manchester Brigade assembled on the cliffs between the beaches before moving inland to the rendezvous known as Shrapnel Valley. The other transports, including the *Crispin* with Headquarters on board, arrived off Gaba Tepe on May 8, and anchored there for the night. In the morning Major-General Douglas, failing to obtain a reply to his ship's signals, visited the Senior Naval Transport Officer on board H.M.S. *Queen*, and the transports were soon steaming southwards, Headquarters disembarking at " W " beach in the afternoon of May 9.

The disembarkation of the Division was practically completed on the 11th, though two companies of the 10th Manchesters and one of the 5th East Lancashires, when about to follow their comrades ashore, were carried off by the naval authorities for some unexplained reason, and were not landed until the 14th. The medical and surgical equipment of the 3rd Field Ambulance was also lost in the same way, and was not recovered for a fortnight. The 5th Battery, R.F.A., and two guns of the 6th Battery had been landed, when orders were received that, as the area occupied by the British was so small, sufficient space would not be available for the batteries, so the Artillery must return to Egypt. It was, however, decided to allow the guns which had already been brought ashore to remain. Lieut.-Colonel Birtwistle, commanding the 1st Brigade, R.F.A., had gone ashore with the 5th Battery, and he was placed in charge of a sub-group of Australian and New Zealand batteries. The mortification of the other batteries was intense, but after four more months in Egypt they again sighted Cape Helles, and this time were allowed to land. For the same reason—congestion on the occupied territory—the 1st, 3rd and 4th Companies, A.S.C., with the exception of the Supply personnel, were ordered back to Egypt.

The vagaries of the naval transport authorities which had sent some of the transports on a tour along the coast were not regarded as an unmitigated evil by those of the wanderers upon whom responsibility weighed less heavily, for they were given the opportunity to survey the scene of operations from various angles, from Tekke Burnu to Fisherman's Hut beyond the headland of Gaba Tepe, where lay the Anzacs, and from Cape Helles to Morto Bay and the entrance to the Straits. They witnessed the bombardment of the enemy's positions from sea and land; and some, with good glasses, were able to follow the movements of the Lancashire Fusiliers during the heavy fighting of the 6th and 7th of May, and could actually see them move forward to attack, their bayonets flashing in the sun, and concentrate on certain points when the advance was held up. On the right the French Colonial troops were seen, carrying all before them with their usual dash, only, alas ! to be driven back a few hours later. They passed close to the mighty *Queen Elizabeth*, that embodi-

The Landing at Helles

ment of concentrated sea-power which—as many anticipated—had proved so comparatively ineffective against an enemy on land, though the big naval shells which burst in and around Krithia Village threw up clouds of dust and smoke and debris seventy feet in height. There also were the French men-of-war and the " Packet of Woodbines," as the five-funnel Russian cruiser *Askold* was termed.

That the landing on open beaches, exposed to chance firing from the Turkish front, and presenting a visible target to batteries at Kum Kale on the Asiatic shore, was accomplished quickly and almost without loss was due to the fine spirit shown by all ranks. The disembarkation was by no means a simple affair. It contrasted strangely with the embarkation at Alexandria, where the trooptrains ran alongside the steamers, and the docks were equipped with all loading facilities. At Cape Helles the transports anchored at varying distances from the shore, and the troops were transferred to steam-tugs and trawlers, each carrying about 500 men to the makeshift piers of trestles or old barges, or to the jetty formed by the stranded *River Clyde* on " V " Beach. Horses and mules were slung overboard and lowered into lighters. The ground swell increased the difficulties and dangers.

As the men scrambled into the tugs many began to realize that they were now confronting the biggest thing that had yet entered into their lives. They joked and chaffed one another, and smoked their pipes, as if crossing to the Isle of Man, while the thunder of the heavy guns echoed against the cliffs. They were not yet " heroes," and few of them had yet been tested by fire; and if, to steady their nerves and conceal from their comrades—and from themselves—the anxieties and doubts that would not be denied, they made fun of the ordeal that lay before them, all honour to them!

Each boatload was welcomed by a Landing Officer, whose one idea was, naturally enough, to get men and baggage clear of his " pier " and beach in order to make room for the next batch and prevent the short stretch of foreshore from becoming hopelessly blocked. The strip of firm sand at the water's edge soon changed to loose sand and shingle, which sloped gradually to the foot of the cliffs, about 150 to 200 yards from highwater mark. The cliffs rose abruptly to the height of fifty to sixty feet, except in the centre of the bays, where higher ground was reached by rough winding tracks. From the top of the cliffs a view of Achi Baba was obtained—a sight interesting enough, and even exciting, at first, but the interest soon palled and gave place to detestation. The top was no place to linger upon, for its occupants were plainly visible to the Turk in front, as well as to the Turk in Asia. Low scrub and grass covered it; beyond, the ground dipped slightly before it began to rise nearly 600 feet to the summit of Achi Baba, about six miles to the northeast. It was mainly uncultivated ground, though a certain amount of young grain afforded good grazing for the horses while it lasted, and there were one or two small vineyards more than a mile inland, the young grapes from these being made into delectable puddings later by enterprising A.S.C. officers. The only trees near the Helles beaches were small groups of wind-swept firs and a few limes, but further inland, near the nullahs, and away on the right, in the French area around Morto Bay, more foliage could be seen. There were many wild flowers, including a lovely pink cistus, wild thyme and very fine wild roses; and here and there the vivid red of a patch of poppies relieved the general impression of green.

For nearly two miles inland this ground formed a narrow, congested bivouac for troops newly landed or in reserve, and a rest camp for those which had suffered heavily. Corps Headquarters, ordnance, supplies, hospital tents, transport vehicles, and long lines of picketed horses and mules, covered large expanses. At first men lay in twos and threes in small natural hollows, in coffin-shaped holes hastily dug to the depth of two or three feet, or in wide shallow trenches which provided some little cover for men lying down. Later, oilsheets were used to cover these trenches as a protection from the sun by day and the cold at night. The difference in temperature was keenly felt by men who had passed the preceding seven months in Egypt. Indeed, on the first night ashore officers and men, unable to sleep because of the cold, stamped backwards and forwards until tired, then huddled together until forced to take violent exercise again. The dawn was exquisite as the first rays of the sun touched the snow-tipped mountains to the east, but few were in the mood to appreciate it. What was then asked of the sun was warmth, not beauty.

Very little protection from shell fire was to be found on the peninsula owing to the nature of the ground, to the position of the allied armies between the guns of Achi Baba and the batteries of the Asiatic shore, and to the entire absence of material for revetting trenches and constructing shelters and dug-outs. Wood and other material could only be brought from Egypt or Mudros in small quantities—small as compared with the vast amount required—and even these seldom found their way beyond the beaches, and sandbags during the first months were as precious almost as drinking-water. Moreover, there was no time for work on defences, and no men were available. The cliffs themselves provided shelter from shell fire from the north, but none from "Asiatic Annie," the heavy gun (or rather guns) which shelled "W" and "V" Beaches continuously from various points along Erenkoi Bay east of Kum Kale, inflicting many casualties and much damage.

Into this too-crowded, unprotected area the Turk consistently pitched his high-explosive shells, and the ear-splitting crash and " coal-box " effect greeted the Territorials on arrival and gave them their first impression of real warfare. It was amazing that the casualty list was not far heavier. Had the enemy at this period been in possession of more and better ammunition the position in Gallipoli would have been untenable. Owing to this shortage in these early days solitary wagons and pack-animals could be moved about freely by day behind the lines, within view and range (with

The Nullahs

open sights) of the guns on the slopes of Achi Baba; for the Turk rarely wasted a shell on the chance of destroying one man or horse, and, by extending to a distance of 400 yards, even a battalion transport could often go forward and backward unmolested by day. The incessant rifle fire at night made the area immediately behind the front lines more dangerous then than by day.

Farther away to the north the British front was intersected by three streams, or, except during and immediately after rain, three more or less dry beds of streams, running north-east to south-west. The largest of these was Gully Ravine (Saghir Dere) close to and parallel with the western coast, emptying into Gully Beach about two miles north of Lancashire Landing. The Krithia Nullah (Kirte Dere) began near Krithia Village, and intersected the centre of the British area for a distance of three miles, then, a mile north of " V " Beach, turned to the south-east and emptied into Morto Bay. The third, Achi Baba Nullah (Maltepe Dere) ran parallel to, and from 500 to 1000 yards to the east of the Krithia Nullah, and it also debouched into Morto Bay. No nullah emptied into " W " or " V " Beach, and none intersected the high ground adjacent to those beaches. As the one road in the occupied territory, the Krithia Road, was registered, and in full view of the Turks, these gullies formed the only concealed approaches from the bivouacs and rest camps to the front line. The congestion of these " main streets " made traffic slow and laborious. Normally the approach would be along the bed of a tortuous stream, showing here and there a trickle of water, and at one spot in the Krithia Nullah even a small bathing-pool; but the sight of driftwood and debris deposited six feet and more above the bed-level gave warning to the observant. Disastrous experience soon showed that a few hours' heavy rain could convert these nullahs into raging and devastating torrents; and when the spate subsided channels of deep mud would be left, with here and there a quagmire into which mules and horses sank.

That one may have too much of a good thing while suffering from a lack of it may be a paradox, but there were times when it was true enough in Gallipoli. Water there was below the surface, to hinder the construction of deep trenches, in which men might stand or sit or walk without offering their heads and bodies as targets to the sniper; there was at times water in exuberant excess to wash away stores, equipment, and even trenches and dug-outs; but clean water was more precious than wine. There were one or two derelict farms which had wells, but the demand was so great that the supply soon gave out. Unfortunately no steps had been taken to protect wells from pollution when the area was first occupied, but afterwards a guard was placed over them, and the water chlorinated before issue, through fear of contamination. A small supply for the brewing of tea was obtained by digging a hole in the trench, below the parados, and placing therein an old biscuit tin with perforated bottom. In this way a little water could be collected—and every pint was treasure. As there were many of our own and the enemy dead lying out in the open, and also latrines in the immediate neighbourhood, it is a great tribute to the value of chlorination and typhoid inoculation that men drank this water with impunity. The normal trickle through the Krithia Nullah provided water for washing but not for drinking, as the stream flowed through the Turkish lines into ours, and was very dirty. A few springs of good water were found in the banks of the nullah, and one of these never failed to supply about 100 gallons an hour. Later, new wells were dug, a gang of well-sinkers, chosen from men of the mining districts, doing useful work. Some of the best of these wells were sunk on the side of a precipitous cliff at Shrapnel Point, near Gurkha Bluff, within a stone's throw of, but fifty feet above, the sea.

Before the Division landed there had been little attempt at sanitation; there were not nearly enough men for fighting purposes, and no one had time to worry about such things until too late. The flies had then arrived.

The southern point of the peninsula had been very sparsely inhabited. There were two villages, Sedd-el-Bahr, between "V" Beach and Morto Bay, and Krithia, below the slopes of Achi Baba. Elsewhere a few isolated buildings remained, and arches of an ancient aqueduct which had formerly brought water to Sedd-el-Bahr, still stood. But the inhabitants of the nullahs had not fled. Who that heard them will ever forget the frogs of the nullahs at night? A vivid memory of this will remain when things of more importance are forgotten. The average Lancashire man had read that frogs croak, and had accepted the statement tolerantly, as we acquiesce when told that, in spite of appearances, Sirius is really larger than the moon, or that the earth goes round the sun. Now they heard them, and considered "croak" too feeble and inexpressive a word. Some had perhaps read Aristophanes, and had assumed that the frogs of sunnier climes might voice their joys and sorrows less decorously than those which reside in suburban ponds near Manchester. At first the origin of the noise * gave rise to much conjecture, a popular notion being that the Gurkhas were responsible. Anything out of the common might be attributed to them. Had it not been printed in the newspapers that the Gurkhas observed a strange rite in respect of the shedding of blood whenever they drew their kukris, to show to the curious stranger or to put a still keener edge on the blade? And did they not throw these heavy, curved knives at the enemy? Accepting such statements as facts it was quite simple to believe that you yourself had seen them do these strange things. So the noise was made by the Gurkhas, and doubtless some unfortunate Turks were having a most unpleasant time.

Other interesting and unusual fauna were the tortoises, lizards, tarantulas, and scorpions. The tortoises were decidedly popular,

---

* Some declared that what the frogs said was "Bivouac! Bivouac!" A member of a new draft going up Krithia Nullah for the first time by night was heard to say : " I wish these 'ere b—— ducks 'd shut up; they'll give away uz position."

and the lizards entertaining, but no one loved the others. At a later date some ammunition was wasted on the flocks of migrating cranes and storks that flew over in wedge-shaped phalanx, until shooting at them was forbidden. The number of birds which lived and nested on the peninsula, undeterred by, and apparently indifferent to, the noise, carnage and destruction and the presence of armies where men had hitherto been infrequent visitors, was remarkable. Linnets, goldfinches, turtle-doves, magpies, jackdaws, and other familiar birds were common. During the summer many rollers were seen, and were called " parrots " from the brilliance of their plumage. Black-headed buntings, having yellow plumage, were mistaken for canaries. Birds of prey abounded, from the griffon vulture seen in May on the cliffs of Helles to the abundant kestrel. Levantine sheerwaters, known to the Turks as " the souls of the damned "—a name which gained in significance as the months passed —flew in flocks round the cape. The winter brought homely English birds, robins and dunnocks, starlings and chaffinches, to remind men of home.

Another noise which for a time puzzled the lads from Lancashire was a weird, penetrating cry heard in the morning and evening. There were various conjectures as to its origin, but finally the more enlightened decided that it was the muezin calling the Faithful to prayer.

Having given some idea of the conditions in Gallipoli and the nature of the country, we return to the narrative of events.

On May 11 the East Lancashire Division was ordered to take over the whole of the British front line, except that portion held by the Indian Brigade, which came under the command of General Douglas for a few days. The line was taken over in the course of the night and of the morning of the 12th. It was a pitch dark night with heavy rain, and few of those who took part will forget this first experience.

On the evening of the 12th the Manchester Brigade made a demonstration to draw attention from an important movement by the Indian Brigade on their left. The high cliff overlooking the ravine of " Y " Beach was strongly held by the enemy, and the machine guns of this formidable redoubt formed an obstacle that must be overcome before further progress could be made. The feint of the Manchesters served its purpose by distracting attention from the storming company of the 6th Gurkhas, and so enabling the hardy little mountaineers to scramble up the cliffs unopposed and rush the redoubt. They held the Turks at bay while their comrades of the other three companies swarmed up the rocks and completed the capture of the position, which received the name of Gurkha Bluff. It was not only a fine bit of work, but also a success of the greatest value. On the same evening the Lancashire Fusilier Brigade opened fire to support a forward movement by French troops on their right.

On May 15 a readjustment of positions was ordered, and on the nights of May 16–17 and 17–18 the reliefs were carried out. The line of trenches was now in four sections. That on the left, held by the 29th Division, including the 29th (Indian) Brigade, ran from the Ægean coast eastward for 1600 yards to the eastern edge of Fir Tree Wood, 300 yards north-west of Krithia Nullah. The next section, held by the East Lancashire Division, extended the line for 1500 yards from the right of the 29th Division, through the Krithia Nullah to the Achi Baba Nullah, which it included. The Royal Naval Division's section continued the line for 700 yards to the Telegraph Line; and the right section, thence to the coast of the Straits, above the ruin known as " De Tott's Battery," about 2100 yards in length, was held by the French Corps Expeditionnaire.

Later this line was termed the Redoubt Line. Saps terminating in T-heads were run out towards the Turkish trenches, and parties told off at night to connect the T-heads and dig themselves in, until two new advanced lines had been made. By the end of May a series of redoubts had been constructed at intervals along the old front line, and these were garrisoned in readiness to meet any temporary success of the enemy. The occasion did not, however, arise. The Manchester Brigade occupied the first line of the second section, with the Lancashire Fusilier Brigade on its right, and the East Lancashire Brigade as reserve. It may be mentioned that at this period the total ammunition available for a battalion consisted of 200 rounds per man, with twelve boxes of 1000 rounds each in reserve in the firing line, and twelve boxes at Battalion Headquarters.

During the three weeks after the disembarkation of the Division had been completed there was little actual fighting, no attack being made by either side. The arrival of the Territorials had strengthened the position sufficiently to discourage Turkish hopes of dislodging the invading force, but no forward movement on a large scale could be contemplated until the ground recently won had been consolidated and the difficulties of transport and supplies reduced. As the line stretched from sea to sea no flanking movement was possible. It was therefore a case of playing for position for a time. Each infantry brigade in turn assisted the French, the R.N. Division, and the Indian Brigade to develop their plans and effect necessary changes, and each in turn relieved the brigade in the first line.

But though there was a lull in the fighting after the 8th of May the shelling of the trenches, rest camps, cliffs, and beaches never ceased for long. Even bathing parties * suffered from the shelling, and the Turkish rifles blazed away day and night without cessation, causing much loss to working-parties and men in bivouac far behind the first line, and even in the R.A.M.C. tents below the cliffs. At

* General Bailloud, commanding a French Division, informed General Douglas that his men were always shelled when bathing in Morto Bay until, soon after the arrival of the 52nd Division, a kilted battalion went down to bathe, and from that day the firing ceased. He concluded that the Turks were under the impression that the wearers of " skirts " must be women, and, being of a gallant disposition, they refrained from shelling the bathers.

BATHING POOL IN KRITHIA NULLAH.

THE KRITHIA NULLAH.

EVENING "HATE."

dark one could hear from the cliffs of Gully Beach the continuous "plop" of bullets striking the water. There were also casualties from hidden machine guns; and the courage, enterprise, and skill of the Turkish snipers were the cause of many fatal wounds. Owing to the shallowness of the average trench it was difficult even for the most careful and experienced to keep under cover, and most injuries received at this time were head wounds. The Turkish snipers hid in the scrub—some carrying camouflage so far as to paint themselves green—or lay in holes apart from, and generally in advance of, their trench system; and their patience, persistence, and ingenuity evoked reluctant tributes from their foemen. Fir Tree Wood was a happy hunting-ground of the snipers, some of whom had remained in their hiding-places during our advance, in order to pick our men off at short range during the night. The Territorials received valuable tips from the Regulars on the best methods of dealing with snipers, and before long their numbers, and the losses they inflicted, were kept in check.

During this period the men not in the front lines were kept busy unloading supplies at the beaches and transporting them to the dumps, road-making, trench and well digging, and performing many other fatigues. The sappers, who had landed on the 9th and 10th of May, had their hands more than full. The 1st Field Company was in bivouac near Morto Bay on the right, and the 2nd Field Company on the left flank near Pink Farm, a solitary building which became a famous landmark and rendezvous during the campaign. They directed the construction of trenches, of lines of rifle-pits in front of the trenches, of dug-outs, and trench-bridges for armoured cars, improvements of the rough country tracks, work on wells and appliances for distribution of drinking water, and the manufacture of bombs. The digging, deepening, and repairing, and, when material was available, the strengthening of trenches was a never-ending task, which had to be performed under fire from artillery, machine guns, and snipers. The soil was mainly a stiff yellow loam, which stood well unrevetted until rain came, when it was transformed into peculiarly bad mud, and the water would not drain away. Gorse and heather, outcroppings of rock, and in one or two sectors, the tough fir-roots, which interlaced and formed a network at varying depths, added considerably to the difficulties.

The Field Ambulances on landing had equal difficulties to encounter, and the way in which they contrived to overcome them and to makeshift successfully afforded proof of their resource. Dressing stations had to be made in clefts in the cliffs, with tarpaulin sheets stretched from boulder to boulder for shelter. The shortage of appliances and equipment during the first weeks was a serious handicap. As soon as their equipment arrived they moved up to the rear of the bivouacs in the centre of the line. The battalion stretcher-bearers had quickly "made good." They had had to stand the usual chaff while training, but within a week of landing they had become "heroes" in the eyes of their comrades. The

Field Ambulances, lacking tackle, had not been able to provide bearers to evacuate from First-Aid Posts, and the battalion stretcher-bearers carried the wounded a distance of three miles to the beach.

Practically everything required for the army in Gallipoli had to be brought from the base at Mudros, the harbour of the Island of Lemnos, nearly forty miles away. Even water was conveyed overseas to supplement the inadequate local supply. Rations, ammunition, equipment, and material of all sorts were transferred from the ships to flat-bottomed lighters and landed, frequently in rough weather, and generally under fire from the Asiatic coast. The small A.S.C. unit therefore did not enjoy much leisure. No. 2 Transport and Supply Company had given evidence of its efficiency, for, though within ten days after landing it had lost forty-one animals killed, it was found that they possessed one more than the original number landed. Many loose mules were straying around, and the company upheld the rather unenviable reputation of which it boasted in pre-war days of never passing any unconsidered trifles by.

A Divisional Supply dump had been established on the top of the cliffs above " W " Beach, and there it remained until the evacuation. Though in a very exposed position and under daily shell fire it enjoyed a remarkable immunity. The rations were " man-handled " from the beaches to this dump, where they were issued to the Regimental Quartermasters, who brought with them their limbers when they had any, but usually A.S.C. limbers took rations to the R.Q.M.'s dump, about a mile inland, where they were divided in proportion to the strength of companies. Here battalion transport men loaded the pack-animals and led them across country for two or three miles to Battalion Headquarters, a short distance in the rear of the trenches, where the stores were unloaded, and the Transport Officer's responsibility ended. At Battalion Headquarters a party from each company in the trenches was waiting to carry the rations to Company Headquarters, where the C.Q.M.S. issued to the platoon sergeants the share for their men, and the platoon sergeants in due course divided the articles among the section commanders.

On paper this simple daily routine is a mere matter of efficient organization, but in active practice it was something more. The Turk had a very good idea of the routes to be taken, and as he fired more vigorously during the night than in the daytime, the transport, whenever possible, moved up soon after noon while he indulged in his siesta. Rations had, however, often to be taken up at night, and casualties among the A.S.C. men and trench ration parties were frequent. None of the pack-animals had previously been under fire. The load must be packed with equal weight on either side or it will not reach its destination, for the mule, though a convinced individualist, has nothing to learn from the best-organized trade union in the matter of direct action or the lightning strike. The loads consisted of full boxes and half-filled boxes of bully-beef tins, tins of biscuits, jars of rum, sacks of loaves, whole cheeses, tins of jam, bags of tea and sugar, sides of bacon, and on mail-days bags of letters and parcels. The correct balancing and securing of such articles, even on a placid, well-trained horse in a paddock at home, where no more disturbing explosions are to be feared than those caused by a distant motor-cycle, demands no mean skill and sense of proportion. But when shells are bursting close at hand, and mules and horses do their best to prevent the loading and dislodge the loads, it is a very different affair. When the loading has at last been accomplished and the animal is asked to move he will probably kick and buck until the load goes to the winds. Both mules and horses behaved uncommonly well under fire. On the rough tracks the mule was far steadier than the horse and could carry an equal weight. He was more particular about the perfect balance of his load, and would not attempt to carry an uneven pack.

Having finally completed the packing and persuaded the animals to start on the journey to Battalion Headquarters the Transport Officer's troubles take another turn. He has to find his way in the dark across an open bullet-swept zone with animals that jib and shy as the shells burst, or lie down as the fit takes them, and at times succeed in scattering their packs. These must be collected and laboriously replaced, the driver meanwhile employing the most spirited and forcible terms of endearment in his vocabulary. At times the convoy will be held up by heavy shelling of the area that has to be crossed. Leaving the open they enter one of the nullahs up and down which hundreds of troops are moving, and progress is slow and exasperating. But in spite of all obstacles the transport men daily got the rations through to their comrades in the line. Nor should a word of gratitude to the Indian drivers of the A.T. carts and the Zion Mule Corps be omitted. These men gave efficient help in the transport of stores and material from the beaches to the dumps, and their courage under fire was admirable. The pride the Indians took in the smart and clean turn-out of their mules and carts was the more noticeable as they did not appear to be subject to the ordeal of inspection.

The journeys of the ration-parties from Battalion Headquarters to Company Headquarters were no less exciting than those of the battalion transport parties. Bearing heavy boxes or bags on heads or shoulders they crossed from trench to trench in the open, tripping over wire, stumbling into holes, dodging rifle fire, and, too often, falling victims to the sniper. But the rations arrived and the men were fed.

The rations were monotonous and ill-suited to the climate. They consisted of bacon (for breakfast), bully-beef and biscuit, with a little jam and cheese, a tin of Maconochie's vegetable rations being at first, but not later, considered a treat, but Maconochie was particularly unsuited to a hot climate. Fruit—even good tinned fruit— and fresh vegetables would have done much to preserve the health of the men during the intense heat of the summer. In due course every man became a more or less expert cook, and to be on visiting terms was a privilege not unattended by risk, as it involved the sampling of many weird experiments and decoctions. Bread from the tents on Bakery Beach was first issued on May 21, and was received with acclamation.

Firewood was very scarce, as there were few trees or bushes, but it had to be obtained somehow for the trench fires ver which the men brewed their tea and cooked their food. It w s therefore not uncommon in the Helles area, in spite of orders issued to diminish waste, to see a caseful of tins of bully-beef tipped out on the roadside, that the invaluable wooden case might be split up for fuel. Butts of rifles which lay beside their dead owners met the same fate. Evidence of the awful waste of war abounded—weapons, ammunition, equipment, food, clothing, trodden under foot, and left to rust and decay. Where man could not expose himself by day these things remained unsalved for months, but elsewhere they were collected and returned to store. The best place where wood could be " won " was above Bakery Beach. A sentry was put over the wood-pile, but interesting conversation and a few cigarettes would occasionally distract his attention for the needful time.

On May 21 the Brigade Commanders received instructions from the Divisional Commander on various points connected with the latest methods and conditions of siege warfare, such as the use of bombs, sandbags, and loopholes, and the action of snipers. One officer, one N.C.O. and four men from each company were instructed in bombing, under the officer commanding the R.E., and each infantry brigade was allotted 400 bombs. It was found, however, that no more than 225 bombs were available for distribution among the three brigades. The bombs were made from empty jam tins sent down from the trenches to Lancashire Landing, where they were filled (chiefly by the divisional butchers and bakers at first) with old nails, bits of shell and of barbed wire, and other scraps of metal and an explosive charge. At first a time fuse was fitted through the top of the tin, and this had to be lighted by the aid of a match, but before long a detonating fuse was fitted. Matches were scarce and valuable, and in wind and rain many were wasted before the fuse could be lighted. These bombs were first issued in very small quantities about an hour before the attack began on June 4.

On the 25th of May occurred the memorable cloud-burst on Achi Baba, and in a few moments the nullahs were in spate, the trenches flooded, and thousands of men soaked to the skin. It was an Act of God which could not be foreseen or provided against, and the hardship inflicted upon the troops was very great. For a time the Krithia Nullah was impassable, and many dead Turks were carried down. The Lancashire Fusiliers Brigade Headquarters was under four feet of water for several hours, and the Signal Office was washed away. One battalion was enjoying beef-steaks in the dug-outs when a roar of water was heard, and a stream twenty feet wide quickly filled every dug-out. With British tenacity the men held on to chunks of bread and of steak as they scrambled for higher ground.

The Submarine Menace

Towards the end of the month the submarine menace developed into a very real danger to the men-of-war in these waters. The battleship *Triumph* was torpedoed on May 25 as she lay at anchor with nets out, off Anzac. She sank in ten minutes with a loss of ten officers and sixty-eight men. Two days later, the *Majestic*, Rear-Admiral Nicholson's flagship, lying off Cape Helles, fell a victim to the same German submarine, and sank in six fathoms. Fortunately all but forty-eight men were saved. This disaster was witnessed by many of the Territorials on the beaches and cliffs. As other British and French battleships were attacked by submarines about the same time, it became clear that naval co-operation must be dispensed with, or considerably reduced, as ships at anchor offered too easy a target for torpedoes.

The *Queen Elizabeth* had been ordered home on the first hint of danger, and now all the large ships were sent back to the safety of Mudros, and the regatta-like gathering at the mouth of the Dardanelles melted away. The Turk promptly seized the opportunity for propaganda purposes. An ingeniously worded pamphlet, printed in English, French, and Hindustani, and dropped from aeroplanes, notified the invaders that all their battleships and transports had been destroyed, that the Germans had gained control of the seas, and that no further supplies need be expected. " Don't take our word for it, but see for yourselves. Last week you saw a large fleet of all kinds of vessels off Cape Helles. Look for it to-day. You have fought bravely; give yourselves up now to an enemy who respects your valour and will treat you well." Tommy laughed. He had got his rations for the day, and the morrow would take care of itself.

On the 25th of May the designation of the Division was changed, and as the " 42nd (East Lancashire) Division " it took precedence in numerical order of all other Territorial divisions. The Lancashire Fusilier Brigade became the 125th Infantry Brigade; the East Lancashire Brigade the 126th; and the Manchester Brigade the 127th. On May 27 the 126th Brigade was split up among various battalions of the 29th Division in order to bring those depleted battalions up to strength pending the arrival of drafts from England.

D

CHAPTER III

GALLIPOLI

(June 1915—January 1916)

THE situation in Gallipoli on the 1st of June, 1915, was disappointing. Much more had been hoped for than had been accomplished, and the loss incurred for so small a gain had been three times as great as the *maximum* for which the authorities had made preparation.

After five weeks of toil and struggle, valour and self-sacrifice, unsurpassed in history, no more had been achieved than the securing of a mere foothold on the peninsula. Only incurable " optimists " in England could ignore that fact, but, discouraging though it was, the prospect would have been less gloomy had there been any reasonable hope of a steady inflow of drafts to fill the great gaps in the ranks, and of reinforcements of sufficient strength to permit a breathing-space to the overworked, worn-out remnants of the heroic 29th Division. Instead, the Russian collapse under Hindenburg's blows in Courland, Galicia and Poland took away all hope of support from the north and east, and set free Turkish divisions in the Caucasus and Asia Minor for employment in defence of the peninsula. Bulgaria, too, was about to join in on the side of her ancient enemy against her former friends; submarine activity had become a very real menace to communications and had deprived the invaders of the support of the heavy naval guns; and the shortage of shells, especially of high explosive, placed them at a great disadvantage. The daily allowance was limited to three rounds per gun, and at times to one round, whereas the French 75's were firing continuously.

The casualties of the Mediterranean Expeditionary Force already numbered 38,600, and though it was calculated that the enemy had lost at least 55,000 men, the damage done to the defending force was not in proportion to that received by the invading force in view of their relative resources. The difficulties had been underestimated, and the preparations inadequate, and as the present position at Helles was an impossible one, it was necessary to move forward and, by repeated assaults, to push the enemy's lines farther and farther from the landing-places. With this object in view an attack on a large scale had been planned for the beginning of the month. As a preliminary to this Lieut.-General Hunter-Weston,

The Plan of Battle

commanding the 8th Army Corps, held a conference at the Corps Headquarters on May 27, to settle details of an advance along the whole front in order to bring the first-line trenches within assaulting distance of the Turkish trenches. By 11.10 p.m. the movement was reported completed, and the troops were digging themselves in. Casualties had been few, but next morning it was found that in the darkness mistakes had been made and the new line was, in places, from 50 to 150 yards in rear of the positions indicated. On the night of May 28–29 a fresh advance to rectify mistakes was successfully carried out by the 127th Brigade, but this time the casualty list was much heavier.

On June 3 orders for the attack were issued. The French objective was the line of the Kereves Dere Nullah. The first objective of the 8th Army Corps (of which the 42nd Division formed the centre, with the 29th Division and the Indian Brigade on their left, and the R.N. Division on the right) was the main line of Turkish trenches, about 200 yards from the British first line. The second objective was the enemy's third line.

At 8 a.m. the next morning (June 4) the heavy guns and howitzers would open the bombardment of certain strong positions. At 11.5 a.m. an intense bombardment of the enemy trenches would begin. At 11.20 all guns except those on the approach lines would cease fire, and the infantry would cheer, raise their bayonets above the parapet, as though about to assault, with the object of inducing the Turk to occupy his front trenches, which would be heavily bombarded by all guns and howitzers, the machine-guns firing in bursts as targets presented themselves. At 12 noon the first line of infantry would advance, without firing, to the assault of the first objective, the batteries lifting to range on the trenches farther back. At 12.15 the second wave would advance, pass through the first line, and attack the second objective.

Divisional conferences were held at the Headquarters of the 125th Brigade, and General Douglas issued and explained his orders, and disposed the troops under his command as follows: First wave—two battalions of the 127th Brigade consisting of a half-battalion each of the 7th, 5th, 8th and 6th Manchesters, from right to left in the order named. The objective for this line was the front line of the Turkish trenches. A half-battalion of the 5th Lancashire Fusiliers was to follow in support on the left flank. The second wave consisted of the remaining half-battalions of the 127th Brigade. Their orders were to rush through the front line of Turkish trenches and gain the second objective, which was less than a mile from Krithia. A half-battalion of the 6th L.F., as working party, and the 1st Field Company, R.E., were to follow the first wave; the other half-battalion and the 2nd Field Company were to follow the second wave, to consolidate the lines gained. All the above troops were under the command of Brig.-General Noel Lee. The remaining half-battalion of the 5th L.F. was to form the garrison of the line of trenches held as the firing-line before the attack.

The 9th Manchesters were to occupy the second line, which was strengthened by redoubts. The 7th and 8th Lancashire Fusiliers were to be in Divisional Reserve. The 9th Manchesters was the only battalion of the 126th Brigade acting with the Division, the 4th and 5th East Lancashires and the 10th Manchesters being still split up among the skeleton battalions of the 29th Division.

The bombardment that opened at 8 a.m. on June 4 was the heaviest and most prolonged that the peninsula had witnessed. At 11 a.m. every available gun both on land and sea was firing, including six batteries of four guns each of the famous 75's, generously lent by the French Commander. These were firing high-explosive shell. The whole Turkish line was enveloped in smoke, and it seemed impossible that any positions could withstand its fury. The village of Krithia and, indeed, the whole of the hillside appeared to be a mass of flame and dust. The plan to cease fire on the front trenches at 11.20 a.m. had the effect intended, and the enemy prepared to meet the expected assault. A hail of bullets swept over the trenches of the 127th Brigade, and a few moments later the renewal of the bombardment caught the Turks as they were manning the trenches or hastening through the communication trenches to reinforce their thinly held front line.

The last half-hour of waiting was a severe test of nerves, and it was a relief both to the imaginative and the stolid when the hour of noon arrived. But the Manchesters had already been proved. The operations of the end of May, the digging in No Man's Land to push the first line closer to the enemy, while the Turk knew perfectly well what was intended and had been able, by the light of a waxing moon, to thin out the working-parties, had been highly dangerous and trying to the nerves. The losses had been deplorable, but the will to overcome the difficulties and to face the dangers with resolution had prevailed, and had given officers, N.C.O.s and men confidence in one another. Each platoon, each company, knew that it would not let the others down when the big event should come off. And now the hour had struck. Promptly at twelve o'clock the leading wave of the 127th Brigade went over the top for the first time, and advanced steadily and in good order. They were met by devastating rifle and machine-gun fire, but those who escaped the bullets pressed on in a steady line and by bitter hand-to-hand fighting made good their first objective. In places the wire was untouched by the bombardment, and men died cutting it that their comrades might pass through. The second wave followed at the appointed time. Within five minutes the Turkish first-line trenches had been captured, and the second in half an hour, and during the afternoon the fourth line of Turkish trenches had been penetrated. Sappers accompanying the successive waves found and disconnected buried mines, and assisted in the construction of new trenches and the reversal of captured ones. On the left the 29th Division had seized their first objective, but their further advance was checked, as the barbed wire on their left remained

Battle of June 4, 1915

undamaged, and the Indian Brigade was held up by this obstacle. The professional soldiers of this division paid generous tribute to the amateurs of the 4th and 5th East Lancashires and 10th Manchesters, who fought with such spirit and determination within their ranks.

On the right, however, an initial success was soon followed by a reverse which had disastrous consequences. The R.N. Division had gone forward with a dash that did credit to these young untrained soldiers, and with a considerable measure of success. On their right the French had rushed a formidable redoubt, called from its shape "the Haricot," but unfortunately their colonial troops, magnificent in attack, lack the confidence and dogged resolution in adversity that characterize our " native " troops from the Punjab and Nepal. They gave way before a furious bombardment and counter-attack, and the Haricot, once more in Turkish possession, proved a fatal obstacle. With their right flank exposed to the concentrated fire of innumerable machine-guns the Naval Division, cruelly reduced in numbers—one brigade losing sixty officers— were compelled to fall back to their original line, leaving the right flank of the 42nd Division in the air, the gap being 300 yards from front to rear. The Turk possesses individual initiative and resource in full measure, and he was quick to take advantage of the situation. Also, he was amply provided with bombs, whereas at this date our men had none—a serious handicap in close fighting. His bombing parties began to eat their way into this flank, which was also enfiladed by rifle and machine-gun fire, and in spite of the most determined opposition of the Manchesters, of the L.F. who were in support, and of a party of Engineers under Lieutenant Oscar Taunton, who threw back the enemy's grenades until wounded, the position became critical.

In the meantime the 7th Lancashire Fusiliers had been moved up to the old fire trenches when these were vacated by the second wave, and at 2.45 p.m. two companies of the 8th L.F. were sent to fill the gap between the right of the 127th Brigade and the R.N. Division. At 3.35 p.m. it was seen that the enemy was massing troops in a nullah on this flank, seriously threatening the foremost line. The French Commander had, however, promised to make a fresh attack on the Haricot at 4 p.m., and this, by enabling the R.N. Division to advance, should relieve the pressure. Our Allies were unable, however, to make this attack, and the position of the 7th Manchesters on the right becoming quite untenable, the Divisional Commander, after consulting the Corps Commander, at 6.30 p.m. ordered the withdrawal of the foremost line to the main Turkish trench. The retirement was made with the greatest reluctance; indeed, the few remaining officers had great difficulty in making the men realize that the order to withdraw must be obeyed. The idea of giving up the ground they had won was almost unbearable, for the four Manchester battalions had resolved to hold on to their gains, whatever the cost might be. " C " Company of the 6th Manchesters had penetrated to a considerable distance beyond the bifurcation of the nullahs, but, being enfiladed from the higher ground on the right, found it impossible to retire. Its commander, Captain H. B. Pilkington, was mortally wounded in the head, but, propped up in the trench, he continued to direct and encourage his men. The company was practically wiped out.

The cost had indeed been great. Of the 770 men of the 6th Manchesters only 160 answered to the roll-call that night. A company of the 8th Manchesters which at noon leapt out of the trenches nearly 200 strong, could only muster 18, and from the other units there were similar reports. Early in the afternoon Brig.-General Noel Lee had received a shell-wound in the throat from which he died on June 21 in hospital at Malta. When he fell, Lieut.-Colonel Heys, 8th Manchesters, assumed command, until, an hour later, he was compelled to return to his battalion, as hardly any of its officers were left; and he was killed soon after he rejoined. The last remaining officer of this battalion, Captain Oldfield, was killed shortly after he had organized the withdrawal of the battalion. Lieut.-Colonel Lord Rochdale, 6th Lancashire Fusiliers, was ordered to succeed Colonel Heys, and he remained in temporary command of the 127th Brigade until June 21. The 7th Manchesters had also lost their C.O., Major Staveacre, who had succeeded to the command of the battalion on May 28, when Lieut.-Colonel Gresham was invalided to Malta.

The work of the Battalion Medical Officers and stretcher-bearers was beyond praise, but what can be said of the grit of the wounded ! One M.O. records that from the 120 men who passed through his Regimental Aid Post, many being badly wounded and obviously in great pain, he did not hear even a whimper. Much difficulty was experienced in getting the wounded down the crowded and battered trenches and communication ways. The advanced Dressing Station of the 3rd Field Ambulance was in the Achi Baba Nullah, half a mile above Backhouse Post; that of the 1st Field Ambulance was at Clapham Junction. It was a rough journey for wounded men from either of these posts to the Central Clearing Station on " W " Beach; only hand carriage was available for those who could not walk, and there were many casualties among the bearers, though they were not fired upon deliberately. The wounded could not be attended to quickly enough to prevent a line of stretcher cases, waiting to be dressed, forming outside the stations.

The Territorials had proved themselves in the Division's first pitched battle, not merely with credit, but with distinction. Though the assaulting waves had been exposed to converging fire from higher ground on either flank their attack had been brilliantly successful. At the end of the day the front had only been advanced by 400 yards, yet the Manchesters had gained 1000 yards, and could have advanced still farther. Indeed, there can be little doubt that the Turkish centre had been pierced, and that, had not the troops on their right been compelled to fall back, or had there been reserves to bring forward, they would have seized the high ground behind the

Turkish Counter-attacks, June 6, 1915

village of Krithia, the key to the Achi Baba position. The Division had captured 217 prisoners, including 11 officers.

The 5th of June was mainly given over to the consolidation of the front to meet the expected counter-attack. On the evening of the 5th the first line was still held by the 127th Brigade, but during the night part of it was relieved by the 125th Brigade. There were two weak points—

(1) A pronounced salient where the right of the 42nd Division linked with the left of the R.N. Division. A strong work was in process of formation to strengthen this.
(2) The ground between the Vineyard and the right branch of the Krithia Nullah had many facilities for bringing enfilade and reverse fire to bear on our line. This became the scene of the hardest fighting.

At 3.45 a.m. on the 6th the enemy began to shell our line : at 4.25 a.m. strong bodies of Turks were working their way down the Krithia nullahs. At the same time an attack was delivered on the trenches held by the 8th Manchesters, but this unit had just been reinforced by three platoons of the 7th Lancashire Fusiliers, and the attack was easily repulsed. Some Turks succeeded in getting part of the trench held by the 5th Manchesters, but were driven out again by the combined action of the 5th Manchesters and the 5th Lancashire Fusiliers. At 6.20 a.m. the 88th Brigade, on the left, were obliged to fall back slightly, and as this exposed the left flank of the 5th L.F., they were forced to fall back below the bifurcation of the nullahs. Here they were reinforced by a weak company of the 7th Lancashire Fusiliers. Bombing attacks and bayonet charges continued throughout the morning, and reserves were brought into the front lines until the Divisional Reserve consisted of only 60 men of the 7th L.F. Casualties were heavy, Lieut.-Colonel Fallows of the 8th L.F., and his second-in-command, Major Baddeley, being among the killed. The three battalions of the 126th Brigade should have rejoined the Division on the 5th, but they, too, had been fiercely attacked, and, though suffering severely, were upholding the credit of the Lancashire Territorials. As the 29th Division could not spare any of these three battalions, the Chatham Battalion of the R.N. Division was attached to the 42nd Division at noon on the 6th, and held in reserve.

By 1 p.m. the situation had improved, and the number of Turks in and around the nullahs had greatly diminished. The 5th and 7th L.F. were now ordered to take the offensive; the small redoubt near to the bifurcation of nullahs, which had been captured by the enemy, was attacked and retaken. By the evening of the 6th the enemy's attack, which had been made in great strength and with much bravery, had been repulsed. His losses had been considerable, and his only gain was the small indentation by the Krithia Nullah. For three days the fight had raged without intermission. Worn-out, hungry, thirsty, sleepless men had fought and dug and fought again until the line had been firmly established and held by the physically exhausted remnants; and the battalions that had suffered most had time to rest and lick their wounds.

On June 7 counter-operations were undertaken after dark with the object of straightening the line from the Vineyard towards the nullah. The attack was divided into three parts, the right being entrusted to 100 men of the 9th Manchesters, and 20 men of the 1st Field Company; the centre and left each to a company of the Chatham Battalion. The 9th Manchesters succeeded, but the left and centre failed to attain their objective. On the night of June 8–9 the 127th Brigade was withdrawn to Corps Reserve, and its place in the firing-line taken by the 126th Brigade, the three detached battalions having rejoined.

The casualties in the 42nd Division during the four weeks amounted to—

	Killed.	Wounded.	Missing.
Officers	68	121	6
Other ranks	610	2691	688
	678	2812	694

Total, 4184.

In his Official Despatch, General Sir Ian Hamilton made special mention of the part taken by the 42nd Division in the action of the past few days.

" The Manchester Brigade of 42nd Division advanced magnificently. In five minutes the first line of Turkish trenches was captured, and by 12.30 p.m. the Brigade had carried with a rush the line forming their second objective, having made an advance of 600 yards in all. The working parties got to work without incident, and the position here could not possibly have been better."

After describing the withdrawal of the R.N. Division, Sir Ian proceeds—

" The question was now whether this rolling up of the newly captured line from the right would continue until the whole of our gains were wiped out. It looked very like it, for now the enfilade fire of the Turks began to fall upon the Manchester Brigade of the 42nd Division, which was firmly consolidating the furthest distant line of trenches it had so brilliantly won. After 1.30 p.m. it became increasingly difficult for this gallant Brigade to hold its ground. Heavy casualties occurred; the Brigadier and many other officers were wounded or killed; yet it continued to hold out with tenacity and grit. Every effort was made to sustain the Brigade in its position. Its right flank was thrown back to make face against the enfilade fire, and reinforcements were sent to try and fill the diagonal gap between it and the Royal Naval Division. . . . By 6.30 p.m., therefore, the 42nd Division had to be extricated with loss from the second line Turkish trenches, and had to content themselves with consolidating on the first line which they had captured within five minutes of commencing the attack. Such was the spirit displayed by this Brigade that there was great difficulty in persuading the men to fall back. Had their flanks been covered nothing would have made them loosen their grip."

In a private letter from Sir Ian Hamilton to the Divisional Commander the following sentence occurs : " As a matter of fact I never saw any finer piece of work than that performed by the Manchesters that day."

Later on the evening of June 4 this message from the Divisional Commander was conveyed to all ranks—

The following message from Lieut.-General A. G. Hunter-Weston, C.B., D.S.O., received at 8.33 p.m. on June 4, is published for information—

" Please express to the 42nd Division, and particularly to the 127th Brigade, my appreciation of the magnificent work done by them to-day. The 127th Brigade attacked with gallantry, and held on to the objective ordered with tenacity. It was a very fine performance. Please convey this to all the troops of the Division when possible, and tell them that I deeply appreciate their gallant conduct and devotion to their duty. The renown they have gained for the Division will not only reach the ears of all in Lancashire, but throughout the British Empire. I feel sure that the same tenacity will be maintained to-night and throughout the Campaign."

On the night of June 12–13 the 127th Brigade embarked for a period of rest and reorganization on the island of Imbros. Any who fondly imagined that the term " rest " implied a period of repose and pleasant recreation were soon disillusioned, for fatigue parties were much in request at the Imbros base, and guards had to be provided for the various stores. While there, the men were inspected and addressed by the Commander-in-Chief, who assured them of his appreciation of the Brigade's gallantry on June 4. Its place in the line was taken by the 155th Brigade, which with the 156th Brigade had arrived at Helles in advance of the Headquarters of the 52nd (Lowland Territorial) Division. When the 127th Brigade returned on June 22 and 23, Brig.-General the Hon. H. A. Lawrence (later Chief of the General Staff in France) took over the command. The 5th and 6th Lancashire Fusiliers and the 10th Manchesters next had their period of rest; the first-named at Mudros and the others at Imbros. When they returned on July 9 and 10, the 7th and 8th Lancashire Fusiliers and the 5th East Lancashires took their turns, the Fusiliers' period of recuperation being cut down to four days. On July 13 Brig.-General Viscount Hampden assumed command of the 126th Brigade.

Though there were many minor operations during June and July no action on a large scale took place after June 8 on the divisional front. Enemy activity was kept down by local counter-attacks and bomb-raids. In one of the former the 126th Brigade's attack between the Vineyard and Krithia Nullah on June 18 was anticipated by the enemy, and the 10th Manchesters suffered severely. The first trench raid of the Division was made about this time. Lieutenant Bennett Burleigh, 7th L.F., with six volunteers, crawled up an old communication trench and bombed a small redoubt held by Turkish snipers. The party returned without a scratch, though several men of the 8th L.F., who were giving supporting fire, were killed or wounded. This raid was the more notable in that it took place an hour before noon, and, as was hoped, the Turk was caught asleep. On July 2, the same officer (who was killed in action a few days later) accompanied by two men, went out twice by daylight and once after dark along the Turkish communication trench which ran through the Vineyard, and brought back valuable information. On the 5th the 7th Manchesters helped to repulse a fierce attack on the 29th Division on their left, and the battalion wiped out about 150 of the enemy. On the night of the 10th, Lieutenant O. J. Sutton and Sergeant Grantham, both of the 9th Manchesters, made a daring and successful reconnaissance of a new Turkish trench, and on the following night went out again and ascertained by measurement its exact position.

About the middle of the month the first Monitors arrived, each carrying two huge guns, and before long other strange marine objects appeared—the " blister ships " and the " beetles." The former were cruisers which even at anchor could ignore the submarine menace, and the latter were motor-lighters with a drawbridge at the bows, and they could carry 500 men to the landings, protected from bullets and shrapnel by the iron decks and sides. The need for such protection increased with the daily evidence of the enemy's improved supplies of guns and ammunition. On one morning seven hundred shells dropped on Lancashire Landing alone. On July 23 the Division had been reinforced by 47 officers and 1500 other ranks from the second line in England, but these did not nearly make good the losses. The 18th Battery, R.F.A., and the 1/4th E. Lancs (Cumberland and Westmorland) Howitzer Brigade had also arrived from Egypt during the month, and with them Brig.-General A. D'A. King, D.S.O., who was given the command of all artillery in the right-half sector of the Corps. The 5th Battery under Major Browning, and the two guns of the 6th Battery had been continuously in action, and had firmly established the credit

Battle of the Vineyard, August 6-7, 1915

of the Territorial Artillery. On July 24 Major-General Douglas had assumed temporary command of the 8th Corps until August 8, the command of the Division during that period being taken by Major-General W. R. Marshall.

On August 6 the period of comparative inactivity came to an end. The primary purpose of the Gallipoli campaign was to obtain possession of the Narrows, and thus secure command of the Dardanelles and cut off communication with the Asiatic shore. It had been hoped to achieve this by pushing forward from the south, but the original force had been far too small for the purpose. During May, June and July the Turkish garrison had been much increased, and also the supply of guns and shells, and the defences on Achi Baba greatly and most ably strengthened, whereas the British reinforcements and drafts to fill the gaps had been relatively small. There was little prospect of success by a frontal assault from Helles, and the loss that would be incurred by a futile attempt would cripple the Allies and remove all chance of ultimate success. The Commander-in-Chief decided upon an attempt to reach the Narrows at Maidos, five miles across the peninsula from Anzac, the formidable Sari Bair range intervening. A new landing was to be made on August 6 and 7 at Suvla Bay, a few miles to the north of Anzac cove, and it was hoped that the force landed here would seize the northern slopes of the Sari Bair range, while the troops from Anzac would storm the central and southern heights. On August 6 an attack was to be made from the right of Anzac in order to divert attention from both the landing and the true objective; and a vigorous offensive was ordered at Helles, with the object of containing as large a Turkish force as possible within the southern area and of drawing their reserves from the north. There appeared to be good prospects of a decisive success, and hopes were high.

The line of trenches from the Achi Baba Nullah to the Krithia Nullah (both inclusive) was held by the 125th Brigade on the right and the 127th on the left, the 126th being in reserve. The French were on the right of the 125th Brigade and the 29th Division on the left of the 127th. The 5th Manchesters, who were acting in conjunction with the 88th Brigade (29th Division) had for objective a Turkish trench on the right of that Brigade. The bombardment began at 2.80 p.m. on the 6th, and soon H.E. shells could be seen bursting in the trench which the 5th had been ordered to take. At 3.50 p.m. they attacked, but on reaching the objective, found that they had been enticed into a dummy trench, without cover, and exposed to enfilade fire. To prevent the right flank of the 29th Division being left " in the air," Captain Fawcus, commanding the first line of the 7th Manchesters, was ordered, about 8 p.m., to get into touch. Arriving at a trench which he expected to find occupied by the 88th Brigade, he called out : " Are the Worcesters there ? " and was heavily fired upon. Moving to the left he still found the enemy in occupation of the trench, and fell back. On his way to rejoin the second line he came across a small party of the Worcesters and took them with him. The two lines regained the firing-line in the small hours of the morning, having lost 40 men out of 200. That Captain Fawcus returned safely was amazing, his clothes being riddled with bullets.

A few hours later the Battle of the Vineyard began, the bombardment by British and French batteries opening at 8.10 a.m., and increasing in intensity at nine o'clock when the naval guns joined in. The fire on the trenches south-east of Krithia Nullah was both heavy and accurate, but the trenches within the triangle formed by the fork of the nullahs suffered but little. Half a battalion of the 126th Brigade was attached to the 125th Brigade on the right, and another half-battalion to the 127th Brigade on the left. One battalion of the 126th Brigade was to hold the original line. Two batteries of machine-guns assisted by bringing a cross fire to bear on the enemy's trenches.

At 9.40 a.m., the troops went forward with their usual dash, wearing tin back-plates that could be seen by the artillery " spotters." On the right the Lancashire Fusiliers gained their first objective, but the 5th and 8th found that their portion was merely a very shallow trench raked by enfilade fire. Parties of the 6th and 7th reached their second objective, but enfilade fire and superior numbers compelled them to fall back. One of the few officers to reach this objective was Major W. J. Law, 7th Lancashire Fusiliers, who took part in all the subsequent fighting in the Vineyard. Soon after 11 a.m. portions of the first objective were retaken by a strong Turkish counter-attack, but the Vineyard remained in our hands. The 5th and 7th L.F. made a gallant effort to recover what had been lost and were partially successful. At 1.30 p.m. another enemy counter-attack in close formation was caught by our guns and brought to a standstill. The Turks suffered severely in counter-attacks upon the Vineyard, and for some hours gave up the attempt in this quarter, but resumed it late at night with no more success. The 5th and 8th L.F. reoccupied a portion of their first objective in the evening. Parties of the 4th East Lancashires and 10th Manchesters gave great assistance both in attack and defence. On the left the Manchesters showed similar dash and determination, but owing to the greater difficulties of the ground between and about the nullahs and to the intricacy of the Turkish trench system, which, with the nests of machine-guns, had escaped our shells, they were unable to hold any of the trenches taken in the initial assault, and their losses were grievous, the attacking lines being mown down by the enemy's machine-guns.

The casualties during the two days were—

	Officers.	Other Ranks.
Killed	20	203
Wounded	36	770
Missing	24	511

The first V.C.

The result was that a tactical point of some importance had been won and held by the tenacity of the 125th Brigade, and that a large Turkish force had been pinned down when urgently needed in the north. The Turks had, indeed, been massing troops in front of the Division as they had intended to attack our lines in force, on the 6th or 7th of August. Sir Ian Hamilton telegraphed to the Corps Commander: " Your operations have been invaluable, and have given the Northern Corps the greatest possible help by drawing the main Turkish effort on yourselves. I was sure you were ready for them to-night. Well done, 8th Corps."

But though the sacrifice had not been altogether in vain, the advance from Suvla Bay and Anzac had failed, and the conquest of the Dardanelles seemed more remote than ever. And yet for one half-hour it had seemed so near! Of all the many lamentable tragedies of the campaign surely the most dramatic, the most appealing, was that on Chunuk Bair, at dawn on the 9th of August, when companies of the 6th Gurkhas and 6th South Lancashires had stormed the cliffs and driven the Turks headlong before them. From the top of the saddle they looked down upon the promised land. Below them the goal—Maidos, and the Narrows! The way lay open and victory was in sight—was already achieved!—and the Turkish Army in the south would be cut off! But these four hundred men alone of all the Allied troops that landed on the peninsula were destined to view the promised land. Flushed with triumph, Gurkhas and Lancastrians intermingled raced down the slopes after the fleeing Turks. And then the blow fell—truly a bolt out of the blue—a salvo of heavy shells crashing with infernal accuracy into the midst of them, mangling and destroying the exulting victors. Where that salvo came from will probably never be known with certainty, but there can be little doubt that the shells were British. The remnants of the little force could only make for shelter; there was no shelter in front, and the chance had gone, never to return.

To return to the 42nd Division. In and about the Vineyard held by the 6th and 7th Lancashire Fusiliers, the fighting surged and swayed for several days. The Turk fought gamely, with grim determination, and the casualties on both sides were heavy. The C.O.s of the two battalions had been ordered to remain at their Headquarters in communication with the Brigadier, and the Adjutants, Captains Spafford and Gledhill, held on tenaciously. Spafford was killed, and the order to retire was sent, but Gledhill's pertinacity got this order withdrawn, and the Vineyard was held. A successful and very gallant stand against great odds was made by " A " Company, 9th Manchesters, on the night of August 7–8, when the first V.C. awarded to the Division was won by Lieutenant W. T. Forshaw, who was in temporary command of the company. Two M.C.s and two D.C.M.s were also won by the company. Forshaw was holding the northern corner of this small oblong with a bombing party when he was attacked by a swarm of Turks who converged from three trenches. For the greater part of two days he kept them at bay, and even threw back, before they had time to explode, the bombs they threw at him. In the words of the Official Report—

> "He held his own, not only directing his men and encouraging them by exposing himself with the utmost disregard of danger, but personally throwing bombs continuously for forty-one hours. When his detachment was relieved after twenty-four hours, he volunteered to continue the direction of operations. Three times during the night of August 8–9 he was again heavily attacked, and once the Turks got over the barricade; but after shooting three with his revolver he led his men forward and recaptured it. When he rejoined his battalion he was choked and sickened by bomb fumes, badly bruised by a fragment of shrapnel, and could barely lift his arm from continuous bomb throwing."

On the 8th and 9th the 126th Brigade relieved the 125th and continued the struggle, and Lieutenant S. Collier, 6th Manchesters, gained the M.C. for a good bit of work on the right of the Vineyard. A trench held by a group of men of the 126th Brigade was fiercely attacked by enemy bombers, and its capture appeared certain. Collier, however, organized and led the defence, and though he had never before handled a bomb, he displayed much aptitude with this weapon; and in spite of persistent attacks, continued throughout the night, the Turks were beaten off. On the night of the 12th the enemy attacked in mass and captured the Vineyard, but the next day were bombed out of it, and it was finally consolidated and held. Throughout the operations the Divisional Engineers had worked and exposed themselves as fearlessly as ever. Their services were continuously in demand, and they had never been found wanting. The bulk of the work on this occasion had fallen on the 1st Field Company. The Signal Company, too, had proved how competent all its branches were. Much of its work is not done in the limelight, and it may be mentioned that the average number of messages passing through the Signal Office daily had been about three hundred. In times of stress this number was greatly increased.

On August 13 the 42nd Division was relieved in the trenches and went into Corps Reserve. The following 8th Army Corps Special Order was issued next day—

> "The 42nd Division has now been withdrawn into Reserve after having been in the firing-line for three months without relief. During this time the Division has taken part in three big attacks, and has been subjected to the continuous strain of holding, improving and extending our line and communications under constant fire.
>
> "Though some units have distinguished themselves more than others, the Division has, throughout this arduous period, displayed a dash in attack and a spirit of determination and

CAPT. FORSHAW, V.C., 1/9 BN. MANCHESTER REGT.

GULLY BEACH.

Sickness and Pests

endurance in defence which is worthy of the best traditions of the British Army. The persistence with which the enemy were held off during the recent determined attack, and part of the ground lost gradually recovered in face of strong opposition, was a fitting conclusion to the period during which the Division has been in front line.

"The Lieut.-General Commanding wishes to express to Major-General Douglas and his staff, as well as to all ranks of the Division, his appreciation of their good work, and he looks forward to seeing them again display the same soldierly qualities in active operations against the enemy at an early date."

The Division, however, was not destined to enjoy a long period of rest, as orders were received at noon on the 19th to take over the trenches of the Left Section in relief of the 29th Division which had been ordered to Suvla. This was completed by 8.30 p.m. More than a thousand officers and men had rejoined from hospital in Alexandria, and small drafts arrived from England, but the Division was still much below strength; and as reinforcements for the Division practically ceased after August, it is indeed amazing that the units held together in view of the terrible losses through fighting and disease. The second line, from which alone drafts for the Territorials could be obtained, was formed into a Division (the 66th) for employment in France. To all intents this meant that battalions must dwindle into companies and companies into platoons or even sections. But there was no corresponding reduction in responsibility. For instance, a Field Company of twenty or thirty sappers, most of whom would be worn out by overwork and sickness, must still do the work of a hundred fit men. The sappers had not enjoyed even the brief period of rest accorded to other units.

Enemies more insidious than the Turk, and regarded with far greater detestation, had appeared during the past two months. The ravages of sickness had reduced the fighting strength of the Division more than had the bullets of the enemy. Dysentery and jaundice were rampant, and an epidemic of septic sores ran through the Division. The seasoned veterans fared better than the new reinforcements, who succumbed at an appalling rate. There had been no break in the hot, dry weather. Many of the wells had gradually become defiled, others had run dry, and this no doubt contributed greatly to the amount of sickness. The insanitary conditions inseparable from the type of warfare waged in so confined and exposed a space, the continuous strain exacted from all, the lack of sleep, the tropical heat, the monotonous and unsuitable food, the lice, and, above all, the plague of flies, with which no sanitary measures and precautions could cope, all were in their degree responsible for the deplorable results. The country was one huge graveyard in which hundreds of corpses of friends and foes lay unburied, and the air was heavy with the stench. Flies clustered in noisome masses on everything that attracted them, on the food and in the mess-tins as these were carried to one's mouth, on sores, on faces and hands—blue and green monsters too lazy to fly or crawl away, and to kill fifty was but to invite five thousand to attend the funeral. Under such conditions men lived and moved, and even kept a stout heart. Weak and emaciated, they crawled about the trenches, but when work or fighting was to be done they never shirked, and did not give in until compelled to do so. They had by now absorbed some measure of the philosophy of the East, and, borrowing a phrase from the enemy when things seemed at their worst, they encouraged one another with the remark: " Never mind; there's always tomorrow." In these days the small " band of brothers " who had come safely through the fighting were drawn closely together, and the rest of the world seemed very remote. The personal inspiration of certain officers and men counted for much, and the memory of the example of zeal and energy and good courage when the prospect was most dreary, set by officers of the Indian Army, in temporary command of units that had lost their senior officers, is gratefully preserved by those who survived. Many officers who left England with the Division gained in no ordinary degree the admiration and affection of their comrades, but the name of Philip Vernon Holberton stands out pre-eminently. His repeated acts of gallantry, his constant thought for others and entire disregard of self, his genial presence and cheery words of encouragement when these were most needed, stimulated weary comrades to carry on hopefully, and made him an inspiration to officers and men alike.*

The amalgamation of battalions was put off as long as possible, but later, in October, there was no alternative. The 5th and 8th Lancashire Fusiliers were then combined under Lieut.-Colonel F. W. Woodcock, and the 6th and 7th under Major Alexander; the 5th and 6th Manchesters under Lieut.-Colonel C. R. Pilkington (Lieut.-Colonel Darlington having been evacuated with fever), and the 4th East Lancashires and 9th Manchesters were split up among other battalions.

In the new area, which had previously been held by the 29th Division, now at Suvla, there were many changes, on the whole for the better. The men were not sorry to see the last of Krithia and Achi Baba Nullahs, of the Vineyard and other scenes of carnage. Yet the names conjure up other memories, not wholly painful—of heroic attempt and gallant performance, of courage, self-sacrifice, and devotion to duty unsurpassed in any theatre of war, of cheerfulness in adversity, of enduring friendships, of doggedness and

---

* Holberton could trounce an offender very effectively, but his comments never rankled nor ever affected the admiration and affection in which he was held. While Adjutant and at the same time O.C. of his battalion, he placed a newly-joined subaltern in charge of a working-party. An hour later, to his surprise, he saw the party returning from the task. " You don't mean to say you've finished ? " he said to the sub. " No, sir, but the men said they were tired and would work better after a rest and tea." " Yes," said Holberton, " they wanted to find out if they had to deal with an officer or a d—— fool! Now they know."

ENTRANCE TO GULLY RAVINE AT GULLY BEACH.

GULLY RAVINE. HEADQUARTERS OF SIGNAL CO. AND 2ND FIELD CO. R.E.

determination, of great pride in the comrades who had fallen, whose graves, marked by biscuit-box crosses, lay thick in the Krithia Nullah beyond Clapham Junction. The Eski, Australian and Redoubt Lines, Wigan, Stretford, and Oldham Roads, Burlington Street, Greenheys Lane, Ardwick Green, Clapham Junction, Cooney's corner (where it was wise to make good speed), Romani's Well, which could always be relied upon for a supply of deliciously cool water, the olive-grove beside it, most peaceful and popular of bivouacs—these were seen for the last time, but the memories that cluster about them will never be wiped out. The mention of the names brings back the scene, the sounds, the smells—the gullies thronged with men and animals, the R.A.M.C. carrying the wounded down to the dressing stations, the transport toiling up with rations, the linesmen of the Signal Company coolly and efficiently laying lines and repairing wires under shell and machine-gun fire, the despatch riders driving furiously over ground that no motor-cycle was ever meant to negotiate, those good men of the Zion Mule Corps, the Hindus driving their well-cared for, well-trained and (to them) docile mules, or at rest making chupatties, the smell of wood-fires— and of manure incinerators—the lines of animals, neighing or braying, the dumps, the incessant crack of rifles, and, above all, the flies and the mud.

A new nomenclature had now to be learnt and to be created. Fusilier Bluff, Geoghegan's Bluff, the Gridiron, the Birdcages, Border, Essex, Hampshire, Lancashire, Douglas, Frith, Ashton, Burnley Streets or Roads soon became familiar signs. The derivation of most of the names is sufficiently obvious, but the " Eski Line " puzzled the men until some genius among them propounded the brilliant theory that " it's the pet name of one of the Staff-officer's wives." As it was understood that he meant " of the wife of one of the Staff-officers," the illuminating suggestion was adopted as satisfactory, and men were heard to murmur the name *Eski* ecstatically. Gully Ravine took the place of Krithia Nullah as the main road to the firing-line. The bed of the gully in September and October was deep in loose red sand which made very heavy going for tired troops, but when the mud came one sighed for the vanished sand. The transport was frequently thigh-deep in liquid mud in those evil days. On both sides stretched the horse and mule lines, and stores and dumps were placed at suitable spots. At the last bend of the gully a wag erected a cairn and labelled it *Third Tower*. This was hailed with delight by parties changing over, as all men who had trained on the Cairo–Suez Road understood that the end of their journey was close at hand. A thirty-yard rifle-range was constructed in the ravine for the training of the reinforcements from the third line, who had had little or no experience of the service rifle, and the modest beginning of a Divisional School came into being in one of the small offshoot gullies where Major Fawcus held his bombing-class.

E

A " rest " was more of a reality in the new area, and it was comparatively safe, but in Gallipoli the word *rest* held a very different significance from that attached to it at home. It had now become too closely associated with hard work to be really popular, and the *dolce far niente* illusion had been quite dispelled. It meant heavy fatigues day and night, much digging, the unloading of lighters and the carrying of heavy loads; but a Beach Fatigue had its compensations, for it was possible at times to get a bathe if one was not too fastidious to object to coal-dust and refuse from lighters, nor to the close companionship of the dead horses and mules that floated around. These were constantly being towed out to sea, but the homing instinct, or the current, brought them back again. " W " Beach even boasted a canteen (run by enterprising Greeks), and men who had time to spare and were possessed of patience might, after waiting for hours in a queue, come back with a bit of chocolate and a tin of fruit—rare and precious luxuries. One day would-be purchasers found the military police in possession. The Greeks had been arrested as spies, and were not seen again. In due course the Division ran its own popular canteen on Gully Beach.

As a rest-bivouac Gully Beach was a great improvement upon all previous resorts, and its attractions read like a holiday advertisement. A sea front, excellent bathing in the Mediterranean, superior accommodation on ledges cut in the cliff face—not unlike a colony of sea-birds—and those who applied early enough even got first-class quarters in a hole in the rock. Inside the ravine, where the bends gave complete protection from shell-fire, caves had been dug in the cliff sides, one above the other up to forty feet, and even more in places, above the bed of the gully. By night the illuminations in these irregular tiers of dug-outs, with the black outline of the cliff-tops beyond the highest tier of lights standing out distinct against the star-lit sky, gave the ravine an effect of glamour and romance—almost of sentimental prettiness—that contrasted strangely with the grim reality of day. " Doesn't it remind you of Belle Vue ? " was a comment frequently made by the men, all of whom were familiar with the chief attraction which Manchester provides for strangers. It was possible to walk upright along the coast road (or Marine Parade) past the little colony of the Greek Labour Corps to Lancashire Landing, but this shore road could not be used for wheeled traffic. The sunsets seen from the beach, or, better still, lying among the heather on the cliffs above, were at times gorgeous. Perhaps it was the peace of twilight, the red sun sinking behind the hills of Imbros or snow-capped Samothrace, that turned one's thoughts and conversation homewards at the evening gatherings, and sharpened the longing for the good times that must surely be coming. Prime favourite of all items at the jolly sing-songs arranged by the various units was " Keep the Home Fires Burning," and this was generally kept back for the closing chorus. These entertainments were excellent and they did good. Much hidden genius was brought to light, and a store of original and topical humour tapped.

In October a start was made with the construction of winter quarters, in the lower end of the ravine, for the Brigade in reserve, the R.A.M.C., etc. The supply of sandbags had improved and a minute quantity of corrugated iron sheets was rationed out to units.

The Divisional Commander naturally took an interest in the construction of his own quarters, and, among other questions to the sapper employed thereon, he rashly asked about the composition of the mortar used. It is here necessary to disclose a trade secret and state that the mortar depended upon the horse-lines for one of its components. This secret was revealed without any attempt at concealment, and thenceforward the sapper worked unhindered, while the General in the distance wondered what other horrid secrets had been hidden from him.

A certain corporal of the R.E. who was engaged on D.H.Q., had achieved an enviable reputation as one who could deal effectively with both officers and men. To him infantry officers—not merely second-lieutenants, but even field officers—were as clay in the hands of the potter, but when confronted with the Divisional Staff he met his Waterloo. He found that the Staff Officers' Union demanded—

(a) That each officer's hut should be completely rebuilt without any inconvenience to the officer concerned.
(b) That each officer should be treated better than any other officer.
(c) That every one's hut should be begun at once and finished forthwith.

Reluctantly he admitted defeat, and applied to be transferred to work as close as possible to the firing line, " for the sake "—as he put it—" of peace."

The Staff Officers of the Division could relish a joke at their own expense, and they were as much tickled as any one by the libellous report that the following official scale of rewards paid to Turkish snipers had been discovered : For killing a private, 5 piastres ; N.C.O., 10; lieutenant, 25; captain, 50; field officer, 100; Red Tab, court-martial and execution for " assisting the enemy."

In August there had been a fair supply of vegetables and raisins, but as a general rule the onion was the only vegetable obtainable. A small consignment of strawberry jam actually reached the trenches. By one of those lucky accidents that occur all too rarely the labels had been removed from the tins, and as the happy warrior enjoyed the unaccustomed treat his fancy toyed with the picture of the anguish and indignation of the profiteer and the conscientious objector on learning that their strawberry jam had been sent in error to the brutal soldier, and on being asked if they would take " plum-and-apple " instead. Plum-and-apple was now anathema. No longer would the *poilu* proffer his delicacies in barter, and even the Senegalese declined to trade. The flies were less fastidious.

Cookhouses were now established in Gully Ravine; the battalion *chefs* made the most of the ingredients at their disposal; and as the nights grew chilly the hot, well-cooked meals were more and more appreciated. Improvization was the crowning art of that weird-looking soldier, the cook, and one essential qualification for the job was the ability to " win " wood. In justice to him it must be admitted that he generally possessed this qualification, and he did good work. Cookhouses were no safer than other spots behind the line, and the cook's job was not a cushy one. In one cookhouse in the ravine a shell exploded when some dixies of rice were on the fire. The cook, uninjured in body but indignant at the mess made, gazed disgustedly at the debris. His only comment was : " Might have been a b—— wedding here ! "

Sickness diminished with the coming of the cooler weather, and as health improved moods of depression abated, and the irresponsible cheeriness of the British soldier, in spite of all he had gone through and all that lay before him, shone forth under conditions the reverse of exhilarating. Perhaps the rum-punch had some slight share of responsibility on one occasion. A party of transport men, howling a chorus on their way down the ravine in a drizzling and depressing rain, on being challenged by a sentry at the Eski Line, proceeded to serenade him. The sentry, whose job gave little scope for hilarity, inquired in disgusted tones : " What the —— are you so happy about ? Is the war over ? "

The unhappy experience of a quartermaster's storeman provides a moral—or even more than one. He had noticed two delectable rum-jars in the orchard by Pink Farm, with a Scottish sentry posted over them. After profound meditation he decided upon a frontal attack, and, accompanied by a fellow-conspirator, walked up to the sentry and said : " I've been sent for the rum for the puir laddies in the trenches. They'll be awfu' glaad to get it, and it'll do them guid." He then told his colleague—incidentally addressing him as " Jock "—to take one jar while he took the other, and off they went towards the nullah, the sentry appearing quite satisfied, and curiously lacking in that nasty suspicious spirit so prevalent among persons in charge of valuables, and so discouraging to enterprises of this sort. Half-way to the nullah they entered a deep ditch, with the intention of working their way round to the dump, where water was already boiling in anticipation. But the jars were heavy and temptation could no longer be resisted. A cork was pulled out with great care and some difficulty—and they found themselves in possession of two bottles of creosol. Their remarks are unprintable.

A new subaltern arrived about this period, and was handed over at the Battalion Dump to the post-corporal, who was on his way to H.Q. in the line. Presently a shell passed overhead, and the corporal explained that " it's not addressed to us; it's addressed to t' beach," some miles away. The sub., being a bit on his dignity, thought fit to tell the corporal—an ancient member of his battalion,

GULLY BEACH. DIVISIONAL HEADQUARTERS.

GULLY BEACH. INDIAN A.T. CARTS.

GULLY BEACH. QUARTERS OF THE 2ND AND 3RD FIELD AMBULANCES.

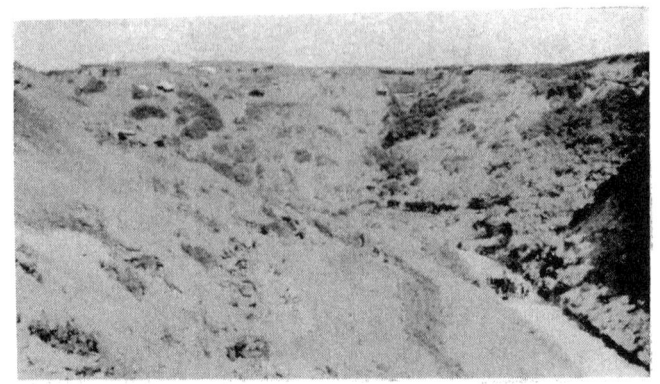

GULLY RAVINE. THE "ROAD" OR RIVER BED.

GULLY RAVINE. A "DUMP."

GULLY RAVINE. HEADQUARTERS 1ST FIELD CO. AND WAY UP TO THE ESKI LINES.

Mining Operations

and more in the nature of a family friend than anything else at Battalion H.Q.—that he need not be funny. A little later, probably within range of a deceased mule, the sub. unbent, and said : " Rather queer smell here, corporal? " " Yes, sir," was the reply, " this is where we bury uz officers."

Instruction in sinking shafts and making galleries had already been given by expert miners. A Mining Company was now formed, extra pay being granted to the men, and it was reasonably expected that this would be filled from the many colliers in the Division. A Staff Officer who was wont to boast that experts could be produced for any kind of job, inspected the company and proceeded to question the men. To the first he said—

" Well, my man, how do you like your task? "
" Oh, it's not so bad, sir."
" Extra pay all right, eh ? "
" Yes, but you can't spend it, sir."
" I suppose the work comes quite naturally to you ? "
" No, sir, I'm a solicitor's clerk."

The second man was a music-hall artiste, and the third a barber. Much discouraged, the officer ceased to interrogate.

The enemy exploded mines on the 3rd, 15th, 18th, 21st, 22nd and 29th of September, all opposite their trench in front of our right, known as " The Gridiron." Three of these damaged our parapet, and all caused interference with our field of fire. The repairing of the damage done on September 22 was made possible by the enterprise of bombing parties of the 6th Manchesters under Lieutenant Collier, who kept up a steady hail of bombs from the lip of the crater, where they had little shelter. On the left, at Fusilier Bluff, the Mining Company had got out protective galleries in time to baffle the Turco-German miners.

At first our mining policy had been defensive, but on this same day one of our shafts reached the barricade of a favourite Turkish bombing station. A mine was exploded, the barricade levelled, and a crater forty feet in diameter formed. The sky was darkened by the earth thrown up, and men in support and reserve trenches were covered with the falling clods. Brisk rifle fire from the enemy showed that the trenches were thickly occupied at the time, and their losses must have been considerable. A rush was at once made to the crater and a barricade built across it. Captain Cawley, 6th Manchesters, M.P. for Prestwich, was shot at night by a Turkish sniper, when shooting over the parapet with his revolver, and the crater became known as " Cawley's Crater."

On the 17th of October General Sir Ian Hamilton relinquished the command of the Mediterranean Expeditionary Force amid universal regret, and left for England. He had won the respect, and indeed the affection, of all ranks of his army, by whom he was regarded as a true friend and comrade, prompt in appreciation and unfailing in sympathy. To General Douglas he wrote : " You and your Division have always been consoling thoughts in the anxious moments we have lived through in common, and I want you to have all the luck in the world." On Sir Ian's departure, Lieut.-General Sir William Birdwood assumed temporary command in the peninsula until the arrival of General Sir C. Monro.

During October the South-Eastern Mounted Brigade (dismounted) was attached to the 42nd Division. The Brigade consisted of the East Kent, the West Kent and the Sussex Yeomanry, under Brig.-General Clifton-Browne. It remained attached to the Division until the evacuation, and officers and men proved the best of comrades. A system of fortnightly reliefs was now instituted, the 125th and 127th Brigades holding the right sub-sector, with H.Q. at the zigzag in the Gully; the 126th Brigade and the S.E. Mounted Brigade the left, or coastal, sub-sector, with H.Q. at Gurkha Bluff.

On the west of Gully Ravine the line was advanced by an average of forty yards on a front of 300 yards. In no place was the enemy's line more than 125 yards from the Division's trenches, and in places it was less than ten. On the 29th and 30th of October the Turks exploded mines near the Gridiron, blowing in fifteen yards of fire trench, killing two men, and burying six. Three of these were soon extricated, but, in spite of continued efforts, the other three—all miners—were given up for lost. As the Divisional Commander was passing along the trench three days later, he saw to his great delight two of the missing men being brought from the mine-shaft on stretchers. The third, Private Grimes, 5th Manchesters, though obviously on the border of collapse, stoutly refused to be carried. These men had had no food for three days and only one bottle of water between the three. It was largely due to the determination and grit of Private Grimes that they had had the dogged persistence to dig through twelve feet of earth with the aid of one pocket-knife, and so win to safety.

The month of November was not marked by military events of special importance, our constant activity having chastened the enemy's offensive spirit. Reports from Turkish prisoners indicated that the thorough training that had been given in the bombing school had contributed largely to this result. Mining was very active, and the divisional miners now held the upper hand. On the 25th the enemy injected through a hole in one of the galleries an aromatic gas, which affected the eyes, but not the lungs. Parties of three or four hundred officers and men from each Brigade were sent, in relief, to a newly formed Training School at Mudros for two or three weeks at a time, and derived much benefit therefrom.

During the first half of November there had been occasional heavy showers and some frost. On the 15th–17th a violent storm, accompanied by a deluge of rain, drove the sea higher and higher up the shore, swamping the bivouacs on the beach. In the Gully conditions were even worse. Bales of hay, sacks of bread, drowned mules, were washed down the ravine into the sea. On the night of the 26th a still fiercer storm raged in the peninsula, a storm as

Y RAVINE. LOOKING DOWN TO THE SEA.

IN THE FRONT LINE. MAN USING A PERISCOPE.

IN THE TRENCHES. AN ENTRANCE TO A MINE SHAFT.

SHELTERS TO PROTECT HORSES FROM SHELL FIRE.

LOOKING DOWN FUSILIER
BLUFF TO THE SEA.

IN THE TRENCHES.
MAKING TEA.

GULLY RAVINE.

GULLY RAVINE.   STRETCHER BEARERS.

Floods and Frost

disastrous to the combatants as any that ever affected armies in the field. The flood-gates of heaven indeed opened, and at Anzac and Suvla the trenches were quickly waist deep, and the current swept down like a mill-race—kit, equipment, rations, even men, being washed away. In places the trenches filled, and the troops must drown or stand on the top, a sure target for the Turk had he not been in a like predicament. As in a prairie fire or other of Nature's more appalling manifestations, the beast of prey and its natural victim flee side by side, or cower together, so Briton and Turk regarded one another as fellow-sufferers rather than as implacable enemies. The gale became a hurricane; the crash of thunder, the blinding flashes of lightning, heightened the sense of catastrophe, and the bitter cold made it the more unbearable. Piers and landing-stages were destroyed and the beaches strewn with wreckage. During the 27th the rain came down steadily; then the wind veered to the north and brought snow and cruel blizzards. A hard frost followed, and at Anzac and Suvla men were frozen to death; others lost their limbs—some their reason—and cases of frost-bite were very numerous. In the south the conditions were less disastrous than further north, but the suffering of the troops was intense. Altogether about 10,000 sick had to be removed from the peninsula as an outcome of the four days' tragedy. When the floods subsided Gully Ravine was a bed of deep mud, and its passage —a vital matter to the Division—could only be accomplished with infinite labour.

The activity of the hostile artillery increased as superior guns and munitions of war arrived from Germany, and the bombardments became more accurate and deadly. On December 14 Lieutenant W. R. Hartley, 7th Lancashire Fusiliers, led a patrol with great boldness and judgment close up to the Turkish trenches and located the entrance of a mine-shaft in the Gridiron, only six yards from a crater occupied by our men. Captain A. W. Boyd, of the same battalion, accompanied by Corporal W. Downton and Privates F. Mottershead and C. Bent, volunteered to carry out the destruction of this mine-head on the night of the 15th. Unobserved by the enemy they succeeded in placing a charge of forty pounds of gelignite in position in the Turkish trench, the charge being laid by Mottershead, who had originally discovered the mine-shaft. In addition to the electric wire a thin rope was attached so that a slight jerk would cause the charge to fall into the shaft; and as it was essential that the rope should be laid in a straight line Mottershead had to return to his trench *over* the Turkish barbed wire and in full view of the enemy. This was successfully accomplished; the rope was jerked, and the charge fired. On the following night Lieutenant Hartley (killed three days later) ascertained that the entrance to the shaft had been completely filled. Mottershead was awarded the D.C.M., and the gallant act was specially mentioned in 8th Corps Orders, the last paragraph of which stated that : " This enterprise is only part of the good work that has been done recently by this battalion under the command of Major W. J. Law, and the keenness and energy displayed are deserving of all praise."

Lord Kitchener had visited the peninsula in the middle of November, and on his return to England had reported in favour of evacuation. On December 8 General Monro issued orders to evacuate Suvla and Anzac, and on the 16th the withdrawal of 80,000 men, nearly 5000 animals, 2000 vehicles and 200 guns began. The highest estimate of probable loss that might be incurred in this most difficult and critical of operations was fifty per cent.; the lowest, fifteen per cent. Preparation was made at Mudros to accommodate from 5000 to 10,000 wounded, yet the evacuation was carried out without loss. It was one of the finest and most wonderful achievements of this or any other war, and all ranks shared the credit—though in very different degrees—from General Birdwood down to the humblest Indian mule driver.

Two minor operations were arranged for December 19 to take place simultaneously with an advance of the 52nd Division by the Krithia Nullah and the evacuation of Suvla and Anzac. Mines were laid at the Gridiron and at the east end of Fusilier Bluff. The intention was to take advantage of the explosions to establish bombing stations in the craters formed. The "jam-tin" bombs were now obsolete, and those used were the Mills and "cricket-ball" types. The task at the Gridiron was assigned to the 125th Brigade, the troops attacking being drawn from the 7th Lancashire Fusiliers, with some of the 1/2nd (West Lancashire) Field Company, R.E. The 6th Battalion held the original line and supplied catapult parties to fire from behind. Major Law was to have directed operations, but this able and gallant officer was killed two hours before the time fixed for the attack, and Captain Gledhill assumed temporary command of the 7th Battalion, Captain Boyd being in charge of the attacking party. The artillery gave strong support. The mine was exploded on the far side of a great crater which had a Turkish and English trench on either side. The explosion blew in the enemy trench and extended the crater, which the attacking party crossed, and then pressed down the horns of the Turkish trench and constructed barricades. By 6 p.m. the new line was well established in spite of rifle fire and enfilade fire from machine-guns. A Turkish attack at 9.40 p.m. succeeded in driving our men out, but Captain Boyd with great resource and promptness organized a counter-attack, and within fifteen minutes the lost ground had been retaken and a further gain made. In fact, the bombing parties had to be restrained from going too far down the enemy trenches in pursuit. A lot of work had to be done to make the crater tenable, and assistance was sent. A bomb team of the Sussex Yeomanry did remarkably good work in consolidating the left trench under heavy machine-gun fire, which continued all night. By daylight they had succeeded in deepening and sandbagging the trenches and in digging through from Cawley's Crater into the new one. Of two mines laid only one had exploded at first, but after the counter-attack our men

GULLY RAVINE. THROUGH THE MUD.

LIEUT. SMITH, V.C., 1/5 BN. EAST LANCASHIRE REGT.

were withdrawn into safety and the second mine was fired. It caught a number of Turks who were seen pressing up a sap, probably with the intention of counter-attacking again. Lieut.-General Sir Francis Davies, the Corps Commander, telegraphed his congratulations and gave permission for the new crater to be called officially " Boyd's Crater."

Similar operations at Fusilier Bluff were not, however, successful. Parties of the 9th and 10th Manchesters, supported by bombers of the 5th East Lancashires and the W. Lancs. Field Company, R.E., went forward pluckily, and several got within a yard or two of the enemy trench, but had to be withdrawn. The retirement was effected with coolness and judgment by Lieutenant Simpson, R.E., who, though wounded, checked a bayonet rush of the enemy. The casualties in both places amounted to one officer and twelve men killed and four officers and eighty-seven men wounded. The artillery and trench mortars gave valuable assistance throughout. The following message from General Birdwood, Commanding the Dardanelles Army, was received on the morning of the 20th December : " Well done, 42nd Division ! "

On the 22nd December Lieutenant Alfred Victor Smith, 5th Battalion East Lancashire Regiment, dropped a bomb when in the act of throwing it. It fell to the bottom of the trench in which were a number of men. He shouted a warning, and he himself got into safety, but, seeing that the others could not, he returned and threw himself on the bomb just as it exploded. He was killed instantly, but his comrades were saved. It is not too much to say that the account of this act of heroic devotion sent a thrill through the Empire, and there was general satisfaction with the decision to confer the V.C. after death. The 126th Brigade was justly proud of the fact that both V.C.'s so far gained by the division had been won by officers of its battalions.

Christmas festivities were held on different dates by the various units according to their positions in the line or in reserve. Taking into consideration the adverse conditions that prevailed, an excellent bill of fare was provided—roast beef, plum-pudding with rum sauce, a pint of beer for each man, and various delicacies from canteen stores. Christmas day was bright and frosty, and the Divisional Band turned Gully Ravine into a pleasure resort by playing Christmas carols at appointed spots in the ravine. One battalion thought that greater delicacy might have been shown in the choice of carols. They had been relieved from the front line on Christmas Eve, and had just settled down in " rest " bivouacs near Gully Beach to a much-needed sleep, when, in the early hours of Christmas morning, they were ordered to turn out and move to a distant bivouac far up the ravine. As they put on their equipment in a most unchristian frame of mind, the band started to serenade Divisional Headquarters with " Christians Awake ! " and as the men prepared to move off the tune changed to a less familiar air. " What are they playing now?" asked an officer. "'God rest you, merry gentlemen,'" came the reply in a voice choked with emotion. With twilight a silence fell. No gun fired, no rifle cracked, until the moon showed over the shoulder of Achi Baba, when missiles of destruction of every kind, from the cricket-ball bomb to the giant shells from monitors out at sea, pitched into the enemy lines.

Hostile aircraft, both bombing and observation planes, had greatly increased in number since the evacuation of Suvla and Anzac, the Turks being naturally anxious to learn what was happening at Helles. A note attached to an old bomb was thrown from the enemy trenches into the trenches occupied by the Sussex Yeomanry. It contained this message: " Good-bye, Sussex Yeomanry. Sorry you can't stay, but we'll meet again on the Canal."

The Turk was not looked upon with the blend of amusement (at his egregiousness) and detestation (of his manners and brutality) with which the Boche was regarded by all who came in contact with him. Rather was he respected as a brave foeman and esteemed as a sportsman. Among other things to his credit, he had treated wounded prisoners well and had respected the Red Cross flag. The flag of the Advanced Dressing Station at " Y " Beach was in full view of the Turks for three months, but there was no shelling and no casualty from shells. When the Field Ambulance of the South Eastern Mounted Brigade took over in December, the Union Jack was hoisted *in addition to* the Red Cross flag. The change was made at midnight, and promptly at dawn the Turks opened fire. The first two shells were short; then came three " overs," and the sixth —and last—brought down the flag-pole. The Medical Officer who records the above also testifies that during a long and heavy bombardment of " Y " Ravine hostile shells were dropping all along the tracks in the vicinity of the Advanced Dressing Station, the shooting being " dead accurate," but not one shell came within sixty yards of the Red Cross flag that flew over the Dressing Station.

Rumour had had little rest since August, 1914, yet she remained very vigorous and active. She had been particularly busy in Helles since the evacuation of the northern landings. To obtain ready credence, the rumour-monger must support his theory with convincing circumstantial evidence, as, for example, that he had been told by a friend, whose platoon-sergeant's brother was a batman at Divisional Headquarters, that there had been a terrible increase in the slaughter of the staff chickens. The 8th Army Corps Special Order of the Day, issued on December 20, reassured those who regarded evacuation as an admission of defeat, and, it must be confessed, disappointed those who felt that the object of the landings on Gallipoli had already been defeated and that they could therefore serve a more useful purpose elsewhere. The Order indicated that there was no intention to abandon Helles. Confirmation of a resolve to retain a hold on the peninsula appeared in the shape of the arrival off Helles of transports carrying fresh troops, the 13th and the veteran 29th Divisions; and now Rumour whispered of still another

The Evacuation

attempt to march across Achi Baba. But on December 27 and 28 innumerable fatigue parties were detailed to collect all stores and baggage at dumps for transport to the beaches, as the 42nd Division was to be relieved at once by the 13th Division under Major-General Stanley Maude. With much labour the baggage was taken to " V " Beach, only to be ordered to " W " Beach.

At 5 p.m. on the 29th the remnants that were left of the once proud battalions of East Lancashire Territorials moved off on their last march in Gallipoli—a sorry procession. The distance to " V " Beach from which most of the men embarked was about five miles, much of it through deep mud, and it was sheer grit that pulled them through, for their frames were wasted and enfeebled through sickness, exposure and unceasing strain; their feet, sodden through weeks of standing in muddy and water-logged trenches, were tender and painful; they were, it is true, quitting the scene of much misery and suffering, but they were not leaving as victors. Though they had done and endured all that was possible their object remained unachieved, and they were depressed by the sense of failure. Not unreasonably they felt that the Territorials had been neglected by the authorities at home—that had drafts been supplied in full measure from their second line they might have won through. At the date of the first landing, again on June 4, and again in August when the ambitious advance was made from Anzac and Suvla, victory had been in sight, and the lack of reserves had robbed the Dardanelles army of the triumph for which they had paid so heavy a price.

On arrival at the crowded beach they awaited their turn to board the " beetles." The French had a number of haystacks on the shore, and had posted a sentry to give warning of the coming of the shells by blowing a horn the instant that he saw the flash from an " Asiatic Annie " across the Straits. The bursting of the shell had been timed to follow the flash by twenty-three seconds, so the sounding of the horn was the signal for a rush to the haystacks or other available cover. These were seconds of extreme tension until the crash came and men realized that they at any rate had respite for a time; though in the dark it was impossible to know what damage had been done elsewhere. Piers were struck and great gaps made as parties were about to cross. Throughout the long night the embarkation proceeded, most of the men crossing the hulk of the *River Clyde*.* The wind was rising, and the transfer from the lighters to the larger transports was made dangerous by the roll of both vessels, and much argument ensued between the Royal Navy and the Mercantile Marine. In due course it was accomplished and, as the dawn showed pink in the east, the convoy steamed away towards Mudros. Eight months

---

* Was there ever a ship that lived through such shelling as this old hulk was subjected to for the period of nine months during which she lay aground at " V " Beach ? Or on whose decks so much blood had been shed ? The sale of the *River Clyde* to a Spanish firm at Malta seems hard to justify and shows a regrettable lack of imagination.

ago nearly 14,000 Lancashire Territorials had disembarked on the inhospitable shores which were now receding. The Division that left Gallipoli barely numbered 5000, though every battalion and unit had received drafts from the second and third lines in England, or from Egypt, and thousands of casualties had rejoined from hospital. Few of the 14,000 who had landed in May with such high hopes and in such good spirits, took part in the last melancholy parade to the beaches, or sailed on this December day to Mudros, but those few thought of what might have been, and of the great-hearted comrades and brothers-in-arms whom they had left behind. Many now lay in the cemetery above Lancashire Landing, a glorious resting-place from which, when alive, they had looked out upon the intense blue of the Ægean Sea, with the peaks of Imbros and Samothrace to the west, to the south and east the coast of Asia Minor and the straits, and direful Achi Baba to the north; others had been buried where they fell. Soon the lovely blossoms of the rock-rose and the gorgeous poppy would be covering their graves.

Perhaps to none of the survivors would these memories be more poignant than to two of the padres, the Rev. E. T. Kerby, M.C.,* and the Rev. F. W. Welbon, M.C., who had been untiring and absolutely fearless in giving comfort to the dying, in performing the last rites under fire, and in sharing the dangers and privations of the men in the front line.

The Divisional Artillery remained behind, and also a small detachment of Engineers and the 1st and 3rd Field Ambulances, all attached for duty to the 13th Division. The more modern guns must first be saved, and as each battery was withdrawn a battery of the old 15-pounders of the 42nd Division was substituted, so there was no cessation of fire during the day. For several nights no artillery fire was permitted between 9 p.m. and 2 a.m., in order to accustom the Turk to quiet nights with little or no firing. When the final evacuation took place three of the old guns were taken away successfully and the remainder destroyed. Some of the gunners and the greater part of the R.A.M.C. left a few days before the curtain fell on the final scene of the great tragedy of Gallipoli. The last men of the 42nd Division—and among the very last of the allied forces—to leave the peninsula were detachments of artillery and R.A.M.C. and a small party of Engineers.

On the 7th of January the last fight was fought on Gallipoli. After seven hours' heavy bombardment the Turks attacked, but they found the front line more heavily manned than it had been for months past, and the attack failed. Probably they were surprised by the vigour of their repulse, as they must have been convinced by now that the Helles force was in process of evacuation. It is likely that the strong opposition encountered led the Turk to believe that the British departure was less imminent than he had hoped, and that he would have to wait a little longer before he could catch

* Padre Kerby read the Burial Service over nearly one thousand graves of the Manchesters in Gallipoli.

LANCASHIRE LANDING SHORTLY BEFORE THE EVACUATION.

his enemy on the run. If his suspicions were lulled in this way it was fortunate that he chose for his attack the day immediately preceding the final evacuation. Heavy casualties were inflicted on both sides, and the East Lancs R.A.M.C. men were hard at work without a pause from 5.30 p.m. to 3.30 a.m. on the 8th. Their good work in attending to the wounded of the 13th Division brought them the personal thanks of General Maude, who also sent a letter of appreciation to the Divisional Commander. Lieutenant R. Hartley, R.F.A., distinguished himself and upheld the Division's reputation, by putting out a fire, which had started in a wagon full of ammunition, at great personal risk.

About noon on January 8 orders were received to destroy everything that could be of use to the enemy, and an orgy of destruction began. Huge dumps were made, or added to, the largest of these being at " W " and " V " Beaches. Hundreds of cases of bully beef, condensed milk, biscuits, and other rations, ammunition that could not be taken away, limbers, wheels, and anything else that would burn, were piled up, and the mass soaked in paraffin. Many horses and mules had to be shot, to the bitter grief of their drivers.

Preparations were made for the firing of the dumps at daybreak on the 9th, some hours after the hour fixed for the embarkation of the last batch of troops. As in the case of so many of the " innovations " of the Great War—steel helmets, breastplates, catapults, darts, hand-grenades, for instance—a time-honoured device was resorted to. Candles were left burning in tins, their rate of burning having been carefully timed, so that when the flame should reach a certain point it would ignite a train of oil and waste, which led to a mass of combustible material placed around and among the wooden cases. By means of a similar artifice fixed rifles in the firing-line continued to pop off at irregular intervals in order to delude the Turk into the belief that the trenches were still occupied.

A walk up Gully Ravine and the Mule Trench to the front line in the afternoon of January 8 provided new and strange sensations. Practically all the fighting troops were in or close up to the firing-line, the support and reserve lines and the usually crowded billets at Geoghegan's Bluff, the Eski lines, and similar spots being completely deserted. One could walk half a mile without meeting anything other than one of the limbers told off to trundle up and down the tracks in order to give the enemy the impression that traffic was still normal.

Late at night the troops began to leave the firing-line. When they had passed, the men in the second line filed out, and after them followed the small parties—each of one officer and four men—of the East Lancashire R.A.M.C. to pick up stragglers and assist any sick or injured. Last of all came the handful of sappers who had charge of the closing of the gaps in the entanglements of Gully Ravine. In places the enemy trenches were only fifteen yards from the British line, and it seemed too much to expect that the Turks should remain in ignorance of the complete departure of the opposing army.

The night was pitch dark. The men moved along the communication ways and passed through the gaps with a seeming deliberation and slowness that was most irritating to the more imaginative, whose nerves were on edge. There is some comfort in a crowd, though it may be more liable to panic. The handful of R.A.M.C. and R.E. who toiled in the rear were dominated by one thought—how many hours or minutes would go by before the Turk would discover that the British trenches had been deserted, and that he would simply have to follow swiftly to cut off all stragglers and perhaps capture or destroy the greater part of the retreating army? These were the most trying hours that the Lancashire men had ever known. "If ever man knew terror, I knew it that night," said one of the officers, and the others admitted that his experience was theirs no less. It cost them a real effort to appear calm and collected, and to talk to their men in tones of apparent unconcern. No sound pierced the stillness of the night save the occasional crack of a Turkish rifle, or of one of the fixed rifles left in the trenches, and now and then the bursting of a shell on one of the southern beaches.

The last party to arrive at Gully Beach found that the lighter which should have taken them off, was on a reef. "Saturday night, and we've missed the last train home!" sighed one of the men, as, in the small hours of the morning of the 9th, they set off along the shore road to "W" Beach, where the last two lighters, already packed like tins of sardines, awaited them. R.A.M.C. men and sappers got on board—one of the former complaining that the night had passed without the promised excitement—and as they steamed away the dump on the beach went off with a most appalling din. As a spectacle it was magnificent, the entire stretch of coast being lit up; and immediately the Turks awoke to the situation, "went mad," and began to shell the whole of the Helles portion of the peninsula furiously and indiscriminately.

Thus, on the 9th of January, 1916, the last men of the 42nd Division left Gallipoli. Yet is much of the ground in the south-western extremity of that peninsula still held for Lancashire by thousands of her best and bravest, who, in the bloom of youth or prime of manhood, died fighting cleanly and without hatred for love of country, faith in her cause, and the honour of their corps.

LIST OF GALLIPOLI CASUALTIES, M.E.F. (LAND FORCES, NOT INCLUDING FRENCH)

Killed, 28,200; Wounded and Missing, 89,349 . 117,549
Sick (of whom a large number died) admitted to Hospital 96,683

214,232

Casualties of the 42nd Division in Gallipoli: 395 officers, 8152 other ranks, killed, wounded, and missing.

CHAPTER IV

THE SUEZ CANAL AND SINAI

(*January,* 1916—*March,* 1917)

THE Division remained at Sarpi Camp, Mudros, until the middle of January. Gallipoli had left the body weak and the spirit dulled; every unit was much below strength, and most had less than half, and some barely a quarter, of their full establishment. Death, wounds and sickness had played havoc with the organization, and squad, platoon, and company drills disclosed the fact that the men had lost much of their barrack-square smartness, but drills and exercises, guards and pickets soon put an edge on the dulled blade. The weather was not particularly good, but the decent tents, the thorough and much-needed wash, the immunity from shell and rifle fire, the freedom to walk upright, to take exercise and play games, the arrival of six weeks' mail, the canteens, the unfailing interest in the shipping that went in and out of the great natural harbour daily, all combined to promote content and happiness.

On January 13 the advance parties and the 5th and 6th Lancashire Fusiliers sailed on H.M.S. *Mars* to Alexandria, and then proceeded to Mena, where they took over a large canvas camp and prepared it for the reception of the Division. The 126th Brigade, the greater part of the R.F.A. and other details embarked on January 14, but the weather at Mudros grew worse, and the order to embark the 127th Brigade was received in the early hours of a morning of violent storm, during which tents were blown down in some camps and the men drenched. In the murky half-light of dawn camps were struck, and companies moved off in a driving hurricane of hail and sleet. Some boarded a tug, packed so that they could not even turn their backs to the stinging hail, and were taken " joy-rides " round the great harbour in unsuccessful search for their troopship, were landed, and again embarked, transferred to a cattle-boat to be lodged and boarded on biscuits and bully-beef for five days, and then transferred to the right transport. Others marched through the quagmires across half the breadth of Lemnos and embarked at North Pier, and, indeed, some pessimists are convinced that they marched three times round the island. An improvement in the weather soon restored cheerfulness, and with a light heart the remainder of the 42nd Division left Mudros, the last link with Gallipoli, on the morning of the 18th of January.

Alexandria was reached in about forty-eight hours; thence by train to Cairo and by road to Mena, where the Division settled down in camp near the Pyramids of Gizeh. There the 2nd (Manchester) Brigade, R.F.A., the ammunition columns, the A.S.C. train, and other details which had been left behind in Alexandria, or had subsequently arrived from England, were re-united to the Division. For the past eight months the A.S.C. had been employed on local transport work, and had supplied drafts for No. 2 Company at Helles, for the A.S.C. in Salonika, the expedition in the western desert against the Senussi, the transport camps at Mudros, and a small detachment had been sent to Suvla Bay. " A " Squadron, D.L.O.Y., which had also taken part in the fighting against the Senussi, rejoined the Division a few weeks later. The show-places of Egypt were new to a large proportion of officers and men, who made the most of what opportunities were afforded to see them. Happy recollections of the autumn of 1914 were revived by the others, and also memories of good friends and comrades whose shallow graves lie thick in Helles. On the whole these were pleasant days of recuperation, but the Division did not long enjoy the flesh-pots of Egypt—if that term may be stretched to include the French teas and ices at Groppi's and similar delights. Orders were received to move to Tel-el-Kebir, but after a few units had arrived there the destination was changed to Shallufa, a few miles north of Suez, the Division concentrating in a camp in the desert east of the Canal during the last days of January and the first days of February.

The Division now formed part of the 9th Corps, commanded by Lieut.-General Sir Julian Byng, whose Headquarters were at Suez. Soon after the arrival of the Division the command of the 9th Corps passed to Lieut.-General Sir Francis Davies, and Brig.-General V. A. Ormsby succeeded Brig.-General G. S. Elliott in command of the 127th Brigade. The Division was now equipped for the first time with *pukka* first-line transport vehicles, and the field-kitchens were a much-appreciated novelty. The advance-parties at Shallufa had had their fill of hard work, for the stores had to be taken across the Canal and man-handled up the steep banks. For a short period in the early morning and late evening the Canal could be crossed by a pontoon bridge built by the Australians, but during the greater part of the day the crossing had to be made by means of a stage hauled across by a chain which lay on the bed of the Canal. This stage often carried a motley collection of troops, natives, camels, and stores, and the hauling was heavy work, which, at a later period, was relegated to Field Punishment prisoners from the Divisional Compound. The Engineers who were in this region in the winter of 1914–1915 found that little had changed. There had been insignificant enemy raids, and no new works of importance had been carried out. At Kubri the swing-bridge, made of lighters fifteen months previously by Major Wells—to last a few months, according to his instructions—was still working, and as the chesses wore out they were covered with filled sandbags, so that the progress of animal traffic over the bridge partook of the nature of a steeplechase. The Divisional Band paid a series of visits to the units, and it was surely the first time that these sandhills had echoed with waltz music and the airs of musical comedy. On such occasions the troops made quite a happy picture, for the strain of Gallipoli had almost worn off, and the men, now bronzed to a ripe saddle-colour, danced and laughed and sang, and a more cheerful and contented set of fellows could hardly be imagined.

The Canal defences had hitherto been on the west bank, with bridgeheads on the east bank, close to the Canal. It was recognized that the Canal must be defended from the eastern side, so a line of self-contained works was constructed in the desert, far enough out to prevent the enemy from bringing guns into action within seven miles of the waterway. Behind these first-line posts was a series of supporting works, while bridgeheads on the Canal formed the third line. In each section of the defence a mobile force was held in readiness for counter-offence. The posts were connected by telephone with the Brigade Headquarters and with one another. Visual signalling was also largely used by the Divisional Signal Company, the heliograph being of great service for long distances in this land of brilliant sunshine. In due course roads and light railways were run out to the posts, and three-inch water-pipes were laid. The posts were named after the depot towns of battalions, but, owing to subsequent reliefs, the units did not as a rule occupy those named after their depots. Each post had a garrison of, approximately, a battalion of infantry, a battery of artillery, a troop of yeomanry, and a section of engineers. The Transport of the 42nd Divisional Train was left at Alexandria, where its services would be more useful than in the desert, the Supply accompanying the Division to the Canal zone and in subsequent operations.

The Field State of February 29 shows a considerable increase in the strength of the Divisional Artillery, and that various units had been attached.

	Officers.	Other Ranks.
Divisional Headquarters	14	120
Divisional Signal Company, Cable Section and Airline Section	5	229
Artillery and Divisional Ammunition Column	108	2,520
Royal Engineers	16	296
125th Brigade and Signal Section	124	1,764
126th Brigade and Signal Section	117	2,244
127th Brigade and Signal Section	114	1,584
A.S.C. Supply Details	9	77
R.A.M.C.	24	537
Carried forward	531	9371

F

	Officers.	Other Ranks.
Brought forward	531	9371
Attached—		
3rd County of London Yeomanry	5	93
1/2nd W. Lancs. Field Coy., R.E.	6	143
Monmouth R.E.	3	83
Sanitary Section, R.A.M.C.	1	22
19th Mobile Veterinary Section	1	12
1st Essex Regiment	26	934
2nd Hampshire Regiment	25	900
Total	598	11,558

Later the Divisional Squadron of the D.L.O. Yeomanry rejoined the Division, and the 3rd Dismounted Brigade, mainly Yeomanry, was also attached.

It is unnecessary to refer to the importance of the Suez Canal, not merely to the commerce of the Empire, but also to the policy and strategy of the Allies. But it may be well to explain here, very briefly and roughly, the general situation so far as it affected the defence of this main communication between East and West. Prior to the outbreak of war there were British frontier posts in Sinai as far east as El Arish on the coast about ninety miles due east of Port Said, and more than a hundred miles by road from the Canal. The sole purpose of these posts was to supervise and regulate traffic between Egypt and the Turkish Empire, and as such traffic automatically ceased on the outbreak of war with Turkey, the handful of troops was withdrawn. The invasion of Gallipoli had compelled the Turks to abandon for a time any idea they may have entertained of conquering Egypt. Now, at the beginning of 1916, although the withdrawal of the Allies from the Dardanelles and the entry of Bulgaria into the war on the side of her ancient enemy had set free a large Turkish army for employment in Asia, the situation had not greatly changed. The heavy losses sustained in Gallipoli had been a serious drain upon the finest troops of the Ottoman Empire; the Russians had entered Armenia victoriously, and it was not possible for Turkey to prepare and equip new armies to arrest the Russian progress and at the same time to cross the Desert of Sinai with any reasonable prospect of success. For, if the evacuation of Gallipoli had released a large Turkish force for offensive purposes, it had done no less for the British, and the conquest of Egypt was still a remote possibility only. But, as the Turks had been improving their communications through Palestine, there remained the probability that they might attempt to establish themselves in strength within striking distance of the Canal. They hoped that a successful attack here might bring about a rebellion in Egypt. While the Egyptians remained passive spectators there was no chance of a Turkish victory.

There are three routes by which a hostile force might approach the Canal.

(1) The northern caravan route along the coast through El Arish to Kantara, the route by which Joseph's brethren, and later the Holy Family, and in more recent times Napoleon, had travelled from Palestine to Egypt.
(2) The central Hassana–Ismailia route.
(3) The southern Akaba–Suez route.

Lack of water along the greater part of the central and southern tracks renders them impracticable for any but a small, mobile, desert-bred force, and against raiding parties of this description the chain of posts under construction would be a sufficient defence. But the El Arish–Katia–Kantara route is of a different character. Oases are more numerous, and in the vicinity of Katia and Romani, within twenty miles of the Canal, wells are plentiful, and the water, though brackish, is drunk by animals, and to a certain extent by natives. No army, British or Turkish, could occupy this region until water-pipes and a railway had been laid, but the possibility of a rapid dash had to be provided against, so the system of defence on the northern route was extended to a point much farther east than was necessary in the central and southern sections, and it included the coast of the Bay of Tina and the water-bearing area around Katia and Romani.

Kantara was the base for this northern section, El Ferdan for the central, and Shallufa, where the 42nd Division was stationed during February and March, for the southern. Here trenches were dug and revetted with wooden frames and hurdles backed with canvas; miles of barbed-wire entanglements were put up; hutments of matting over wooden frames for mess and recreation, sun-proof standings for horses, and fly-proof larders were erected at the posts on the Canal banks. Gangs hauled the chain-ferry, and every one was kept steadily at work. In fact, the whole of the Canal zone for a hundred miles from Port Said to Suez has been described as a vast hive of workers; and the company humorist—who, by the way, always alluded to the desert as "the croft"—would ask plaintively: "Is it true, sir, that we're staying here till we've got all the desert into sandbags?"

Water for men and animals was obtained from the Nile, *via* the Sweet Water Canal, which runs a few hundred yards west of the Suez Canal. Darius the Persian is credited with the construction of the Sweet Water Canal, which he used for transport between the Mediterranean and the Red Sea. After Actium the remnant of Cleopatra's galleys took refuge therein. It fell into disuse for centuries, and was restored by de Lesseps as a water-supply for his workmen while the Suez Canal was under construction. There were filtering plants at all pumping stations, and as Nile water contains the parasite of the dreaded disease bilharziosis, there was a strict rule against bathing in the Nile or the Sweet Water Canal. Water for the troops was at first brought in barges from Suez and stored in tanks on both sides of the Suez Canal, being distributed by camel transport to the outposts in *fanatis*. A *fantasse* (plural, *fanatis*) is a stoppered flat box of zinc which holds from ten to twelve gallons and usually leaks a little. A camel carries a *fantasse* slung on either side. As the scheme grew the engineers laid a six-inch water-main across the desert, and thus the ancient prophecy that Palestine would never be freed from the Turkish yoke until Nile water flowed into it was fulfilled.

The third line of works was within easy walking distance of the Canal. It was good fun for the veterans of Gallipoli to bandy repartees from the water with the newly-trained drafts for India and Mesopotamia who, looking down upon them from the towering decks of big transports, asked when they were going to " do their bit," instead of taking a seaside holiday at an Egyptian pleasure-resort. Much booty in the form of tins of cigarettes thrown by passengers on liners was gathered in by bold swimmers. The weather was cool, and, in spite of very strenuous labour in the loose sand, the stay at Shallufa was a pleasant holiday as compared with conditions in Gallipoli. The sandstorms of March were decidedly unpleasant, however, for the sand penetrated everywhere. To attempt to keep it out of food, equipment, clothing or lungs was quite futile, and a sandstorm would quickly fill the trenches that had been dug at the cost of several days' steady labour. These sandstorms began with amazing regularity about midday and continued until 6 p.m. All cooking had to be done before or after these hours.

During the Shallufa period many officers and men returned to duty from hospital. These would feel that this record of the 42nd Division would be incomplete indeed were no reference made and no tribute paid to the founder and the workers of the admirable Convalescent Home at Alexandria, established in June, 1915, by Lady Douglas, whose solicitude for the welfare of all ranks under her husband's command will be remembered with lasting gratitude by the Division. The hospital was supported by the units and by subscriptions from friends at home. In addition to the return of those who had been absent through wounds and sickness, units were further strengthened by small drafts from home—but numbers still remained much below strength. The Division was weakened by the return to England of time-expired Territorials, including a number of the best men. Two officers who had been in command of their units throughout the Gallipoli campaign also left the Shallufa camp for England in the spring of 1916—Lieut.-Colonel S. L. Tennant, R.E., on leave, and Major England, A.S.C., who left to take charge of the 66th Divisional Train, the duties of Senior Supply Officer devolving upon Captain A. Gillibrand.

The Artillery here received their 18-pounder guns—handed over by the 29th Division—and their training and reorganization were taken seriously in hand, with firing practice in the desert. The three Field Ambulances remained on the Canal bank, and when not engaged in training or in attending to the cases brought in on camels or by light railways from the desert posts, were able to enjoy the bathing in the Canal. Sick were conveyed by steam launch from Kabrit and Genefa to Shallufa, and many of the high-temperature cases were dipped and sponged in the cooling, refreshing water of the Salt Lake. The Division settled down to a diet of "ginger, spit, and polish," the hard work, the swimming, games, sports, concerts—including a singing competition "for the championship of Asia"—proved wonderfully efficacious in restoring the vitality and the smartness of the Division after its long spell of trench life. Invariably, however, there is the man who has to acquire polish at the cost of much tribulation to himself and to his immediate superiors. There was, for instance, the sentry who failed to turn out the guard for the Divisional Commander. In excuse he explained: "Well, sir, I didn't see at first that you were a *Staff Colonel*," then, being of an amiable disposition, he leant forward and added in confidential tones: "You see, by rights I oughtn't to be here at all. I'm the sanitary man!" It was felt that this man was not a success, either as sentry or diplomat.

During the last days of March and the first days of April, the Division left Shallufa to camp in the desert about two miles north-west of Suez. With the assistance of a Belgian contractor and native carpenters the infantry, under the supervision of the engineers, rapidly erected a large number of huts with double roofs of matting and also long lines of stables. A macadam road was made through the camp and was eventually extended to Kubri. A thorough course of company, battalion, and brigade training was carried out here, the physique and efficiency of the troops improving greatly in consequence. Much of this training was carried out in the desert west of Suez and along the ancient tower-marked road that leads to Cairo—the "far end" of the very road which had become so familiar to the Division in the first autumn and winter of the war. The machine-gun sections had constant practice; and it was here that the Brigade M.G. Companies took definite form as separate units. Emphasis was laid on the training of the young officer; and the offensive spirit was successfully fostered and stimulated. Once more it was proved that close-order drill and punctilious discipline, diversified and relieved by games and sports, formed the basis on which that military ideal must be built up. Rugby, soccer, hockey, and even donkey polo were played, and the Rugby team of the 5th Manchesters won great renown. Canteens now provided cigarettes, biscuits, chocolates, and other articles much appreciated by the troops. A Dramatic Society was formed, and plays specially written by Major G. B. Hurst were given at the "Theatre Royal." The rehearsals and presentation gave great fun.

While at Suez the Artillery brigades and batteries were renamed. The 1st E.L. Brigade became the 210th Brigade, and the 2nd, 3rd, and 4th became the 211th, 212th, and 213th respectively, each having three four-gun batteries designated A, B, and C, with the exception of the 213th Brigade, which consisted of two howitzer batteries. After the Division left the Shallufa camp it was found that the defences there were not progressing with sufficient rapidity, and at the end of May the 7th and 8th Lancashire Fusiliers and the 127th Infantry Brigade were sent to Kubri and Shallufa to assist the 54th Division. In spite of the great heat, the Lancashire men, now more or less acclimatized, got through more in a few days than the recently arrived troops had accomplished in a month, and they received deserved praise from the G.O.C. of the section for their work at Manchester, Salford, Ashton, and other posts.

The heat in June was terrific, and a temperature of 120 degrees in the shade—the difficulty being to find the shade!—was normal, and on one or two occasions a midnight temperature of 105 degrees was registered. During this hot period the scouts and signallers of the 125th Brigade, while taking part in a training scheme, were sent out to the Ataka Hills, some seven or eight miles from camp, two parties operating as opposing forces. Movement among the hills proved more arduous than had been anticipated, and the men suffered much from the blazing sun—the rays being refracted by the rocks—and also from want of water. The greater part of them got back to camp with considerable difficulty. A Yeomanry patrol and an aeroplane were sent out on June 16, and parties of Arabs two days later, to look for the missing, and the bodies of two men who had died from heat and exhaustion were brought in. After this no training was permitted between the hours of 8.30 a.m. and 6 p.m. For the remaining ten hours of the day the average man could do little except lie, lightly clad, envying the Russians in the Caucasian snows, and dreaming of the invention or discovery of an ice-cold drink that could be produced in unlimited quantities even in a desert, and would remain unaffected by the temperature. But—

" Who can hold a fire in his hand,
By thinking on the frosty Caucasus ? "

Khamsin winds made life almost unbearable, and bathing was the one resource, for even bridge became too strenuous a game, though nap was played occasionally by the energetic ones.

On June 19 the Division was ordered north to take over from the 11th Division the El Ferdan Section, the central section of the Canal zone, midway between Ismailia and Kantara. The move was completed by the end of the month. The 7th and 8th Lancashire Fusiliers took over the defences at Ballah, a station on the Canal, and the 5th and 6th Lancashire Fusiliers at Ballybunnion, a desert post about six miles to the east. The 6th and 8th Manchesters and the 126th Brigade were stationed at El Ferdan and Abu Uruk, about five miles north-east of El Ferdan. The artillery was split up among the posts, the 210th Brigade at Ballah and the 211th at El Ferdan, and during this period the howitzer batteries were rearmed with 4·5 Q.F. howitzers. The 1st Field Company, R.E., was at Ballah and Ballybunnion; the 2nd Field Company at Abu Uruk, and the recently arrived 3rd Field Company at Ferdan, where were also the 2nd and 3rd Field Ambulances. The Division was now occupying

El Ferdan

the ground where, according to tradition, the Israelites crossed the Red Sea. The 5th and 7th Manchesters went as far north as Kantara, where they were attached to the 52nd Division, and the friendship with the Lowland Scots, begun and cemented in Gallipoli, was here revived. They also took over posts from the 11th Manchesters, the first of the " Kitchener " battalions of their own regiment.

The Engineer-in-Chief, Major-General H. B. Wright, called to his aid the engineers of the Egyptian Government. Civil contractors, labour and plant were brought down to the Canal and material was requisitioned from all parts of the globe—from Australia, timber and wire-netting, the latter to be used for road-making over the loose sand; from India, water-pipes, matting and meat-safes; reed-matting from the Sudan; the whole of her stock of Decauville (two-foot gauge) railway material from Egypt; engines and pumps from England; and from the United States, through Mr. J. Pierpont Morgan, a shipload of water-pipes which were so precious as to require a cruiser as escort. It was, however, upon the R.E. of the Division and Corps that the brunt of the work fell, though it might almost be said that the whole Division was temporarily transformed into a corps of engineers. The system of communication maintained by the Divisional Signal Company was extensive, all posts and outlying positions being connected with Headquarters by cable, often buried in the sand for many miles, and by visual signalling. Also all posts had their own system of inter-communication by telephone. Though the great heat continued during the six weeks in this section there was often a cool breeze on the higher ground, and conditions generally were far preferable to those prevailing in the dusty, fiery atmosphere of Suez.

Toward the end of July information was received that a large enemy force, led by German officers, and armed with German and Austrian artillery and machine-guns, was moving, with a rapidity that was surprising when the difficulties of the march of an army across the desert are realized, westwards from El Arish. Before long aircraft located Turkish troops at Oghratina Hod—a hod being a plantation of date palms—about ten miles east of Romani, held by the 52nd Division. Aerial activity increased on both sides, and traffic swarmed on the Romani road. The Turks meant to force a fight in the worst possible season for British troops, and their march across the desert was a notable military achievement.

It was now decided to transform the 8th Corps, of which the 42nd Division formed part, into a Mobile Column, under Major-General the Hon. H. A. Lawrence (a former Brigadier of the 127th Brigade) for operations in the desert east of the fortified posts. Camels were to be provided to carry all stores, such baggage as was absolutely necessary, engineering, material, food, ammunition, and water. Kit was cut down to the bare minimum. Wheeled transport was removed as useless, and gun-carriages and limbers were fitted with pedrails and equipped with extended splinter-bars to allow four animals to pull abreast, each team consisting of twelve horses. Sand-carts and camel cacolets would be provided for the R.A.M.C., and for the engineers new equipment for well-sinking on an extensive scale, with camels to carry the well-lining materials, troughs, pumps, tools, etc.

In the last week of July the Division was hurriedly ordered north to Kantara, the El Ferdan and Ballah area being handed over to the 54th Division and the 3rd Australian Light Horse Brigade. On the 29th and 30th of July the Mobile Column scheme was issued to unit commanders in rough outline, details being left to them. A Base Depot was formed at Ballah for the R.A. of the Mobile Force, and A Battery, 210th Brigade, and certain Ammunition Column details remained at the depot. The horse transport of the remainder of the Division and the heavier baggage were left at the base camp at Kantara.

The 127th Brigade, now complete, as the 5th and 7th Manchesters had rejoined, was the advance brigade at Hill 70. On July 31 it moved forward along the new railway to Gilban, together with the Divisional Squadron, a battery of the 212th Brigade, R.F.A., the 3rd Field Company, R.E., and the 3rd Field Ambulance. On the evening of August 3 the 6th Manchesters proceeded to Pelusium, near the coast and six miles north-west of Romani, to prepare defensive works east of the railway line, and to cover the detraining of the rest of the Brigade. Early in the morning of August 4 the sound of artillery fire from the direction of Romani announced that the Turkish attack had begun. The remainder of the Brigade was hurriedly ordered to Pelusium, and at 3.27 p.m., as the last battalion was detraining, Brig.-General Ormsby received the order to march at once in support of the Anzacs, who were heavily engaged in the neighbourhood of Mount Royston, to the south of Romani. At 3.30 p.m., within three minutes of receipt of the order, the 5th, 7th, and 8th Manchesters moved off *without any transport*—as none of the camels had arrived—and also without their dinners, the stew which had been prepared for them being left untouched. They passed through the 6th Manchesters, who were ordered to remain in their positions covering Pelusium, in order to escort and assist in organizing the expected camel transport. Artillery, cavalry, and engineer detachments arrived at Pelusium and moved forward, but nothing was seen or heard of the camels until 11 p.m., when two long files, each of 1000 camels, turned up. It was pitch dark, the transport was new to the Division, and the task of sorting out the animals, allocating them to the various units, loading them with fanatis, rations, ammunition and blankets, was a stupendous one. But the 6th Manchesters understood what every moment's delay in delivering the goods—especially the water—might mean to their comrades, and they put their backs into it. By 4 a.m. the camel conveys for the 127th Brigade and the attached troops had been despatched on their trek into the desert, and the 6th Manchesters had moved off to rejoin their Brigade.

The Turkish army numbered about 18,000 men, including 4000

Battle of Romani, Aug. 4, 1916

in reserve, and was well equipped. The soldiers had been assured that during the great Fast of Ramadan they should destroy the infidel and march victoriously into Egypt. But General Lawrence, whose cavalry and aircraft had been in touch with the advancing army since July 21, had made very thorough preparations for its reception, and the Battle of Romani was fought strictly in accordance with his plans, the enemy conforming with pleasing docility to the tactics he laid down for them. General Lawrence had a large force of artillery, cavalry, and infantry in an entrenched camp at Romani, secured on the north by the sea, and conspicuously protected on its eastern and southern fronts by strong redoubts and entrenchments. The south-western front, being left open ostentatiously, invited attack. The enemy could not ignore the force at Romani and march on towards Kantara and Dueidar, where the 42nd Division and two brigades of cavalry were stationed, as they would then be taken in rear and flank by the troops from Romani and in front by the Kantara force. They fell into the trap. Their aircraft reported the strength of the British position to the east and south of Romani and its apparent weakness to the south-west. On the night of August 3 they had attacked the cavalry outposts to the south of the camp, and had slowly driven them in. On the morning of the 4th they made a strong feint, with the greater part of their artillery, against the redoubts held by the 52nd Division on the east, while their main body moved to the south-west to attack the front that had been invitingly left open. The Anzac Light Horse, withdrawing slowly and skilfully, and now fighting on foot, led them on until they were involved among the sandhills, and at noon the cavalry and R.H.A. from Dueidar closed in from the south-west. The attacks on Katib Gannit, held by the 52nd, had now been repulsed with heavy loss by the Lowlanders, and it was at this stage that Major-General Chauvel, commanding the Anzacs, asked that the 127th Brigade might be sent with all speed to help "mop up" the Turk, who so far had been fighting stoutly as usual.

To return to the 127th Brigade. The three battalions had set off immediately the order was received, the 5th and 7th Manchesters leading. Heavy though the going was under the pitiless desert sun, they arrived upon the scene sooner than the Anzac commander had thought possible. As they drew near they could see the Turkish shrapnel bursting above the Anzacs, who, now that reinforcements were at hand, regained their horses and began to mass for a charge or pursuit. At about 2000 yards from the enemy position the leading battalions extended into lines, the 7th on the left, the 5th on the right. But the Turk did not wait. Worn out as he was by the marching and fighting of the past few days, the sight of the new British troops moving steadily towards him, line after line in regular waves, shook his faith in the assurance of victory. As the Manchesters attacked the ridge of Mount Royston the Battle of Romani was over. Those Turks who doubted their ability to get away in safety held up their white sandbags in token of surrender, seven officers and 335 men, with many horses, mules, rifles, and much ammunition falling into the hands of the Brigade. The Anzac cavalry accounted for the rest of the Turkish force at Mount Royston, having swept round the hill and cut off the retreat. Hundreds of Turks were seen being rounded up and marched back by a handful of troopers.

It was a great and decisive victory, in which, though the 42nd Division had played only a minor part, their share had been most opportune. The 127th Brigade had entered at exactly the right moment, and their march across three miles of deep, loose sand, under a blazing sun, in the hottest season, coming into action within one hour thirty-three minutes of receiving the order at Pelusium, was a noteworthy performance, which richly merited the following letter from the G.O.C., Anzac Mounted Division—

Romani, 18. 8. 16.
MAJOR-GENERAL SIR WM. DOUGLAS, K.C.M.G., C.B., D.S.O.
  Commanding 42nd Division.

  " MY DEAR GENERAL,
    " Just a line to ask you to be kind enough to express my thanks to Brig.-General Ormsby and the 127th Brigade for the prompt manner in which my request for support was complied with on the afternoon of the 4th inst., in spite of the heat and the soft sand-dunes the men had to march over.
    " I understand the Brigade moved within three minutes of getting the order from you, and I found them actually in position at least an hour before I expected them.
          " Yours very sincerely,
              " H. G. CHAUVEL,
                " Major-General."

The Turk had been decisively beaten, and on August 4 the menace to the Canal had passed, and it was now our turn to take the offensive. That evening plans were made to follow up the success by a forward move which, though slow and wearisome at first, and discouraging in its second stage, finally developed into the brilliant campaign in Palestine and Syria under Allenby, with its amazing succession of shattering victories.

The Manchesters rested after their toilsome march as best they could, with little food and water, until 3.30 a.m., when they stood to, awaiting the order to advance. It was, perhaps, fortunate that this was delayed in transmission as, while they waited, a string of camels laden with fanatis was sighted. There was no food, but the omission passed unheeded in the delight of obtaining water, though the supply was only enough to allow three-quarters of a bottle to each man. This small ration had to be husbanded carefully, for it might have to last them the whole or the greater part of the day.

March to Katia, August 5-6, 1916

By 7 a.m. on the 5th the 127th Brigade was on the move. During the night the enemy had retired to Hod-el-Enna, where he was holding a line northward toward Katib Gannit. The 42nd Division was ordered to advance and envelop the Turkish left flank in conjunction with the mounted troops, the Anzac Mounted Division operating on their left, and the 5th Mounted Brigade on the right, linking up with the 3rd Australian Light Horse. The 125th Brigade, which had arrived at Pelusium on the previous evening, had made an early start in the small hours of the morning, and was now on the left, the 127th Brigade being on the right, and the 126th Brigade in Corps Reserve at Pelusium. The heat, especially in the valleys, was stifling, and many men were sunstruck or completely prostrated by the heat. Souvenirs picked up earlier in the day—Turkish bayonets, swords, belts—were quickly discarded. The heavy, yielding sand greatly hindered the horse-drawn guns of the 212th Brigade, R.F.A., and for the same reason the cable wagons could not keep up, the teams being utterly exhausted. The Divisional Squadron reached Mount Royston at noon, after patrolling the railway line throughout the previous night, and they too had to halt for a time, the horses being badly in need of rest, food and water. In the evening the squadron arrived at Hod-es-Seifania, together with a hundred troopers of the Bikanir Camel Corps. The infantry gained their objectives, and on the ridge of higher ground saw the cavalry pursuing the Turks and our guns flinging shrapnel among them. Out at sea, a monitor, looking like a toy boat, could be seen bombarding the enemy positions—first a flash, then after a long interval the roar of the great gun, then an ear-splitting explosion among the fleeing Turks. The Division now held the line Hod-el-Enna to Mount Meredith, and cavalry patrols reported that the enemy rearguard was holding the line Bir-el-Rabah -Katia–Bir-el-Mamluk. The 125th Brigade on the left and the 127th on the right rested for the night on Mount Meredith and Mount Royston, and the number of Turkish dead lying on these hills showed how heavy had been the casualties. The evening was cool—in fact, the night was even chilly after the extreme heat of the day. There was little to eat or drink. The news came that Katia was to be taken next day, that the enemy was holding the oasis basin strongly, and that the march to Katia would be more exacting even than those of the past two days. The prospect was not alluring, for there was no sign of water to replenish the empty bottles, many of the native transport drivers having been stampeded by enemy shell fire. The prospect of an advance across the desert without food or water was far more alarming than the Turk, however strong might be his position and his numbers. Thirsty, hungry, and exhausted the men of the two brigades scooped hollows in the sand and snatched a few hours sleep.

At 3 a.m. on August 6 the infantry with the 1st and 3rd Field Companies, R.E., were preparing to move, each man wondering if he would be able to hold out, when a beatific vision of distant fantasse-laden camels was hailed with rapture. The pestiferous *oont* is an ungainly beast, with disgusting manners and a vile temper, but there are moments when one could almost wish that he would allow himself to be caressed, and this was one of such occasions. Though the allowance of water was disappointingly small, there being barely a pint per head, still it made all the difference to the spirit of the troops. The start was made at 4 a.m., the 42nd Division on the right, the 52nd on the left, with cavalry on both flanks. Viewed from a ridge, the advance on Katia was picturesque. The plain was covered with long lines of infantry, mounted troops on the flanks, batteries of field-guns with traction-engine wheels hauled through the sand by huge teams of horses. Far away to the rear came endless strings of grunting, bubbling camels, and miles in front, a tantalizing sight, lay the green oases that brought to mind the desert pictures of childhood. The prediction that the march would be more exhausting than any yet attempted proved only too true, and officers who had been through the worst of the Gallipoli campaign, and at a later date had eighteen months' experience of trench and open warfare in Flanders and France, declare that they have known nothing to surpass in horror the sufferings of the 127th Brigade on the 6th of August, 1916. The 125th Brigade, moving by a more direct route, reached the shade of the Katia oases in the forenoon, and found that the Turk had not awaited their coming. But while the Fusiliers rested there, the Manchesters were still trudging wearily through the soft sand, every step seeming to sink deeper and deeper, until it needed not only physical strength but also will-power to drag one's legs along. In the depressions between the ridges there was not a breath of air. The sun grew more and more malignant, and the men became more and more dejected and taciturn. Hundreds collapsed from sunstroke, or because every ounce of energy they had possessed had been expended. The instructions to husband the meagre allowance of water had been explicit, and every one knew that the bottles could not be replenished until Katia should be reached. It was forbidden to drink without first obtaining the permission of the platoon or unit commander, and the best results were obtained where the officers insisted firmly on exact obedience to this order. The men behaved splendidly, and even when their powers of endurance seemed to have reached the limit, they forced themselves heavily and listlessly onward, stedfastly resisting the ever-increasing temptation to drink. A regimental Medical Officer described their appearance as " that of men being gradually suffocated, their faces turning a dusky blue; they were panting for breath and falling unconscious on the track. All that could be done was to try to collect them in groups and place their heads under any low scrub that could be found." At one spot the torture was most cruelly augmented by an unfulfilled hope of relief. The sight of great quantities of attractive fruit, outwardly resembling oranges, was hailed with hoarse cries of delight. The " oranges " were seized upon ravenously, and in a few cases bitten into—and thrown away with curses. It was that most bitter of fruits, calumba—bitter as the disappointment

KATIA.   KATIA. BIVOUACS.

CAMEL CARRYING WATER TANKS.

CAMELS CARRYING FANATIS WAITING AT THE WATER POINT.

ROMANI. WATER TRUCKS ON THE BROAD-GAUGE RAILWAY.

ROMANI. EAST LANCASHIRE ARTILLERY.

it had caused, for the prospect of allaying the agonizing thirst intensified the anguish. Then it was that the officers, who were in no better case than their men but were upheld by their sense of responsibility, silently blessed him whom they had so often found occasion to curse, the " funny man " of the platoon or company. Luckily these men are to be found in every British unit, and when things are at their worst they extract humour from hardship until even the most despondent begin to feel less depressed.

As they struggled gamely on General Douglas rode from company to company to cheer them with the news that more than 3000 prisoners and a vast quantity of material had already been captured, and to show the men that their commander recognized the strain to which they were being subjected, and appreciated the gallant response they were making. About midday an oasis, a mile from Katia, was sighted, and men staggered on towards the trees and the hoped-for water. But there was no sign of water. Rumour quickly passed from man to man that water lay within two feet of the surface; and distressing scenes were witnessed of men half mad with thirst desperately digging into the sand with entrenching tools and even bare hands in a vain attempt to find water. Fortunately the camels arrived an hour later bringing an allowance of a pint for each man, and undoubtedly this saved many lives.

Refreshed by the water and a lie down in the shade, parties of volunteers went forth into the hateful desert again, in spite of their great fatigue, to seek out and bring in those who had fallen by the way. Through the night desultory rifle fire in front told that the cavalry were still in touch with the Turkish rearguard, who had put up a good fight at Oghratina, and managed to get away most of their guns and transport, though followed and harassed by the R.H.A. and cavalry as far as Salmana. Complete victory had crowned the operations, as the following figures show—

Enemy's strength	. .	18,000
Enemy's losses	. . .	3,930 (prisoners)
		1,251 (killed and buried)
		4,000 (wounded)
Total losses	. . .	9,181

The captured material included a complete Krupp Mountain Battery with 400 rounds of ammunition, 9 German machine guns with 32 extra barrels, 30 boxes of belt ammunition, and 9 shields, 2300 rifles, 1,000,000 rounds Small Arm Ammunition, large numbers of pack saddles, sandbags, clothing, equipment, rockets, barbed wire, stretchers, tools, swords, etc.; one aeroplane engine and 3 petrol tanks, 100 mules and horses and 500 camels.

The following telegram was received from H.M. the King—

" Please convey to all ranks engaged in the Battle of Romani my appreciation of the efforts which have brought about the brilliant success they have won at the height of the hot season and in desert country."

Katia, which was bombed daily, was occupied until the 14th August, on which date the Divisional Headquarters and the units that had taken part in the operation moved back to Romani and Pelusium to engage in very arduous training, and to put the finishing touches to the new equipment after the extremely severe test that had been undergone. The units were distributed as follows on the evening of the 15th August—

Pelusium :

Divisional Headquarters.
Signal Company.
Headquarters, R.E.
Divisional Squadron, D.L.O.Y.
126th Infantry Brigade.
A Battery, 211th Brigade, R.F.A.
2nd Field Company, R.E.
2nd Field Ambulance, R.A.M.C.
Attached—100 Bikanir Camel Corps.

Romani :

C Battery, 210th Brigade, R.F.A.
A Battery, 212th Brigade, R.F.A.
1st and 3rd Field Companies, R.E.
125th and 127th Infantry Brigades.
1st and 3rd Field Ambulances, R.A.M.C.

The remainder of the Artillery and Divisional Ammunition Column were at Kantara and Ballah.

Reference has been made to the arrival of the camels on the night before the march of the 127th Brigade to Mount Royston. The Ship of the Desert henceforward played so important a part in the operations of the Mobile Column that gratitude demands a few words of appreciation. A hundred, more or less, with from thirty to forty native attendants, were apportioned to each battalion, and the troops by now would have been unimpressed if a squadron of elephants had been dumped upon them. The camels and their satellites were placed in charge of the odd-job subaltern, the sergeant surplus to Company strength, and the few simple men who would volunteer to trudge alongside a grunting, grumbling, snapping mass of vermin and vile odours, and listen to its unpleasant internal remarks, while gazing upon its patchy hide and drooping, snuffling lips. British soldiers are notoriously fond of animals, and will try to make a friend of anything with four legs, or even with none,* and no doubt some of these volunteers had visions of their sloppy, shambling charges eagerly responding to affection, answering to a pet name, and turning soft eyes of devotion upon the beloved master while he fondled it. If so, they were quickly disillusioned, and soon they became prematurely aged men, bitterly regretting the impulse that had led them to volunteer. The native gentlemen had apparently been chosen for their knowledge of the English language—some could even count up to four in that tongue!—their gambling propensities, their detestation and ignorance of camels, and their appearance of abject misery. By the camp fire, at the end of the day's march, they became more cheerful as they compared thefts, smoked vile cigarettes, and babbled of the riotous time they would have in Cairo when they returned with their accumulated wealth. They were handy men, however, and the Lancashire lad regarded them with kindly tolerance, touched with the wondering pity he extends to all who have never watched Manchester United play Bolton Wanderers.

On the coast, two or three miles to the north of Romani, lies the hamlet of Mahamadiyeh, which sprang into fame as the most popular seaside resort in Africa, the battalions, with the exception of those of the 126th Brigade guarding the railhead, being sent there in turn for rest, recuperation, and sea-bathing. Further advance eastward by the Division was impracticable until the railway and pipe line had been pushed farther ahead, the present limit being a few miles beyond Romani. Meanwhile, a position was sited east of Oghratina to cover the extension of the railway, and this was reached by the Division, less the 125th Brigade, 1st Field Company, R.E., eight batteries, R.F.A., and the 1st Field Ambulance, on September 11. A prospecting party of Engineers had located considerable supplies of water, and the few trial wells were rapidly increased to forty-three, supplying 9000 gallons an hour. The water was slightly brackish, but was drunk by horses and camels. Water for the men was supplied to units at the railhead tanks. The 125th Brigade had been moved to section defences, the 5th Lancashire Fusiliers to Kantara, the 6th to Dueidar, the 7th to Hill 40, and the 8th to Ballybunion. A few weeks later the Brigade was reunited at Mahamadiyeh, where D.H.Q. was established.

For more than two months the Division shared with the 52nd

* One man, indeed, tried to cultivate friendship with a horned viper. He had actually tied a string to its tail—how he managed this goodness only knows! —and was showing it round when it rose in its wrath and bit him. The fact that he was near the M.O.'s tent saved him, but he was left with a "dud" finger for life. All sorts of queer pets, lizards, tortoises, praying-mantis, etc., were kept by the men when their units were stationary, and one of these—a large lizard—proved to be of a rare species, and found an honourable refuge in the Cairo Zoo. Desert mice and rats of various kinds abounded, and were often tame and amenable, but of larger animals only a few gazelles and, once, an Egyptian wild-cat, were seen. Nearly every cookhouse acquired a pet goat, the diminutive black one of the 10th Manchesters being the most admired of these. The 6th L.F. goat "joined up" at Imbros and saw service in Gallipoli as well as in Sinai.

Division and the mounted troops the duty of protecting the railway and water-pipe from raiders, the troops occupying a succession of forward positions along the coastal road in advance of and covering the railway, each Division returning to Romani when relieved by the other. To pack up, load the camels, and move off to a fresh bivouac quickly became second nature. Steadily the railway was pushed forward towards El Arish, and alongside it a road was constructed, the sand being conquered at last by the ingenious device of wire rabbit-netting laid and pegged down. In this way the fatigue of marching was much reduced. The large main through which a daily supply of 40,000 gallons was pumped from the Sweet Water Canal through filters to Romani, was carried forward by the Engineers, who also erected reservoir tanks at the railhead. This supply was barely sufficient for the men, and none of it could be spared for the animals, so exploring parties of sappers went ahead to sink innumerable wells and erect signboards giving a rough estimate of the supply per half hour and the degree of salinity. They also prepared maps of a region that had hitherto been practically unmapped. It was an engineer's war, and the amount of work done by them in the face of difficulties that had been considered insuperable was indeed amazing.

The health of the troops had suffered greatly by the prolonged strain under a tropical sun, and a number of men had been sent into hospital with dysentery. There had also been a few cases of cholera, presumably contracted from Turkish prisoners and camping grounds. A number of men, pronounced medically unfit for the arduous duties of the Mobile Column, were formed into a composite battalion and stationed at Kantara, where they were engaged upon guard duties and training. In October a much-appreciated scheme of rest and holiday cure was recommended by the medical authorities. Parties of officers and men were sent to Alexandria for a week's real relaxation, and during this week they were practically free to do as they liked. It was a novel military departure, as there was neither work nor duty for officers or men. The change of surroundings, the freedom, and the sea-bathing worked wonders. The coming once more into touch with civilization had in itself a good effect; health quickly improved, and with the cooler weather a complete change for the better was experienced.

In October, Major-General Lawrence, having returned to England, from the 23rd of the month until the arrival of Lieut.-General Sir Philip Chetwode early in December, Major-General Sir William Douglas was given temporary command of the Desert Column, the name by which the Mobile Force was now known, Brig.-General Frith assuming command of the Division. As Brig.-General King had been appointed C.R.A. of the Desert Column, the command of the Divisional Artillery was taken over by Brig.-General F. W. H. Walshe, D.S.O., who had been in command of the artillery attached to the Anzacs.

The mounted troops, co-operating with bodies of infantry from one or other of the two Divisions, kept in touch with the enemy, and pressed him farther and farther to the east as the work of construction went forward. The railway reached Bir-el-Abd, nearly thirty miles east of Romani and more than fifty from the Canal, then to Salmana, then Tilul, and in November the railhead was at El Mazar, about eighty miles east of the Canal. Engagements took place at Bir-el-Abd and at El Mazar, the latter forcing the enemy to withdraw upon El Arish, their base and the most important town in Sinai. As each stage of railway and water-main construction was completed the main bodies of the 42nd and 52nd Divisions also advanced a stage. Viewed from a distance, the slow-moving column seemed to have strayed into the scene from out of the twentieth century B.C., as the long line of laden camels wended their deliberate way along interminable stretches of bare sand, or across salt lakes of dazzling whiteness, or through undulating scrub country which raised fleeting hopes that the desert had been left behind. Turkish aircraft continued to harass the advance, but the bombing was rarely effective, and even the natives of the Egyptian Labour Corps grew accustomed to the raids, and no longer bolted like rabbits for cover when a plane was sighted. Due acknowledgment must be rendered to these Gyppies, who worked with admirable rapidity and cheerfulness, each gang being in charge of a native ganger whose badges of authority were two stripes and a stick which was freely used. While working they invariably chanted, the ganger acting as fugleman, and the heavier the work the louder the chanting. When they were not chanting they were not working. It was at times fortunate that the soldiers did not understand the words chanted. The English soldiers soon took up the idea, and when collective effort was required, it was done to the accompaniment of some extraordinary singing. Towards the end of November the 42nd Division occupied El Mazar, only twenty-five miles from El Arish, and the railway was already pushed on to El Maadan, about ten miles further east, where an important railhead was constructed and arrangements made for the storage of a large water supply to be fed by railway tanks. Three or four times a week every man had for breakfast a 1 lb. loaf baked in Kantara on the previous afternoon.

On December 20 a concentration of all available troops was effected at El Maadan. There were at least 30,000 men, including natives, and 18,000 camels, marching in parallel columns as far as the eye could reach. A rapid forward move and a surprise attack upon the Turkish positions covering El Arish had been planned, and the prospect of celebrating the close of the year 1916, and the completion of the hundred-mile stage of the conquest of the desert, by a good stand-up fight was looked forward to with exhilaration, except by the pessimists who freely betted that there would be no fight. In the small hours of the morning of December 21 the company commanders received orders to prepare to march—but, alas! back to El Mazar, not forward to El Arish, for the bird had flown and the stunt was a " washout." Brig.-General Walshe had gone out in an

G

aeroplane to reconnoitre the position for artillery purposes, and as no sign of the enemy could be seen the pilot brought the machine down until they skimmed along the top of the palm-trees, and made sure that the Turk had cleared out. The disappointment was intense. El Arish was occupied by the mounted troops and the 52nd Division, while the 42nd gloomily marched back to Mazar. In the words of the order : " The Turks having fled, the Division was no longer required to fight them."

They were not downcast, however, for any length of time. A remark of the Divisional Commander, as he commiserated with his men on having missed the promised " scrap," gave rise to rumours and much discussion of the Division's prospects. " Never mind, lads," he had said, " you'll get as much as you want very soon." Could it mean France, Salonika, India, Mesopotamia? Perhaps, even an advance through Palestine—though this was scouted as too wild a notion. But Christmas was at hand, and hopes and chagrin were laid aside for the moment, as men's thoughts were wholly occupied with visions of Christmas festivities. Anticipations were fully realized; the mail and parcels from home arrived at the right time, and the Christmas of 1916 was thoroughly enjoyed. The rest of the stay at El Mazar was not. The Turk had been stationed here in force and had bequeathed a legacy of lice of abnormal size and ferocity, which swelled the fighting strength of the Division to many times its normal number. A delousing apparatus was brought up by train, and the men conceded that it was not wholly ineffective— in assisting the young lice to attain maturity more speedily, and in whetting their appetites. There was also an alarming development of septic sores, probably due to the filthy sand.

Meanwhile the mounted troops had been busy. On Christmas Eve they had struck suddenly at Maghdaba, a dozen miles to the south of El Arish, and had destroyed the garrison there, and, later, had made a brilliant lightning raid on Rafa, about thirty miles to the east, on the border of Sinai and Palestine. The enemy, taken completely by surprise, surrendered after putting up a good fight.

In the middle of January 1917, the 42nd Division marched by stages to El Arish, halting for a few days at El Bitia en route. This place furnished a welcome change from the ordinary desert scenery— palm groves, flat stretches of firm sand peculiarly adapted for football, a roaring sea close at hand, and a fine beach for bathing. El Arish was reached on the 22nd, and this was the furthest point east attained by the Division, though the Engineers, with a Company of the 8th Lancashire Fusiliers, spent a few days at El Burj, ten miles beyond. At El Arish wells were sunk at the edge of the beach where, to every one's surprise, excellent water was found in abundance only twenty yards from the sea. A very bad sandstorm was experienced here, and there were periodical but ineffective bombing raids by aircraft. Before the end of the month the Division, less the squadron D.L.O.Y., was ordered back to the Canal, their destination being Moascar, near Ismailia.

BIR EL GERERAT. BIVOUACS.

A "HOD" OR OASIS OF DATE PALMS.

TURKISH LINES AT MASAID.

EL ARISH.

EL ARISH.

The Work Accomplished

The heavy sand through which the guns had been hauled and the difficulties of the water supply for the horses had provided a hard test of the endurance and skill of the Divisional Artillery, and it is greatly to the credit of the batteries that they had overcome all obstacles. Men and horses had become accustomed to desert trekking, and at the end of a day's march the bivouacs were prepared, the horses watered, and everything running as smoothly as under peace-time conditions. On Christmas Day the batteries had (on paper) been formed into six-gun batteries, but the scheme was not actually put into operation until the Division had returned to the Canal zone.

As in Gallipoli, the Divisional Signal Company had been kept continuously at work and had displayed energy and efficiency beyond praise. Every task that had been set them—and their name was legion!—had been done well. The Supply details of the A.S.C. had accompanied the Division during the six months' operations in the desert, and it may safely be said that no Division was better maintained in the matter of supply. The R.A.M.C. had formed mobile sections in each Field Ambulance, and two of these with camel convoy had accompanied each infantry brigade, and had shared their experiences. In spite of the heat and the shortage of water the desert life had on the whole proved healthy.

The magnitude of the work accomplished in the desert may be estimated by the following figures—

Railways	360 miles
Pipe lines	300 ,,
Roads	220 ,,
Timber Hurdles . . .	800 ,,
Timber for hutting . .	2,000,000 square feet
Wire netting	50,000 rolls
Barbed wire	7,000 tons
Cement	2,000 tons
Sandbags used . . .	30,000,000

The defence of the Suez Canal had now been made secure. The revolt against Ottoman rule in the Hedjaz had broken out, and the Turk was in no mood for further adventurous enterprise. Henceforward he would confine his energies to defensive operations, and would ask nothing more than to hold his own.

The infantry entrained for Kantara, *en route* for Moascar, during the first days of February, and though the hundred-mile railway journey was far from luxurious the troops were glad enough to be spared the weary march back to " th' Cut." They had watched the railway grow mile by mile, and their interest in it was almost that of a proprietor, but this was the first time they had ridden upon it for any distance.* Most of the units halted for a day or two at Kantara,

---

* The 42nd did not regard as a happy compliment to their marching prowess the fact that while the troops of other divisions were occasionally allowed to go

a station with which they were familiar enough. Here the only subject for comment seems to have been the remarkable number of gulls that swarmed overhead at meal times. The mention of these birds will remind many officers and men that the 42nd Division made very useful contributions both to the knowledge of the fauna of the Sinai Peninsula and to the supply of animals to the Cairo Zoo. Many desert mice and rats, lizards and tortoises reached the Zoo alive, and one rat was so exalted by the prospect of introduction to Cairo society that it gave birth to a healthy litter while in the parcel post. Insects of great interest and rarity, and of peculiarly local distribution, were sent to the Ministry of Agriculture at Cairo twice a week for six months; and species entirely new to science were discovered. A battalion of the Lancashire Fusiliers, from the R.S.M. and the Cook-Sergeant down to the sanitary men, took to collecting and nature study with great ardour and much success.

Divisional Headquarters and the Signal Company arrived at Moascar on February 4. On the 6th, 7th, and 8th the various units (less the 2nd Field Company, R.E., which proceeded direct by rail to Alexandria) set out from Kantara on the two-days' march to Moascar along the new road by the side of the Canal. The change from the soft sand of the desert to the hard road was a sore trial to the feet, and a big proportion of the men limped rather than marched into Moascar. All ranks now knew what most had suspected for some time, that the Division was bound for France, and there was general enthusiasm. The prospect of a change from the sand, the glaring sun, the discomfort of intense heat, the monotony and isolation of the desert, was hailed with joy by the majority. A number of officers and men had not been home since September 1914, and knew that there was little chance of home-leave while the Division remained with the Egyptian Expeditionary Force. Yet there were some among those who had been out longest upon whom the spell of the East had fallen, and who were disappointed that, having accomplished so much of the preparatory work, they, like Moses, could only see the Promised Land from afar, and were not allowed to go forward into Palestine.

While at Moascar the Division was inspected by Lieut.-General Sir Charles Dobell, commanding the Eastern Force, and it also marched past General Sir Archibald Murray, Commander-in-Chief of the Egyptian Expeditionary Force. An event of even greater moment for men who had been nearly twelve months in the desert was a week's visit from Miss Lena Ashwell's Concert Party. The troops were grateful and appreciative, and they showed it unmistakably.

In view of the impending change every man now required serge

---

by train, *they* had always to walk. A Tommy, home on leave, got into conversation with an Australian in a London bus. "Are you 42nd Division?" asked the Australian, who had been in the desert in 1916. "That's so," the Lancastrian replied. "Well," drawled the other, "why don't you get out and walk?"

FLASHES OF UNITS IN THE 42ND DIVISION.

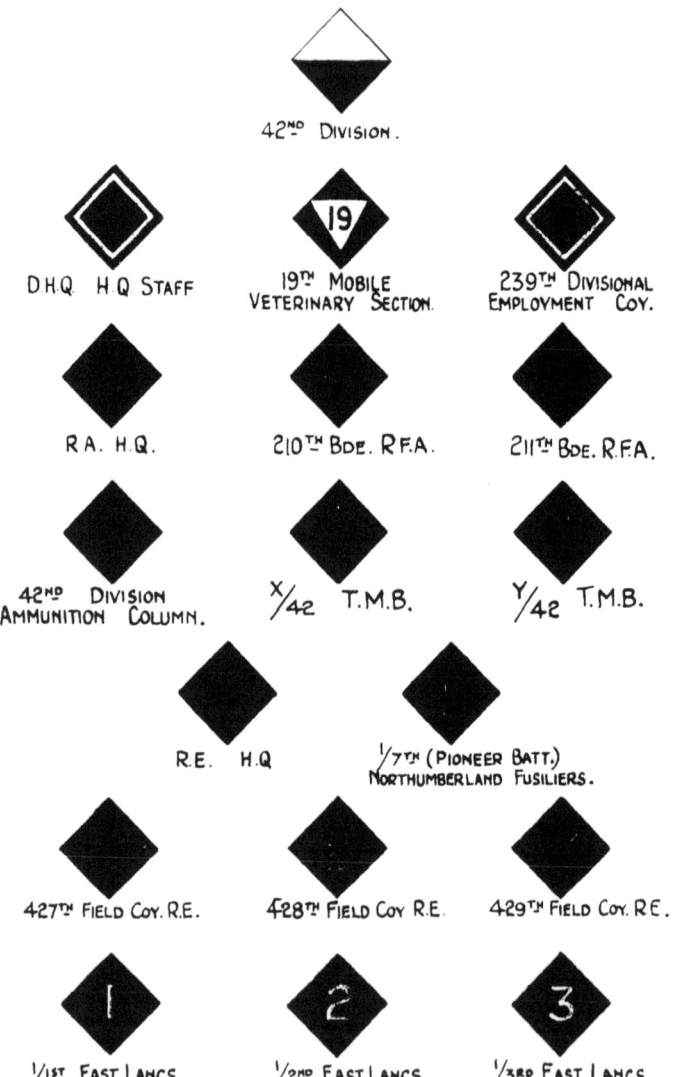

125ᵀᴴ Brigade H.Q.   126ᵀᴴ Brigade H.Q.   127ᵀᴴ Brigade H.Q.

1/5ᵀᴴ Lancashire Fusiliers.   1/5ᵀᴴ East Lancs. Regt.   1/5ᵀᴴ Manchester Regt.

1/7ᵀᴴ Lancashire Fusiliers.   1/8ᵀᴴ Manchester Regt.   1/6ᵀᴴ Manchester Regt.

1/8ᵀᴴ Lancashire Fusiliers.   1/10ᵀᴴ Manchester Regt.   1/7ᵀᴴ Manchester Regt.

125ᵀᴴ Bde. Light T.M. Battery.   126ᵀᴴ Bde. Light T.M. Battery.   127ᵀᴴ Bde. Light T.M. Battery.

MG   **MG**   **MG**

H.Q. 42ᴺᴰ Batt. M.G.C.   A. Coy. 42ᴺᴰ Batt. M.G.C.   B. Coy. 42ᴺᴰ Batt. M.G.C.

C. Coy. 42ᴺᴰ Batt. M.G.C.   D. Coy. 42ᴺᴰ Batt. M.G.C.

42ᴺᴰ Divisional Train A.S.C.   428ᵀᴴ Coy. A.S.C. (H.Q. Coy. 42ᴺᴰ Divˡ. Train)   429ᵀᴴ Coy A.S.C. (125ᵀᴴ Bde. Coy.)

430ᵀᴴ Coy. A.S.C. (126ᵀᴴ Bde. Coy.)   431ˢᵀ Coy. A.S.C. (127ᵀᴴ Bde. Coy.)   42ᴺᴰ Divisional MT Coy. A.S.C.

clothing, winter underclothing and service cap. The field-gun batteries were established on a six-gun basis, and two artillery brigades, the 210th and 211th, were formed out of the three existing brigades of four-gun batteries. The 1st, 2nd, and 3rd Field Companies, R.E., were re-numbered as the 427th, 428th, and 429th Field Companies respectively. Many details left behind during the advance across the desert rejoined the Division, as did also the R.A. Base at Ballah, and the instructors and staff of the Divisional School at Suez. This school had done most useful work, a large number of officers and other ranks having been put through a series of short courses, and much progress had been made in bombing and in the use of the Light Trench Mortar, or Stokes Gun.

To the great disappointment of all ranks it was decided that the A.S.C. should remain in the East, as a new 42nd Divisional Train had been formed in England to join the Division on its arrival in France. There was sincere regret on both sides at the severing of comradeship. The Divisional Train left Kantara early in March to join the 53rd Division, to which it was attached during the operations against Gaza. On the formation of the 74th (Yeomanry) Division it became the 74th Divisional Train, took part in all operations with that Division in Palestine, went with it to France, and remained with it until disembodied. The Divisional Squadron, now with the 53rd Division, was engaged in the first and second battles of Gaza. Later, it was attached in turn to the 60th and 52nd Divisions in Palestine and Syria; it took part in the third Battle of Gaza, in numerous skirmishes, outpost affrays, and pursuits, and shared in the honour of the great campaign that brought Turkey to her knees.

Before the end of February all preparations had been completed, and units had entrained for Alexandria. On March 2, 1917, the last transport left the harbour, and, after two and a half years of service in the Near East, the 42nd Division was at last on its way to the Western Front.

CHAPTER V

FRANCE

(*March—August* 1917)

THE voyage westward across the Mediterranean was made under conditions widely different from those of the outward journey of September 1914, when " glory of youth glowed in the soul," and the glamour of the East and the call of the unknown had made their appeal to adventurous spirits. Familiarity with war had destroyed illusion and had robbed it of most of its romance. The Lancashire Territorials had a very good idea of what to expect in France or Flanders, and were prepared to face minor discomforts and worries with the inevitable grousing which proclaims that all is well, and real privations, perils, and horrors with steadfastness often masked by levity. Though the Mediterranean was at that period infested by enemy submarines, the vigilance of the British and French navies proved a sure shield. One torpedo only was fired at the troopships, and this passed between the log-line and the stern of the *Megantic*. A call was made at Malta, and on March 1 the first transport anchored in the magnificent harbour of Marseilles, and D.H.Q. at once entrained for the North of France.

The railway journey of sixty hours to Pont Remy, near Abbeville, will not be forgotten. Men who had at much cost become acclimatized to the intense heat and dryness of the Sinai Desert, were suddenly plunged into the opposite extreme of an arctic climate. The winter of 1917 was one of the most prolonged and severe on record, and throughout the tedious journey in French troop-trains the men shivered and trembled with the bitter cold. But if France greeted them freezingly there was no mistaking the warmth of the welcome of her sons and daughters. Wherever the trains stopped the inhabitants gathered round to cheer them on their way. The news of the fall of Bagdad had preceded them, and the French women and girls, old men and children, knew that these were victorious British reinforcements from the East, and Bagdad and Sinai were equally remote.

The troops detrained at Pont Remy in a storm of snow and sleet, and marched through deep, freezing slush to the villages in which billets had been prepared. After six months' experience of open bivouacs wherever the day's trek ended, the barn billets were something of a novelty. Reorganization and re-equipment were, of course, the most urgent matters to be dealt with, and the refit was carried out expeditiously. The short Lee-Enfield rifle displaced

General Douglas's Farewell

the longer rifle with which the Division had been armed; and the issue of two strange items, the " tin hat " and the box respirator, provoked some hilarity. Baths, each capable of washing sixty men per hour, were erected by the R.E., and henceforward the Division left its mark in the shape of new or remodelled baths in every area in which it was located. The Divisional Cinematograph and Canteen were also inaugurated here. The last troops from Egypt, the 5th East Lancashires and the 9th Manchesters, arrived on March 15. A new Divisional Train joined from England. This train had already had considerable experience of France, as it had been formed to join the Lahore Division in September 1914. Motor ambulances were supplied to the three Field Ambulances, and a complete train of motor-lorries was attached to the Division. The 42nd Divisional Ammunition Column was formed from a nucleus of the former Brigade Ammunition Columns with the addition of a large draft from the R.A. Base in France. A Heavy (9·45-inch) Trench Mortar Battery and three Medium (6-inch) T.M. Batteries were also formed here, and these became a part of the Divisional Artillery. Three Light T.M. Batteries were attached to the Infantry Brigades.

On the arrival of the Division in France Major-General Sir William Douglas left for England in order to give evidence before the Royal Commission appointed to inquire into the Dardanelles Campaign. Temporary command of the Division was taken over by Brig.-General H. C. Frith, C.B. (125th Brigade), until the arrival of Major-General B. R. Mitford, C.B., D.S.O., who assumed command about the middle of March. Much regret was felt by officers and men that the general, who had been responsible for the training and organization of the Division in time of peace, and under whose leadership during two and a half years of war it had served with distinction in two campaigns and had " made good," should be unable to lead them to the gaining of fresh laurels on the most important of all fronts. They had been fortunate in a commander who had ever taken a personal interest in the welfare of all ranks under his command, and who had identified himself with the Lancashire men and was jealous of their good name. That General Douglas regarded his officers and men with affection is clearly shown in his farewell message—

"In bidding the 42nd Division good-bye I wish to express my heartfelt thanks to my Staff Officers, Commanders, and Regimental Officers for their loyal and whole-hearted support and superb work during the period of my command. My admiration for the conduct, fighting qualities, grit, and endurance of all ranks is profound. Never have I met a more responsive, willing and lovable lot of men than these Lancashire lads, and, to my last days, I shall remember with affection and pride the three and three-quarter years that I have had the honour to command them. I know how well you, officers and men, will add to the great name you have already earned for the Division, I wish you the best of good fortune and a rich reward."

Towards the end of March the Division moved to an area some ten miles east of Amiens, D.H.Q. being established at Mericourt. The 42nd was now a veteran Division in war and in travel, but in the trenches of France it was in the position of a new boy at a strange school. It had learnt much in the old school, and the experience would be useful. Each unit had a record and tradition of which it had good reason to be proud, and the commanders knew that their officers and men could be relied upon. Endurance and courage had been severely tested, but the endurance required for slogging through deep sand under a tropical sun was of a very different nature from that which would now be demanded, and the intense heat of the desert was a poor preparation for the bitter winds, the snow, sleet and freezing mud of the trenches of France. Much had to be learnt in the new school, and much unlearnt.

In Gallipoli the opposing trenches had often been only a few yards apart, and rifle-fire had continued all day and increased in violence at night. In that sector of the Western Front taken over by the Division the recent withdrawal of the enemy had created a No Man's Land, which might be anything from 10 yards to 1000 in width, and unaimed rifle-fire was uncommon. Here, too, patrolling was a matter of nightly routine, whereas in Gallipoli more than an occasional patrol had been impossible. Two of the most novel features were the gas and the amount of H.E. shelling. It was the Division's first experience of gas, and on rare occasions only had it witnessed *annihilating* shell-fire. Never before had any of the original members been in billets, and they found them and their inhabitants a source of interest and comfort. Some felt hurt that the bits of Arabic picked up in the East were of no use here, and they resolutely refused to learn any French. " I've learnt Gyppo, and I'm not going to bother with any more foreign languages." Imagine their delight when on leave in Amiens they found that the paper-boys (who had come into contact with the Australians) knew the meaning of " *Imshi!* " This word, being the imperative of the Arabic verb " to walk," did duty for " 'op it ! " Possibly the most striking differences of all were that the Division got reinforcements after suffering casualties, and was able to get back into " rest " of a real kind after a trying time in the line.

The strength of the Division on Aprii 1 was 727 officers and 16,689 other ranks.

Advance parties had been sent ahead of the Division, and now other parties of officers, N.C.O.s and men were attached for short periods to battalions and units of the 1st Division in the front line trenches that they might see and understand the conditions of warfare on the Western Front, before the Division should be called upon to take its place in the line that stretched from the Belgian coast to Switzerland. The enemy's retirement from the Somme and the Ancre to the Hindenburg Line had upset the plans of the Allies for a spring offensive. The recently-vacated German trenches were visited, and the scenes of appalling devastation, the shattered remains of what had once been flourishing villages and farmsteads, gave the troops their first impressions of France's martyrdom, and filled them with indignation and loathing. They had heard and read of the ruin and desolation in Belgium and Northern France, but the half had not been told. The wanton destruction of fruit-trees and the desecration of cemeteries were acts dictated not by military necessity but by beastliness of mind.

Throughout this preparatory period the troops were kept busily employed upon the badly damaged roads, and—as occasional opportunity offered—in the attempt to make the *entente* still more *cordiale*. Feuillieres, Biaches, Herbecourt, Flaucourt, Dompierre, and Peronne were visited by various units, and the sappers constructed bridges to take heavy guns and lorry traffic over the Somme at Brie and elsewhere. Not only had the enemy blown craters at most of the cross-roads, but, east of Peronne, he had felled the trees that line the main French roads, and these had to be removed. This work of clearing up after the German retreat was of great importance, and the Division gained an insight into conditions on the Western Front as the troops approached the line. Where possible the ruins of farms and houses, swarming with rats, were used as billets, but the road-makers usually slept in cellars, dugouts, and holes. The wretched weather continued and there was heavy snow in April. The horses, so long accustomed to an eastern climate, suffered greatly and began to deteriorate, some succumbing to pneumonia. The boots which had been issued just before leaving Egypt were quite unsuited to a bad winter in Northern France, and they fell to pieces quickly. Each day a number of men had to remain in billets until new boots could be obtained from Ordnance Stores. A number of officers and men, however, refused to be worried by such insignificant details as boots, for were they not going home for the first time since September 1914? During the month batches of these veterans departed for fourteen days amid the rousing cheers of their comrades.

At Peronne, where D.H.Q. was opened on April 14, every building was badly damaged except the Town Hall, which was at once placed out of bounds because of this immunity, as any place that appeared to invite occupation was regarded with suspicion, owing to the typical Boche habit of leaving delayed-action mines and other "booby-traps." Peronne Town Hall did not, however, go sky-high, as was daily expected. In the village of Peiziere some officers of the 126th Brigade took up their quarters in a house that had been left in good condition. Fortunately one of them took the precaution to explore and found a quantity of high explosive hidden under the beams. They cleared out. Next day a shell dropped on the building and it vanished. An R.A.M.C. orderly in the vicinity was lifted several feet in the air by the force of the explosion. "Eh, that wur a near do!" he said, as he picked himself up carefully and resumed his journey.

The Division now formed part of the 3rd Corps of the Fourth Army.

On the 8th of April the 125th Brigade took over a portion of the line from the 48th Division at Epehy, in front of Le Catelet, and a few days later the 126th Brigade also went into the line, in order that as many battalions as possible might have a short experience of front-line conditions before the Division as a whole assumed responsibility for a sector. The front here had become practically stationary, and as neither side had a continuous trench system the connecting of posts proceeded nightly, and patrolling and digging were the chief diversions. The 7th Lancashire Fusiliers was the first battalion to go into the line, which they advanced, after a sharp skirmish, to a copse about half a mile ahead. They were relieved on April 12–13 by the 6th L.F., and during the relief Malassise Farm, in which were a number of men of both battalions, was heavily shelled. The building was destroyed, and the fall of the roof buried about fifty of these men in the cellar. Though the shelling continued with great violence, admirable courage was shown in extricating the buried men, and for this the Military Medal was awarded to a private of each battalion. The Division's first trench raid on the Western Front was made by the 4th East Lancashires at Epehy. On April 28 the 126th Brigade advanced their line successfully, but the 4th and 5th East Lancashires suffered rather heavily.

Throughout April the wintry weather continued, but the unfailing spirit of the British soldier under depressing conditions is shown in the following anecdote related by an officer of the 4th East Lancashires : " The rain was pouring into my dugout, and the water slowly rising, so to avoid a fit of the blues I went along the line to see how the men were faring. A sentry was standing in mud half up to his knees, his hands numbed and wet, and a stream of water ran from his tin hat. By way of comparing notes I asked this pitiable spectacle what he really felt like. ' Like a flower in May, sir,' was the cheerful reply, and I was cured of the blues."

On May 3 the Division took over from the 48th Division a sector in the neighbourhood of Ronnsoy, south-east of Epehy. As Brig.-General Ormsby was engaged in marking out the new front line of his Brigade near Catelet Copse, the enemy suddenly opened a bombardment, and he was struck in the head by a piece of shell and killed. General Ormsby had been in command of the Brigade for more than twelve months, and during that period he had become very popular with his men and had gained their respect and admiration. Lieut.-Colonel H. C. Darlington, 5th Manchesters, once more assumed temporary command until the arrival of Brig.-General the Hon. A. M. Henley, who remained in command of the 127th Brigade until the end of the war.

Two brigades were in the front line and one in reserve, with a system of four-day reliefs. The long winter was over at last; summer had arrived without any introduction by spring, and the weather was now gloriously hot. There was a good deal of local fighting, especially around Guillemont Farm, an enemy post which more than one division had found by no means difficult to capture, but exceedingly difficult to hold. Several night attacks were made by companies and platoons, in one of which, on the night of May 6–7, the 9th Manchesters established forward posts in the face of heavy machine-gun fire, and Private A. Holden was awarded the Bar to the M.M. for volunteering to bring in the wounded, and afterwards going out into the open to make sure that none had been missed. He found a wounded officer and helped to carry him 400 yards on a heavily shelled road, and went out again to assist another injured man to safety. He succeeded in this, but was himself wounded. The enemy artillery was generally active, and on one occasion some men of the 126th Brigade were quite grateful to the German gunners. A heavy shell, which fell among some ruined cottages, threw up a number of gold and silver coins, dated a hundred years ago and evidently a long-buried hoard.

On May 23 D.H.Q. moved to Ytres, about eight miles north-west of Epehy, the Division relieving the 20th Division on a newly-captured sector running from the Canal du Nord, south-west of Havrincourt, to a point south of Villers Plouich, through Trescault and Beaucamp; and here the Division remained until July 8. This was a fairly quiet sector, and during the first few weeks there was no event of any importance to vary the daily round of digging, wiring, and strengthening the trench system and the patrolling of No Man's Land. Havrincourt Wood in the spring of 1917 remained a very beautiful spot amid the chaos of war. Though the " hate " of the Boche was less demonstrative than in many sectors his trench-mortars and machine-guns were generally busy at night, and considerable annoyance was caused on the right of the line by a trench-mortar which—so it was conjectured—was brought up every night on a light railway, and taken back after a few shots had been fired. At sunrise the clamour of the guns ceased and the birds at once " took over," the cuckoo being particularly active. Nightingales were common here and in the copses in the line, and as they seemed to regard machine-guns as rival vocalists, they would sing in competition. The bell-like whistle of the black and yellow golden oriole was often heard, and in the centre of the wood the war at times seemed far enough away. The A.S.C. turned their hands to hay-making, and helped to cut and harvest some acres of excellent clover, rye, and lucerne. The 3rd Field Ambulance were more envied by their fellows, as they harvested—for their own consumption—the crop of a very prolific strawberry bed in the garden of the ruined villa which they inhabited at Ruyalcourt.

A quartermaster of the 127th Brigade had chosen the ruins of a farm at a cross-roads near Havrincourt Wood for his dump. He was warned by the Town Major that this spot had probably been mined by the enemy, and particularly warned not to make use of the cellar, which was a likely place for a " booby-trap." However, nothing happened, and of course his men not only went into the cellar but took planks and bricks therefrom to improve their quarters in the rooms above. One evening the Q.M. returned from the line to find his staff in a state of nervous collapse. As soon as he had prevailed upon them to sit up and take a little nourishment they related this painful story: The former owner, armed with documents and accompanied by gendarmes and British Military Police, had visited the old home, descended into the cellar, and dug up jars containing jewellery, coins, and banknotes, within a few inches of the spot from which the storemen had taken the planks. The butcher had even held a candle to assist the search, and his reflections on " what might have been," as the jars of buried treasure were brought to light, completely unnerved him, especially when the owner handed him a couple of francs with thanks for the trouble he had so kindly taken. For some time after this these storemen displayed a rabbit-like tendency to burrow in any old corner, but luck was not with them.

One night when the Brigadier of the 127th Brigade was in the front line the enemy put down a fierce bombardment of gas shells and H.E. The night was dark, but calm and clear, and large working parties were out wiring and digging. These came back " hell for leather," and General Henley found his passage through the trench cut off by the crowds. Colonel Dobbin, deeming the scene unseemly for a Brigadier, suggested a dash over the top. Unfortunately fresh wire had just been put down, and, close to the support line where the long-range shells were dropping, both fell heavily into a double apron-fence. They extricated themselves painfully, leaving portions of clothing and some blood on the wire, and eventually arrived, " improperly dressed," at Battalion Headquarters, to be met by the adjutant with the tactless remark: " There has been a bit of a bombardment, sir, but it doesn't concern our front." The Brigadier, who limped for several days, suggested that his companion should write a sketch of the episode under the title, " *Young officers taking their pleasures lightly.*" Though the Colonel did not take advantage of the suggestion, another officer did.

Brig.-General H. C. Frith, C.B., returned to England in June to assume command of a Home Service Brigade, and Brig.-General H. Fargus, C.M.G., D.S.O., took command of the 125th Brigade until the end of the war. General Frith was the last of the General Officers who had served with the Division from the outbreak of war. For three years he had commanded the Lancashire Fusilier Brigade, which had become much attached to him, for he was quick to recognize and give credit for good work, and he possessed a remarkable memory for faces, invariably knowing each officer by name after the first meeting. The 6th Manchesters learnt with regret that their popular M.O., Captain A. H. Norris, M.C., who was home on leave, had been retained by the War Office for duty at home. A better-known and better-liked Medical Officer never served with any battalion, and the regret was not confined to officers and men of the battalion, for the sick and wounded of many units were grateful for the energy, solicitude and complete disregard of self—and of red tape—which he had displayed in looking after their comfort and welfare in Egypt, Gallipoli, Sinai, and France.

On the 1st of June the order was received to advance the divisional front by about 300 yards, the operation to be completed by 6 a.m. on the 10th. The order indicated that strong opposition might be expected, and details were left to the Brigadiers. The 126th Brigade on the right adopted the orthodox method of sapping forward each night, making a T-head at each sap to connect and form a continuous line later. The expectations of opposition were realized. Photographs taken by enemy planes brought heavy trench-mortar and machine-gun fire on the working-parties, and serious casualties were inflicted. A position near Femy Wood was occupied at night by the enemy, who were thence able to harass the working-parties. On the evening of June 3rd Corporal A. Eastwood, 9th Manchesters, took a patrol of three men to this point and lay down to await events. At 9.30 p.m. a German patrol emerged from the wood. The corporal ordered his men to hold their fire until the enemy were within thirty paces, when they opened fire with good effect, and remained until 2.30 a.m. covering the work and silencing a machine-gun and snipers. The hard and rocky nature of the ground in this part of the line was a further obstacle, but in spite of all difficulties good progress was made, and the troops were complimented upon their work by the Chief Engineer of the Corps. On the left, Brig.-General Henley, profiting by the experience of the 126th Brigade, decided to complete his part of the operation at one bound. On the night of the 8th–9th he advanced his line the full distance, and all four battalions of the 127th Brigade began to dig in furiously. The covering party was in position at 10.30 p.m., and digging began at 11 p.m. under the supervision of the 427th Field Company, R.E. Before dawn twelve outposts on a front of 1500 yards were linked up by a continuous trench, and, leaving a skeleton garrison in the new trench, the companies returned to their positions practically unharmed. The finishing touches were added next night, and the new line was completed by the stated hour. This good work was rewarded by a Special Order of the Day from the Corps Commander.

The night patrolling in No Man's Land furnished admirable opportunities for testing and training officers and men. These patrols appealed to many adventurous spirits, while others looked forward to their first experience with natural apprehension. Many patrols were therefore sent out with the primary object of giving the men confidence and experience, and this policy was completely successful. There was also a considerable amount of sniping, especially in the vicinity of Havrincourt Wood, where German snipers for a time had the advantage and made the most of their opportunities. They were, however, beaten at the game by Sergeant Durrans, 6th L.F., who on June 14 crept 450 yards into the long grass in No Man's Land and patiently bided his time. When the snipers disclosed their positions by firing he gave a fine display of marksmanship for two and a half hours and picked off half a dozen of them. He was wounded in the right knee.

On the night of June 12 an officer of the 5th Manchesters, who were then holding the " Slag Heap," was detailed to reconnoitre Wigan Copse, in No Man's Land, examine the wire—concealed by the long grass—and find the gaps. He led a party of six men to the copse, but could find no gaps, the wire being apparently uninjured. He crawled round it to the back of the copse, and eventually discovered an opening through which he crept, accompanied by a corporal, the rest of the party being posted outside. A narrow trench and some rough shelters were located, but there was no sign of life until the officer, desiring to take back a souvenir of his visit, disturbed a pile of stick-bombs. A tarpaulin then moved and a voice challenged them. The officer fired several shots with his revolver, and yells indicated that at least one of the Germans had been hit. The fire was returned, and in a moment the wood seemed alive with the enemy. As the exit was too close to the German front line for comfort the patrol crept away and lay in the long grass until the noise died down, when they withdrew untouched. On the following afternoon the enemy guns registered on the copse, and in the evening bombarded the British line and put down a box-barrage, under cover of which a company of the enemy charged the copse, yelling " Hands up, the English !" They suffered severely from rifle and Lewis-gun fire. Information was obtained later from prisoners that the garrison of the copse had been so scared by the sudden appearance of Englishmen in the wood that they had bolted, and had reported that the British were in possession of the post. Hence the elaborate counterattack of the empty copse.

In the afternoon of June 22 a particularly daring raid was carried out by Sergeant J. Sugden (later Lieutenant) of the 10th Manchesters. Annoyance had been caused by a small trench-mortar, and as it was suspected that this was fired from a derelict elephant hut a few hundred yards from our most forward post, Sugden—a born scout —resolved to make sure. He found that there was a sentry guarding a dug-out near to the elephant hut, and that the man seemed inclined to take his duties easily. Returning, he chose two companions, whom he posted on a flank, while he crawled unobserved to within a few yards of the dug-out. He then quietly informed the sentry, in fluent German, that he was covered, and that he would be shot if he showed the slightest hesitation in obeying orders. He showed none, so Sugden ordered the other occupants of the post to come out with their hands up. At first they seemed inclined to dispute the matter, until told that they were surrounded and that unless they obeyed promptly they would quickly find themselves blown into a region even lower than their dugout. The threat had its effect; they meekly obeyed, and Sugden had the satisfaction of bringing four very sullen Germans, carrying a trench-mortar, across No Man's Land in broad daylight. The Corps Commander sent a complimentary letter to the Battalion Commander praising the initiative and the aggressive tactics of his men, and congratulated Sugden personally, and also gave him special leave for fourteen days.

At the end of June the 7th Manchesters were instructed to supply a party to raid Wigan Copse and bring back three prisoners. Lieutenant A. Hodge (later Lieut.-Colonel, commanding 1/8th Manchesters), who was chosen to carry out the raid, gave his men some realistic preliminary training. At 11 p.m. on July 3 the guns opened on the enemy's lines behind the copse, and Hodge's platoon, after a crawl of more than half an hour, rushed the copse. Its occupants tried to bolt, but the box-barrage hemmed them in and they had to choose between fighting and surrender. One young German, who had been lying in the grass on outpost duty, was so scared that in his fright he rose and attached himself to the Manchesters, until Hodge took him by the scruff of the neck and flung him to the man behind. But no one wanted the Boche, so he was flung from one to another until finally one of the covering party held him captive. After five minutes' rough-and-tumble, in which none of the 7th was hurt, though a number of the enemy had been bayonetted, or shot by the officer's revolver, Hodge returned with the three prisoners indented for. It had been a model raid.

On the 8th of July the Division was relieved by the 58th Division, with the exception of the artillery, which remained in the line with the 58th Division, and later with the 9th Division, at Havrincourt Wood until the end of August, when they rejoined their own Division in Belgium. The artillery's periods of " rest " were infrequent and uncertain. Whenever the divisional infantry was relieved the guns would remain in the line for a time, attached to the relieving Division. From the artillery point of view the work at Havrincourt consisted mainly of concentrated fire at night on back areas of the enemy line and in artillery duels. Corporal Charles Gee, " B " Battery, 210th Brigade, twice won distinction during this period. On July 22, near Hermies, a hostile shell set a gun-pit on fire, and Gee, with Bombardier W. Pate, disregarding the explosions, succeeded in covering the burning material with earth, and so saved a considerable amount of ammunition. On August 13, during a heavy bombardment of the battery position, a shell burst in a dugout occupied by one man, blowing off one of his legs. Accompanied by Gunner W. Armitstead, Gee went to the injured man's assistance, and while they were removing the debris a shell burst near and knocked both over. They managed to extricate the man, bandage his wounds, and convey him to safety, being all the time under heavy fire and suffering from fumes.

The Ytres sector was looked back upon as a " bon " front by comparison with others with which acquaintance was made later. Here the Divisional Concert Party, which afterwards achieved fame under the title of " *Th' Lads*," was first organized. " Th' Lads " soon became a feature which the Division could ill have spared, and the delightful entertainments given under the fine trees of Little Wood are recalled with genuine pleasure.

From July 9 to August 22 the Divisional Headquarters were in the Third Army reserve area at Achiet-le-Petit, where the 127th Brigade was stationed, with the 125th Brigade at Gomiecourt and the 126th at Courcelles. This area, which was visited by the King on July 12-13, had been wholly devastated. What had once been a village was now a heap of broken bricks and rubble; a few stark walls standing grimly against the skyline and a name painted in bold black lettering on a white ground informed the passer-by what village had once stood here. The fields were scarred with trenches and shell holes, and all the indescribable debris of an abandoned battlefield was spread around. Most of the troops were under canvas, but as there were not enough tents for all a number had to live in little " shacks " made of odd bits of corrugated iron and any other scrap material available. The fine weather continued and the six weeks in this area partook of the nature of a holiday, though the days were fully taken up by intensive training, special attention being paid to training in attacks upon fortified posts and strong points. Instructional visits were made to the scarred battlefields of the Somme, Brig.-General Henley taking a number of his officers to Thiepval and giving his personal experiences of the fighting there. The various training stunts—battalion, brigade, and divisional—enabled the troops to gain a thorough knowledge of the ground in this area, and this familiarity with the topography stood them in good stead when seven months later they were called upon to withstand the German onrush on this very ground. Time was found for divisional and brigade sports, inter-battalion football and cricket matches, boxing contests in the large crater at Achiet-le-Petit; and the visits of " Th' Lads " to the Brigade Headquarters were keenly appreciated. There had never been such a time for sports as this, and it was hard to realize that " there was a war on." Newly-painted vehicles, perfectly turned-out animals, bands playing, troops spick-and-span, all combined to lend a gala aspect to this period.

On August 22 the period of rest came to an end, and the Division entrained for the most detested of all fronts—Ypres.

CHAPTER VI

YPRES

(September 1917)

THE Division reached Watou, a village in the Poperinghe area, on the 23rd of August, and, with the exception of the artillery, which went straight into the line near Potijze Chateau, under the 15th Division, remained in that district for a few days' training prior to going into the line at Ypres, rather more than a dozen kilometres to the east. Parties of officers and other ranks from all units were attached to units of the 15th Division in order to learn the geography of the sector. Except for the nightly bombing raids by hostile air squadrons this would have been an uneventful week.

At the end of August the Territorials from East Lancashire marched from Poperinghe into the Flemish city which had become a tragic household word throughout the British Isles. The name of Ypres had a deeper, fuller significance for the men and women at home than that of any other foreign town, and however queerly it might be pronounced the word was rarely uttered without stirring emotions of pride, admiration, horror and pity. In the streets and country lanes of the homeland were vast numbers of men, clad in garments of bright blue or grey, who had been maimed and battered in defence of the ruins of an ancient city of which they had never even heard before the autumn of 1914; the wards of hundreds of hospitals were filled with the wounded and gassed, who spoke unwillingly of the horrors of Ypres; and thousands of British homes mourned the loss of one or more who had fallen there. Ypres stood for death and mutilation and agony, and all that was most cruel and horrible in war. To wives and parents it was the Valley of the Shadow of Death, where their husbands and sons fought a never-ending fight with the Powers of Darkness, and never gave ground, yet never gained the victory.

On July 31, 1917, the Third Battle of Ypres had opened with a terrific bombardment of the Hun positions, which had lasted ten days and had obliterated every sign of life and every green thing that grew. But the ill-luck that dogged the British arms had been consistent; the fine weather on which the complete success of the long-prepared offensive largely depended, came to a sudden end, and when the troops made the attack an unusually heavy rainstorm

H

had turned the scarred, shell-pitted ground into a vast quagmire, and the thousands of shell-holes into ponds. The tanks, from which so much had been anticipated, struggled gallantly against the adverse conditions, but many of them were " bellied " at an early stage, and some of those which went furthest into the Boche lines suffered the ignominious fate of conversion into German pill-boxes and sniper-posts. A little ground had been gained, a great deal of unavailing heroism had been shown, there had been much slaughter of British and Germans, and that was all.

Sooner or later almost every fighting unit of the B.E.F. had been moved to Ypres. Veterans, indeed, considered that no soldier had been properly " blooded " until he had taken his place in the line at the famous salient; and there were probably few soldiers with any length of service in France or Flanders who had not passed the traffic-man at the cross-roads leading to Hell Fire Corner, where the tide of motor ambulances ebbed and flowed so regularly. On the night of September 1 the 42nd Division passed through the Menin Gate on their way to the front trenches, now between four and five kilometres from the town. The Menin Road had been subjected to almost incessant shelling for more than two years. The German gunners had registered every square yard of it, and of every other road and track that led towards the front, and the men declared that if a large fly crossed the Menin Road in the daytime the Boche would at once put down a barrage of 6-inch shells. At night their guns would search every stretch of the road systematically on the chance—which was almost a certainty—of getting a bag. Night after night rations and ammunition were brought to the troops in the trenches through a hail of shells, which too often caught men, animals and vehicles and blotted them out. Night after night the roads were converted into shell-holes, but still the work of repairing them went on unceasingly; the gunners brought their teams along at the gallop; the transport men arrived with their precious loads and returned to pass through the inferno again, and often the ration limbers came back bearing burdens very different from those they had borne on the outward journey. And for every hundred struck by Death amid that never-ending hail of shells a thousand tricked him by hairbreadth escapes. At dawn there would often be a brief respite—a semblance, or rather a mockery, of peace. For an hour or two the crashes and rumblings ceased, as though the guns were pausing for breath through the very violence of their fury, and, while pausing, were plotting some still more devilish form of hate.

The whole terrain through which the Division passed on its three miles' journey to the trenches was stiff with guns. The 18-pounders had been brought close behind the infantry, and they stood in mud and shell-holes almost wheel to wheel. They appeared to be innumerable, and it was something of a shock to the Lancashire gunners to find so many guns within a radius of one hundred yards. The 4·5-inch howitzers were in groups, also close to the front; further back were the 6-inch howitzers, the 60-pounders, and the

YPRES. THE CLOTH HALL.

YPRES. RAILWAY WOOD DUG-OUTS.

POTIJZE ROAD. THE A.D.S. AT THE WHITE CHATEAU.

POTIJZE ROAD. BAVARIA HOUSE, AN R.A.M.C. COLLECTING POST.

YPRES. BORRY FARM OR "PILLBOX."

The Ypres Salient

guns of heavier calibre, though there was a battery of 9·2-inch howitzers only twenty yards behind one of our R.F.A. batteries. The huge naval and 15-inch guns were well to the rear of Ypres, but though they could not be seen their tremendous power appealed to the imagination of the infantryman, who regarded them somewhat in the light of influential friends or patrons who, if occasion should arise, would see that he had fair play and would keep the ring. The enemy had also concentrated a similarly vast array of artillery in this sector, which he too regarded as the most important and most to be dreaded of all. Day and night the guns of both sides barked and thundered, and the strain on the gunners would have been considered unbearable before the Great War had taught the lesson that the limit of man's endurance cannot be calculated. British and Germans lost more guns and gunners here in a week than an army would have lost in a year's campaigning in any previous war. At night, high above the flashes of our 18-pounders, the beautiful coloured stars and golden rain of the German signal-rockets recalled memories of Belle Vue nights. In the daytime the swans calmly paddled in the moat round the eastern ramparts of Ypres, though the 60-pounders blazed away within a few yards of the water's edge.

The Division, now part of the 5th Corps of the Fifth Army, had a strength of 703 officers and 16,972 men on September 1. The sector taken over from the 15th Division was about 1500 yards in width, from a point south-east of the Ypres–Menin railway on the right to a point 500 yards north-east of Frezenburg on the left. The roads were soon left, and the units proceeded to their positions by the duckboard paths which were the arteries from the bases to the front line, and along which generals and privates, stretcher-bearers and casualties, rations and ammunition, passed. It was more easy to lose one's way than to keep to the track, and soldiers of both armies strayed into their opponents' lines. A German officer, returning from leave, walked into the territory of the Division one night, and at breakfast time he was being interrogated at D.H.Q. Along the whole dreary length of duckboards the probability of slipping into one of the countless shell-holes filled with water and deep slime, was an ever-present menace which might prove fatal. At intervals small signboards were erected with the distinctive number or letter of the path in luminous paint. The front line was merely a series of linked-up shell-holes, with Battalion and Company Headquarters in pill-boxes captured from the enemy in the recent offensive. Despite such discouraging conditions a covey of partridges would often be put up at dawn by men returning along " J " trench, between Cambridge Road and the Menin Road.

One shrinks from the attempt to describe the conditions that prevailed in the Ypres salient. No part of it was ever at rest. By day, aircraft sought to spot every movement that was attempted on either side, and day and night the guns sprayed the trenches, the roads, the duckboard paths, with shrapnel and H.E., the grim resolve to kill dominating every other thought or desire. The ghastly evidences of the fighting in three great battles and nearly three years of warfare were brought to light by the bombardments that tore and flung up the earth. The flares at night showed up in silhouette the figures of ration and ammunition carriers and of transport men, and brought swift destruction upon them. The runners who bore messages from one headquarters to another took their lives in their hands every time. Even for those few who were endowed by nature with the sixth sense of locality the odds were against their safe arrival and return. But the average town-bred lad has little sense of locality, so the carrying of a message meant wandering in a maze in which lurked enemies real and imaginary, varied by tumbles into shell-holes. Yet the runners generally got their messages through, and when one failed it was because another casualty had been added to the list. But if the Ypres Salient was detested by the British soldier, the enemy, although not penned within the narrow salient, regarded this sector with even greater abhorrence, and German prisoners declared that their troops, on being sent to the Ypres front, considered the order as equivalent to " certain death or worse."

One night, at Hell Fire Corner, an ammunition depot was set on fire by enemy artillery, which continued to shell the dump and its vicinity furiously. In spite of the bombardment and constant explosions a party of the divisional transport loaded up alongside the depot, and got all teams and wagons safely away. Fighting patrols and working-parties went out nightly, and many were the unrecorded acts of heroism. There were also minor operations, which with one exception were quite small affairs. The 125th Brigade was ordered to attack on September 6 the positions known as Iberian, Borry and Beck House Farms, strong posts protected by the usual elaborate system of outworks. Two similar assaults in this vicinity had already failed—one by the 15th Division, in which a little ground had been gained by the Black Watch and the Gordons, who had lost very heavily and had been driven out in the morning by a counter-attack; and the second, on September 5, against Hill 35 by the 61st Division, had been no more successful. Prior to the date fixed for the attack by the Lancashire Fusiliers a daring reconnaissance in daylight was carried out by Sergeant Finney, 8th L.F., who, accompanied by a rifle-grenadier and two Lewis-gunners, pushed out to within twenty-five yards of Beck House. Although he knew that for the last hundred yards he was under observation, and could see the enemy manning the shell-holes, he worked parallel to the position until forced by rifle fire to withdraw and lie down in No Man's Land. The following night Finney went alone to this post and lay out to study the enemy dispositions at night. He brought back valuable information, and was awarded the D.C.M. His bold move the previous day had evidently affected German nerves, for the enemy put up a many-coloured firework display and disclosed their general dispositions and barrage line, which previously had only been known vaguely.

Iberian, Borry, and Beck House

Practice barrages had been carried out by the artillery for three or four days before the 125th Brigade launched its attack, and rarely have gunners worked with such keenness as the divisional artillery displayed in the early hours of September 6. Four rounds per minute was the order, but eight, nine and ten rounds found their way into the enemy lines, and the gunners state that never were the guns so hot as on that day. The 5th and 6th L.F., with the 7th and 8th in support and the 6th Manchesters as carrying parties, advanced under the heavy barrage. A thunderstorm on the previous day made the going heavy, and the German machine-gunners, from the security of their apparently invulnerable concrete pill-boxes, were able to direct a devastating fire upon the advancing waves. Within a few minutes many officers and men were down, one company being reduced to thirty men commanded by a corporal. The survivors pressed doggedly on, but their courage was unavailing, and the Iberian and Borry positions were never reached. In the centre the troops attacking Beck House had a less exposed approach, and by 7 a.m. they had gained a footing and had captured the garrison. They now suffered heavily, however, from the machine-guns in the posts not included in the objective, as well as from those in Borry and Iberian, and all who had penetrated into Beck House were killed or captured in a counter-attack by three companies of fresh storm-troops. The order was received to abandon the attack on the other posts, and the survivors withdrew reluctantly and with difficulty from an impossible position, having lost nearly 800 officers and men. Much gallantry had been shown by all ranks, and a number of distinctions were awarded for deeds of which the following are merely typical examples.

Private James Dolan, 5th L.F., though twice blown up by shells and badly bruised, succeeded in bringing his Lewis-gun into action. After the rest of the team had become casualties, he worked the gun alone with great vigour and—to quote the official report—" in an extraordinarily cheerful manner " against two strong counter-attacks. Private W. Walliss, of the same battalion, worked as stretcher-bearer during the attack and for twenty-four hours subsequently, after the attack had been held up and two of his fellow bearers had been killed. He was subjected to harassing fire the whole time, and his disregard of risk and untiring devotion to duty saved many lives. Sergeant George Ward, 6th L.F., went out six times into the open under heavy enemy barrage and sniping to bring in wounded men, and was himself badly wounded on completing his sixth successful journey. Lance-Corporal E. Taylor, 6th L.F., seeing enemy reinforcements threatening, rushed his Lewis-gun into a shell-hole and opened a deadly fire, breaking up the attack. After all other members of his team had been killed or wounded Taylor stuck to his gun until ordered to withdraw. Sergeant J. H. Ashton, 3rd Field Ambulance, " worked unceasingly and without rest for forty-eight hours, often under heavy fire, in charge of squads removing the wounded."

The assistance given by the 6th Manchesters, who had been lent to the 5th and 6th L.F., was warmly acknowledged by Brig.-General Fargus and the Battalion Commanders. Lieut.-Colonel Hammond Smith, commanding the 6th L.F., in a letter to Lieut.-Colonel C. S. Worthington, D.S.O., commanding the 6th Manchesters, regretting the heavy loss suffered by the companies attached to his battalion, added : " To-day I asked for help to bury some of our dead, involving a carry of three-quarters of a mile through the barrage area. Seventy-two of your men volunteered, and that speaks for itself. We could not bear to think of burying men in this area where they were bound to be blown up again, otherwise we should not have asked."

The Division had had an object lesson in the peculiar strength of the German defensive system and the futility of " minor operations." The losses from continuous shelling and from unproductive local assaults were heavy during the next ten days. There were deeds of valour, too, but the pill-box problem was no nearer solution. Gunner S. Hardcastle, " B " Battery, 211th Brigade, during a heavy bombardment of the battery position near Potijze on September 7, left cover to go a hundred yards through the shelled area to get water for a wounded comrade, and three days later, seeing an ammunition dump belonging to the battery on his left struck and set on fire by a hostile shell, he ran across and was first to begin the dangerous work of extinguishing the fire. But for his prompt action a large amount of ammunition would have been lost. During an attack on an enemy blockhouse on the night of the 11th–12th September, Private T. M. Howard, 9th Manchesters, volunteered to bring in an officer who lay wounded about forty yards from the blockhouse, from which severe machine-gun and rifle fire was maintained. Howard reached the officer and carried him 200 yards over exposed ground illuminated by enemy flares. On the following day Corporal W. White, 8th Manchesters, made five successive journeys through a continuous barrage, and each time brought in a wounded man. On the night of September 11 a covering party protecting workers in No Man's Land found a wounded private of the Inniskilling Fusiliers, who had been lying out since August 11, unable to crawl into safety. In spite of thirty-one days exposure and starvation—except for the meagre rations found upon the bodies within reach—he recovered.

Among the casualties of these ten days were Lieut.-Colonel R. P. Lewis, 10th Manchesters, killed by shell fire, and Brig.-General A. C. Johnson, D.S.O., seriously wounded within two days of his arrival to take over the command of the 126th Brigade in succession to Brig.-General Tufnell, who was Chief Staff Officer of the Division on the outbreak of war, and who had returned home for a much-needed rest. Brig.-General W. W. Seymour succeeded to the command of the Brigade a few days later. On September 18 the Division was relieved by the 9th Division, and D.H.Q. moved to Poperinghe, the infantry concentrating in camps in that region preparatory to a march northwards to the coast. The artillery remained in the Ypres sector for nearly three weeks, when they rejoined the Division at Nieuport. The East Lancashire Artillery did some of its best work in the Ypres Salient, and its best was very good. Losses in guns and personnel were heavy, especially from the accurate and relentless fire of the enemy's 5·9 howitzers, for there was no cover and no protection other than the accuracy of their own fire. They were content to give more than they received, and they gave it with hearty goodwill. As an indication of their activity it is interesting to record that on one night, September 13, more than 1100 horsed vehicles conveyed supplies to the Divisional Artillery, in addition to the supply of ammunition by motor-lorries and pack-animals. Night after night, in pitch darkness, over cut-up and waterlogged ground, amid constant shell-storms, the daily supply of ammunition was brought up, and the gunner had little rest and less sleep. Dumps were set on fire by the daily bombardment, and officers and men vied with one another in fighting the flames, while shells from the enemy and from the burning dumps exploded right and left. Guns sank axle-deep in the mud—Napoleon's *fifth* element—and were salved under deadly fire. After the rest of the Division had left for the coast, the artillery took part in continuous fighting from September 20 onwards, advancing to forward and exposed positions on Frezenberg Ridge on the 25th. These were the days of the greatest artillery battles of the war, and it was not unusual for a single battery to fire 5000 rounds in twenty-four hours. There were many casualties from gas, as the batteries were in small depressions in the ground, and these were never really free from gas. Men wore masks sometimes for five hours at a stretch—until they had to discard them through sheer exhaustion. In the course of a few days the four batteries of the 210th Brigade lost 120 men in gas casualties alone. When relieved on the 29th September batteries could barely muster more than 100 N.C.O.s and men. Majors Boone and Simon had been killed and Brig.-General Walshe and Major Highet severely wounded, Lieut.-Colonel A. Birtwistle, C.M.G., assuming temporary command of the Divisional Artillery.

Of numerous instances of devotion to duty and disregard of personal safety three examples (on September 25–26), taken haphazard from the Honours List, must suffice. Padre A. C. Trench, attached to the 211th Brigade, R.F.A., followed up the infantry to their forward positions and worked all day under shell fire, setting a fine example of cheerfulness to all ranks, bandaging the wounded and ministering to the dying. Sergeant H. Bentley was in command of " A " Battery, 210th Brigade—the officers being casualties —when an ammunition dump close to the guns was set on fire. Bentley kept the guns working, and with Corporal A. Butterworth tackled the burning dump and put out the fire, saving ammunition at a time when it was most valuable. A similar act was that of Sergeant W. L. Breese, Corporal E. Fletcher, and Driver A. Hughes, of "C" Battery, 210th Brigade. A gun-pit and an ammunition dump were fired during a bombardment, and the fire spread to the camouflage of the guns and to ammunition pits on both flanks. At great personal danger from bursting shrapnel and H.E., the three extinguished the newly-started fires and saved two guns and much ammunition.

Lighter incidents were not wholly absent on Frezenberg Ridge. A barrel of beer had arrived; naturally enough the Boche could not ignore so important an event, and before the barrel could be put in a safe position it was shelled. Men ran to cover, but kept an anxious eye on the barrel, which was soon punctured. The sight of beer running to waste was too much for one gunner, who ran to the barrel, calling out : " Hey, chaps, coom on ! Jerry has knocked t'bung-hole in ! " He remained by the barrel, stopping the leak until the shelling ceased, and ever afterwards marvelled at the lack of a sense of proportion shown in decorating men for saving guns and ammunition while one's sole reward for rescuing a barrel of beer is to be hailed as a public benefactor.

While in the Ypres Salient the three Field Companies, R.E., as usual did all manner of work, from the maintenance of duckboard tracks to the construction of concrete emplacements. The Signal Sections displayed the efficiency that one learned to expect from them. A Lamp Signalling Station on the ramparts did useful work, and the carrier-pigeon service proved surprisingly quick and reliable. The linemen had a particularly hot time, as communications were exceedingly difficult to maintain in this sector; and their coolness, courage, and skill in repairing the constantly damaged lines gained several decorations, and also the admiration of their comrades of all arms.

Equally cool must be the stretcher-bearer. Casualties had to be conveyed by hand carriage over the duckboard tracks before wheeled carriers could be used. Yet day and night the bearers kept a continuous stream of wounded flowing to the rear. The distance between the front and the region of comparative safety made the evacuation of the wounded a matter of difficulty. The Field Ambulances were, however, equal to their task, and though the Advanced Dressing Stations at Railway Dugout, Bavaria House, and Potijze Chateau were cramped for space and were frequently gassed and always shelled, all the wounded were dressed and got away. The pressure in rear was so great that some bandages were not changed until the men reached England.

The Army Service Corps had a most trying time, but in spite of serious losses the supply services never failed. Reference has already been made to the dangerous and difficult work carried out so competently by the battalion transports.

The period at Ypres ended on a note of depression. One felt that the Division was beginning to doubt its ability to achieve the impossible. It was not the imminent menace of death from above

FREZENBERG RIDGE.

YPRES. SQUARE FARM, USED AS BATTALION HEADQUARTERS AND AID POST.

NIEUPORT. THE FIVE BRIDGES AND R. YSER.

NIEUPORT. "THE REDAN."

in the form of shell or bomb, or from the trenches in front in the shape of machine-gun bullet. But the secrecy and furtiveness of every movement, the ghastliness of the abomination of desolation all around, the sickening sights and smells, the saturation of the whole terrain with gas to such an extent that men often preferred to lie out in the open under fire rather than risk suffocation in dugouts—these combined to awaken a vague, inarticulate protest against the cruelty and futility of war. Had the men been able to get at those responsible for turning a peaceable countryside into something viler than any man's imaginings of hell, indignation and righteous anger would have left little room for the depression generated by the sense of impotence—the beating one's head against a concrete wall, the waste of effort and of lives thrown away in futile local assaults. The men were glad to quit the Ypres salient, but they did not leave it in a happy frame of mind. Every one felt that the Division was not at its best; that it was capable of better things had opportunity been given.

CHAPTER VII

NIEUPORT

(October—November 1917)

ON September 26 and 27 the Division took over the coastal sector of the Nieuport front, relieving the 66th Division, composed of the second line of the East Lancashire Territorials. The relief was therefore a hurried family gathering, a meeting of elder and younger brothers. The first-line and second-line battalions were keenly interested in each other's doings and experiences. Friends met friends; many were related; more had friends and acquaintances in common; so they "swapped lies," and the time was all too short to exhaust the store of anecdote, reminiscence, and inquiry. The 66th Division left for Ypres, and a fortnight later " made good " in the advance at Passchendaele.

D.H.Q. was at La Panne, a picturesque seaside village. The billets were very good, and for the first time since the Division's arrival in France the excitement of shopping was experienced. The sea-bathing was excellent, and the Belgian Army baths (in a theatre) were well patronized. The Division now held the left of the Allied Line, Barrel Post, on the seashore at the mouth of the Yser, being the extreme left post. On October 1 Major-General Mitford proceeded to England on leave, and temporary command was assumed by Brig.-General W. W. Seymour. Nothing of importance occurred here, and on October 7 the Division was relieved by the 41st Division, and took over the neighbouring divisional front from the 32nd Division. The new sector included the town of Nieuport with the Lombartzyde and St. Georges sub-sectors. Belgian troops were on the right.

The Nieuport sector was a curious one, and those who had expected a comparatively " cushy " time were disappointed. The town itself had ceased to exist, for it had never a day's immunity from the enemy artillery, and the bombing was hardly less continuous. It was also heavily gassed, the place being filled with gas on most nights. Here the large Gotha bombing-planes were first sighted, going to or returning from Dunkirk, where bombs had been dropped during twenty-three of the thirty nights of September, the enemy pilots being greatly assisted by the guiding lines of the canals and coast. The strained look, the expression of dull despair, on the faces of the war-harassed peasantry of all the devastated areas of France and Belgium, was particularly noticeable in this region. Nieuport had been very thoroughly tunnelled by the French during their occupation, and though at first the low, slimy, and very dark tunnels were distinctly unpopular, all ranks were thankful for them as they became more intimate with the situation. The tunnels, running parallel to the streets, had been made by connecting up the cellars. They were—at times—lighted by electric lights, but even then fully equipped troops found difficulty in passing through.

The left, or Lombartzyde, sub-sector lay to the north and north-east of Nieuport, across the wide and deep Yser canal. It was held by the 125th and 127th Brigades in turn. The less important St. Georges sub-sector, to the east and south-east, was in charge of the 126th Brigade, two battalions being in line and two in reserve. In each sub-sector the front line consisted mainly of breastworks and island-posts, as much of the area was below sea-level, and it was impossible to construct trenches in the flooded marshy ground. The front has been comprehensively described as "one big flood," and when, as frequently happened, a big shell knocked in the bank of one of the many dams, this description was no exaggeration.

Just across the Yser were the Redan and Indiarubber House; the former being a large triangular redoubt—apex towards the enemy—with an artificial moat, the latter a barn-like structure apparently inviting demolition, but in reality built of solid concrete ingeniously disguised, from which the shells—so rumour says—rebounded harmlessly. This building, which was lighted by electricity, was used as headquarters of the battalions in line in the left sub-sector. The Redan was linked to the town by three wobbly duck-board bridges, laid on floats, without side-rails, and with many gaps between the boards. These bridges, Putney, Crowder, and Vauxhall, rose and fell several feet with the tide, at times making the approaches and exits, down and up very steep gradients of the Yser's muddy banks, a matter of the greatest difficulty. They were shelled all day and machine-gunned all night, with the result that they were frequently smashed, for the Germans had the exact range. Troops, working-parties, and ration-parties had to make their way across the swaying planks, carrying full equipment, and often two petrol-tins full of water, or bags of rations, a trench-board, or a box of ammunition. It was therefore unhealthy to linger when crossing, and some who had to take frequent trips across began to think that Ypres was not so bad a place after all.

On the east of the town several smaller canals joined the Yser, and at this point the Five Bridges—so-called, though there were really six—had to be crossed. There were also other less important bridges over these canals, by which the front of the St. Georges sector was reached. This right sector included the site of one of the finest golf-links in Europe, but much of it was now under water. The destruction of dams and locks brought the tide into the canals, causing them to overflow and flood our defensive works; and the Boche amused himself at times by refraining from molesting the sappers while they repaired a dam, in order to knock it down as soon as completed and filled. The repairing and rebuilding of dams and bridges was a severe drain upon the resources of the Engineers and the infantry working under their supervision. The 428 and 429 Field Companies had each more than thirty bridges of various kinds under their charge. Infantry were attached to the Field Companies, and every unit supplied a permanent working-party of a platoon with an officer to serve with the Tunnelling Companies, which, among much other excellent work here, helped the R.A.M.C. to construct three deep A.D. Stations in the Nieuport cellars. The R.A.M.C. had their first experience of mustard-gas, and were also called upon to treat and evacuate several hundred cases of phosgene gassing.

There was little activity on these fronts other than artillery duels and aircraft bombing. The line was often under fire from heavy mortars, and the bridges, dams, roads, and back areas were constantly shelled. The enemy's 15-inch guns bombarded Dunkirk, twenty miles behind the line, and the shelling of back areas increased in violence until on reaching the front line it frequently attained an intensity unsurpassed on any sector of the British front. The enemy had the advantage of slightly higher ground at Lombartzyde village, so his works and trenches were not affected by the floods. As he could see any movement on our side, and as on the least sign of this his machine-guns and " whizz-bangs " promptly opened fire, our men lay " doggo " behind the breastworks, or in small pill-boxes, during the daytime. This absence of movement gave one a sense of isolation and even the unpleasant feeling of being left behind by one's comrades and forgotten. At night there had to be considerable movement, and the Lancashire men speculated on the length of stay that would be required to transform them into amphibians, and when they would begin to develop web-feet. Patrols sent out to reconnoitre posts alleged to be occupied by the enemy had a particularly difficult and nerve-testing task. Often they had to wade through the floods, and sometimes to swim across the canals, the one compensation being that as No Man's Land was always flooded there was little chance of any surprise attack. Listening posts close up to the German lines were reached by means of duckboards resting on the marshes, and these at times crossed ditches eighteen feet deep. Shell-holes in the front areas were quickly filled with water and converted into ponds of varying depths. As at Ypres, the heavy shells tore great pits in the roads and blocked them. One night a guide was sent to conduct some transport past a newly-made and particularly deep crater. Presently he warned the drivers that the hole was close at hand—and a moment later disappeared. Out of the depths arose an agonized wail. " Stop ! for heaven's sake, stop ! I'm down the —— hole myself ! "

There were no communication trenches to most parts of the

NIEUPORT, SHOWING REMAINS OF PUTNEY AND CROWDER BRIDGES AND RUBBER HOUSE IN THE DISTANCE.

INDIA-RUBBER HOUSE, USED AS BATTALION HEADQUARTERS.

General Solly-Flood arrives

line in the left sub-sector, and on dark nights it was easy to lose one's way. On the night of the 10th–11th of October, Lieut.-Colonel G. E. Hope, M.C., commanding the 8th Lancashire Fusiliers, while visiting his outposts with two officers at a point very near to the enemy line, saw a post ahead and called out : " What post is that ? " On this challenge the German flat-topped caps were seen instead of the expected " tin-hats." The three officers got clear, but, the night being very dark, they stumbled into another enemy post. Bombs were thrown and a machine-gun opened on them, and in the mêlée the three were separated. Hope, who had been leading, was last seen in the midst of the enemy, who were fighting one another in the confusion, and he was never heard of again. His companions got away, one by waiting until there was sufficient light to give him his bearings; the other by the desperate expedient of trusting to the enemy's knowledge of the British lines and making for a spot where the " minnies " were falling.

The 15th of October, 1917, is a notable date in the history of the 42nd Division, as on this day Major-General A. Solly-Flood, C.M.G., D.S.O., assumed command. The new Divisional Commander when war broke out was a Major in the 4th Dragoon Guards, who were the first in the British Army to kill any of the enemy. As C.O. of this regiment he had also fought at Messines, Ypres, and in all the battles of the Yser in 1914 and 1915, and at Loos in 1915. In the Somme battles of 1916 he had commanded the 35th Infantry Brigade, 12th Division. For some months prior to taking command of the 42nd Division, General Solly-Flood had been Director of Training at G.H.Q. in France. Mingled with gratification there was some uneasiness on the part of officers, who feared that the new Divisional Commander might demand an abnormally high standard of " spit and polish " and take occasion to " strafe " them as mere Territorials, should the latest drafts fail to conform to a Guards standard. They were quickly reassured. They soon found that they were commanded by a man who understood men and how to get the best out of them; who meant to lead and inspire rather than to drive; one who knew well how to show appreciation of every trier, and how to stimulate him to try still harder, and instruct him how to make the best possible use of his efforts. Officers and men alike began to want to satisfy their Chief and to merit his approval, for he gave them the impression that he knew they would bring credit to the Division and that he was not only their General but their friend. From the outset he identified himself with the Division and was proud to command it.

Prior to August 1917, all drafts for the Division, and men returning from leave, had been passed through the Corps Rest Camp, and the training of officers and men had been carried out in England or at the Army and Corps Schools. These systems had not been found entirely satisfactory, and it was decided that drafts be sent direct to divisions. In August 1917, the 42nd Division Rest Camp accordingly came into being, and in October was changed into the

Divisional Reception Camp, Lieut.-Colonel H. Grant Thorold, D.S.O., then assuming the command, which he retained until the end. In this camp at Ghyvelde the training of the drafts in such subjects as *Musketry, Bayonet fighting, Signalling, Machine- and Lewis-guns, Scouts, duties of N.C.O.s,* etc., was carried out. A Lewis-gun demonstration in November by men of the 7th Manchesters was the first of its kind in the Division, and was very instructive. The Division was fortunate, not only in the officer commanding this camp, but also in its instructors, most of whom came from battalions of the Division. But, perhaps, the chief responsibility for the training which was put to such good account a few months later rests with Captain Edwards, Coldstream Guards. In his classes for junior N.C.O.s, corporals, lance-corporals, and selected privates were put through a short intensive course on all subjects, from cleanliness in billets to tactical exercises with live ammunition and bombs. Sports were also included, this being a subject to which the Divisional Commander attached very great importance. At the end of the month's course competitions were held and prizes awarded, the best all-round student receiving a watch from the Major-General. Competitions between units in classes and sports became very keen, with excellent results, and Commanding Officers stated later that they invariably found that the best students at these classes made the best leaders in action.

Two or three instances, selected more or less at haphazard as typical of many, must suffice to illustrate the general character of service in the Nieuport Sector, memories of which are usually associated with the bridges, canals, and dams, each bridge having its own history worthy of individual record if space permitted, and such history would be particularly interesting to the engineers of the three Field Companies. At 4.20 p.m. on October 22, Putney, Crowder, and Vauxhall bridges were destroyed by shell fire while a relief was in progress, and the enemy continued to shell the area to prevent repairs. Lieutenant J. F. H. Nicholson, Corporal Brightmore, and Sappers J. Bennett and J. Rylance, of the 429 Field Company, at once volunteered to repair the bridges, and in spite of heavy shell fire they had restored communications across Putney bridge by 5.55 p.m. All four were decorated.

Bath Dam (Dam 66) was, perhaps, the worst job the R.E. had to tackle in the whole sector, as the enemy made a special target of it. This dam controlled the flow of the River Yser into the Yser Canal, and by its means the water in the flooded polders was kept at a sufficiently high level to form a military obstacle. On October 31 a breach fifteen feet in width was made by 8-inch shells, causing the flooding of the country up to the third-line trenches. Lieutenant Mellor, 427 Field Company, promptly organized a working-party of sappers and men of the 6th and 7th Manchesters, and at once started on its repair, the enemy, of course, doing their utmost to obstruct. The indefatigable C.R.E., Lieut.-Colonel D. S. MacInnes, D.S.O., who never failed to turn up at any hour of the day or night when his presence could assist and inspire, took charge of one of the reliefs, and set an example of energy and coolness under fire.* The breach was rebuilt with sandbags before the rapidly rising tide could take effect. On November 3 York Dam was damaged, but the same night a working-party closed the gap with 2000 sandbags; but on November 13 both York and Hull Dams were heavily shelled and wiped out, and on the 15th, Dam 66 and Mellor Dam were blown up by concentrated artillery fire. The height of the tide hindered the work of repair, which on this account could not be completed before the Division was relieved.

On October 31 Lieutenant K. MacIver, of "B" Battery, 211 Brigade, R.F.A., during a bombardment of his battery position, which destroyed two of the three guns, ran out to attend to a wounded man of another unit. He was knocked down by a shell and his left arm rendered useless, but, assisted by a driver, he removed the wounded man to safety. Soon afterwards two dumps caught fire and MacIver, foreseeing that the flames would assist a hostile plane to register the battery, ran out into the shelled area and, though one arm was useless, he extinguished the flames at both dumps. On November 2 Private T. Brotherton, 5th E. Lancs., while in charge of a limber taking rations up the line, was wounded by a shell which dropped three yards in rear of his vehicle. Although in great pain and under heavy shelling all the time, he coolly unhooked his mules, one of which had been injured, refusing attention for himself until he had done everything possible for the animals. He then had his wounds dressed, and obeyed the order to report to the nearest Field Dressing Station with great reluctance, as he wished to return to his transport lines for another mule so that he could carry on. On the same day Crowder Bridge was shelled while a party of the 6th Manchesters was in the act of crossing singly, and one man was seriously wounded and knocked into the water. Sergeant E. E. Parry, R.A.M.C., attached to the 6th Manchesters, at once rushed on to the bridge, and remained supporting him and crouching over him until the shell-storm ceased. The man was saved, and Parry received the M.M. for this brave deed. On more than one occasion Captain Brentnall, R.A.M.C., carried wounded men across a bridge on his shoulders when he considered the shelling too severe to permit a bearer-party to cross in safety.

On November 4 an enemy shell fired an ammunition dump near White House, in the right sub-sector. Captains L. Green and M. B. Bolton, with a number of N.C.O.s and men of the 4th East Lancashires, hastened to the spot, isolated the fire, and prevented the destruction of the entire dump. They worked for forty minutes under heavy shell fire, sometimes carrying burning boxes of smoke bombs away from the flames. Both officers were decorated, as were C.S.M. R. Graham, C.S.M. A. Potts, Sergeant R. Driver, and Privates J. Berry and G. Kay. On the same day Private Isaac

* It was alleged and universally believed that Colonel MacInnes after each day's hard work used to spend his few hours of "rest" in repairing Dam 66.

Whitehall, A.S.C., whilst driving a motor ambulance, came under shell fire at India Post, and was badly wounded in the shoulder. He succeeded in driving the ambulance under very heavy shelling to the A.D.S., where he had to be carried in, his machine being destroyed a few moments later. So serious was his wound that an operation had to be performed.

The Nieuport Sector was in many ways an exceedingly interesting part of the line, but space does not permit of more than an allusion to a number of places and events that will be long remembered. Among these were the rest billets at East Dunkirk and Wulpen, the camps in the sand dunes, Fisher's Post, Suicide Corner, Cocked Hat and Triangle Woods; the Lombartzyde Road at night, a storm-centre of " whizz-bangs " and machine-gun bullets; the assistance given by artillery and machine-guns to the Belgians in their raids and attacks on Dixmude; the heavy naval guns on board monitors, on the coast, and in the dunes; the outbreaks of sand colic among the animals in the transport lines.

It was in this sector that the Division made the acquaintance of several Medical Officers of the U.S. Army. These were attached to Field Ambulances and battalions, and became very popular.

Early in November the system of " *Retaliation Fire* " was abandoned as unprofitable. The British positions here being entirely dependent upon the maintenance of dams and bridges, we had many more vulnerable points than had the enemy. " *Punishment Fire,*" consisting of crashes of devastation fire of all guns and howitzers, including heavies, on certain well-known tender spots, was substituted, and was more effective.

On November 19 the 133rd French Division (" La Gauloise ") relieved the 42nd Division, which was now ordered to La Bassée. The occasion was an interesting one, as the men were keen to notice differences in methods and kit. In the middle of the relief the Germans began heavy shelling, and the Divisional Commander, risking the starting of an artillery battle, applied his scheme of Punishment Fire and silenced the enemy in twenty minutes. The relief was completed without further molestation, all ammunition in the left sub-sector being brought across the Yser in an overhead cradle. There were no regrets on leaving Nieuport. " Remember Belgium ! " muttered a Fusilier, in allusion to the posters he had seen when home on leave. " Can I ever bloomin' well forget it ? " The cool bright weather was ideal for route-marching, and the day's march of about twelve miles was usually completed about 2 p.m. After a short rest, followed by cleaning up and polishing, the troops would make for the nearest estaminet, there to drink *vin rouge* or *vin blanc* and converse in a strange compound of English, French, Arabic and sign-language with the thoroughly competent Hebe, of any age between nine and ninety, who attended to their wants. While resting for two days at Aire the Festival of St. Catherine was celebrated, and the local custom which ordains that any youth, by presenting a girl with a flower, may claim a kiss, was voted a bright idea, many staunch Protestants from Lancashire admitting that there was more to be said for some of the Roman Catholic customs than they had hitherto imagined. It was said that the flower-gardens of the village were devastated, but the villagers condoned this departure from the strict respect for private property normally shown by the British soldier. Indeed, the men's conduct in France won high praise from the civilians, who termed them *très gentils*. There was a bad moment when a borrowed bucket fell down a well, and the owner began to express very eloquently her opinion of such carelessness. Fortunately the cook-sergeant had " won " a *buckshee* bucket on his way through France, and the presentation of this much superior article softened the good lady's heart.

The five days' road-marching acted as a tonic; the splendid feeding and undisturbed rest night after night revived the spirits and raised the tone of the troops by the time that they arrived in the La Bassée Sector. On November 29 they relieved the 25th Division in the line.

CHAPTER VIII

LA BASSÉE

(*December* 1917—*March* 1918)

THE front of the La Bassée Sector ran north and south for nearly 5000 yards, and was intersected in the centre by the Bethune–La Bassée Canal, at a point roughly three kilometres west of the town of La Bassée. The left, or Givenchy, sub-sector contained the ruins of Givenchy, once a mining village, now an important tactical point on a spur of the Aubers ridge. The right sub-sector, which included the canal and the village of Cuinchy to the south, was known as the Canal Sector. The opposing lines had been practically stationary since 1915, and here could be traced the history of trench warfare from its early and crude forms to its latest developments, as the story of the earth's surface is revealed in strata and fossils to the geologist. The trenches and landmarks bore names familiar to very many battalions and units of the B.E.F., as, for instance, *Windy Corner, Harley Street, Orchard Keep, Moat Keep, Poppy and Marie Redoubts, Death or Glory Sap, Red Dragon Crater, Mill Sap*, and many others. In the reserve line—part of the " Village Line " which ran as far south as Lens—stood Cambrin, Pont Fixe, Le Plantin, Festubert, and Cailloux, all in ruins, though in Cambrin, within 2000 yards of the front line, a few civilians still clung to their homes and strove to subsist by providing light lunches and selling eggs, chocolates, and oranges to the troops. This sector was popularly known as " Egg and Chips Front."

D.H.Q. was at Locon. One infantry brigade held each sub-sector and the third was in Divisional Reserve, with a system of reliefs described by an appreciative officer as " beautiful and soothing in its clockwork regularity." The villages of Beuvry, Le Preol, Essars, Le Quesnoy, Gorre, and Oblinghem provided some of the best billets the Division experienced in France or Belgium, and the comparatively large town of Bethune was near enough to offer its considerable attractions to the troops in reserve. Bethune and its inhabitants had always enjoyed an admirable reputation among officers and men of the B.E.F., and when the Division first entered this area the town was not seriously damaged. At a later date, however, it suffered so severely from aircraft bombing and a long-range gun that many of its inhabitants were forced to leave;

LA BASSÉE CANAL, LOOKING TOWARDS PONT FIXE.

HARLEY STREET AND WINDY CORNER.

LA BASSÉE SECTOR. THE BRICK STACKS.

LA BASSÉE SECTOR. SITE OF GIVENCHY CHURCH.

GIVENCHY. "J" SAP.

GIVENCHY. MOAT FARM.

The Trenches in Winter

and a company of the 8th Manchesters on its way from the front to its billets in the vicinity of the town was surprised by a low-flying plane, which dropped a bomb that killed or wounded nearly half the company. By the end of the year 1917 Bethune was like a city of the dead.

Though the phrase " nothing to report " occurred with unvarying monotony during the Division's sojourn in this region, and though the experiences here seem to have had little in common with those of the closing stages of the war, it was in the Bethune–La Bassée area that the 42nd Division was raised to its highest standard of efficiency, *esprit-de-corps*, and enthusiasm, and that it received training and inspiration to accomplish the deeds by which it won distinction in the great battles of 1918, and helped to break the iron might of the German armies and bring about the final triumph.

The trench system here was " Bairnsfather-land " pure and simple. The very names conjure up vivid pictures—the trenches deep in melting snow; No Man's Land, with its almost continuous line of craters, full of stagnant, green, stinking water, the sides of crumbling earth and slimy mud converting them into death-traps for night-patrols; the front line with its saps—eerie and lonely posts for the sentries who kept watch. As in the leading case of the Curate's Egg, some parts were better than others. South of the Brickstacks, and south of the La Bassée–Bethune road, for instance, the accommodation in dugouts and tunnels was quite comfortable. Company Headquarters there were sometimes mistaken by delighted visiting Brigadiers for public picture-galleries, so elaborately were they decorated with illustrations from *La Vie Parisienne* and kindred works. But north of the canal the water-level was only a few feet below the surface, and the " trenches " were little more than parapets of turf and sandbag breastworks. They had been made at a time when little thought was given to " batter " and " berm," and, under the influence of rain, frost, and thaw, shell fire and trench-mortar fire, duckboards had disappeared under pits of mud, and walls had collapsed and blocked the trenches in a tangle of wood, rabbit-netting, and mud. It seemed enough to ask a man merely to keep alive in the awful discomfort of the trenches in winter, and under such conditions to carry on the offensive and defensive work of the garrison. But far more than this was demanded, for there was no end to the work of maintaining existing defences and constructing a new system. Give the infantryman a rifle and bombs, and point out where and how he can use them, and his inevitable grouse is no more than the Englishman's traditional method of disguising his real cheerfulness. But hand him a spade or barbed wire and stakes, and ask him to dig, or erect " apron " fences, and he ceases to be his old cheerful self. However nicely the detested term " working party " may be camouflaged, nothing will ever reconcile him to fatigues, and it must be remembered that he was attired for war, not for manual labour. The impedimenta he carried, including the box respirator strapped across his chest in the " alert " position, placed him under a heavy handicap. Yet he does the work—no soldier better! He loathed it, but he put his back into it, and found matter for facetious comment in his own and his chum's personal appearance. For the leather jerkin which had been issued when the frost came had now been supplemented by a pair of " boots, gum, thigh," and he looked like a Yarmouth fisherman in a tin hat.

In this sector sick and wounded were generally conveyed to the Base Hospitals by the Inland Water Transport's comfortable hospital barges. This was a mode of transport much preferred to the alternative of conveyance over bumpy roads. One badly-wounded man, on being put aboard one of the barges, expressed the hope that there were no shell-holes in La Bassée Canal, as he would hate to be bumped. The men in the trenches regarded the " bargees " with some envy, and inquiries were made as to the qualifications necessary to obtain this coveted job.

An extensive scheme of concrete shelter construction was taken in hand by the engineers, especially in the support line, known as the Village Line. Owing to the presence of water a few feet below the ground level, tunnelled dug-outs were seldom practicable, so a system of 5·9-shell-proof, ferro-concrete structures was begun. The Brigade in rest-billets supplied working-parties, and some idea of the amount of labour required is shown in the records of the 428 Field Company, where the number of man-loads of material used in the making of these shelters for one brigade front alone is given as follows—

Cement . .	5,036	sandbags
Shingle . .	19,384	,,
Sand . . .	9,692	,,
Total . .	34,112	sandbags,

each averaging 60 lb. in weight, a quite sufficient load for a man to carry over a mile of trench duckboards on a slippery day in winter. A pioneer battalion (three companies) was lent by the 55th Division, one pioneer company and one field company being with each infantry brigade in line, the remaining pioneer company working in back areas under the orders of the C.R.E. By some men duty in the line was preferred to any other form of employment. A batman from rear headquarters was returned to duty for some misdemeanour. Being seen in the line a few days later looking particularly fit and cheerful, he was asked how he liked the change. " It's a cinch! " he replied. " Keep your buttons clean and call the C.S.M. ' Sir,' and it's a soft job."

Though there were no infantry operations beyond occasional raids, the trench warfare was not lacking in incident, and snipers and patrols were active. Here the enemy snipers gave little trouble,

PTE. W. MILLS, V.C., 1/10 BN. MANCHESTER REGT.
DIED OF WOUNDS

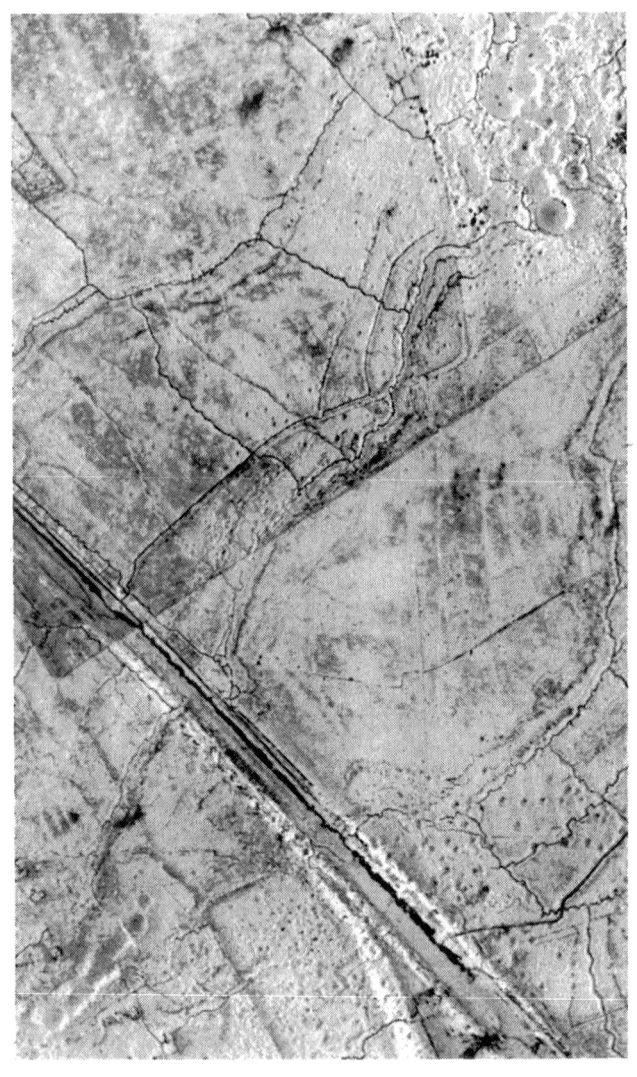

BETHUNE-LA BASSÉE CANAL, SHOWING NO MAN'S LAND, THE CRATERS, ORCHARD KEEP, ETC.

and our patrols, of which several went out nightly from each front-line battalion, rarely encountered the enemy in No Man's Land, where British mastery was tacitly admitted. Particular attention was paid to the systematic collection of intelligence by patrols, and a standard form of patrol report was introduced, and was incorporated later in the 42nd Division Pocket Book. Gas projectiles were freely used by the enemy, and on the first occasion these caused heavy casualties. But this incident gave the 10th Manchesters the opportunity to show their grit and tenacity. They seized the chance with both hands, and grievous as was the loss sustained, the story of the night of December 10 is one that Oldham men look back upon with pride. The battalion had only been in the front line for an hour or two when the enemy, knowing that a relief had just taken place, bombarded their trenches with gas-drums preliminary to an attack. Practically every man in Red Dragon Crater, occupied by men of "C" Company, was affected by the poison-gas, and most were out of action when the Germans attacked. But though choking, blinded, and reeling—and well aware from lectures on the subject that exertion under such circumstances is likely to be fatal—every man who could stand made for the parapet, and with bombs, rifles, and Lewis guns put up a memorable fight, one after another sinking back into the trench to die from the poison. But they held their post and beat the Boche, and every man who took part merited recognition. Private Walter Mills, realizing the deadly nature of the gas and the danger of the post being lost, sprang at once to the top of the trench, and fought magnificently to save the situation. Though suffering acutely from the gassing, he remained there, throwing bombs and beating off the attack, and fell back to die just as victory was assured. He was selected for the posthumous award of the V.C., and four other men of the company received the Military Medal.

A snowstorm in December was followed by a frost of more than a fortnight's duration. When the sudden thaw came, with torrents of rain, the old trenches collapsed in many cases and were almost waist-deep in mud and water. Huge craters, due to former mining and counter-mining activity, abounded in the sector, and these were waterlogged, as was most of this marshy region, and the work of the night patrols was rendered still more difficult and exciting. Every available man was put to work, and the 55th Division lent their pioneer battalion and a field company.

Christmas arrived before the thaw, and, with twenty degrees of frost, the weather was appropriate to the occasion, and the blood tingled as it ought to do. The festival was celebrated by each unit on the date most convenient to itself, so the festivities continued well into January. Quartermasters had become expert in buying pigs " on the hoof " and fattening them. Bethune yielded oranges, apples, and nuts, and even beer at a price. Rations were supplemented lavishly from canteen funds, and there was no lack of cash, for it was intended that the men should have a good time. Mess-rooms were gay with garlands and bunting; dangers and hardships were forgotten, and the troops gave themselves over to merriment and good-fellowship. During the entertainment that followed one of the Christmas dinners an officer, much impressed by the radiant happiness, physical fitness, and morale, remarked : " I wonder what the parents would think if miraculously transported into this room? They would imagine that being at the front is regarded as the most glorious fun in the world, and that their boys are having the time of their lives."

The pantomime, *Cinderella*, given by *Th' Lads*, under the direction of Major Maude, D.A.A.G., Captain Webster, R.A.M.C., and Captain Makin, 9th Manchesters, drew large and enthusiastic houses, and richly deserved its popularity, the acting, staging and dresses being remarkably good. It was held at Le Quesnoy, within range of the enemy's field-guns, and parties of officers and men were taken by motor-lorry from their billets in adjacent villages. In addition, each unit organized concerts and entertainments, and the 7th Manchesters were specially prominent in this respect, Major Hurst's delightfully funny sketch " *Gwendolen de Vere of Greenheys Lane* " being hugely enjoyed. Each Brigade or unit had its favourite songs and its own peculiar jokes, many of which were incomprehensible to the outsider. Perhaps none was quite so esoteric as the weird Lament of the 10th Manchesters, known in three continents and many countries as " *On Owdham Edge beaut 'at* " (sung to an old Methodist tune combining swing and solemnity), wherein the gruesome fate of the lad who, without head-covering, courts Mary Jane upon that eminence is foreseen by the fond parent in a way that vies with Darwin's logic in tracing the super-excellence of the roast beef of Old England (pre-war) to the prevalence of old maids in rural districts, *via* cats, mice, honey-bees, and clover. First a cold, then death, burial, eaten by worms, worms devoured by ducks, which in turn appear upon the family dinner-table. " Then we's soon be ettin' thee," begins the last verse of this lugubrious but fascinating lyric. No doubt it recalled the loved, if unlovely, streets and mills of Chadderton, Mumps, Glodwick and Hollinwood, and visions of home and of potato-pie. A young " roughyed " who had taken a Blighty one at Nieuport got home-leave from a South of England hospital just after Christmas. " Eh, lad, but aw'm glad to see thi agen," was his mother's greeting. " Did they feed thi well ? " " Feed me, mother ! I've never 'ad such feedin' in aw me life as this Christmas. 'am an' eggs for breekfast, turkey an' sossidges, plum-puddin' an' mince-pies for dinner. Cakes an' grapes an' apples an' oranges as much as we could put away. Then yesterday we wur taken to a big house for dinner, and 'ad it all o'er agen, an' other things too." " Eh, lad, but they've done thi well ! " " Aye, everything we could want—except one thing, mother, as I'm fair longin' for, and that's a gradely tater-pie." " That's aw reet, lad ! There's one a-waitin' for thi i' th' oven. Aw knowed as they wouldna be feedin' thi proper."

LA BASSÉE SECTOR.   THE MILL.

LA BASSÉE SECTOR.   GIVENCHY CRATERS.

LA BASSÉE SECTOR.   GORRE CHATEAU.

Festivities and Social Life

The social life played an important part in developing and stimulating the morale of the Division. New drafts to replace casualties had first to acquire the *esprit de corps* of the Unit, and then of the Brigade and Division; and the hearty fellowship and jollity shown by all ranks at Christmastide had a distinct military value. The 42nd had again become one of the happiest of divisions, and good comradeship prevailed from top to bottom, whether in the line, where danger and hardship were cheerfully accepted as part of the day's work, or in billets, where care was cast aside. To take one instance, who can forget "Harley Street" after dusk? Within rifle range of the enemy, and under observation in the daytime, it would hardly seem the place in which to congregate. With divisional baths and a reading and recreation room in full swing, the street was a crowded thoroughfare, and when night fell limbers and wagons passed through in an unending stream. Men lounged in the doorways of ruined houses, smoking, passing remarks on things in general and critical comments on drivers and animals. The air hummed with the buzz of conversation, broken now and again by snatches of popular ditties from gatherings of convivial souls. The spirit of good-humour was passed on to the folk at home. A machine-gunner had been punished by his officer, and, knowing that the same officer would have to read the letter in his capacity as censor, he wrote to his mother : " We have got a new Section Officer, such a nice fellow. We get on splendidly together, and he thinks me so capable that he has got me the job of cleaning pack-saddles this week."

The strength of the Division on January 1, 1918, was 732 officers and 14,314 other ranks. On January 14 Major-General Townsley, of the American Army, with his Chief of Staff and A.D.C., was attached to the Division for ten days. On the 22nd the campaign on behalf of St. Dunstan's Hostel for blinded soldiers was closed. £775 had been raised in the Division, this amount being £130 more than had been raised by any other division of the 1st Corps.

The Divisional Artillery, which covered the whole of the front, had far more fighting than the infantry. The policy was one of " Offensive—Defensive." The enemy's guns, and above all his trench-mortars, were very active, and long acquaintance with this sector enabled him accurately to register the targets he periodically engaged. His " minnies " were the pet aversion of the men in the trenches. But here the Germans had not the advantage they possessed at Lombartzyde, and punishment was meted out to them. As a counter-measure a standing order was issued that for every T.M. shell fired by the enemy he must receive five in return, and with the exception of the few occasions when prevented by limitation of ammunition, all T.M. crews loyally and gladly carried out the order. Good use was made of the Punishment Fire scheme inaugurated in the Nieuport sector. A selection, carefully based on all available intelligence, was made of those targets which would cause the enemy the most immediate damage and inconvenience.

These were registered, and when the enemy shell fire exceeded what was considered the limit of normal harassing, prompt and effective retribution was dealt out to him by guns of all calibres from the 15-inch howitzers to the 18-pounder field-guns.

Of the three machine-gun companies of the Division—the fourth arrived in February—two and a half companies were in action covering the front. A few of their guns fired indirect S.O.S. barrages, and the remainder were sighted for direct fire in carefully chosen positions distributed in depth. Every inch of ground over which the enemy must advance was swept by machine-gun fire, direct or indirect, frontal or flanking. To take two examples only—the ground from the canal at Death or Glory Sap up to and beyond Red Dragon Crater was swept by the direct flanking fire of two guns cunningly emplaced in the railway embankment on the south side of the canal; and the northern face of the bastion of Givenchy was swept by the indirect fire of four guns near Festubert Keep. In addition to their defensive duties the machine-gun companies carried out day and night harassing programmes.

A brief reference must be made to the work of the 179th Tunnelling Company, R.E., in the right sector. Most of their heavy work, such as the construction of tunnelled dug-outs and emplacements, and the maintenance of infantry sub-ways, proceeded unseen by the men of other arms, for the entrances to the deep-mining system were closed to the curious. The strata in which mining operations were possible had become so honeycombed with galleries and listening-saps that no new offensive mining could be undertaken without instant detection. The methods of keeping touch with enemy activities were full of interest. In a little chamber off the main gallery a man sat in front of a board on which was a plan of the mine system. A telephone receiver was fixed over his ears. By inserting a plug into the board at any of the sapheads he could listen by a microphone to the enemy's subterranean activities in the vicinity of this particular sap. A pump at work in an adjacent trench, an enemy miner patrolling the gallery or tiptoeing to an adjacent saphead—even such sounds as these could be detected with uncanny distinctness.

The system of holding the line by tactical localities and immediate counter-attack, which afterwards proved so successful as compared with continuous line, was made the subject of strenuous training. The reorganization was planned with the double object of reducing the number of men required to garrison the trenches, and at the same time of strengthening the defence by a series of self-contained, mutually supporting localities, disposed in depth and connected, so far as possible, by underground, shell-proof passages, with wire-entanglements so sited as to bring an approaching enemy under the fire of these localities. The term "locality" is used to denote an area of ground of tactical importance which is organized for defence in depth to form a centre of resistance. The guiding principle is that its front and flanks should be held by infantry posts and

Raids

machine-guns while reserves are kept in hand ready for counter-attack within the locality. A large number of concrete machine-gun emplacements, command posts, etc., were constructed, and as there was no adequate system of light railways or tramways serving the front, a heavy strain was thrown upon the transport in bringing up R.E. material alone. The value of this work was seen later during the German offensive on the Lys in April, 1918, the sector being then held by the 55th (West Lancashire Territorial) Division. Major-General Jeudwine, commanding the 55th Division, in a letter to Major-General Solly-Flood, stated that the work of the East Lancashires had greatly assisted the West Lancashires to defeat the onslaughts of the enemy—and thus hold inviolate that most important tactical feature, Givenchy—and that he had pleasure in acknowledging the debt they owed to their predecessors.

There were raids on both sides, but while those of the enemy revealed a lack of determination and of the true offensive spirit, ours were entered upon and carried through with zest. In the southern sector the Germans were particularly inactive, but the Division opposite Givenchy showed rather more enterprise.* Twice they attempted to raid " J " and " K " saps, and on the first occasion succeeded in entering our trenches, only to be promptly ejected. Other attempts further north were equally futile. On the British side the raids provided welcome breaks in the monotony of trench routine. The most important raid by our troops took place on February 11 in the left sector, opposite Festubert. The artillery put down a " box " barrage, enclosing an area by three walls of bursting shells, and Captain D. B. Stephenson, with two other officers and ninety-seven men of the 9th Manchesters and an officer and six sappers of the 429 Field Company, went " over the top " in two waves. In places the wire had been imperfectly cut, so men lay flat on the " concertinas " to keep the wire down while their comrades scrambled across. As the barrage enclosed the enemy within the " box," they could not get away nor could reinforcements reach them, so they had no choice but to fight man to man, and at this the Germans were no match for the Ashton men. At least twenty-five were killed, seven prisoners and two machine-guns were secured, and the sappers blew up three enemy dug-outs with gun-cotton. It was a good night's work, carried out with great dash.

On the following night, Lieutenant A. Elliott, 7th L.F., with Sergeant T. Gerrard, Corporal J. Phipps, and two men, reconnoitred a mineshaft situated well within the enemy's lines, near the Brickstacks. After exploring the tunnel he left a guard over it and went back for a demolition party, returning with an officer and three men of a tunnelling company and seven Fusiliers carrying explosive. Elliott helped the tunnellers to lay the charge, and then sent back all the men except Phipps, who remained with him to guard the

* About the middle of January the 126th Brigade found themselves opposed in this sector by the 126th German Infantry Brigade.

entrance while the tunnelling officer lit the fuse. The mineshaft was completely destroyed and the whole party returned in safety. Elliott and the two N.C.O.s had been associated in two night adventures on February 1–3, in the course of which they discovered the mineshaft and explored the tunnelling system for 150 yards. Afterwards they located and bombed an enemy post, inflicting casualties.

On February 15 the Division was relieved by the 55th Division and withdrawn to 1st Corps Reserve in the Busnes–Burbure–Fouquieres area, with D.H.G. first at Hinges and later at Labouvriere. The divisional artillery were relieved a few days later, but the pioneers and the sappers remained at work in the line during the whole of the Division's period of rest. The billets in the rest-area were good, sports were encouraged, and concerts held in the local halls. Training was carried on vigorously. Suitable ground for musketry and field work existed in the divisional area, and full use was made of it. The training always had in view open and semi-open warfare, and it included the hasty occupation of defensive positions in depth, counter-attacks on small and large scales, the use of ground for manœuvre, and of different weapons in attacks on strong points. This training proved most valuable in the operations following upon the enemy offensive in March. The Division also provided large working parties for work on the rear lines of defence within the Corps area.

Shortly before the Division was relieved it had received its pioneer battalion, the 1/7th Northumberland Fusiliers, transferred from the 50th Division. This battalion, commanded by Lieut.-Colonel Liddell, D.S.O., had been given little time to carry out its reorganization from a four-company infantry battalion to a three-company pioneer battalion before being set to work on the 1st Corps defences. The territorial spirit is strong, and the Northumberland men did not conceal their chagrin at having to leave the division in which they had won renown at High Wood and elsewhere, but they soon threw themselves into the work and play of their new division with such zeal that they rapidly won popularity and a reputation for great courage and efficiency. Their work was of the greatest value to the Division, both when resisting the German onrush, and no less when the tide turned. They also showed much prowess in all games and sports.

A more extensive reorganization had now to be made. So great had been the drain upon the man-power of the empire that it had become necessary to reduce the establishment of infantry brigades from four to three battalions. A number of officers and men of the 6th Lancashire Fusiliers, the 4th East Lancashires, and the 9th Manchesters were posted to other battalions of the Division, and the remainder transferred to the 66th Division. As the 126th Brigade thereby lost two battalions, the 8th Manchesters were transferred to it from the 127th Brigade. The brigades were then made up as follows—

Reorganization

The 125th Brigade—
    1/5th Battalion Lancashire Fusiliers
    1/7th   ,,   ,,   ,,
    1/8th   ,,   ,,   ,,

The 126th Brigade—
    1/5th Battalion East Lancashire Regiment
    1/8th   ,,   Manchester Regiment
    1/10th   ,,   ,,   ,,

The 127th Brigade—
    1/5th Battalion Manchester Regiment
    1/6th   ,,   ,,   ,,
    1/7th   ,,   ,,   ,,

As most of the battalions were all considerably below strength they received as reinforcements three battalions (less Commanding Officers, Adjutants, and Quartermasters) from the 66th Division— the 3/5th Lancashire Fusiliers, the 2/8th Manchesters, and the 2/10th Manchesters—which were divided among the nine battalions. The departure of three battalions which for three and a half years had shared in the labours, dangers, and honours of the Division was a matter of deep regret both for those who left and those who remained, but there was some consolation in the thought that they now formed part of the sister-division, and would thenceforward fight side by side with the second-line battalions of their own units. The four separate machine-gun companies were now reorganized as a machine-gun battalion, one company being with each infantry brigade, and one in Divisional Reserve. There were also changes in the trench-mortar batteries. V/42, 9·2-inch T.M. Battery had been left in the La Bassée sector. X/42 and Y/42, 6-inch T.M. batteries were transformed into six-gun batteries, Z/42 being divided between them. The departure of the C.R.E., Lieut.-Colonel D. S. MacInnes, C.M.G., D.S.O., to become Deputy Engineer-in-Chief at G.H.Q., caused general regret. Few men of the Division had so thorough a knowledge of the front line, and whenever any particularly difficult and dangerous work was in hand, he would be there by day or by night to assist, and especially to encourage. Another of the best-known figures in the Division, the A.D.M.S., Colonel T. P. Jones, C.M.G., had left, and had been succeeded by Colonel W. R. Matthews, D.S.O., who maintained the R.A.M.C. in the highly efficient state to which it had been brought by Colonel Jones and his subordinates, and the Division soon had reason to congratulate itself upon the appointment. In January, too, Lieut.-Colonel R. F. Guy, D.S.O., had been appointed G.S.O. 1. A hard worker, he backed up his chief with loyalty and energy, and soon gained the entire confidence of the Brigadiers and C.O.s.

The Divisional Reception Camp at Allouagne was proving very valuable as a training centre, and even casuals passing through from hospital or other leave were given a brief refresher in musketry and gas training, and a general smartening up. That instruction in " General Knowledge " was needed by some of the newer drafts is shown by the following true story, which is also a tribute to the energy and activity of the A.A. and Q.M.G. of the Division. An N.C.O., at the close of an hour's instruction in a barn at Le Quesnoy, asked one or two general questions—

Instructor. " Who commands the battalion? " (Correctly answered.) " Who commands the battalion when the colonel is away? "

A Voice (after an interval of silence). " Sergeant-Major——"

Instructor. " Wrong."

Another Voice. " Colonel Slaughter."

Instructor. " Wrong again. Major X. commands in the colonel's absence. Now, who commands the Brigade? "

Several Voices. " Colonel Slaughter ! "

Instructor. " Wrong. It is commanded by General Henley. Now, who commands the Division? "

Loud Chorus. " Solly-Flood."

Instructor. " Right. Who commands the Division if the General is away."

Full Chorus. " COLONEL SLAUGHTER ! ! "

About this period a violent attack of mange among the R.E. horses carried off eighty per cent. of one field company's animals. Stringent orders were given to prevent its spread, and the drivers were separated into two lots, one to look after the infected horses, the other to guard those which had not yet developed symptoms. All the clothing was stoved, and for one day drivers had to do their best to keep warm in their shirts and pretend that they were " Jocks." The Divisional Commander was always pleased to see the transport men on terms of intimacy and affection with their animals, and he frequently asked the names of the horses. One day he heard a driver address his mare as " Phœbe," and remembered that the man had recently assured him that its name was " Dolly." He pointed this out, whereupon the driver explained that in the meantime he had changed his girl.

Though it is always gratifying to come across men thoroughly devoted to duty and conscientious in its performance, enthusiasm may be carried to extremes. Two worthy men on the pioneer staff of their battalion were detailed to superintend a foot-bath, and being very conscientious, they determined that no foot-bath in the B.E.F. should have a better record. Each day they proudly reported the number of men who had used the bath, and the average was high. But for some reason numbers began to dwindle, so the pioneers resorted to the expedient of seizing passers-by and compelling them to wash their feet. The average went up again until on one unhappy day they grabbed three of the adjutant's runners.

The coming event was already casting its threatening shadow

before it. The feeling was in the air that the Germans were preparing for the mightiest of all their amazing military efforts, and as one could only conjecture where the heaviest blows would fall, the whole army was on the alert. The 42nd Division was in a state of readiness to reinforce any part of the 1st Corps front should the necessity arise. In addition, one infantry brigade and machine-gun company were warned to move at short notice by motor-bus and route-march to reinforce the Portuguese * on the immediate left of the Corps. On the night of February 25–26 the Portuguese trenches were heavily bombarded, and in the early morning the 126th Brigade moved to its supporting positions in the area around Vieux Chapelle and La Couture, arriving at 10 a.m. However, nothing more serious than a raid was attempted, and in the afternoon the Brigade was withdrawn.

The Divisional Artillery came out of action for a period of training near Choques, and on March 1 the Division passed from Corps into G.H.Q. Reserve. The Divisional Commander availed himself of the opportunity to deliver to officers and N.C.O.s a lecture the purport of which is expressed with admirable terseness in its title, " Wits and Guts." The General gave a vivid picture of the fighting of 1914, and foretold that it was highly probable that the Division before long might find itself similarly situated, and would then have the opportunity to emulate the deeds of the " Old Contemptibles." The lecture was given to every officer and N.C.O. of each infantry and artillery brigade, and to other units in turn, and a précis was afterwards issued in the Foreword to the Divisional Pocket Book. It was in the course of this address that Major-General Solly-Flood gave the Division its motto, " GO ONE BETTER," a motto adopted with enthusiasm by all ranks as a very real expression of the spirit that inspired the Division.

The training during February and March included some keenly contested and most useful competitions. The basis of training and sport was the platoon. The spirit of the attack was the platoon. There were platoon efficiency competitions, from guard mounting and clean turn-out to contests of skill with all weapons; platoon boxing, football, cricket, sing-songs, and similar rivalries, and also transport competitions. In this way every individual had to take part, and none looked on all the time. There were other interests, too. Larks were singing, and though the wanton lapwing was not in evidence, the fuller " crimson " was showing on the robin's breast —in short, spring was in the air, and more than one young man's fancy lightly turned to thoughts of love, and the French maidens were not coy. The rather hazy notions that had been entertained

* Pigeons, working in pairs, were proving very useful at this period, and " Signals " thought it might be a good thing to teach our Portuguese allies something about the pigeon service. They accordingly sent two pairs of birds to the Portuguese Staff, with instructions as to their use, and awaited results. The pigeons did not return to the loft, but next day a very polite note arrived, thanking " our comrades, the British officers, for their *hospitality*."

of the French as a light-hearted, frivolous race had been turned inside out. True, they had seen little or nothing of French males under fifty-five years of age, but they had discovered that French women and girls were the most practical, shrewd, clear-headed, and capable in the world. Young girls and middle-aged and elderly women were combining the heavy farm-work of men—and doing it well !—with the house-work of the capable house-wife, the art and craft of the trained milliner and dressmaker, and a mastery of finance worthy of a chartered accountant. The rapid and facile mental arithmetic displayed by girls in " totting up " the sum total of a complicated series of purchases in one lightning utterance, apparently composed entirely of sibillants that reminded the audience of " Sister Susie's sewing shirts," took the breath away and compelled admiration. Nor was the admiration wholly one-sided. The Lancashire lad was pronounced *gentil* and *aimable*. He would fetch and carry, amuse the children, mind the baby, and perform a hundred and one odd jobs to help the overworked women, and many friendships were formed. But training, sports, and dallying were rudely interrupted by the call received on March 21, when, at about 6 p.m., warning orders were received that the Division might be suddenly called upon to move southwards into action. The warning was emphasized on the night of the 21st by a terrific bombardment by German aircraft of all back areas, railheads and junctions.

The great German offensive had begun. On the morning of March 23 the Division started to join the 6th Corps, Third Army, in the Somme area, the infantry, R.E., and R.A.M.C. personnel proceeding in motor-lorry and 'bus, the artillery and transport by road.

Total strength of 42nd Division, March 1, 1918—

	Officers.	Other ranks.
Divisional Headquarters	33	111
Royal Artillery, H.Q.	5	19
210th Brigade, R.F.A.	35	778
211th ,, ,,	38	773
Div. Ammunition Column	29	778
Royal Engineers, H.Q.	3	10
427th Field Company	8	208
428th ,, ,,	6	197
429th ,, ,,	7	213
42nd Signal Company	9	274
125th Brigade, H.Q.	3	21
5th Lancashire Fusiliers	45	958
7th ,, ,,	43	907
8th ,, ,,	42	934
125th T.M. Battery	3	43
Carried forward	309	6,224

Strength of Division, March 1, 1918

	Officers.	Other ranks.
Brought forward	309	6,224
126th Brigade, H.Q.	3	22
5th East Lancashires	44	975
8th Manchesters	46	982
10th ,,	54	980
126th T.M. Battery	4	46
127th Brigade, H.Q.	3	21
5th Manchesters	43	958
6th ,,	49	982
7th ,,	41	980
127th T.M. Battery	5	61
Machine-Gun Companies	38	753
1/7th Northumberland Fusiliers (P.)	43	945
Divisional Train, A.S.C.	20	385
,, Supply Column	4	220
R.A.M.C.		
1st E.L. Field Ambulance	8	239
2nd ,, ,, ,,	9	246
3rd ,, ,, ,,	7	234
19th Mob. Vet. Section	1	26
239th Divn. Employment Coy.	2	312
Total	773	15,514

CHAPTER IX

OPENING OF THE GERMAN OFFENSIVE

(*March* 21—*April* 9, 1918)

BEFORE dawn on March 21, 1918, a terrific bombardment along more than fifty miles of the British front, from east of Arras to south of St. Quentin, heralded the opening of the mightiest attack in the history of warfare. More than one hundred divisions—including many transferred from the Russian front—highly trained for the special purpose for which they were to be used, were suddenly launched against less than fifty. The German storm-troops were concentrated in depth on narrow fronts opposite what were judged to be the most vulnerable points in the British line; fresh troops passing through those of the exhausted or shattered divisions that had been used to break open the gaps. Before they could be brought to a standstill still further troops, with hordes of machine-guns, moved forward through the wreckage of the others, forcing their way to the flanks and even to the rear of the British positions. The greater the number shot down the more they seemed to multiply. The enemy was staking everything upon the success of this gigantic onslaught, and he was fighting with a courage, skill, determination, and confidence in numbers which would mean the triumph of Barbarism unless met by still greater resolution and endurance. Forced back by the weight of numbers, the Fifth Army, under General Sir H. de la P. Gough, on the right of the area attacked, and to a lesser extent the Third Army, under General Sir J. H. G. Byng, on the left, withdrew step by step, fighting desperately to stem the overwhelming onslaught, and again fell back still farther as their flanks and rear were enveloped. Village after village, town after town, recovered for France at a heavy price in the earlier British offensives, fell once more into the hands of the enemy; thousands of prisoners, many guns, and great quantities of material were lost.

Divisions in reserve were hurriedly brought forward to block the gaps, and to stem the onrush or check its pace. A certain amount of confusion was unavoidable. The enemy once more seemed to have established control over the weather, the ground remaining firm and dry and a mist screening his movements. At times it was impossible to carry out orders literally, as between their issue and receipt the situation had changed entirely, and defensive positions which brigades or battalions of the relieving divisions had been ordered to take up, were found to be in the occupation of the enemy.

On the morning of the 23rd March the infantry brigades of the 42nd Division, packed into many hundreds of motor-busses and lorries, pressed southwards through St. Pol to Doullens, and then turned north-east along the Arras road to Beaumetz-les-Loges, where they turned south-east in the direction of Ayette, a village more than eight miles south of Arras and nearly eight miles north-west of Bapaume. At this stage of the journey they were met by straggling groups of refugees, women, children, and old men, hastening with the more portable of their poor possessions out of the reach of Hun savagery and rapacity. Some of these homeless wanderers appeared haggard and despairing; some numbed and hopeless; others simply bewildered. It was a pitiful and pathetic sight, which aroused feelings of mingled pity and anger, and intensified the Lancashire men's longing to get to close quarters with the oppressor. They were to have their wish. Those who had joined the Division since August 1915 found the few remaining days of March more crammed with incident and fighting than the whole of their previous careers.

As they drew nearer to their destination progress became more and more difficult, the roads being packed with troops moving in the same direction; and with an increasing stream of traffic retiring before the enemy's advance. The Divisional Commander and G.S.O. 1. (Lieut.-Colonel R. F. Guy, D.S.O.) had gone on some hours in advance of the Division to reconnoitre, glean information, and attempt to unravel the tangled skein of conflicting reports. At 5 p.m. on March 23, D.H.Q. was established at Adinfer, about two miles north-east of Ayette. The 125th and 126th Brigades debussed at 7 p.m. and proceeded to Adinfer Wood to bivouac. In the wood were many green woodpeckers, which greeted the men with their jeering cry. " Aye, *you* can —— well laugh ! " growled a Salford man, for the night spent in this wood was not a cheerful or restful one. There was a keen frost, and as fires were forbidden, most of the men tried to find warmth by walking up and down during the night. Before midnight the 127th Brigade debussed on the Ayette–Douchy road and took up an outpost position, facing south-east, with two battalions in the outpost line on the Ablainzevelle–Moyenneville Ridge, a few miles south-east of Adinfer, with Brigade H.Q. at Courcelles Aerodrome. Owing to the congested state of the roads the transport was unable to rejoin the Division until the night of the 25th. The Division was therefore without horses or wagons; there were no telephones and no mounted messengers. The Divisional Commander succeeded in borrowing horses from the 40th Division for the many reconnaissances made prior to taking over command of the sector. But great as the difficulties were, they were many times greater when it came to actual command in battle.

K

The situation was obscure, changing as it did from hour to hour. As the enemy thrust forward, gaining here and there, by weight of numbers, a position of tactical importance threatening a flank, plans must be hurriedly re-cast and movements diverted or stopped. At 2 p.m. on March 24 orders were received from the Corps Commander, Lieut.-General Haldane, for the relief of the 40th Division by the 42nd that night on the right sector of the 6th Corps front. The Divisional Commander went round the 40th Division's advanced lines, and at 2 p.m., in the 40th D.H.Q. two miles east of Bucquoy, he issued orders to his Brigadiers. The 125th and 126th Brigades were moved up to Logeast Wood to facilitate the relief, and Divisional H.Q. was moved to Monchy-au-Bois. At 6 p.m. notification was received that the 40th Division would leave outposts in front of a line east of the Arras–Bapaume road, running north and south through the villages of Ervillers, Behagnies, and Sapignies, a few miles north of Bapaume, which was now in the enemy's hands, and these would be withdrawn when the 42nd were in position. The 125th Brigade was ordered to take over the right sub-sector and the 127th the left, the 126th being in Divisional Reserve. A Special Order of the Day was issued by Major-General Solly-Flood—

" On this, the first occasion on which the Major-General has had the honour of leading the Division into action, he desires to wish all ranks the best of luck. When the enemy attacks, the Divisional Commander is convinced that the Division will give such an account of itself as to make the enemy regret that they tried conclusions with East Lancashire. " This is the opportunity we want to ' Go ONE BETTER.' "

Along the road from Bapaume, through Achiet-le-Grand, batteries of heavy guns were being withdrawn to positions farther back, and processions of wounded, and the personnel of stationary hospitals and clearing stations, were moving to the rear as the infantry brigades set off at dusk. They proceeded in a north-easterly direction towards Gomiecourt, where they expected to be met by guides who would lead them to the positions they were to take over from the 40th Division, which had been in action for forty-eight hours about Mory—more than two miles east of Gomiecourt—and had suffered heavily. Twice had Mory been taken by the enemy, and twice re-taken by counter-attack, and fighting was still in progress there. The region through which the Brigades passed was familiar to many, though it wore a very different aspect now, and as the rifle-range used during the previous summer and the old camp of the 125th Brigade were passed, the contrast between the conditions then and now was the subject of much comment. Instead of the lines of canvas tents one could see dimly the heavy artillery in action and, when the gun-flashes lighted up the surroundings, the horses harnessed ready to remove the guns in case

GOMIECOURT CHÂTEAU.

ERVILLERS, WHERE THE 1/10 BN. MANCHESTER REGT. REPULSED EIGHT ATTACKS.

SAPIGNIES, THE SCENE OF HEAVY FIGHTING FOR 125TH BRIGADE.

LT.-COL. P. V. HOLBERTON (THE MANCHESTER REGT.) COMMANDING 1/5 BN. LANCASHIRE FUSILIERS. KILLED IN ACTION.

(*From a snapshot*)

ACHIET-LE-GRAND.   THE RAILWAY CUTTING.

ACHIET-LE-GRAND.   THE RAILWAY EMBANKMENT.

ESSARTS. DUG OUT USED AS BRIGADE HQRS. DURING FIGHTING BETWEEN MARCH 28 AND APRIL 7.

BUCQUOY CROSS ROADS: THE SCENE OF SEVERE HAND-TO-HAND FIGHTING ON APRIL 5, 1918, BY THE 125TH BRIGADE.

of emergency. Soon after the leading battalion had left Gomiecourt a Staff Officer of the 40th Division brought word that "as the enemy are reported to have broken through between Sapignies and Behagnies," the order for the relief had been cancelled, so he diverted the direction of the 125th and 127th Brigades. The report that the enemy had broken through at Sapignies was later found to be incorrect. The 127th Brigade, deflected to the right—that is, to the south instead of to the east—moved across the open in artillery formation, and the 125th before long passed diagonally across their lines. The enemy were pressing to the north and north-west through the gap made by their break-through at Bapaume, and the leading brigades had turned south and south-east to stand across their path. Near Forest Lodge the 126th Brigade met the same Staff Officer, but as Brigadier-General Seymour knew that the other Brigades had changed direction, he considered that they would be able to deal with the situation on the right, and decided to carry out the original orders. The 127th Brigade was therefore on the right of the divisional front, facing south and south-east; the 125th in the centre, facing south-east and east; and the 126th (supposed to be in Divisional Reserve) on the left, facing east and north-east. Commanding officers, subordinate officers and men of all three Brigades deserve the greatest credit for the skilful dispositions made under such unfavourable conditions. The difficult operation of taking up defensive positions on ground that had not been reconnoitred had been accomplished in darkness.

About midnight on the 24th-25th the 127th Brigade was in position, facing south-east, with outposts on the Bihucourt–Sapignies road, and the 6th Manchesters on the right, near Bihucourt, established touch with the 41st Division. At 1 a.m. on the 25th Sapignies and Behagnies were reported clear of the enemy by the Lancashire Fusiliers, who took up a line facing east on the high ground east of the Arras–Bapaume road, covering those two villages. Stragglers from other divisions passed through and gave much conflicting information as to what had happened and was happening. A telephone message from Corps H.Q. stated that the enemy had possession of Ervillers, as well as of Mory, but this report, like many others received from the rear at this time, proved unfounded, for patrols of the 10th Manchesters discovered that Ervillers was clear of the enemy. This battalion was then ordered to push two companies forward and take up a position on the south-western edge of the village, and send patrols through it. This was done and touch obtained with the 31st Division.

Thus the Division went into battle on the morning of March 25 with all three infantry brigades in the line. It possessed neither transport for units nor horses for reconnoitring, and the lack of means of rapid reconnaissance and inter-communication was sorely felt. Though the Motor-Cycle Dispatch Riders of the Signal Company proved invaluable, the Signal Company was unable to function properly until its transport arrived; and during the following two or three days a heavy expenditure of cable was caused by the continual moving of Divisional and Brigade Headquarters. The Division was not covered by its own artillery, and two infantry brigades of the 40th Division and one of the 59th Division were still in the line. However, Major-General Solly-Flood took over the command of the sector, and the Division was then transferred from the 6th Corps to the 4th Corps under Lieut.-General Sir G. M. Harper.

At dawn the enemy attacked along the whole divisional front. The 10th Manchesters pushed two companies forward through Ervillers to the north-eastern outskirts, and brought up a third company on their right into a trench which ran parallel with the Ervillers–Behagnies road. In this trench were men from various brigades, practically "done in" after four days of hard fighting without rest; but when Lieut.-Colonel Peel enrolled these oddments among his own men it was found that they could still fight gallantly. At 8.45 a.m. a message was received from the 125th Brigade reporting that other troops were falling back, and asking whether the Division was to conform. The Divisional Commander replied that the Division would fight on the position taken up, and no withdrawal would take place without orders. This message was repeated to the other infantry brigades, and two M.G. companies were moved up to cover the flanks. Machine and Lewis gunners had carried their guns into action a distance of seven to ten miles, and in the absence of transport all ammunition had been carried by the troops. It was not the ideal prelude to a thirty-hours' battle against odds.

Between 9 a.m. and 10 a.m. (March 25), owing to the withdrawal of troops of the 40th Division, the enemy penetrated the north end of Sapignies, in spite of a gallant attempt to check their advance on the part of the 5th L.F. and a company of the 7th, who held an angle in the line a little way beyond the village. The enemy massed his machine-guns, and brought up a battery of field-guns, concentrating his fire upon this point. "A" Company of the 5th L.F. was enveloped on three sides, but fought until all ammunition was spent. A dozen men got away, and a few were captured, but the rest of the company became casualties. Lieut.-Colonel Holberton, commanding the 5th L.F., brought up two companies of the 8th L.F., who were in support, and Major M. G. Bird and Captain Fairhurst, the O.C. and Adjutant of the 8th, collected headquarters details and led them forward. The counter-attack was a brilliant one, and Sapignies was regained, and a line established east of the village. Major Bird, who was awarded the D.S.O., was unfortunately seriously wounded. Shortly afterwards the enemy again succeeded in entering and pushing through Sapignies, but was met by the 5th Manchesters on the Sapignies–Bihucourt road, and driven back into the village.

As the enemy was reported to be assembling east and south-east of Bihucourt, a company of the 6th Manchesters under Captain

March 25

S. L. Bridgford was ordered there. It arrived simultaneously with the Germans, and, in spite of their great numerical superiority, immediately attacked them. Fighting desperately, the company was forced out of the village step by step, but in a brilliant counter-attack the ground was regained by sheer grit, backed by superiority with the bayonet. Again overwhelming numbers prevailed, and the survivors of the company were once more driven out. With the handful that remained Bridgford made another gallant effort, but he was severely wounded and died in the enemy's hands. The prompt and determined action of this company gained time for troops to be moved in support, and prevented the enemy debouching from Bihucourt. Had they been able to do so and reach Achiet-le-Grand, they could have commanded the reverse slopes of the ridge on which rested the centre of the Brigade. The O.C. 6th Manchesters was ordered to deny Achiet-le-Grand to the enemy at all costs, and the Pioneer Battalion (7th N.F.) was placed at his disposal. The 6th Manchesters, however, accomplished their task, though heavily engaged and under increasing artillery fire, without calling upon the Pioneers.

Towards midday the situation about Bihucourt on the right of the divisional front having become critical, the Tanks in Logeast Wood were ordered to counter-attack, and the 62nd Division, which had moved up to Bucquoy during the morning, was called upon to support the right flank of the Division about Achiet-le-Petit. This manœuvre was successful, four Tanks with a detachment of the 127th Brigade inflicting heavy casualties. About 2 p.m. scouts of the 5th East Lancashires on the left confirmed the report that the enemy had seized Behagnies and were advancing on Gomiecourt in strong force.* Lieut.-Colonel Clare, commanding the 5th East Lancashires, seeing that this move threatened to cut off his own battalion and also the 10th Manchesters between Gomiecourt and Ervillers, immediately sent forward headquarters details to hold

* The following extract from an infantry officer's letter home, giving his impressions of the enemy's methods of advance, is worth quoting here: "The Boche came on in ones and twos and small groups, apparently disorganized, and yet with wonderful speed and method. In a few moments hundreds would filter down into a depression of the ground, and from there advance in small sections, running anyhow, one after another, and making an exceedingly difficult target. Our artillery cut him to pieces when they saw him massing, but it was very difficult to inflict heavy losses with the rifle—though at times we had good practice, and all we had to do then was to take a rifle and shoot at odd parties of Boche. The German army is a wonderful organization. The pace at which they came on, and how they managed to pile up line after line of men in successive attacks, was almost incredible. One minute you would be watching the crest of a ridge and see a few men sauntering over the top in twos and threes, and two minutes later you would find the face of the ridge swarming with men, and more and more pushing on behind. As fast as their lines were shot down, other lines took their place."

NOTE.—This method of "infiltration," to which the writer refers, had formed part of the Division's training while in the La Bassée sector, was still more assiduously practised in May, June, and July, 1918, and was put into operation with signal success as soon as the British Offensive began.

the enemy back for a few precious moments. The handful of scouts, police, signallers, and runners reached the ridge in front of the enemy and, having good targets at short range, did great execution. Time was thus gained for two companies of the battalion to advance from the cross-roads south-east of Gomiecourt in artillery formation, shaking out into extended order below the crest, and doubling forward into fire positions from which they opened rapid fire, breaking up two lines of infantry in extended order not more than 200 yards away. Two Lewis guns were then brought to bear upon a large body in close formation farther back, scattering it. The remaining companies were brought up, and the battalion linked up with the 125th Brigade. The enemy's losses were heavy, and the position appeared to be satisfactory.

Meanwhile the 10th Manchesters had achieved fame by their defence of Ervillers, and Oldham folk will always regard with pride the distinction their men earned here. Eight separate determined attacks upon the battalion had been made by superior numbers, but the 10th, assisted by a company of machine-gunners which had been pushed up to cover their left flank, had repulsed them all, losing good men, but inflicting far greater loss upon the enemy. For this day's work the 10th Manchesters had the honour to be one of the very few battalions mentioned individually in Sir Douglas Haig's despatch. But, owing to the withdrawal to the Courcelles line of a brigade of the division on their left, they were forced to withdraw from the village about 9.30 p.m., and take up a position 1000 yards east of Gomiecourt. The Divisional Artillery, which had arrived about noon, and had immediately come into action, now covered the divisional front, some of the batteries being within 800 yards of the front line, and Battery D/211 had every gun knocked out.

About 10 p.m. (March 25), the 125th Brigade, which had dug in on the ridge between Gomiecourt and the Ervillers–Behagnies road, with the 7th L.F. on the right, the 5th on the left, and the 8th in support, was again heavily attacked. Lieut.-Colonel Holberton, with his habitual disregard of personal safety, walked along the line encouraging and heartening his men, and was shot through the head and killed instantly. Colonel Holberton, who went out with the Division in September 1914 as Adjutant of the 6th Manchesters, was a fine soldier and cheery, gallant comrade, whose death was deplored by all ranks throughout the Division.

At 11 p.m. the Division was still fighting on the ground it had taken up the previous night, with a large extension of front, which had been increased from the original 4000 yards to nearly 10,000, with both flanks in the air, and the Divisional Reserve consisting of two half-companies of machine-guns, one company of pioneers, and a Field Company R.E. as escort to the guns. The right was now thrown back, with two Field Companies and the 7th Northumberland Fusiliers holding the railway, covering the gap between Achiet-le-Grand and Achiet-le-Petit. On the right the 127th Brigade held

March 25-26

the spurs covering the former village, its left joining up with the 125th Brigade, which was fighting in the outskirts of Behagnies and Bee Wood, and the 126th, slightly echeloned back, continued the line to the trenches and Sunken Road just west of Ervillers. The Divisional Artillery were now ordered to withdraw to positions south of Ablainzevelle and, a few hours later, to the Essarts Valley. The transport rejoined late at night. The arrival of fresh divisions and the withdrawal of those which needed rest had blocked the roads for a time. Most of the roads crossed in Bucquoy village, and before noon on March 25 these were completely congested by masses of vehicles which could neither get on nor get out. The confusion appeared hopeless, and had the enemy seriously shelled or bombed these roads the result would have been appalling. The prompt freeing of the roads was essential, and the " A " and " Q " Staffs and the A.P.M. were ordered to concentrate their energies on this job. Ditches were filled in, barbed wire cut down, traffic diverted across country, and efficient controls posted. By 4 p.m. a steady stream of traffic was moving along the roads, and by 10 p.m. the Divisional Transport reached its rendezvous. The R.A. and R.A.S.C. were then admirably prompt and efficient in locating and supplying units under the most trying and difficult conditions. In particular the congestion on the Hannescamps-Essarts road during those days could only be overcome by combined skill, determination, and coolness. On this road the Divisional Artillery lost more drivers and horses than in any other place. But even under such abnormal conditions rations and ammunition never failed to reach the troops, and hot meals were frequently served to the men in the front line. For four days Dispatch Riders * were in the saddle day and night, and their endurance, pluck, and skill in dodging the traffic and getting their messages through had been of invaluable service to the Division.

The enemy was again working round the flanks, and, in the early hours of March 26, in accordance with orders from the Corps Commander, the withdrawal of the Division began, and was carried out in three successive bounds—first, to the line Achiet le Grand-Moyenneville railway; then to the Forest Lodge-Courcelles line, and finally to the Bucquoy-Ablainzevelle line. The troops were in position here at 10 a.m., and on this last line the enemy was success-

* The Dispatch Riders sometimes had the luck that dash and courage deserve. But not always ! A corporal writes : " We were passing the canteen at Achiet-le-Grand as it was about to be burnt, so of course we looked round for what we could win, and in the dark stumbled over a box. When in the dim light we made out the name ABDULLAH on the side, we quickly strapped the box to a carrier. On arrival at Headquarters the box drew a crowd, and we learnt for the first time what decent fellows we were, and how everybody liked us. What was more to the point, we were offered up to five francs a tin for the contents. After a struggle with jack-knives, willingly lent, we got the box open. It was full of the cheapest kind of razor-strops . . . During four years in France as Dispatch Rider I have been with several Divisions, and never met better sports than the Dispatch Riders and Headquarter staff of the 42nd. I tried hard to get back to the 42nd later, but couldn't manage it."

fully held.* The withdrawals were accomplished in good order, and, in the case of the 127th Brigade, units slipped away before the enemy was aware of their retirement, rifle fire being maintained on their late positions for some time after they had gone. Some units, however, were followed up hotly, and enemy pressure forced retiring troops to halt from time to time and open covering fire from different parts of the line, inflicting heavy casualties upon the Germans. A withdrawal in daylight, in close touch with the enemy, is a ticklish operation under any conditions, and the retirement of the troops on either flank some hours earlier added greatly to the difficulties. The companies of the M.G. Battalion did good work in covering each retirement, and the support from the artillery was always effective. Enormous losses were suffered by the enemy at each stage. During the day strong enemy attacks were delivered in front of Bucquoy, but were stopped by artillery, machine gun and rifle fire.

On the morning of the 27th March the headquarters of all three infantry brigades were established in deep dugouts in the vicinity of Essarts, about 2000 yards north-west of Bucquoy. From 8 a.m. enemy aircraft showed great activity, and at 10.15 a.m. heavy hostile shelling began. During the morning an enemy assembly for attack, in Nissen huts south of Ablainzevelle, and a massing near Ablainzevelle Cemetery, were broken up by our artillery. At 2.40 p.m. shelling of the front line became very heavy, but the enemy massing for attack in Ablainzevelle Wood and Village were dispersed by the Divisional Artillery, assisted by the German guns which, shooting short, did much damage to their own infantry. At 3 p.m. an attack from Logeast Wood was shattered by artillery, machine-gun, and rifle-fire. During the night a patrol of the 6th Manchesters entered Ablainzevelle, killed several Germans, and brought back two machine-guns, the officer in command being severely wounded just before regaining his own lines. The initiative shown in this little affair gained the Divisional Commander's congratulations for the battalion.

The boundaries between the 4th and 6th Corps had been continually changing. This caused much alteration of wagon-lines, rear headquarters, etc., and the difficulties were not lessened by such alarmist rumours from the rear as that the enemy had broken through into the Ayette Valley to the north, and as there was a right-angle bend in the British line south of Bucquoy, on the right of the Division's front, this would mean that both flanks of the Division were enveloped. The rumour was denied by the 126th Brigade, who stated that they were in touch with the 4th Guards Brigade, 31st Division. Patrols sent out to Ayette and Le Quesnoy Farm found that the line on the left of the Division had not been penetrated, and at 2 a.m. on the 28th the 126th Brigade and the

* It was not easy to make the men understand why they had to retire. They were holding their own and punishing the enemy. The Divisional Commander, on going the round of the troops later in the day, was asked by one of the men : " Why did you order us back, sir ? Weren't we doing right ? "

BUCQUOY-AYETTE ROAD, USED AS LATERAL COMMUNICATION BY FRONT-LINE TROOPS.

ESSARTS CRUCIFIX, USED AS HQRS. OF 211TH ARTILLERY BRIGADE DURING MARCH-APRIL FIGHTING.

ESSARTS VALLEY, SHOWING POSITIONS OCCUPIED BY DIVISIONAL ARTILLERY.

GOMMECOURT WOOD, SHOWING OLD GERMAN FRONT LINE (1916) AND FONQUEVILLERS.

GOMMECOURT WOOD, LOOKING TOWARDS HANNESCAMPS.

JULIUS POINT, LOOKING TOWARDS PIGEON WOOD.

March 28

4th Guards Brigade reported the position satisfactory, the Guards Division having extended to its right and joined up with the 4th Guards Brigade, thus closing the gap. Two companies of the 125th were sent to reinforce the 126th. The trenches now taken over by the Division were as bad as they could possibly be, having been disused for years. They were, moreover, open to fire on three sides, and as rain had been falling for some time, and showed no sign of stopping, they were knee-deep in mud and water.

At 8.15 a.m. on the 28th after a heavy bombardment of the divisional front, an enemy attack developed from the direction of Ablainzevelle, and was broken up by rifle, machine-gun, and Lewis-gun fire. A second attack at 10.15 a.m., the enemy advancing in three waves from Logeast Wood, was repulsed, chiefly by infantry fire. An hour later large parties from the same direction were met in the open and driven back, except at one point where the enemy obtained a footing in our lines. The 6th and 8th Manchesters at once counter-attacked with the bayonet, and all Germans who had entered our lines were killed or captured. At 1.30 p.m. a bombing attack was made against the left of the 127th Brigade. The 6th Manchesters again counter-attacked and captured two machine-guns and an officer. While one of the hottest attacks of the day was in progress Corporal A. Brooks, 6th Manchesters, noticed that his men were short of rifle-oil and that the bolts of the rifles, from incessant use, were not working freely. In the face of the enemy machine-guns and rifles the corporal calmly moved along the line of his platoon with an oil-can, personally oiled the bolts—and survived. At 7.10 p.m. concentrated machine-gun fire inflicted heavy losses on the enemy assembling in Nissen huts between Ablainzevelle and Logeast Wood.

As Fonquevillers had become a shell storm centre D.H.Q. was moved to St. Amand. During the night of the 28th March the Division took over 1500 yards of front on its right flank from the 62nd Division, and a Field Company R.E. was moved up in close support of each infantry brigade. The 123rd Brigade, 41st Division, was placed at the disposal of the Divisional Commander as a reserve. Within the space of forty-eight hours the enemy had made eight attacks upon the Division, but only on the one occasion had he entered our line, to be driven out immediately at the point of the bayonet. The number of effectives in the three infantry brigades and their condition were now reported as follows—

    125th Brigade, 1017. Fairly fresh.
    126th   ,,   1037. Much shelled, ready to fight, but cannot march.
    127th   ,,   1100. Very weary.

But in spite of weary bodies cheerfulness pervaded the Division, though most of the men could not understand why they had been ordered to withdraw on the 26th, after proving that they could do more than hold their own against Jerry. Open warfare of this sort was more to their taste than the monotonous trench warfare had been. " Simply topping fighting ! " was an officer's opinion. " Bit of change like, this 'ere, from the trenches," observed one Wigan man to another after four days of hard fighting without sleep. After due consideration the other replied : " Aye, mate, this is a bit of aw reet ; it favours a b—— picnic."

The sappers had been sent up in support, and though instructions had been given that they were not to be used in the front line, they made their way into it and even sent out patrols. They and the 7th Northumberland Fusiliers, who were also being used as frontline troops, captured prisoners. The battle surplus of battalions had been formed into a composite battalion, to be used as a fighting unit if required, but this was not found necessary, as the enemy's progress was stayed. March 29 was a comparatively quiet day. The great German Offensive had been definitely checked on this part of the Third Army's front by the determination and fighting qualities of all ranks and all arms. On the night of the 29th–30th the Division was relieved by the 41st Division and given a couple of days in the second-line trenches, in the Hebuterne–Gommecourt sector, with the exception of the 126th Brigade and " B " Company, M.G. Battalion, which remained at Essarts at the disposal of the G.O.C., 41st Division. The Divisional Artillery now occupied positions around Essarts, and there was no chance of even two days' rest for them.

The Division had entered upon these operations under exceptionally difficult circumstances. South of Arras the whole British front was being pushed back. Information was indefinite and conflicting. Owing to the congestion of the roads, the constant changes of positions and the consequent difficulties of keeping in touch, the troops had had to rely for a time on emergency rations solely. They had been pitted against specially selected and trained storm-troops, greatly superior in numbers and imbued with the confidence and enthusiasm which a triumphant advance is bound to inspire. On several occasions both flanks of the Division had been left in the air, but even then it had proved its ability to hold its ground stubbornly and cheerfully until ordered to retire; and its withdrawals had been carried out in good order and with exemplary steadiness. The Divisional Commander was more than pleased with his officers and men ; he was now confident of their fighting spirit and skill, as they were confident in his leadership; and when the Division was relieved he issued the following Special Order of the Day—

> " On being withdrawn from front line of the great battle in which the Division is engaged, the Major-General wishes to congratulate all ranks of all arms and services in the Division on the magnificent work they have done.
> " The co-operation between all arms on the battlefield, and

the soldierly spirit displayed by all ranks, resulted in no ground being given up by the Division without an order, and in enormous losses to the enemy, whose advance has thereby for the moment been brought to a standstill.

"The Divisional Motto to 'Go ONE BETTER' has been truly established. The Divisional Commander is convinced that all ranks, at all times and in all places, will live up to it."

Lieut.-General Sir G. M. Harper, commanding the 4th Corps, telegraphed—

"The Corps Commander congratulates 42nd Division on their magnificent behaviour during the last few days of fighting. Numerous heavy attacks have been made by the enemy, and have been completely repulsed with heavy loss, and the capture of prisoners and machine-guns. He heartily thanks the troops for their courage and endurance, and is confident that they will continue to hold the line against all attacks."

The Division returned to the front line on the night of April 1–2, the 125th Brigade and the 1/7th Northumberland Fusiliers holding the right sub-sector, and the 126th Brigade and the three Field Companies, R.E., the left, with the 127th Brigade in support. All three infantry brigades had their headquarters in Essarts, a village on which a disproportionate amount of "hate" seemed to be concentrated. On the night of the 2nd the 125th Brigade raided a new enemy work east of the Bucquoy–Ablainzevelle road and established a strong point in the work; and at 2 a.m. on the 3rd the 32nd Division, on the left of the 42nd, made a successful attack upon Ayette, capturing 200 prisoners, and establishing a line east of Ayette.

At 5 a.m. on the 5th of April the 125th Brigade front and the neighbourhood of Essarts were heavily shelled, gas being freely used. The 126th Brigade, moving into support trenches at Essarts, suffered very severely, the 10th Manchesters losing more men than in the whole of the previous twelve days fighting. H.E. and gas shells alternately poured down for the space of five hours. The night was pitch-black, as the men stumbled along the muddy trenches, unable to see or breathe. The trenches, already a foot deep in mud, were described as "slime and blood, carpeted with bodies." But when the bombardment lifted, the men extracted their dead and wounded comrades, and resumed their tasks, their resolve to "best the Boche" being no whit abated. The Composite Battalion, also near Essarts, had fifty casualties, and the Divisional Artillery also suffered, though less severely. At 8 a.m., under cover of a trench-mortar hurricane bombardment, which inflicted very heavy casualties, not only among the front-line troops but also in the reserve companies, and completely destroyed a machine-gun section, the enemy attacked and succeeded in throwing back the left of the 8th Lancashire Fusiliers, the two companies being wiped out almost to a man. The 7th L.F. and the right company of the 8th were able to hold their ground, and the latter began to work its way up the trench to the north, but was forced to fall back when nearly surrounded, owing to the retirement of the left company of the left battalion of the division on its right. All lines being down, communication was bad, but at 11.40 a.m. orders were issued that the survivors of the 8th L.F. must eject the enemy at once. They counter-attacked, and at noon reached the main cross-roads in Bucquoy, where hand-to-hand fighting took place amid the ruins of the village. Lieut.-Colonel St. Leger Davies * was mortally wounded by machine-gun fire, and Captain G. W. Sutton, M.C. assumed command and successfully organized the consolidation of the line regained until he, too, was severely wounded. Very fierce fighting continued, and two platoons of the 5th L.F. were brought up. The counter-attack progressed favourably until the line of the Bucquoy–Ayette road was reached, when it was held up by machine-gun fire. Touch had again been lost with the battalion on the right, and the 5th L.F., bringing up their remaining company, formed a defensive flank in touch with the 7th L.F., and the attack was brought to a standstill. The fighting, which had been very bitter all day, gradually died down, and at 8 p.m. the front was quiet, touch being regained on the right flank during the night.

The morning of the 6th was quiet except for artillery fire on both sides. Later information revealed the fact that the attack of the previous day on the divisional front formed part of one of the fiercest and last attacks with which the enemy followed up his initial offensive. Its repulse proved of very great importance. The 5th East Lancashires were put at the disposal of the 125th Brigade, and their place on Henley Hill, the key to the position between Essarts and Ablainzevelle, was taken by the Composite Battalion. Later in the day the 126th Brigade was moved to Souastre, and on the following night the other infantry brigades were also relieved by the 62nd Division, D.H.Q. being opened at Pas Chateau, about ten miles west of Bucquoy. On the night of the 8th the R.E., the M.G. Battalion, and the Pioneer Battalion were relieved, and also a company of the 8th Manchesters, which by some mischance had not been relieved on the previous day. Being naturally annoyed at this delay the company vented its displeasure upon the Boche by raiding Ablainzevelle, inflicting many casualties, and capturing prisoners and a machine-gun.

The casualties in the Division from March 24 to April 8 numbered 126 officers and 2839 other ranks, but heavy as this total was, the loss inflicted upon the enemy by the Division was far greater. The evacuation of the wounded had proceeded smoothly in spite of the heavy traffic and congestion at the Dressing Stations, and very few casualties had fallen into the hands of the enemy. No man did better work for the wounded than Padre E. C. Hoskyns, M.C.,

* Colonel Davies, formerly an officer of the 6th Manchesters, went out with the Division in 1914, and served in Egypt, Gallipoli and Sinai. He was a gallant soldier with a charming personality, and his loss was keenly felt.

attached to the 7th Manchesters. At Achiet-le-Grand, on March 24, he collected a large number of casualties of many units and of various divisions, tended them under heavy fire, and, though himself slightly wounded, remained with them until they could be evacuated. Later, he collected wounded and stragglers, organized carrying-parties, and got the last party safely off just before the enemy arrived. Good work was done by the Military Police, who had a very difficult task in managing traffic about Bucquoy, Essarts, and Hannescamps, and who performed acts of conspicuous gallantry. The Signal Company had shown its usual efficiency, intrepidity and capacity for hard work.

Machine-gunners and Lewis-gunners were sorely tried by the need to carry their guns a distance of seven miles or more into action before undergoing the sufficiently severe strain of continuous fighting. The M.G. Battalion, splendidly led by its Commander, Lieut-. Colonel W. K. Tillie, D.S.O., had done its full share in the gallant and successful resistance made at Ervillers, Bucquoy, Ablainzevelle and elsewhere. The efficacy of the Lewis-gun was clearly brought out, and was enhanced by the initiative of the personnel who used it. It was also satisfactory to note the effective use of infantry weapons, particularly the rifle, and the reliance placed upon them by the men after the first few hours fighting. The attention that had recently been given to rifle practice proved invaluable, for the men discovered that provided they applied the lessons learnt, the enemy had little chance of getting to close quarters.

Two of the factors that contributed to the Division's success may be summarized as follows—

(1) The spirit of mutual trust and camaraderie, from the highest to the lowest, which had been fostered in the Division. While the spirit of emulation to carry out the Divisional Motto animated every unit, each knew that it could rely confidently upon the others.

(2) The rigorous training of the Division in the offensive method of defence in depth, and the system of holding tactical localities by units—as opposed to long lines—combined with preparedness for immediate local counter-attack.

Every branch of the divisional organization had been severely proved in the fire of this epic struggle, and had stood the test gloriously. It is impossible to praise too highly the conduct of all ranks throughout the operations, the initiative of the subordinate commanders in directing and controlling their commands, and the tenacity, keenness and fighting spirit of all arms and all ranks. Whether repelling attacks, or counter-attacking, or withdrawing in accordance with orders, their cheerfulness and high spirits never flagged. They were quite confident that they could " lick Jerry " at any time or in any place, and however weak and exhausted the flesh might be the spirit was always willing. The reply given by a brigade to H.Q. inquiry as to its state of exhaustion is typical : " Can't march, but can fight."

CHAPTER X

ENTR'ACTE

(*April* 9—*August* 20, 1918)

THE Division remained for a week in the Pas–Henu–Couin–Vauchelles area, a period sufficient to enable it to get rid of the clay and mud spread thickly over equipment, clothing, and person, and of the stubble that was beginning to camouflage faces; also to wipe off some of the arrears of sleep and to carry out the necessary reorganization and re-equipment. Signs of the need for sleep and rest were very plain. "Their eyes," said a Battalion Commander, " seemed to be falling out of their sockets with the strain. But there was a splendid smile on all the tired faces, a smile of confidence and victory." They had been put to the hardest of all tests as regards courage, endurance, physical fitness, and soldierly efficiency, and had emerged with flying colours. They knew now that they were better soldiers than the enemy.

Brigade groups were inspected in turn by the Divisional Commander, who told them that he was proud to command them, and explained to them what they had done, what was then happening, and what might be expected to happen. So far as the Division was concerned the German offensive had been utterly broken; they had not surrendered an inch of ground until ordered to do so. At Ervillers and Sapignies the attack had rebounded off them, and had flowed round their flanks. And when, at Bucquoy, the attack had been renewed they had again beaten it, and it had flowed round their right flank past Rossignol Wood to Hebuterne. He was confident that the Division would once more demonstrate its ability to " go one better " than any German division or divisions that might come up against it. During the week considerable reinforcements arrived from England, mainly composed of young soldiers without previous experience, and these were absorbed into the various units.

On April 15 the Division returned to the front line a few miles west of the positions held at the end of the first week of the German offensive, relieving the 37th Division in the Centre Sector (Gommecourt–Hebuterne) of the 4th Corps front. Gommecourt, now a name only—for the Hun had demolished it so ruthlessly that in 1917 the French Government had decided to preserve the scarred

FONQUEVILLERS CHURCH. THE CAVE UNDER THE CHURCH WAS FOR A SHORT TIME USED AS BRIGADE HQRS.

FONQUEVILLERS-SOUASTRE FORK, THE SCENE OF MUCH SHELLING AT NIGHT.

CHÂTEAU DE LA HAIE.

GOMMECOURT WOOD.

GOMMECOURT PARK FROM HÉBUTERNE.

Gommecourt-Hebuterne 143

site as a national monument—lies three miles west of Bucquoy, and must not be confounded with Gomiecourt, a village nearly five miles east of Bucquoy, now occupied by the enemy. The relief was accomplished at midnight, enemy shelling having caused a few casualties as the troops passed through Fonquevillers. D.H.Q. was opened at Couin Chateau, and the Reception Camp in the woods east of Marieux. On the right the New Zealand Division held the high ground above Colincamps, and the 62nd Division was on the left, in the 42nd Division's old line, Bucquoy–Ayette. The positions taken over had been the German trenches when No Man's Land lay between Fonquevillers and Gommecourt Wood in June 1916. The old front lines of the enemy, which now formed our reserve lines, consisted of well-revetted deep trenches with eighteen inches of mud on the old duck-boards. But his reserve lines, now forming our front line from Rossignol Wood to a point 500 yards east of Biez Wood, were shallow trenches, lacking in revetment, fire-steps, barbed wire defences, and anything in the shape of localities or strong points. Work was concentrated on these deficiencies, and the old German light railway from Gommecourt Park to Biez Wood was soon put into working order. It carried many loads of water, rations, and R.E. material nightly. There were several tunnelled dugouts in the sector, those stretching from back to front of Gommecourt Wood being a fine example of German thoroughness. The cellars under the ruins of Fonquevillers church were cleared and made gas proof, and they proved valuable later.

The enemy, relaxing the vigour of his attacks upon the Third and Fifth Armies, had concentrated a huge force in the north, and on April 9 had struck swiftly at the front of the Second Army, between Givenchy and Ypres. The Portuguese at Neuve Chapelle were unable to withstand the attack, and the Germans poured through the gap. But on their right the West Lancashires of the 55th Division held their positions at Givenchy—the defences which their Lancashire comrades of the 42nd Division had designed and nearly completed—with splendid valour and tenacity against four times their numbers, and refused to give ground. At this point the line held, and the enemy could make no impression upon it. Further north, Armentières and other towns and villages which had been occupied for years by British troops had to be abandoned, and the enemy pressed forward to Merville and Bailleul. These were among the darkest days of the war, and the Special Order of the Day, issued by the Commander-in-Chief on April 11, contains these significant words—

" Many among us now are tired. To those I would say that Victory will belong to the side which holds out the longest. The French Army is moving rapidly and in great force to our support. *Every position must be held to the last man. With our backs to the wall,* and believing in the justice of our cause, each one of us must fight on to the end. The safety of our homes and the Freedom of Mankind alike depend upon the conduct of each one of us at this critical moment."

A few days later French cavalry, artillery, and infantry arrived from the south, and, though Mont Kemmel was captured from them on April 26, the crisis was over on this sector. Khaki and blue together stopped the onrush, and together endured the terrific hammering until the smiter grew tired. During this period in April the front held by the 42nd Division had been fairly quiet, but the storm might burst upon it at any moment, so all thoughts and energies were concentrated upon perfecting the scheme of defence. The 4th Australian Infantry Brigade was attached to the Division from the 16th to the 25th of April, and the Divisional Front was divided into four sections, each held by one infantry brigade. The Corps allotted certain lines of defence to Divisional Commanders, and in the 42nd Division each of such lines was formed into a Defensive System as follows—

(a) The Front System—an outpost system, including its own supports.
(b) A Supporting System, known as the " Purple System," on the ridge Monchy-au-Bois–Fonquevillers–Gommecourt–Colincamps. This system must be held against all attacks.
(c) The Sailly-au-Bois–Château de la Haie Switch between the Purple and Red Systems.
(d) A Reserve System—known as the " Red Line "—forming the line of assembly of the divisions in Corps Reserve in case of attack.

Infantry brigades were responsible for the defence of their respective sections of the Front and Purple Systems and all intervening ground, and for the organization, construction, and upkeep of all defences. In each system, or zone, mutually supporting localities were held, with each locality its own commander, even down to platoons. Localities were so selected as to defend tactical points, and, as far as possible, were arranged chequer-wise in depth. If the troops on a flank were wiped out or overrun a defensive flank was to be formed from the supports. The artillery were also distributed in depth so that some batteries were available in each zone. Battery positions were fortified, and were to be defended to the last. The R.A. had been instructed in the use of the " hand gun," as the gunners derisively termed the rifle. The machine-gun defence was most carefully and skilfully organized, also in depth, and in no zone were there any covered approaches which could not be swept by machine-gun fire.

Divisional Engineers and Pioneers were allotted to the Brigades as follows—

The Defensive System

Right Brigade (high ground above Sailly-au-Bois) : one Pioneer Company.
Right Centre (Hebuterne) : one Field Company, R.E., and one Pioneer Company.
Left Centre (Gommecourt) : 1 Field Company and one Pioneer Company.
Left (Gommecourt Wood) : one Field Company.

The Field Companies and Pioneers were placed under the orders of Brigade Commanders, the C.R.E. to assist Brigade Commanders as much as possible and to supervise the work of the Field Companies and Pioneer Battalion. The divisional front was covered by seven Brigades of Field Artillery and three Brigades of Garrison Artillery.

As the very severe weather continued the postponement of the expected enemy attack until more favourable conditions should prevail seemed probable. In view of this the Divisional Commander on April 19 ordered that every effort must be made to ensure both security and the comfort and welfare of the men. The instructions to this effect emphasized the importance of : the field of fire and flanking fire of defensive localities; fire-stepping trenches; improving communications; improving defence against gas, particularly the gas-proofing of deep dug-outs. As many men as possible were to be provided with shell-proof dug-out accommodation, and where this was impossible improvised weather shelters to be constructed. The provision of hot meals in forward areas, of dry standings to prevent " trench feet," of a supply of clean socks and clothing, and of baths and drying-rooms in accessible positions. As much use as possible to be made of trench tramways to relieve the strain on transport and carrying parties. " There is so much necessary work to be done that man power and horse power must be conserved by making every use of available machinery."

On April 25 the 4th Australian Brigade was withdrawn and the New Zealand Division took over a portion of the divisional front. It was now decided to hold the reduced front with two brigades, each having one battalion in the front line, one in support, and one in reserve. In turn each of the three brigades went into Divisional Reserve at Coigneux for a few days. The brigades in the front line constructed communication trenches and forward Company Headquarters, and generally consolidated and improved their positions. For work on the Purple Line—nominated as the main line of resistance—one battalion of the brigade in reserve was at the disposal of the C.R.E. A series of strong posts had been taped out by the engineers, and working parties were engaged upon these every night. The Purple Line rejoiced in the possession of Beer, Stout, and Rum Trenches, but whether the names had been given with the idea of raising false hopes in the breasts of thirsty Teutons and luring them on to destruction is not known. The enemy artillery was active, and great quantities of mustard-gas shells were sent over, but still the Germans refrained from attack. The period,

April 16 to May 7 was noteworthy for the amount of work performed and the trials incidental to trench warfare rather than for any offensive operations on either side.

On April 30 the following gracious message from Her Majesty, the Queen, was issued to the troops—

> "To the men of our Navy, Army, and Air Force, I send this message to tell every man how much we, the women of the British Empire at home, watch and pray for you during the long hours of these days of stress and endurance. Our pride in you is immeasurable, our hope unbounded, our trust absolute. You are fighting in the cause of righteousness and freedom, fighting to defend the children and women of our land from the horrors that have overtaken other countries, fighting for our very existence as a people at home and across the seas. You are offering your all. You hold nothing back, and day by day you show a love so great that no man can have greater. We, on our part, send forth with full hearts and unfaltering will the lives we hold most dear. We, too, are striving in all ways possible to make the war victorious. I know that I am expressing what is felt by thousands of wives and mothers when I say that we are determined to help one another in keeping your homes ready against your glad homecoming. In God's name we bless you and by His help we, too, will do our best."

A visit to Divisional Headquarters was made on May 4 by Field-Marshal Sir Douglas Haig, who sent this message to all ranks of the Division—

> "I know how magnificently they have fought, and thank them from me for their gallant performance. Tell them that I consider the situation is now far more satisfactory than at one time I expected it could be. If necessity arises I know that I can rely on the 42nd Division to do as well again as it did before."

On May 7 the Division was relieved by the 57th Division, and the troops returned to the Pas district, where the greater part were now accommodated under canvas in the woods at Pas, Henu, and Couin, while some were in billets. Here they remained until the beginning of June. The Divisional Artillery, however, continued in action, occupying positions successively at Monchy-au-Bois, Hannescamps, Fonquevillers, and Gommecourt.

There was much work to be done on the defences of the Red Line and La Haie Switch, which would be manned by the division or divisions in Corps Reserve in the event of a strong enemy attack. It was essential that every company, every platoon, and indeed every man, should know the exact position to be taken up at any time of the day or night, however short the notice. The lines were thoroughly reconnoitred by all officers, and the manning of battle-positions was practised until all was perfect. The Divisional Commander laid stress on the importance of the prompt and correct transmission of messages and orders, and warned subordinate commanders against placing too much reliance upon the telephone. Visual signalling and other methods of transmission must be practised assiduously and made full use of. The action of the hateful mustard-gas was explained and practice ordered in the fitting of respirators and their daily use on ordinary parades and at musketry. The Major-General complimented the Divisional Artillery on their excellent discipline during gas concentration on battery positions on the night of the 12th of May.

The bad weather had now come to an end, and these delightful days of May, under canvas pitched in sylvan retreats far—yet not very far—from the madding turmoil of battle, gave one, in the short intervals of rest from strenuous work and training, almost the impression of a holiday camp, though all units had to be ready to move bag and baggage at an hour's notice and man the Red Line. Nature, patiently but triumphantly reasserting herself in the face of the forces of destruction, had a soothing effect which helped men to put aside for the moment the memories of the grim happenings of recent days. Moreover, three afternoons of each week were given up to recreational training, games, boxing and other contests. Major S. G. Johnson, D.S.O.,* Divisional Signal Company, did much to encourage and to raise the standard of boxing in the Division, and also to inculcate the right spirit of good, clean fighting, with the result that the boxers of the Division won laurels in the Corps boxing competitions. Concerts were held in the hall at Pas, and the Divisional Concert Troupe and Band visited the troops in Coigneux and Bayencourt, and behind the line in Louvencourt, Vauchelles and Halloy. Concerts were held in the open by the talent of various units, and the 10th Manchesters secured a natural amphitheatre in Pas Woods. Colonel Peel, with the foresight and energy for which he was famous, had already asked the Mayor of Oldham to send out a piano, and this arrived just when it could be put to the best use.†

About the middle of May the 307th Infantry Regiment of the American Army (77th Division) was attached to the 42nd for instruction and training, and for three weeks the Americans took part in all schemes arranged for the Division. The training was divided

---

* During a bombardment of Fonquevillers a considerable portion of a house was blown into Major Johnson's motor, and as he could not spare the time to empty it, he brought the debris to D.H.Q., where he had to endure much chaff on the subjects of looting and furniture removal vans.

† An officer of this battalion wrote home : " My C.O. is the most energetic man I ever struck; he is at it from morning till night, and in the night too. He does not stop for meals, and I invariably go to meals with a notebook and pencil, as all sorts of points strike him suddenly, and down they go in my notebook."

into three stages. In the first, the U.S. platoons were attached to companies of the 42nd; in the second, U.S. companies were attached to battalions; and later the U.S. battalions formed the fourth battalions of infantry brigades. The U.S. Pioneer Section was attached to the Divisional R.E. The Americans were naturally rather green, and their conception of warfare was perhaps more crude than they had imagined, but they proved quick and willing learners, although it was alleged that in one company the platoon-sergeants had to give instruction in sixteen different languages. They contributed nobly to entertainments, and in return for tuition in football, boxing and warfare, they taught the Division to jazz, and a considerable portion of it, including its Commander, to play baseball. Officers and men of the two armies mixed together with cordiality, good-fellowship and mutual respect, these sentiments being further stimulated by a really good dinner, followed by a well-organized entertainment, given to the attached Americans by Colonel Clare and the 5th East Lancashires in the middle of a wood near Pas. When, on June 3, the Americans were ordered to entrain for the south, it was a common disappointment that they would not have the opportunity of fighting side by side with the men with whom they had helped to train.

On June 7 the Division took over the right sector of the 4th Corps front from the New Zealand Division. As this was an exceptionally broad sector, with a frontage of more than 6000 yards, from a point north of Hebuterne on the left to a point east of Auchonvillers on the right, only one infantry battalion could be held in Divisional Reserve. D.H.Q. was opened at Bus-les-Artois. The Field Ambulances took over the Advanced and Main Dressing Stations at Sailly-au-Bois, Bus and Louvencourt, the Transport Sections being also accommodated in the two last-named villages. Artillery on both sides was active, and the 126th Brigade, on the left, had some casualties from shelling on the first night, " C " Company, 10th Manchesters, losing one officer and six other ranks killed, and nine men wounded. There was much gas-shelling of the forward areas, and long-range guns frequently opened on Bus and Louvencourt. But our artillery inflicted still greater damage on the enemy around Serre and Puisieux, and at night our aircraft flew over to bomb the back areas. Trench mortars were also active, and every landmark on the enemy's front was obliterated. The trenches were well constructed and well sited, particularly in the centre at La Signy Farm, where the front line ran along a ridge from which the enemy was under observation as far back as the villages of Serre and Puisieux, whereas the British support lines were in dead ground, secure from rifle and machine-gun fire; and rations and water-carts were able to come up in daytime. Luxuriant masses of hay-grass, clover, weeds and thistles covered the ground, and partridges and quails were plentiful around the trenches.

All vehicles that brought rations and supplies to the front line took back a load of hay to the transport lines. Divisional orders

SAILLY AU BOIS CHURCH. THE CATACOMBS IN THE VICINITY WERE USED BY THE RESERVE BATTALION.

COUIN VALLEY. THE LEFT BRIGADE AND A FIELD CO. R.E. AND PIONEER CO. HAD THEIR QUARTERS IN THESE BANKS.

COLINCAMPS. CONCRETE MACHINE-GUN EMPLACEMENTS AND O.P. CONSTRUCTED IN A FARM.

COLINCAMPS. APPLE TREE O.P. OVERLOOKING GREAT EXPANSE OF ENEMY COUNTRY TOWARDS BAPAUME.

COLINCAMPS. LA SIGNY FARM.

Horsemastership

about this time drew the attention of Transport Officers to the excellent grazing available in a certain map-square. Whether the transport of one particular unit thought that it had found a still " better 'ole " for grazing, or whether it mistook the map-square, is not known, but one day the " Q " staff were more surprised than pleased to see at least one hundred horses peacefully grazing, and the drivers calmly cleaning harness, under the fold of a hill only a few hundred yards from the front line. Divisional orders the next day were very interesting.

The subject of Horsemastership was one in which the Divisional Commander, as a Cavalry Officer, naturally took much interest. He had found the Division somewhat lax in this respect, and had lost no time in bringing about a considerable improvement. On this, as on all other subjects, experts differed, each having his own fads and foibles which conflicted entirely with those of others, so Transport Officers and Farrier Sergeants led a harassed life while trying to reconcile the irreconcilable. One authority would consider two hot feeds per week vital to the well-being of horses, and another that two would be harmful, but a bran-mash every Saturday night would put a spring into the step and a shine on the coat.

A Divisional Horsemaster was appointed. He was a firm advocate of two hot feeds per week, and it was alleged that by walking down the horse lines he could tell at a glance every horse that had had less or more than this allowance. It was soon seen that the Divisional Commander intended to raise the standard of Horsemastership and Horsemanship by help and advice rather than by " strafing," and in this he was loyally supported by the Divisional Horsemaster and the Director of Veterinary Services. Faults were pointed out at frequent inspections, and the remedy clearly explained, with the result that all who had to do with horses were soon taking a keen interest in the fitness of their animals, and in rivalry with other units. Some units managed to obtain Soyer stoves for the hot feeds, but those with a smaller transport had to be content with a trough known as a " Canadian Cradle," in which was stewed a mixture of oats and hayseeds. The latter was not a ration, but was obtained by shaking the hay over a large sieve, and as the weight of seeds obtained from different trusses varied greatly, the unofficial introduction of sweepstakes on the yield per truss added to the keenness of the personnel. When summer came, grazing took the place of the hot feed, and each unit had to find a suitable field and make arrangements. Some congratulated themselves on the excellent bargain made with the farmer, until on arriving at the field they found that it had been let to half a dozen units. It was then no easy matter to find the farmer—who had been paid in advance. But when fences were broken down, and the horses roamed into other fields, or when—on the plea that the owner could not be found —horses were turned into any field that seemed suitable, the farmers were prompt to appear in the transport lines to make complaint. Of course the transport officer could speak French; it was merely the " patois " that baffled him and reduced the argument to a contest of signs and gestures, in which he put up a poor show against the Frenchman. The driver-spectators enjoyed the pantomimes hugely, and would give renderings later for the benefit of less fortunate comrades. A popular explanation given to our allies on such occasions was that the N.C.O. in charge of the grazing party had made a mistake in the map reference, but in time this wore too thin, and a fresh one had to be invented.

But month by month the horsemastership of the Division became more and more efficient. The Divisional Transport competitions did much to improve " turnout " of drivers, horses and vehicles, and when the Division was trekking, the Divisional Commander usually posted himself on the line of route to watch the troops pass. The O.C. unit was called to his side and every small failing pointed out. In a very short time the Division's transport came up to the standard of a Regular division.

Though there were no actions of great importance in June there were individual acts of gallantry, the following being taken from one day's record. On June 16 parts of a burning camouflage dropped into the gunpit of X/42 T.M. Battery, setting guncotton charges on fire. The flames were travelling rapidly towards a bomb store when Corporal A. Metcalf and Gunner W. Chesmer gallantly rushed to the pit, unfused the bombs, cleared the pit of bombs and charges and, regardless of danger, extinguished the flames. But for their prompt, courageous action there must have been grave loss of life and material. A daring and successful raid was made on Fusilier Trench the same day by a party of four officers and eighty other ranks of the 7th Manchesters. As the signal was given for withdrawal Sergeant A. S. Fleetwood saw a wounded comrade, with a broken leg, lying beyond the enemy trench. He rushed again into enemy territory and carried the man to our lines, arriving there twenty minutes after the rest of the party.

A very severe epidemic of influenza diminished the strength of the Division during June, and no one was sorry when, on July 2, the New Zealanders took over the Hebuterne sector and so reduced the wide frontage of the Division to 3800 yards. This permitted an infantry brigade, instead of a battalion, to be withdrawn into Divisional Reserve. Offensive operations were mainly confined to harassing the enemy by constant artillery and T.M. fire, by gas, and by frequent raids, which generally resulted in the bringing in of prisoners. Some of these raids were on a large scale; others were minor affairs in which, after careful reconnaissance, an officer and a few N.C.O.s and men would suddenly and quietly make their way into the enemy trenches, effect their purpose, capture a prisoner or two for identification, and return. In the daylight raids no artillery or T.M. preparation was usual, and the withdrawal as a rule was only covered by machine-gun and Lewis-gun fire. The barrages placed round objectives by the Machine Gun Companies contributed largely to the success of the more important enterprises.

At 3 p.m. on July 9, Lieutenant C. E. Frost and seven other ranks of the 5th Manchesters raided a post in Watling Street (the enemy line east of Auchonvillers), and, having killed all the occupants, next attacked a working-party. Altogether they killed fifteen of the enemy—eight of these being the officer's share—and returned safely with no other casualties than three slightly wounded, including Frost, who was twice struck by bombs. Every member of the party was decorated.

On July 17 a daylight raiding party of eighteen N.C.O.s and men of the 7th L.F., under Lieutenant J. R. Garbutt, earned the congratulations of the Divisional Commander. On the night of July 18–19 a raid by three officers and ninety-six other ranks of the 5th East Lancashires accomplished its object. Lieutenant S. W. Pacey, in command of the leading platoon, though severely wounded, carried on until his men had finished the task for which they had been detailed. Sergeant J. Spiers, in command of a platoon which suffered heavy casualties, led his men through a hail of bullets to their objective, where he was twice severely wounded. He too refused to quit until the job was done, and on return he insisted on the wounds of his men being attended to before his own were dressed.

On the following night a party of thirty-eight N.C.O.s and men of the 7th Manchesters, under Lieutenant N. Edge, captured and consolidated an enemy post five hundred yards in front of our lines. A night later, another raid by three officers and a hundred and twenty-five other ranks of the same battalion captured the enemy system of trenches known as The Triangle, north of the dozen or so of more or less connected bricks which bore the courtesy title of La Signy Farm. Four posts were captured, a number of the enemy killed, and three prisoners brought back. Lieutenant W. Gresty led with gallantry and skill, and Lieutenant H. Gorst, in charge of one of the parties, killed three or four Germans with his revolver, and was seriously wounded by a bullet fired at close quarters. Sergeant J. Horsfield then took charge of this party and led with great dash, inspiring his men with confidence at a critical moment. Next morning the enemy counter-attacked to regain possession of the lost positions, and wounded with bombs most of the garrison of a forward post. Lance-Corporal S. Lockett, who was at the next post, at once attacked with two or three men, and cleared out the enemy. He himself wounded and took prisoner the German N.C.O.

During the 20th to 24th July the 6th Manchesters were advancing their part of the line in a similar manner. In all these operations C.S.M. H. D. Whitford gave proofs of courage and devotion to duty. He organized and led a party under heavy machine-gun fire to bring in a man who had been killed in the attack, and then organized and conducted a carrying party, also under a hot fire, to take up rations and ammunition to the garrisons holding the newly-won posts, and in other ways set an example of courage and resource,

Private W. Tomkinson, when all other members of his Lewis-gun team had become casualties, took his gun to a new position and put out of action the machine-gun which had caused the casualties. Later, he volunteered to lead a party into No Man's Land to recover the body of one of his gun team. Private N. S. Smith twice brought in wounded across the open in daylight under heavy fire.

In an attack by the 7th L.F. on July 22, the leader of a section being wounded, Private G. Heardley carried him into cover under point-black machine-gun fire, and during a daylight raid on the 24th he led his section to attack a party of forty Germans in their trenches and killed several, though before leaving our lines he had been wounded, but did not mention the fact. After the capture of an enemy post on the 22nd, C.S.M. W. Rushton, 5th L.F., organized the consolidation with great ability. The post being harassed by snipers he crawled forward and killed them; the work on the post being much hampered by rifle grenades and trench mortars he moved some distance to a flank and then exposed himself, digging and throwing up earth, and in this way drew the fire off the post until the consolidation was completed.

On the night of July 30–31 a patrol of the 5th Manchesters came under a very hot fire and the officer was killed. Corporal J. Melling took command and withdrew the patrol successfully, and though under very heavy fire all the time, he managed to carry the body of the officer back a distance of 600 yards in the open.

These stirring events were not allowed to interfere with recreational training. In the Corps boxing competition held at Marieux the 42nd Division produced the champion boxer—best form and cleanest fighter—besides winning in several other weights. On the 16th July D.H.Q. had been moved to Authie, and the Divisional Revue, "*Sweet Fanny Adams*," was produced there. It was really very funny and immensely popular with all who were fortunate enough to get to Authie. As usual the Division left its "Q" mark on the district, baths, canteens, recreation rooms and Y.M.C.A. huts being made out of ruined houses as far forward as Sailly-au-Bois and Courcelles-au-Bois. A reference may be made here to the admirable work of a Y.M.C.A. padre, the Rev. G. Barclay, who devoted himself to the welfare and happiness of the men, and who remained with the Division to the end. His first quarters were in a by no means gas-proof cellar at Sailly, an old barn providing canteen, reading, and writing-rooms, where services were held which were much appreciated by all ranks.

The latter part of July witnessed a dramatic change in the military situation. The gigantic enemy onslaughts of March and April had been directed against the British armies, the first being an attempt to drive a wedge between the allies, to capture Amiens, and roll up the British front. At one time the attainment of these objects seemed near, but British tenacity prevailed, and the line held. The second, an attempt to pierce a vital point south of Ypres and gain the coast, also seemed likely to succeed. But though the line

COLINCAMPS. BROAD-GAUGE RAILWAY LEADING TO EUSTON DUMP.

CHESTNUT AVENUE LEADING FROM COLINCAMPS TO MAILLY-MAILLET SUCRERIE.

MAILLY-MAILLET SUCRERIE.

BEAUREGARD DOVECOTE, OVERLOOKING MIRAUMONT.

MIRAUMONT. THE SOURCE OF THE R. ANCRE.

WARLENCOURT VILLAGE, LOOKING TOWARDS PYS.

bent back dangerously it would not break, and the arrival of French reinforcements relieved the strain upon the greatly outnumbered British. At the end of May a third huge concentration of divisions drawn from the Eastern front, of new divisions hitherto held in reserve, and of the divisions withdrawn from the Somme, struck swift and mighty blows at the French on the Montdidier–Reims front, and for a second time Paris was in peril, and one feared that the heart of France was pierced. Then, on July 18, when Paris seemed almost within grasp of the exultant Hun, and Germany boasted that the war was won, Foch struck with the reserves—including British divisions—which he had held back so patiently to use at the psychological moment, and of whose existence the enemy seemed unaware. On July 20 the civilized world breathed freely once more, and the German High Command knew that, whatever it might order the German populace to think, defeat was to be its portion.

But the time had not yet come for the British Armies to begin their great offensive. They made their preparations and awaited the word. Every brigade of the 42nd Division had raided and seized posts and pushed the enemy back fifty or five hundred yards at one point or another. In the latter half of July the 127th Brigade, by means of the attacks already referred to, had advanced their line on a front of nearly 2000 yards to a depth in places of about 1000 yards, almost to Staff Wood and Observation Wood, 800 yards east of La Signy Farm. In August the possibility of a new enemy attack in force was still contemplated, as it was calculated that there were more than thirty German divisions which had not yet been employed. So the work on the defences continued with unabated energy, the Pioneer Battalion, the three Field Companies, the Tunnelling Companies, and the infantry being kept hard at work on tunnelled dugouts and fortified posts, and it was said that the Division was praying that the Germans might attack. The 179 and 252 Tunnelling Companies did fine work, in which Captain Dean was especially prominent. The names *Sixth Avenue, La Sucrerie, La Signy Farm, Quarry O.P.*, and *Euston Dump* recall many incidents, and Captain Buckley and his Divisional Observers will remember the magnificent view obtained over "Bocheland" to Bapaume from *Appletree O.P.* One of the difficulties in the construction of the many strong points in this sector was the wonderful crop of wheat, which was such an obstruction to the field of fire that much of it had to be rolled flat with an agricultural roller.

On the night of August 12–13 the 127th Brigade relieved the 126th in advanced posts which had only been occupied that afternoon. During the relief the enemy returned in great force and made three determined attacks to regain the lost position. They were beaten off with great loss. Corporal M. Shea, 6th Manchesters, in charge of a Lewis-gun section, though wounded in the first attack, stuck to his post and directed the fire of his gun. He was suffering extreme pain, but refused to go to the Aid Post until the third attack was finally beaten off and the situation saved.

The enemy now began to withdraw his battered line to more favourable defensive positions east of the Ancre. He was followed up closely, harassed constantly by artillery, machine-guns and infantry, and given no rest. Patrols found Watling Street untenanted except by dead Germans, and the trenches had been practically obliterated by the howitzers of the Divisional Artillery. By day and night field guns and heavies pounded the German trenches and strong points, and the effect of the " double crashes " fired nightly on roads behind the enemy positions, was shown a few days later when the troops crossed the Serre Ridge and saw the roads littered with damaged transport. Infantry patrols pushed forward and engaged his rearguards; successful raids and local attacks were made; and by August 20 the Division had passed beyond Serre village and had reached a line running just west of the Beaucourt–Puisieux road. The line had been advanced by 3500 yards on a front of 3800 yards, and many prisoners and much material had been captured. A message from Field-Marshal Sir Douglas Haig, congratulating the Division "on the vigour it has displayed in following up the retreating enemy," was much appreciated by all ranks.

For seventy-five days the Division had been in the line, an unusually long period. The heavy work upon the defensive system, the numerous raids and minor operations, the constant harassing of the enemy, the consolidating of the new positions gained, the advancement of the line with its added difficulties of transport and supply, all these—in the hottest months of the year—had imposed a great strain upon all units. But the troops were fired by enthusiasm, and had no desire to be relieved at such a time as this. Their one desire was to get the Boche on the run; and when the rumours of impending advances finally gave place to definite detailed orders and preparations, the weariness and strain were lightly cast aside. The Germans had done their worst, and had made deep impressions on the allied front. The 42nd Division now meant to go for the Hindenburg Line—and to " go one better."

CHAPTER XI

THE BEGINNING OF THE END

(*August 21st—September 6th*, 1918)

" *The Third Army has been ordered to press the enemy back towards Bapaume without delay, and to make every effort to prevent the enemy from destroying road and rail communications.*" The Battle Instructions issued to the 42nd Division on August 20th begin with the above words, and the Division rejoiced that the signal was down at last for the Third Army to join in the Great Allied offensive, and that General Byng's attack was planned to open before dawn on the morrow. The 4th Corps had three Divisions in the front line, the 42nd, the New Zealanders, and the 37th, from right to left. On the right of the 42nd was the 21st Division of the 5th Corps. The Division's attack was planned on a two-brigade front, with the 127th Brigade on the right, and the 125th on the left. There were three objectives. The first was a line roughly parallel to the present frontage of the Division and about a thousand yards to the east, and the advance was made by fighting patrols, brigades being in echelon with the left brigade leading. The second objective included some high ground on the left flank, and mainly concerned the 125th Brigade; and the third, and most important, objective was, on the left, Beauregard Dovecot, a group of shell-shattered trunks —the remains of trees which formerly surrounded the now obliterated Dovecot—on high ground where five roads meet, and on the right a point within a few hundred yards of the village of Miraumont, and looking down upon it.

The organization of the Division was now designed to secure effective co-operation of all arms under the new conditions of open warfare. The Division had done well in the stationary warfare of continuous lines of trenches; it had shaped still better in the offensive-defensive method of Defence in Depth in which it had been so thoroughly trained by its present Commander; now it was to be tested by the novel experience of open warfare. Infantry Brigade Groups were composed as follows—

    Infantry Brigade.
    Artillery Brigade.
    Machine-Gun Company (one or more).
    2 Sections Field Company, R.E.
    Cavalry or Tanks when available.

These were all under the command of the Infantry Brigadier, the Artillery Commander using the same headquarters where possible —a system that had distinct advantages over the old system of using an Artillery liaison officer.

At zero—4.55 a.m. on August 21—the guns opened. Four minutes later the 125th Brigade launched their attack, fighting patrols of the 5th L.F. advancing, under a creeping barrage, which lifted at an average rate of 100 yards every four minutes, against Hill 140, a strong point better known as *The Lozenge*. The opening moves were of a peculiarly delicate nature as, owing to the paucity of guns, the whole of the artillery and most of the machine-gun fire had to be concentrated first to form the barrage for the 125th Brigade, in order to make sure of The Lozenge, which was the key to the position, before being switched off, at the appointed time, to make a barrage for the 127th Brigade, and again switched to the left when the advance on the second objective was timed to start, at two hours after zero. There was a heavy ground mist—sure precursor of a hot day—and the ill-luck as regards weather conditions, which for some years had attended British offensives, was absent at last. But though the mist served as a screen, it increased the difficulties of keeping touch.

The Lozenge was a nest of machine-guns, and there was sharp and savage hand-to-hand fighting when the Bury men got in with the bayonet. They were better and more confident than the enemy at this game, and Jerry knew it; and when he found that he could not keep them from closing he realized that the game would soon be up, and his number also—or else his hands.

The guns switched over to the right, and at the appointed hour, 5.50 a.m., the 6th Manchesters on the right and the 7th on the left went over the top, and the 127th Brigade's first objective was also reached in good time, the barrage again assisting most effectively. A very difficult ravine had had to be crossed, with steep gradients down to and up from the Beaucourt–Puisieux road. This broken ground was defended by nests of machine-guns, but the friendly mist rendered their fire far less deadly than usual, and the Manchesters were able to get to close quarters. Many of the enemy were killed with the bayonet and a large number captured.

At 6.55 a.m. the 125th Brigade started for the second objective, and soon overcame all opposition. The attacks had been made with vigour and courage, but these qualities would have been unavailing had there been any flaw in the organization, planning, and timing, or in the co-operation between the artillery, machine-guns, aircraft and infantry. There was none, and both first and second objectives were secured and consolidated.

But neither brigade was able to gain the final objective at its first attempt, for the enemy was in great strength and, as he clearly regarded the positions attacked as very important, he fought around the Dovecot and in front of Miraumont with much courage and

SGT. E. SMITH, V.C., D.C.M., 1/5 BN. LANCASHIRE FUSILIERS.

determination. Owing to the mist touch had not been maintained between the 125th Brigade and the New Zealanders. When the mist lifted, the company of the 7th L.F., to whom the capture of the Dovecot had been entrusted, found that they were advancing upon an enemy battery, which opened fire at point-blank range. An attempt was made to hold a shell-hole position, but the enemy was in strong force, and a fierce counter-attack practically wiped out the defenders. However, in the course of the afternoon a joint attack by the two brigades drove the enemy from the entire line of the final objective, the 7th L.F., assisted by two machine-gun sections, capturing the Dovecot, while the Manchesters advanced along the top of the ridge, clearing the enemy out of his dug-outs, and established themselves before Miraumont. They repulsed a counter-attack in the afternoon, and later in the day another, made by picked storm-troops, was also beaten off. The capture of the high ground dominating the Ancre was a brilliant beginning to a victorious advance which was destined to continue until the beaten enemy sued for peace. Field guns, anti-tank guns, and a large number of machine-guns and prisoners had been taken. With this considerable success the day's fighting ended. But not its labour, for the newly-won positions had to be consolidated and all preparations made for the inevitable counter-attacks, so work went on steadily throughout the night.

In the course of the battle of the 21st August there had been a general high standard of courage and also many acts of heroism, some of which passed unnoticed, while some were rewarded. The outstanding valour and prowess of Lance-Sergeant Edward Smith, 5th L.F., at the capture of The Lozenge and subsequently, received the recognition they deserved, the Victoria Cross being awarded on the following grounds—

> For conspicuous gallantry, leadership and personal example during an attack on the 21st August and subsequent operations. This N.C.O. while in command of a platoon personally took a machine-gun post, rushing the garrison with his rifle and bayonet. The enemy, on seeing his advance, scattered to throw hand-grenades at him. Regardless of danger he shot and killed at least six of the enemy. Having done this he ordered his men to follow him, and mopped up two more machine-gun posts, again killing and capturing some of the garrison himself. A little later, seeing another platoon requiring assistance, he led his men to them, took command of the situation, and captured the objective, again killing many of the enemy himself. During the enemy counter-attack on the 22nd August he led a section forward and regained the line where it had been penetrated on his platoon front. This N.C.O.'s personal example of bravery, skill and initiative is worthy of the highest praise and reward. His conduct throughout exemplified magnificent courage and skill with his weapons, and in addition he displayed marked tactical

ability and command. All men around him were greatly inspired by his leadership and example.

At 2.30 a.m. on August 22nd the enemy artillery opened fire, and for an hour and a half the infantry along the whole of the divisional front and the batteries around Serre were vigorously bombarded, mainly with gas-shells. At 4.15 a.m. the expected counter-attack was delivered, and was repulsed with very heavy loss to the enemy at all points except at the Dovecot. The Germans debouching from Miraumont were shattered by steady, well-aimed fire from rifles, Lewis-guns, and machine-guns. The four guns of the section of " B " Company, M.G. Battalion, attached to the 125th Brigade, had been taken forward in front of the infantry, and these, assisted by flanking fire from " C " Company's machine-guns, with the 127th Brigade, completely broke up the attack on the right. On the left, however, posts of the 7th L.F. at the Dovecot were overrun after bitter fighting by overwhelming numbers, but the enemy was held on a line which the battalion had consolidated the previous afternoon just west of and overlooking the Dovecot. Two platoons of the 10th Manchesters (this battalion having been placed under the orders of the 125th Brigade) gave great assistance.

At 8.30 a.m. the enemy counter-attacked this new line and also the positions on the left of the divisional front held by the New Zealand Division. The attack was beaten back all along the line, and again the machine-guns contributed conspicuously to the success. The four guns of the forward section of " B " M.G. Company took the enemy waves in enfilade and broke them up utterly, the section capturing a number of prisoners and forcing more than 200 to surrender to the New Zealanders, who expressed their appreciation of the good work and efficient assistance rendered by the section. During this counter-attack a body of the enemy got through a gap between the two brigades, and all of them were killed or captured by a support section of the M.G. Battalion. Information obtained from prisoners proved that the counter-attacks had been made by four battalions of an entirely fresh enemy division—the 52nd German Naval Division—brought down from Flanders. A third counter-attack was made later in the day, but this, too, was beaten off, and in the evening and throughout the night the troops worked hard to consolidate their new positions, and prepared to follow up their successes. There was to be no rest for them or for the enemy.

The 21st and 22nd of August were days of extreme heat. Considerable movement had been made under a blazing sun, with heavy loads, over ground that had been badly gassed, and as fighting and work upon the new positions had been continuous for over forty hours there was a certain amount of exhaustion, and also some suffering from the heat. But there was none of the dejection and depression that usually accompany exhaustion. Instead, there was the consciousness of achievement, of triumph long deferred but now assured, and of buoyancy of spirit which could control the physical weariness and carry the tired body on and on to further and greater achievement. *Der Tag*—for years a subject of jest—had dawned at last, and its glorious opportunities were not to be thrown away because of a physical longing for rest and sleep. That the War must end some day every one knew; that it would end in victory for the Allies few of the soldiers doubted; but hope had been deferred so long, and disappointments had been so many and so great, that *après la guerre* had become a joke, a half-cynical allusion to a period as inevitable as death but much more remote. Now all was changed; the war had taken on an entirely new complexion, and " next spring," or even an earlier date, was spoken of with confidence, for at last, and for the first time, the Boche was on the run. His day was over and ours had dawned. Though his numbers were still equal or superior to ours, though his lines of defence were as formidable as the skill and ingenuity of the greatest masters of defensive warfare could make them, and though he would turn, snarling, and fight like a wolf at bay, our men had complete confidence in their skill with rifle and bayonet, their grit, and their will to conquer. They knew now that they were Jerry's master. There was an accumulation of old scores to wipe off, and though the beaten individual Boche would generally be treated with contemptuous good-humour, there remained the deep loathing of all the vile deeds by which the title of " Hun " had been earned. Exhaustion and physical distress were therefore thrust aside by the call for action.

At 2.30 a.m. on August 23 two companies of the 8th L.F. on the left and two of the 10th Manchesters on the right attacked the Dovecot. The enemy fought hard to retain his hold of this position, but the Salford and Oldham men fought still harder, and the Dovecot was finally won. Casualties were heavy on both sides. A number of prisoners were taken, and also a complete Field Dressing Station. The New Zealanders on the left advanced their right to conform; and their attack being successful they passed beyond the line of the 125th Brigade, which then swung forward its left flank until touch was restored and sent patrols down into the Miraumont Valley. During the night the 125th Brigade was relieved by the 126th (D Company, M.G. Battalion attached), which also took over 500 yards of front from the New Zealand Division, who were thus squeezed out by the 126th Brigade on their right and the 5th Division on the left.

To exploit victories the following method was adopted—

(a) Strong patrols, usually one platoon, would make good the ground by bounds. These patrols to be adequately supported.

(b) When patrols were definitely held up, and the enemy located, the artillery would bombard points of resistance, and patrols would advance under a creeping barrage.

(c) If the patrols were again held up, a set-piece attack would be organized.

In making these attacks the enemy's position would be turned from one or both flanks. Machine-gun sections were to be pushed up behind patrols close enough to give effective support by direct fire. At least one section R.E. to be with the advance-guard, and also parties of Tunnelling Companies, R.E., to locate and destroy road-mines and "booby-traps." The Pioneer Battalion would be available under the Divisional Commander's hand. The Commander of a higher formation must explain attack orders, personally or through a Staff Officer, verbally to the Commander of a lower formation, and wherever possible the objectives must be pointed out *on the ground* to the subordinate commanders who had to carry out the operation. Briefly, the policy was to command the battle from horseback and not by telephone from a dug-out.

The important village of Miraumont, situated to the south-east of the Dovecot on both banks of the River Ancre, and strongly held by the enemy, was the next objective. Its fall would force the Germans to abandon the line of the Ancre, so a stiff resistance was expected. On the night of the 23rd–24th August the 21st Division on the right had crossed the Ancre further south and obtained a footing upon Thiepval Ridge. On the morning of the 24th the British were above Miraumont on three sides, and about midday the 126th and 127th Brigades fought their way round the outskirts from the north and south respectively until they met on the eastern side. The river was low and there was little difficulty in finding fordable passages. To the south these were secured by patrols of the 6th and 7th Manchesters, while the 5th East Lancashires and the 10th Manchesters turned the position from the north. The capture of this place was a noteworthy example of well-planned and well-carried out co-operation between the artillery and infantry of the Division. Heavy guns pumped shells into the centre of the village; field-guns smothered the outer circumference with shrapnel to keep down the enemy machine-gun fire, while the two infantry brigades worked round outside. When the two columns met on the farther side the guns ceased fire, and at noon infantry patrols entered the town from all sides and "mopped up." Some snipers had to be disposed of, and there were a few house-to-house chases, but the majority of those who had been unable to withdraw before the completion of the encircling movement, were found ready, and indeed anxious, to surrender to any one. A stretcher-bearer of the 127th Brigade, who had fallen into German hands when searching for wounded in the mist of the early morning, proudly conducted about twenty of his now docile captors to meet the advancing patrols. A column of about 300 Germans, waving white flags, marched east out of Miraumont and surrendered. Many other prisoners, a complete battery of 5·9-inch howitzers, some 4·2-inch guns, and many machine-guns were captured. Our casualties were light in proportion to the success attained and to the loss inflicted on the enemy. The stretcher-bearers carried the wounded long distances over badly torn-up ground, in great heat, and under artillery and machine-gun fire.

The capture of Miraumont was promptly followed up, and within a few hours of its fall fighting patrols of the 126th Brigade had entered Pys, a village more than a mile to the east, on the heels of the enemy. The straggling village of Warlencourt–Eaucourt, about a mile and a half farther east, was the next objective. The forward move began at 7.30 p.m., the two brigades moving along parallel lines, the 126th Brigade to the north and in advance of the 127th Brigade. In spite of the difficulties of a night advance through unknown country against strong enemy forces, well furnished with machine-guns, the 5th East Lancashires made steady progress, pushing the enemy rearguard in front of them, following up warily but resolutely, and adding to their bag of prisoners from time to time. On the outskirts of the village the opposition increased in intensity, and the enemy line of resistance, 400 yards west of Warlencourt, was found too strong to be attacked without artillery preparation. The troops on the right and left were already some distance in the rear. An outpost line was put out, and both brigades took up positions affording cover from the heavy machine-gun fire with which the enemy swept the valley west of Warlencourt throughout the night. The 126th Brigade lay across the Loupart Wood road, north and north-east of the village, and the 127th on the western outskirts. After dawn the German fire slackened and patrols of the 7th Manchesters advanced. They encountered opposition which weakened by degrees, and at 10 a.m. on August 25 a company of the 7th entered Warlencourt and passed through it. The advance was then stopped, as the north-eastward advance of the 63rd Division squeezed out the 42nd, which withdrew to concentrate in the Miraumont–Pys area, where two days were passed in rest and recuperation.

The Corps Commander wired his congratulations to the Divisional Commander on the successful issue of these operations, and asked him " to convey to all troops under your command my thanks for their work during the past three days and to congratulate them on their success, which could only have been attained by great fighting capacity and endurance."

The Divisional Artillery was quickly called upon to assist the 63rd Division, which was in difficulties west of Le Barque and Thilloy, the troops being mown down by numerous enemy machine-guns posted in a sunken road between the two villages, and no amount of courage could prevail against the storm of bullets. After hurried reconnaissance the 210th and 211th Brigades, R.F.A., were rushed to positions by Loupart Wood, which was being heavily shelled at the time. A race between the two brigades ensued, the batteries trotting and even galloping to the positions by different routes. It was a perfect example of artillery manœuvre. At one moment an empty grass plain; a moment later a plain covered with the guns, wagons, and horses of eight batteries ! The instant the trails were dropped— before the horses had got clear of the positions—the S.O.S. went up, and forty-eight guns were belching fire practically simultaneously.

Each division in turn was brought out of the line for a day or

M

two in order that the offensive might be carried on with renewed vigour. Refreshing and necessary as the respite undoubtedly was, the troops, stimulated by the victories of the past few days and by the prospect of still greater successes, were glad to resume their vocation of "learning Jerry" to make war. The 42nd Division relieved the 63rd on the night of August 27–28 on a line running north and south of the village of Le Barque, a short distance beyond Warlencourt, with the 126th Brigade now on the right and the 127th on the left, each brigade having a frontage of 1000 yards. The enemy held the village of Thilloy, about a thousand yards east of this line, and two attacks by the 63rd Division had failed to dislodge him. Patrols found the village and the brickfields to the north held in force, and preparations were made to turn these positions from north and south. In the early morning of the 29th the withdrawal of the enemy from Bapaume, less than a mile to the north-east of the left flank of the Division, was reported, and patrols of the 5th Manchesters, finding that Thilloy was being evacuated in consequence, pushed through the village. At 6.30 a.m. the 126th Brigade (with " A " and " D " Companies, M.G. Battalion) was ordered to take over the divisional front with two battalions in the front line, and advance on Riencourt-les-Bapaume, the 127th Brigade dropping back into close support. Strong fighting patrols followed up the retiring enemy, but there was to be no "set-piece" attack, except under preliminary bombardment and creeping barrage. The 8th Manchesters on the right came under sharp machine-gun fire from Riencourt in front and from Beaulencourt on their right flank, and were held up. By nightfall the leading companies of the 5th E. Lancs. on the left had crossed the Bapaume–Peronne road and made good the high ground by the reservoir half a mile north-west of Riencourt. A frontal attack on the village from the west by companies of the 8th Manchesters failed, in spite of the most gallant efforts of all ranks, long distance machine-gun fire from Beaulencourt taking them in the flank and rear, and causing heavy casualties.

In the early hours of the 30th August patrols of the 5th E. Lancs. engaged the enemy in the outskirts north of the village. The German positions were, however, very strongly held, and their numerous machine-guns excellently posted and handled, and little progress could be made. Prisoners taken later stated that orders had been given that Riencourt must be held at all costs. Captain Dick, with two platoons of " A " Company, worked his way down a trench leading south-east towards an enemy position, until he could get dead ground almost up to the position. Making good use of this, he rushed the ridge, and the enemy bolted, giving easy targets at short range. He then led his two platoons against another position with such speed that only three of his men could keep up, but they proved too much for the nerves of the Germans, who fired wildly and missed. Captain Dick killed the officer, his three men wounded others, and the hands of the remaining forty-five went up. For this he was awarded the D.S.O. The battalion dug in, and the artillery shelled the ridge immediately north of the village, but patrols sent out to discover the result of the bombardment reported that the enemy machine-gun positions were still held too strongly to give any chance of getting to close quarters.

In the afternoon the 10th Manchesters were ordered to move into position for a night attack upon Riencourt. Crossing the Bapaume–Peronne road they were heavily shelled, and an enemy observation plane kept in touch only a few hundred feet above them. Machine-gun bullets raised spurts and dust all around or glanced off the stones, and several road-mines exploded close to where they passed, sending up great columns of earth. It was Oldham Wakes Friday, and the men talked of bygone wakes and of the people at home, and made grim jests in contrasting past and present. " A " Company, on the left, worked round to the north-east and lay out in a fold of the ground until the barrage should lift. " D " Company, on the right, had to get through a lot of wire, and, being held up for a time, suffered rather severely. H.E. and shrapnel rained upon the German positions so thickly that it seemed as though they must be obliterated, but as soon as the two companies launched their attack, on the lifting of the barrage, they were met by a hail of shrapnel and machine-gun bullets. Bending their heads to the storm the first wave went steadily forward and at dusk forced their way into the village, where dumps of smoke-shells, trench-mortar shells and Very lights, left behind in the March retreat, exploded from time to time. Enemy infantry and machine-gunners fought courageously, taking up one position after another, as they were forced back. But the second wave pushed through the centre of the village, and getting on the flank killed or captured the crews of the machine-guns. As the Germans were bringing up considerable reinforcements from Villers-au-Flos, " C " Company was rushed forward, the three companies were linked up, and the enemy driven off with heavy loss. Soon after dawn " B " Company was moved up from reserve and the line advanced 300 yards on the left flank. The enemy brought up more machine-guns and even a light field-gun which fired at point-blank range, and made desperate efforts to recover the lost ground, but fighting patrols dealt with them, and Riencourt and its outskirts were finally won. Two field-guns were taken, and one of these was promptly turned against its former owners by gunners of the 210th Brigade. The capture of Riencourt was a brilliant affair, carried to a successful issue against great odds by the clever handling of the companies engaged and the dash and keenness of the infantry and machine-gunners. The Divisional Commander was prompt to show his appreciation in a telegram to the Battalion Commander. During the Riencourt operations there were numerous instances of individual daring, initiative, and resource. After the capture of the village, Captain J. A. C. Taylor, D.S.O., whose leadership of " A " Company, 10th Manchesters, contributed greatly to success, led a Lewis-gun section against the enemy on his flank, and drove them out of a trench and sunken road, killing a large number and capturing three prisoners and a machine-gun. After this he led an attack against a machine-gun post, which he captured. Lance-Sergeant H. Harrison, 8th Manchesters, on his own initiative went through an intense artillery barrage and heavy machine-gun fire in daylight and dressed the wounded who had been left behind close to the enemy's position, when the 8th Manchesters were ordered to withdraw on the night of August 29–30. At night he returned with stretcher-bearers and collected all the wounded in the area. For this he was awarded a bar to the Military Medal which he had gained in March for a similar bit of work. A more humorous incident was that of the 10th Manchester stretcher-bearer who brought in a number of prisoners whom he had cowed with an empty beer-bottle—his only weapon. A group of about twenty Germans, who had been holding a post some distance east of the village, had evidently heard of the good times enjoyed by prisoners in England, so instead of retiring to fight again another day, they waited to be gathered in. Somehow they were ignored by mopping-up patrols, and were no doubt hurt by this lack of consideration. While debating on their next step a British contact 'plane appeared, and on its approach they waved handkerchiefs attached to rifles, and walked complacently into their cage.

Their brilliant success in this and other night attacks led the 10th Manchesters to adopt the nickname of "The Night-jars." The Divisional Commander's predilection for night attacks was completely vindicated on each such occasion, and casualties were much fewer than would have been the case in daylight attacks, even under the best artillery barrage. But thoroughly trained, confident, and trustworthy troops are necessary for success in night attacks, and the General's confidence in his officers and men was always justified.

The 8th Manchesters and the 5th E. Lancs. were relieved during the night of the 30th–31st by the 127th Brigade, and they went into Divisional Reserve at Pys, the 125th Brigade becoming support brigade in Thilloy. The relief by the 6th Manchesters was carried out under difficult circumstances, as the battle raged inside and around Riencourt, and the position was obscure. The battalion to be relieved could not supply guides, so Lieut.-Colonel T. Batherwick, M.C., commanding the 6th Manchesters, made an exhaustive personal reconnaissance amid heavy bursts of shell and machine-gun fire, and returned to lead in two companies. He then made a second personal reconnaissance under similar conditions before taking in the remainder of the battalion. For this and for his part in the success at Miraumont the D.S.O. was awarded. After the relief of the two battalions had been completed the 10th Manchesters remained for a day or two in the front line, attached to the 127th Brigade. After the capture of Riencourt there was no further fighting of any importance on August 31, the rest of the day being spent in consolidating the positions taken up around the village.

On September 1 the 127th Brigade, by pushing out to the left, got into touch with the New Zealanders on the high ground north-east of Riencourt. The situation was unsatisfactory on the right, as this

Villers-au-Flos, September 2

flank was much exposed to the enemy in Beaulencourt, which still held out against the 5th Corps. The next objective was Villers-au-Flos, about a mile south-east of Riencourt, and the attack on this thickly-wooded and strongly-held position was made by the 5th Manchesters on the right and the 6th Manchesters on the left at 5.15 a.m. on September 2, after eight minutes' bombardment. The two battalions and a company of the 7th Manchesters attached to the 5th went forward in fine style in the face of a very stiff resistance, under a creeping barrage which lifted 100 yards every three minutes. Very stiff fighting took place the moment the advance began, for the barrage, though heavy and accurate, was not sufficient to overcome opposition, and the infantry had to provide additional covering-fire to enable detachments to advance without losing the barrage. The accuracy and quickness of fire of the Stokes gunners attached to each of the leading battalions destroyed a machine-gun nest and two German trench-mortars which had caused numerous casualties. On the left good progress was made, but on the right the 5th Manchesters had a harder task, their right flank being swept by the fire of a number of machine-gun posts, but this was overcome by a noteworthy instance of co-operation. An aviator, seeing that the infantry were in difficulties, flew over the German posts and attacked them with machine-gun fire, and at the same time a battery of 18-pounders was withdrawn from the barrage and switched on the machine-gun nests, while trench-mortars, machine-guns and neighbouring infantry, on their own initiative, brought their full available volume of fire to bear. This proved too much for the Germans, a number of whom surrendered, and the 5th and 7th Manchesters went forward. Stiff fighting continued, for the enemy made skilful use of the cover of ruined houses, hedges, and bushes, but once at close quarters the Manchesters made short work of the Germans, who suffered heavily. The Stokes gunners, after using up all their bombs, fixed bayonets and joined heartily in the hand-to-hand fighting. They were gallantly led by Lieutenant R. H. Welch, commanding the 127th Light T.M. Battery, who was awarded the D.S.O. Light carriages had been improvised for the 6-inch mortars, and these vied with the Stokes mortars in close support of the infantry. They had to be man-handled across rough ground, but in spite of the weight of mortars and heavy ammunition they were brought into action in forward positions in astonishingly quick time. Two fighting tanks had been detailed to take part in the attack. One broke down, but the other passed through the village with the infantry and gave very valuable assistance by destroying machine-gun posts. A supply tank delivered small-arm ammunition and drinking water close behind the front line. Before noon Villers-au-Flos had been thoroughly mopped up, and the 127th Brigade was consolidating its new positions beyond the village. Three hundred prisoners, a battery of 77 mm. guns, eighteen machine-guns and much material had been captured, and the enemy's loss in killed and wounded was very great.

In a Special Order of the Day Brigadier-General Henley congratulated the 127th Brigade on "adding a new anniversary to those which your gallantry has already made famous. . . . Yesterday, after three months of unbroken fighting in trenches and in the open, and in face of stubborn resistance by Huns more than equal in numbers, you stormed and took Villers-au-Flos with the utmost dash and determination—a feat which would have been notable if performed by battalions at full strength and fresh from a period of rest. When Manchester hears of this new proof of your prowess, she may well be as proud of her sons as I am of commanding such soldiers."

The New Zealanders on the left and the 21st Division on the right had also made good progress, but the 42nd Division had again gone farther forward than either, and in consequence the 127th Brigade was in a pronounced salient, exposed to enfilade fire on both flanks. The machine-gun sections which had advanced with the battalions applied themselves with zest to keep down the enemy's fire, and they dealt with it very effectively. In the early afternoon the New Zealanders on the left made a further attack and came up into line with the 6th Manchesters, thus easing the situation on that flank. In the evening the 5th and 6th Manchesters were relieved by the 7th Manchesters and 8th Lancashire Fusiliers. At night the heavy and field artillery shelled Barastre and Haplincourt Wood in preparation for the morrow's advance upon those places. In the early hours of September 3, however, patrols of the 8th L.F. and the 7th Manchesters found that the enemy had retired and that Barastre and Haplincourt Wood were empty. The fighting at Villers-au-Flos had evidently hit the enemy hard, and the Division made haste to exploit its success. The 125th Brigade was ordered to "leap-frog" through the 127th, and this was completed at 10 a.m., the 8th L.F. finding the advance-guard. It was a most exhilarating advance, reminding one of a Field Day on Salisbury Plain, and a new thrill was provided when a troop of the Scots Greys passed through and exchanged greetings with the infantry. Warfare had become more and more open recently, but this was the real genuine article. Cavalry going into action on horseback was a pleasant and cheering sight, and its significance was realized. The foot-sloggers grinned and waved their hands, wishing them the best of luck. The battalions in the rear were also witnessing sights, perhaps not so striking in their appeal to the eye, but hardly less significant of the change that had come over the scene. The whole British Army seemed on the move, and the roads were packed with transport. There were field artillery drawn by teams of mules, 6-inch howitzers bouncing along behind motor-lorries, dumps in process of removal, tanks, busses, field-kitchens, cable-wagons, observation-balloons attached to motor-cars with the observer at a height of 100 feet, and every variety of vehicle hastening in the wake of the retreating foe. The railways had been entirely destroyed, and much damage had been done to the roads, especially at the cross-roads. The traffic was constantly checked, or if possible diverted, while huge craters were filled in, but all diffi-

To Old Members of the 42nd (East Lancs) Division.

The objects of the 42nd (East Lancs) Division Old Members' Association are :-

1. —To maintain the spirit of comradeship by keeping old members of the Division in touch and by giving them an opportunity of meeting one another at Social Gatherings held from time to time.

2. —To assist Old Members of the Division and the Widows and Dependents of those who served in it. Not only is financial assistance given in deserving cases, but members are helped in every possible way.

By joining the Association you are helping yourself and helping your old comrades too

**

SUBSCRIPTIONS (Annual)

Officers	5/-
Other ranks	1/-

SUBSCRIPTIONS (Life)

Officers	£1
Other ranks	5/-

**

Nearly all the units of which the 42nd Division is comprised have Regimental Old Members' Associations and most of these have arranged that, for old members of the Division, subscription to the Regimental O.M.A. covers membership of the Divisional Association as well without further payment.

If you served overseas with the Division and are not already a member of the O.M.A., apply to the Headquarters of your old unit or write to the Secretary of the

    42nd Division, O.M.A.,
     H. Q. 8th Lancashire Fusiliers,
      Lower Broughton,
        Manchester.

RIENCOURT-LES-BAPAUME.

VILLERS-AU-FLOS.

TRESCAULT ROAD, LEADING THROUGH HAVRINCOURT WOOD.

A SLEEPER TRACK THROUGH HAVRINCOURT WOOD.

TRESCAULT WATER POINT.

culties were overcome, and the transport and supply services got through Barastre without a halt, and at 1 p.m. the village of Bus, three miles beyond Villers-au-Flos, was entered. By 6 p.m. Ytres, the day's final objective, had been gained, and now the Division was on familiar ground. On the left touch had been maintained throughout with the New Zealanders, who had made equally rapid progress, but the division on the right had met with greater opposition, and was 1000 yards behind.

With Metz-en-Couture as the objective the advance was resumed at 7 a.m. on September 4, the 5th L.F. leading. The night had been remarkable for the intensity of the enemy's gas bombardment, and this continued throughout the day. Ytres, Bus, and indeed most of the positions in the divisional area were drenched with gas, and box-respirators had to be worn for hours at a time. In addition to the bombardment the troops were bombed by successive flights of enemy aircraft. Fighting patrols crossed the Canal du Nord without much opposition, but considerable resistance was met with at Neuville-Bourjonval, and the advance-guard was checked in the outskirts of this village. The division on the right had been held up at the Canal, which they could not cross, and until they could accomplish this it would be useless to incur heavy losses in capturing the village while the Division's right flank was in the air. In the evening four strong patrols were sent out under a barrage to make good the village and the trench system beyond, and the two northern patrols penetrated the enemy's trenches and took prisoners. On the morning of the 5th the village was cleared, but the enemy still held a trench system to the east. This was attacked in the afternoon by a company of the 7th L.F., in conjunction with an attack on the left by the New Zealand Division, and all guns of " B " Company, M.G. Battalion, assisted in placing a box-barrage round the objective. The attack was brilliantly successful, the trench system being captured and more than 100 prisoners taken, with very slight loss to the company. On the night of September 5-6 the Division, less the artillery which remained in the line, was relieved by the New Zealanders, and moved back to the Pys–Thilloy area, with D.H.Q. in a German ammunition dump at Riencourt. The Divisional Artillery had some strenuous days with the New Zealanders, the casualties at Metz-en-Couture being heavy. Some of the batteries fired 5000 rounds, and one battery nearly 6000, in a day.

The sixteen days from August 21st to September 5th had been a period of continuous victory in which every unit shared. The ease with which the troops shook out into open warfare after a long period in the trenches was remarkable, advanced artillery sections and often advanced batteries moving in close support of the infantry. The shooting of the artillery and the accuracy of their barrages earned the praise and the thanks of the infantry, and the gunner can hardly wish for a greater reward. The continual night work involved in bringing up the very large supplies of gun ammunition required in modern battles was most wearing for drivers and lorries, but the guns were fed. Light trench-mortars were frequently used in close support of advanced infantry, and when the ammunition was expended the men acted as infantry with marked success. The M.G. Battalion was consistently good. At critical moments officers and N.C.O.s showed admirable resource and initiative, and the guns were handled with skill and daring. The system of pack transport, to which great attention had been paid during training, enabled gunners, where their fire would prove a deciding factor, to take up positions in advance of the infantry.

The water-supply was the chief problem of the R.E., and the exceptional experience of the C.R.E., Lieut.-Colonel J. G. Riddick, with water difficulties in Gallipoli and Sinai proved invaluable to the Division.* This part of France had little surface water. There was none between the Ancre at Miraumont and the Canal du Nord at Ytres, and the shafts of village wells had been blown in by the enemy. By the capture of Miraumont control of the sources of the Ancre was obtained, and the engineers of the 42nd and New Zealand Divisions at once got to work on the erection of dozens of horse-troughs and a number of water-cart filling-points. During the advance beyond Miraumont all water had to be carried forward in Garford lorries to some improvised water-point as near the firing-line as possible. At this point canvas tanks of 2300 or 9000 gallons capacity were erected, and the lorries were at work at all hours of the day and night to keep the tanks filled. Lift-and-force pumps were then installed, and by their means the battalion water-carts were supplied. Credit is due to Lieut.-Colonel R. J. Slaughter, D.S.O., and the "Q" department for their excellent organization, upon which the advance depended. Artillery horses had to be watered at the occasional foul village ponds until damaged wells could be re-opened, a difficult task which the R.E. accomplished by working day and night. The need for water was so urgent that at times the Garford lorries had to be hurried forward along by-roads before the tunnellers and sappers had completed road reconnaissance, and one of these was blown to pieces by a road-mine, and its drivers killed.

The Signal Company established Visual Stations as far forward as possible, and also supplemented electrical communications by using wireless, pigeons, and Mounted Orderlies. The destruction of roads in the line of advance, and the multitude of shell-holes which pitted the face of the country, made conditions exceptionally difficult for the R.A.S.C., but supplies never failed, thanks to the energy and skill with which the 7th N.F. Pioneers repaired and re-

---

* "Riddick was a tower of strength, combining energy, capability, and inventive genius with other soldierly qualities. His gallantry and unassuming loyalty to the Division could not be surpassed. Under his leadership no job of work, from constructing mined dug-outs or bridging rivers in the face of close enemy opposition, to fighting in the front line, came amiss to the sappers of the Divisional R.E."—*Extract from letter of the Divisional Commander to the author.*

Captures and Casualties

made the roads, and to the expert work of the sappers and tunnellers who unearthed innumerable booby-traps on roads and in dug-outs. Supply tanks gave invaluable aid in bringing up trench mortars, water and ammunition of all kinds. The work of the R.A.M.C. was carried out skilfully and with creditable smoothness, casualties being treated and evacuated with a degree of comfort that could hardly have been expected under the conditions of constant movement, the Field Ambulances keeping up with the infantry, and setting up Aid Posts wherever they could find suitable shelter. Stretcher-bearers went through shell and machine-gun fire calmly and deliberately in the performance of their duties. Officers and men from the highest to the lowest, had complete confidence in one another.*

In short, it was efficiency in all branches that enabled the Division to advance a distance of fifteen and a half miles in sixteen days, against a strong and desperate foe, across country which gave every advantage to the defence, and in that short period to capture the towns and villages of Miraumont, Pys, Warlencourt, Thilloy, Ligny-Thilloy, Riencourt, Villers-au-Flos, Bus, Barastre, Ytres, and Neuville-Bourjonval. One thousand two hundred and sixty-one prisoners passed through the Divisional Cages and Dressing Stations, 24 guns of all calibres up to 8-inch, 50 heavy and more than 100 light machine guns, 16 trench-mortars, and a large quantity of material of war were taken. The casualties of the Division were: 20 officers and 233 other ranks killed, 49 officers and 1256 other ranks wounded, but the loss inflicted upon the enemy was calculated at four times that number. It was a magnificent record which well deserved the Divisional Commander's Special Order of the Day, of September 6, 1918—

" In March of this year I had the honour of congratulating you on the valour and good work displayed by all ranks of all arms and services in a defensive battle. To-day I am proud to find that my confidence in you to live up to the Divisional Motto in an offensive battle has been more than fulfilled.

" In seventeen days continuous fighting you have accounted for, at the very lowest computation, more than a whole enemy division.

---

* The relations between officers and men are exemplified in the following extracts from two letters to the mother of an officer, the first being from the officer himself, dated September 4, 1918, and the second from a sergeant after the officer's death—

" Oh, my splendid men ! Even the most unlikely ones did wonders, and I never felt so proud of men ! . . . It speaks volumes for Englishmen and for the righteousness of our cause. The British Tommy is a great man, and don't let any one forget it."

" His thoughts were always for the boys. He helped them in all fatigues as one of themselves. He worked like a slave carrying tents and doing anything to make the boys comfortable. When he saw that one of us was tired he would do his two hours trench patrol himself. . . . I fairly trembled for his safety on many occasions. . . . His first greeting was : ' Well, sergeant, are the boys comfortable ? ' He thought all the world of his platoon, and they just idolized him."

"Officers, N.C.O.s and men of the East Lancashire Division, I congratulate you on your valiant deeds, and in the name of our King and Country, I thank you for the good work you have done.

"As to the future, I remain confident that, if possible, even better work will be done, and the enemy will have further cause to regret meeting the East Lancashire Division."

The Division was no less proud of its Commander, and its confidence in him was unbounded.

CHAPTER XII

THROUGH THE HINDENBURG LINE

(September 7–30, 1918)

ALONG the entire front from the Belgian coast to Alsace the Allied advance progressed with a vigour and speed that surpassed the hopes of the civilized nations, and now began seriously to sap the morale of the Hun. One of the many satisfactory results of this rapid progress was the shortening of the front, in consequence of which divisions were squeezed out of the line at the conclusion of each move forward by the overlapping of divisions on either flank. Sometimes a division that had penetrated farther than its flanking divisions would be squeezed out when these drew level; at times a division that had encountered greater opposition, and had had to fight for every yard of ground, would be overlapped by troops which had advanced beyond it across less difficult country. Divisions were thus given more frequent opportunities for recuperation and reorganization, and for the training of the new drafts which were being hurried across the sea to repair the heavy losses inseparable from even the most successful assault.

Though the casualties of the 42nd Division had been small in comparison with the value of its accomplishment and the loss it had inflicted upon the enemy, it had suffered severely; and a fortnight of rest, recreation, and training in villages through which its recent victorious advance had been made was a boon that was much appreciated. A number of tents were provided, but the greater part of the troops had to dig in, or repair damaged German shelters. There was no lack of material, so weather-proof and fairly comfortable quarters were soon available. Each brigade of the Divisional Artillery was granted a brief respite of three or four days in which to " wash and brush up," and get a little sleep after their exacting toil. D.H.Q. was at Riencourt in a German ammunition dump, at one end of which was a kind of museum containing a specimen of every variety of shell in the dump. The whole area from Bus-en-Artois to Ytres was utterly devastated, and the once flourishing town of Bapaume was a heap of brickdust. Horrible evidences of recent fighting and of the battles of early spring were oppressively apparent. But the Division was now inured to horrors —not callous to suffering, but accustomed to death, and able to look it in the face. Men would risk all to save an injured comrade, and would even do much to assist a badly wounded enemy, but once a man was dead they accepted philosophically the fact that there was no help for it, and they had better think of something else. The interest and physical effort of sports and games, hard work and training helped men to forget. The training was of a thoroughly practical nature in attacks against strong positions, all arms co-operating; and officers and men threw themselves into it with a zest that clearly indicated their determination not only to " go one better " than the enemy, but also to eclipse their own previous performances. The spirit of the men is illustrated by a story told to the C.R.A. by the Commander of the N.Z. Division. A diminutive Lancashire lad was found in the New Zealanders' trenches. On being asked what he was doing there he replied, " Just looking round," and added in explanation : " We're waiting out at rest just behind you chaps until the next attack starts. We're the Storm Troops, you see ! "

Ever since first meeting the New Zealanders in the early spring, about Hebuterne, the two divisions had been firm friends. The N.Z.s were very big men with big strength, ideas, and hearts, but they exhibited great liking for their brothers of smaller stature from Lancashire, and recognized that small bodies may contain very big hearts. They were unfailingly ready to co-operate in any work that would help to beat the Boche. The nickname of " The Pull-Throughs," which they gave to the Division, contained an uncomplimentary allusion to the size of the men—the flannel pull-through measuring four inches by two inches—and at the same time an appreciative reference to the way in which they invariably pulled through each task entrusted to them. Another division with which the 42nd had been brought into the closest touch was the 37th—a very fine division. The relations between the 37th and 42nd were always most cordial, and each knew that it could always rely upon the other's whole-hearted co-operation.

On the night of September 21–22 the Division relieved the 37th Division in the left sector of the 4th Corps front, rather more than a mile east of Havrincourt Wood, and just east of Trescault, places with which the Division had made acquaintance in the spring of 1917. D.H.Q. was moved to Velu Wood, taking over what had been the H.Q. of the German 14th Reserve Corps, a beautifully fitted place in the middle of a copse, completed by the enemy just in time to serve the Division. The 126th Brigade, now under the command of Brig.-General T. H. S. Marchant, D.S.O., held the line, 2500 yards in width, with all three battalions. On the night of the relief Havrincourt Wood was heavily gassed, between 2000 and 3000 Yellow Cross shells being used. In spite of excellent gas discipline casualties were severe, and these included Lieut.-Colonel Peel, D.S.O., commanding the 10th Manchesters, who, though badly gassed, refused to go down the line. From the 22nd to the 26th September the front was quiet, activity being confined

UNSEEN TRENCH, PART OF THE HINDENBURG LINE S.E. OF HAVRINCOURT.

ANOTHER TRENCH IN THE HINDENBURG DEFENCE SYSTEM NEAR HAVRINCOURT.

The Objectives, September 27

to the gunners and to patrols. The latter were vigorous and successful, capturing prisoners and improving the position east of Trescault at Bilhem Farm. Further south, a daylight patrol of the 5th East Lancashires did good work in front of Beaucamp, a strongly held village in the 5th Division's area.

On the night of September 26th the front was taken over by the 125th Brigade on the right and the 127th on the left, preparatory to one of the most ambitious attacks ever made by the 42nd or any other division. This was no less than the piercing of the famous Hindenburg trench system, by smashing a way through a two-mile depth of the most strongly and scientifically defended positions in the history of warfare. The enemy had succeeded in withdrawing his battered troops, and had placed fresh divisions in line opposite the 4th Corps front. These were given complete assurance that the British advance would be held up at this " impregnable " line, which would be their winter position, and against which the Allies would fling themselves in vain. German orders issued at this date laid down that not a foot of ground was to be given up here.

The objectives of the 4th Corps and of the corps on its left consisted of two main ridges—the Beaucamp Ridge to the south and the Flesquières Ridge to the north. These were separated by the Ribecourt Valley. From the Beaucamp Ridge three large spurs projected northward into the valley, and these spurs formed the objectives of the Division. The most easterly of the three spurs (which are separated by deep re-entrants and very steep gradients) was known as Highland Ridge, and this is the highest and steepest of the three. East of Highland Ridge the ground drops abruptly to the narrow Couillet Valley, running south to north into the Ribecourt Valley. Beyond the Couillet Valley the ground rises sharply to Welsh Ridge. The great double row of trenches of the Hindenburg Line extended diagonally across the spurs, facing approximately S.S.W.

The 42nd Division was on the left of the 4th Corps front, with the 5th Division on its right and the 3rd Division (6th Corps) on its left. The " jumping-off " line was roughly about 600 to 1000 yards east of Havrincourt village on the north and of Trescault on the south. The attack was to be made in five bounds, the successive objectives being termed the *Black, Red, Brown, Yellow,* and *Blue Lines,* the summit of Highland Ridge being the Blue Line, which was more than two miles east of the starting line of the 127th Brigade on the left and rather less from the 125th's line on the right. On reaching Highland Ridge patrols were to be sent into the Couillet Valley and on to Welsh Ridge as far as a *Green Line* about two miles beyond the Blue Line. The bounds were to be made by the leap-frog method, companies passing over one another in turn as each objective was secured. " B " and " C " Companies of the M.G. Battalion would accompany the 127th and 125th Brigades respectively; " A " and " D " Companies would take part in the barrage. Zero hour for the Third Army was fixed at 5.20 a.m. on September 27th; but as the 3rd Division on the left and the 5th Division on the right would advance along higher ground than the 42nd, it was arranged that the 42nd should not move until these divisions had had time to make good the higher ground on its flanks. The Lancashire Fusiliers were therefore timed to leave at 7.52 a.m., and the Manchesters at 8.20 a.m.

The attack was preceded by a short intense bombardment by six brigades of Field Artillery, one brigade of Heavy Artillery, and the trench mortars; and at its scheduled time each infantry brigade advanced in successive waves under a creeping barrage of shrapnel and machine-gun bullets. Two Mark IV tanks were allotted to the 125th Brigade and six to the 127th, but two of these broke down at the start, a third developed engine trouble, and by noon a fourth and fifth were put out of action after doing useful work.* The assistance of the others in dealing with machine-gun nests was very valuable, and they were handled with great skill.

Unfortunately the attack of the division on the right was held up all morning by the very strong enemy defences around Beaucamp, a commanding position on the right flank of the 125th Brigade's line of advance. The 7th and 8th L.F. were thus exposed to a terrible enfilading fire from the high ground about Beaucamp, and the leading companies were practically blotted out. Within half an hour of the start all the officers of one company of the 8th L.F., and all but one of each of two other companies, had been killed or wounded. With great gallantry the two battalions persisted in face of a murderous fire, but the failure to drive the enemy out of Beaucamp made it impossible for the Fusiliers to get beyond their first objective, the Black Line, until towards midday. The right of the 127th Brigade, which had made good progress, was thus left in the air. The leading wave of the 5th Manchesters had advanced over Trescault Ridge in fine style, and had gained the first objective within the scheduled time, with considerable, but not disproportionate, loss. The 6th and 7th Manchesters, dividing the front equally, passed through the 5th, and, though badly knocked about by machine-gun fire, both from the front and the unprotected right flank, they made good the Red and Brown Lines in the course of the forenoon, and the 7th Manchesters captured two 77 mm. guns. With bomb and bayonet they turned the Germans out of their huge and elaborate dug-outs in batches of twenty and thirty, about 400 being taken in the first three hours by the 127th Brigade and the Machine-Gun Company, which had gone forward with its usual dash, and had selected its positions and handled its weapons with much coolness and skill. More than 350 enemy dead were buried later in the area between the Black and Brown Lines.

On the right of the 127th Brigade's front the 7th Manchesters

---

* One tank caught fire and had to be abandoned on the ridge east of Trescault. It carried a number of T.M. bombs, and presented a most ludicrous spectacle, hopping about like a wounded rabbit as each bomb exploded.

were wholly exposed to enfilade fire from the high ground to the south—for Beaucamp still defied the division on the right—and their casualties were grievous : 450 men of this battalion went over at 8.20 a.m.; only 150 were left at the end of the day, and of 16 officers only 4 remained. Two determined counter-attacks were made against the 7th Manchesters on the Brown Line, but " B " Company flung back a defensive flank and held the ground, the machine-gunners doing great execution. Further progress was impossible until touch had been regained with the 125th Brigade. By 11.30 a.m. the 1st Cheshires had mopped up Beaucamp, and the Lancashire Fusiliers were now able to make progress towards the Red Line, and cleared up Boar Copse with the assistance of one of the tanks. At 1.30 p.m. they had passed the second objective and were approaching the Brown Line, overcoming fierce resistance and inflicting heavy losses on the enemy. By 2.30 p.m. a company of the 6th Manchesters, consisting of 2 officers and 30 other ranks, had reached the Yellow Line, on the extreme left of the divisional boundary, joining hands with the 187th Brigade of the 3rd Division in Ribecourt, and about the same time an equally weak company of the 7th Manchesters was on this line, and the enemy was being turned out of his network of dug-outs. The German machine-gunners were specially selected and trained men of undoubted valour, and as a rule they would work their guns and fight to the death. But the infantry, though they would fight well under the protection of the machine-guns, were cowed by the bayonet when close quarters were reached, and would then surrender with curious docility, and often, indeed, with eagerness. The Manchesters could spare no men as escorts for prisoners; they simply waved them to the rear, and the Boches meekly obeyed, too glad to be out of the fighting to attempt to take advantage of the disproportion between captors and captives by acts of treachery. There were exceptions, of course, and on one such occasion a mud-begrimed private approached his officer with : " Beg pardon, sir, 'ave I your permission to shoot one of the prisoners who threw a bomb at us after putting 'is 'ands up? " " Certainly," replied the officer. The man looked relieved. " That's all right, sir. I 'ave shot the blighter."

The 127th Brigade was now linked up with the 62nd Division, which had passed through the 3rd Division and now occupied Ribecourt. During the afternoon there was a lull in the fighting. The company objectives were in some cases on a frontage of 600 yards, and numbers were now so small that commanders had not men enough to attack on so broad a front. Little parties gained ground as they could, but reorganization and reinforcement were necessary before a further assault on a large scale could be made. On both sides the artillery was on the move, our batteries pushing forward, theirs retiring to avoid risk of capture. It was becoming evident that the enemy's strength was failing, and that the spirit had been hammered out of him. It had been a soldier's battle of ding-dong fighting against an enemy possessing the advantage of the strongest possible positions combined with superiority in numbers of men and of machine-guns. To win success against such odds required skill with weapons—bullet, bayonet, and bomb—and also the finest qualities of initiative, resource, determination, and endurance on the part of subordinate leaders and men, and this skill and these qualities had been shown in a high degree. When company, platoon, and section commanders fell, junior N.C.O.s and even privates had proved that they could lead. By sunset more than a thousand prisoners, including two battalion commanders and a complete headquarters staff, had been passed through the divisional cage. The artillery had contributed splendidly to the successful issue of the day, and the rapidity with which they had moved into action in new advanced positions had been remarkable.

Orders were issued to attack the Blue Line during the night. As the 6th and 7th Manchesters had lost so large a proportion of their officers and men, the 10th Manchesters were placed at Brig.-General Henley's disposal for the operation, and this battalion was brought up into the Yellow Line and moved into its positions for the assault in pitch darkness. On the right of the divisional front the 5th Lancashire Fusiliers passed through the 7th and 8th Battalions on the Brown Line, in preparation for the attack. Zero hour was altered from 1.30 a.m., September 28, as originally fixed, to 2.30 a.m., at the request of the division on the right; and at the latter hour, the waning moon being now up, the 10th Manchesters and the 5th L.F. moved off with fine dash under a creeping barrage.* The attack was successful along the whole front, and by 6 a.m. the Oldhamers had secured the final objective and the Bury men had passed the Yellow Line and were approaching Highland Ridge. " B " Company, M.G. Battalion, again distinguished itself by engaging two German field-guns and destroying the crews. The company commander, Major E. W. C. Flavell, personally engaged one of the guns and forced the enemy to abandon it. Both guns were captured later. Throughout the operations of these two days

* The following description of the barrage is taken from an officer's letter, dated 30-9-18—

" Dawn had not quite broken, and a half moon was shining in a cloudless sky. All was as quiet as the grave when suddenly a big gun fired, and instantaneously, from one end of the horizon to the other, the barrage started. . . . Looking back it seemed that the sky was on fire for miles and miles, and the ground shook. In front there was one long flickering crashing line of bursting shells—a wall of fire 70 yards in front of us. What a barrage it was! I believe we could have followed it to Berlin. . . . A barrage is a terrifying thing to be under, as always a few men are knocked out by splinters or 'shorts,' but it is necessary to keep right under it and prevent the Boche putting his head up before you are on top of him. We would advance, then kneel down to wait for the barrage to creep forward, and by the light of the bursting shells I could see right down the line, and it was a wonderful sight. The men were in as straight a line as though dressed on parade, every man motionless on one knee, the moon glinting on bayonet and steel helmet. As we went forward again, the line would break up as men darted in and out of trenches and shell-holes to clear out the Boche, and then ' back again to the line of the barrage ! ' That is the secret of success."

Welsh Ridge, September 28

the machine-gunners of all companies fought their guns splendidly, and took a number of prisoners. Lieut.-Colonel W. K. Tillie, commanding the M.G. Battalion, did work of great value in making most daring reconnaissances. The 10th Manchesters took more than 250 prisoners and the 5th L.F. a large number and also a 77 mm. gun with gun-team. The enemy, plainly demoralized, could be seen from the edge of Couillet Valley moving in straggling parties eastwards and upwards towards Welsh Ridge, where a stand was to be expected. The 10th Manchesters at once sent patrols into the valley and across the railway, and at 8.15 a.m. " A " Squadron, 3rd Hussars, was ordered up from Velu and placed at the disposal of Brig.-General Henley. At 10.30 a.m. the cheering report arrived that the Oldham patrols had gained a footing on Welsh Ridge. The Brigadier ordered the cavalry to report to the O.C. 10th Manchesters, and to assist that battalion in the task of reconnaissance, and he began to move larger bodies of infantry across the valley.

In the early afternoon the 126th Brigade took over the left front and passed through the 127th. It had been ordered to take over the whole of the divisional front and establish itself on Welsh Ridge, but the Lancashire Fusiliers were not to be denied. The 5th L.F. had reached the top of Highland Ridge, and here the 8th L.F., in spite of their serious losses thirty-six hours earlier, passed through them and followed the 3rd Hussars in close support to Good Old Man Farm, a post of considerable importance on the ridge. The Hussars had captured one side of the farm, the other being still in the enemy's possession, and they held on until the infantry arrived and took over. By 6 p.m. the 8th Manchesters (who had passed through the 10th), and a little later the 8th L.F., had reached their objectives and won the summit of Welsh Ridge. The 125th Brigade had captured between 400 and 500 prisoners during the day, 35 machine-guns, 6 trench-mortars, and a field-gun. Welsh Ridge had been made good at a comparatively slight cost, and at 3 a.m. on September 29 the New Zealand Division relieved and passed through the 42nd; and from this most advantageous " kicking-off " ground they continued the victorious advance. The battle had been very involved, and no definite line could be found on the top of Welsh Ridge, behind which the New Zealanders could form up before "leap-frogging" the 42nd. Therefore, after dark, all 42nd troops east of Surrey Road, on the western slope, were withdrawn to that road, and here the New Zealanders were given exceptionally favourable assembly and " kicking-off " positions, and a perfect artillery barrage.

In two days of incessant fighting the Division had pierced the much-vaunted Hindenburg Line to a depth of 5000 yards, and the Booty Officer's report stated that 1712 prisoners from five enemy divisions, 8 field-guns, one 4·2-inch howitzer, and 92 machine-guns had been taken. But this was certainly an under-estimate, as nearly 1500 Germans passed through the 127th Brigade command post on one day, September 27. It was impossible to estimate accurately the numbers captured by any given formation, as the Germans were so thoroughly beaten and so glad to be out of the fighting, that they took charge of themselves and marched into captivity without escort. The Division had lost 12 officers and 179 other ranks killed, and 33 officers and 874 other ranks wounded and missing. The enemy's losses in killed and wounded had been enormous.

The Division withdrew to Havrincourt Wood for ten days' rest, reorganization, and training of the new drafts. General Solly-Flood, congratulating his troops on the successful storming of the Hindenburg Line, and on " the soldierly conduct and gallant fighting qualities displayed," assured them that " Once more you have proved the Divisional Motto, and have struck a hard blow for our King and Country. I am proud to be your Commander." He also presented ribbons of decorations awarded for conspicuous service. Each recipient of an honour, when the ribbon was pinned to his tunic, was given a card bearing the Divisional Sign and Motto, and the signature of the Divisional Commander, on which an account of the deed was typewritten, and these cards are highly prized. Between March and September 1918, as opportunity offered, many hundreds of these were presented by the General; and the stories of these deeds of valour and devotion to duty would fill several volumes. The more thickly such acts were crowded into the space of a few days, as on March 25-26, August 21-24, August 30-September 2, and September 27-28, the less chance has the historian to record individual instances, such as stand out when raids, not battles, are the stirring events of the period.

The loss of many good comrades was sorely felt, but individual grief was for a time swamped by the common exultation. For four years the tide of battle had ebbed and flowed more or less evenly. Successful but costly attacks had been followed by equally successful and costly counter-attacks; the finer heroism on the one side had been balanced by great material advantage on the other, and it seemed as though trench warfare must go on for ever. At last the thrill of victory upon victory was being experienced, and the knowledge that they had played a worthy part, that they had been strong and of good courage, was very pleasant. From all parts of the Allied line came the same story of victory, and the news of Allenby's 45,000 prisoners in Palestine, and of Bulgaria's unconditional surrender, now arrived to crown the jubilation.

CHAPTER XIII

ACROSS THE RIVER SELLE

(*October 9–23, 1918*)

ON the 9th of October the Division marched out of the rest area to take over the left sector of the 4th Corps front, held by the New Zealand Division. After the breaking of the Hindenburg Line the pursuit had been carried on by the Third Army with such vigour that the enemy had been unable to make any prolonged stand, and the front was now at least a dozen miles east of the Couillet Valley. Throughout these operations the Divisional Artillery had assisted the New Zealanders. Evidence of the haste with which the enemy had retired was furnished on the second day's march, when the battalions passed through Lesdain, as most of the houses here had been left standing, though interiors had been looted. While the unending column of troops and transport moved eastward across the ridges and valleys of the Somme country, past battered villages and farmsteads, a stream of old men, women and children poured to the west. These were the liberated civilians, freed at last from the Prussian yoke. Though many of them seemed too stunned by ill-treatment and the loss of all they had possessed to understand or feel interest in what was passing around them, the greater number greeted the British soldiers enthusiastically, and urged them to drive the *sales Boches* out of their beloved France, whose soil had been defiled. Ruined and bereft though they were, French pride and passionate love of their country still burned brightly, and the chief emotion was joy that the *cochons prussiens* were being hustled ignominiously out of France. The second night was passed in Pélu Wood and Chateau Briseux, with D.H.Q. at Esnes. Away to the north Cambrai was burning so fiercely that the spire of one of its churches stood out black against the background of flame. A semicircle of fires in the further distance told of the destruction of villages and homesteads, and the Lancashire men understood something of the loathing and hatred that animated the homeless French and perhaps saved them from the deadening effect of utter despair. The third day's march brought the Division to Fontaine-au-Pir and Beauvois, where a halt was made while arrangements were completed for the relief of the New Zealanders around Briastre, on the western bank of the River Selle.

The River Selle winds through and about Solesmes, Briastre, Neuvilly, Le Cateau and other villages east and south-east of Cambrai, and here the Germans made one of the last desperate attempts to check the British advance. The line of the Selle was strategically one of the most important positions along the whole front, the key position to Maubeuge, Mons, and above all Valenciennes, the centre of the enemy's main lines of communications for all the northern area. The German troops were ordered to fight to the death in the very strong defences prepared east of the Selle, and their best troops were put into the line here, including the 25th German Division, which claimed that it had fought through the war with an unbroken record of victory. This famous, hard-fighting division had been held in reserve that it might be thrust in at the vital moment, fresh, fit and confident, to turn the scale, and it was now brought into line against the 42nd Division. To increase their confidence the German Higher Command issued the following statement : " All past experiences, all prisoners' statements, prove that the British infantry does not push on as it meets with resolute resistance. Only by offering a tough defence shall we achieve an honourable peace." General Solly-Flood issued this statement to his troops with the comment : " The Division, as it has always done, will overcome the toughest defence the already shaken Hun can offer, and teach him once more what the Divisional Motto means."

The New Zealanders had already secured a precarious footing at one or two points on the eastern bank of the Selle, opposite Briastre, and on the night of October 12–13 their front was taken over by the 125th Brigade, two companies of the 8th L.F. crossing the river. The enemy made violent attempts to dislodge them, and, by driving them back across the Selle, prevent or delay the bridging of the river. The first attempts were on the night of the relief, but these were repulsed without much trouble. On the afternoon of the 13th the enemy made much more desperate counter-attacks. At 4.15 p.m., after a heavy bombardment, their infantry and machine-gunners counter-attacked in force. Though the troops of the division on the right were forced to withdraw their forward posts, the two companies of the 8th L.F. stood firm, and inflicted very heavy losses, a Lewis-gun section contributing largely to this. Fresh counter-attacks, no less violent, were made, and enfilading machine-gun fire compelled the posts on the extreme right to withdraw a short distance and take up a defensive flank, which checked the enemy. At nightfall patrols again worked forward and established posts close to the original line. In the course of the next few days the brigade succeeded in establishing posts across the river along the whole divisional front, between Briastre and the railway triangle just south of Solesmes.

The enemy now disclosed a greater artillery strength than he had shown during recent weeks, and on the 13th and 14th Briastre was heavily shelled and gassed. Captain H. Neame, R.A.M.C., accompanied by a French officer, Lieutenant Pinto, and some N.C.O.s and men of the 2nd and 3rd Field Ambulances, twice entered the

Bridging the Selle, October 17-19

village during the worst of the shelling, and helped to evacuate more than 150 civilians. Among these were at least thirty infirm persons and children, who had to be sought out, and then carried into safety. On the 15th Lance-Corporal W. Armstrong, 5th L.F., being ordered to reconnoitre a suspected machine-gun post in a house on the Solesmes–Belle Vue road, led his section so skilfully that they not only found the post, with a loaded gun in position, but also seized an opportunity to enter quietly and abstract the gun before the garrison realized what was taking place. They were then fired upon, but the withdrawal was managed with equal skill, and the gun carried off without a casualty to the section.

As the banks of the Selle drop rather sharply to the water it is not an easy stream to bridge or cross, especially as the enemy held the higher ground, with direct observation, not more than 400 yards away, and in some places their machine-gun posts were only 100 and 150 yards from the river. On the nights of the 17th and 18th the Divisional Engineers erected four footbridges with handrails, and prepared material for others, and also for two pontoon bridges to take wheeled traffic and field-guns. About the centre of the sector was a weir; north of this the width of the stream was from 15 to 20 feet, and here the bridges were made of German telegraph posts, 30 feet in length, with boards nailed across. South of the weir the width was greater, and the bridges were made of trestles and duckboards. On the night of the 19th—the assembly for attack taking place at midnight—four more footbridges and the pontoon bridges were erected. The pontoon wagons were brought down soon after dusk, their wheels padded with canvas filled with straw to deaden the noise. There was a great deal of rain, the river north of the weir rose nearly four feet, overflowed its banks, and inundated the surrounding country, so that the bridges already constructed had to be raised and extended. By the gallantry and good work of the Engineers all was completed in time, in spite of violent machine-gun fire and shelling with H.E. and gas. Respirators were worn for several hours, but there were only six casualties among the sappers. The route to each bridge was taped out to guide the assembling troops and ensure speed in getting into the " kicking-off " positions east of the Selle; and a lantern was placed at the head of each bridge, which was numbered. Thanks to the efficiency and thoroughness of the sappers, the infantry were able to cross the river and deploy for the attack without confusion or delay.*

The bridging being completed, the advance of the Third Army was resumed on October 20, with zero hour at 2 a.m. The direction of the Division's advance, which from the opening of the Third

---

* One of the pack-mules, when crossing, deliberately jumped into the water, dragging his driver in. It was the second time the mule had behaved in this way. The driver got the animal and its load to the enemy's side and, while shells and bullets were whizzing around, he admonished his charge on its folly. " This is the second —— time you've done this," he said. " If you fancy yourself as a —— submarine, you're —— well mistaken. Coom on ! "

Army's offensive had been practically due east, was now turned to the north-east, towards Maubeuge and Mons. The attack was planned in three phases.

First Phase.—The 126th Brigade, which had relieved the 125th in the front line, would advance, with the 5th East Lancashires on the right and the 10th Manchesters on the left, and a company of the 8th Manchesters in support of each battalion, at zero plus three minutes, under a barrage lifting at the rate of 100 yards every three minutes. The first objective, termed the *Blue Line*, was the railway cutting running southwards from Solesmes—a very strong defensive system, with deep dug-outs in the cutting; the second objective, termed the *Green Line*, was the high ground beyond a sunken road which ran roughly parallel to the railway, about 1500 yards north-east of the "kicking-off" positions. Between the Blue and Green Lines the barrage would lift at the rate of 100 yards every five minutes. Handshakes would be established with the 5th Division on the right and the 62nd on the left on the divisional boundary lines at each objective.

Each battalion would advance in four waves, as follows: On the right the first wave ("B" Company, 5th E. Lancs.) to go forward with six sections in arrow-head formation to the railway cutting, while one platoon would seize Belle Vue Farm, near the cross-roads a few hundred yards west of the railway, mop up the cross-roads, and then work from left to right and form a defensive flank on the spur just beyond the railway; the second wave ("C" and "D" Companies), advancing in extended order, to carry on the advance to the *Green Line*, through the ravine that stretched diagonally between the two objectives; the third wave ("D" Company) to advance in line of sections in single file, and, after mopping up the ravine, to extend either flank of the leading companies and provide fighting patrols to clear the flanks and find touch with the 10th Manchesters and the 5th Division; the fourth wave ("D" Company, 8th Manchesters) to form a defensive flank between the spur and the right of the *Green Line*. On the left, the first wave of the 10th Manchesters ("C" Company on the right, "A" Company on the left) to carry both objectives; the second wave ("B" Company) to reinforce the first, and mop up and occupy the cutting; the third wave ("D" Company) to leapfrog over the second and clear the ravine; the fourth wave ("B" Company, 8th Manchesters) to assist in mopping up and to support the others as required.

Second Phase.—The 127th Brigade to pass through the 126th and advance from the *Green Line* at 7 a.m., under a barrage at the rate of 100 yards in five minutes, to the *Red Line* (of which the hamlet of Marou formed the centre), about 1200 to 1500 yards further to the north-east. After a pause of fifteen to thirty minutes, to continue the advance to the *Brown Line*, which would secure the important tactical point of the sunken cross-roads on the top of the hill between Marou and Romeries, at the rate of 100 yards in four

THE CEMETERY NEAR BILHEM FARM ON THE TRESCAULT-RIBECOURT ROAD.

R. SELLE FIGHTING. BELLE VUE.

R. SELLE FIGHTING. FIRST OBJECTIVE, THE RAILWAY CUTTING.

R. SELLE FIGHTING. THE RAVINE.

Plan of Attack, October 20

minutes, making the total advance for the morning about 4000 yards on the left, and rather more than 3000 on the right. Handshakes to be established with the flanking divisions where the lines cross the divisional boundaries.

Third Phase.—The advance beyond the *Brown Line* to be carried on by the 125th Brigade, objectives and date depending upon the general situation on the front of the Corps.

Two companies of the M.G. Battalion were allotted to the 126th Brigade and one to the 127th. The reserve company, with a company of the New Zealand M.G. Battalion, would cover the advance from high ground west of the Selle. The importance attached by the Commander-in-Chief to the offensive east of Cambrai was shown by the vast array of artillery concentrated there. As the artillery was let loose upon the enemy positions the thunder of the heavy guns seemed to shake the ground, and it was amazing that ammunition could be brought up in sufficient supplies to feed the voracious monsters. The night of October 19–20 was very dark, and to assist the infantry to keep direction, the artillery fired bright "incendiary" shells to mark the flanks and also the centre of their barrage, and these proved useful guides. The attacking battalions had already rehearsed the assault on preceding days, and each moved off through Briastre in the darkness, mist and rain, crossed the Selle, and arrived at its "kicking-off" position between midnight and 1 a.m., the 5th East Lancashires without loss. The left flank, however, was heavily shelled, and the 10th Manchesters suffered rather severely. It was raining hard, but many men were so tired that they fell asleep as they lay in a beet-field awaiting the signal.

At 2 a.m. (October 20) the barrage came down 300 yards in front, and the first waves went over as one man. The bandsmen of the 5th East Lancashires, who were on duty as extra stretcher-bearers, had brought up their instruments, and played the Regimental March under teeming rain and heavy fire. Enemy machine-guns opened at once and caused about fifty casualties among the 5th East Lancashires, and a thick belt of wire had to be got through in the dark. But the sections were on the railway in good time, and with a terrific yell the Burnley men entered the steep cutting and went for the defenders with the bayonet, and in a very short time a red Very light signalled back that the railway was captured. Meanwhile the platoon detached to carry Belle Vue Farm—a formidable position, strengthened by three cunningly devised machine-gun nests—had achieved its object, though both its commander and sergeant had fallen before the objective had been reached. The barrage slowed down to the four-minute rate, and the second wave advanced in extended order and captured the ravine. They were then enfiladed by machine-guns, but this hardly checked the advance, and the Green Line was carried, the battalion having passed through six defensive belts, at all of which opposition was encountered. On reaching the final objective they were harassed for a time by machine-gun fire from the left, and in the blackness of the night a number of the men lost direction and wandered into the 10th Manchester's territory. Touch was soon established, however, with this battalion, and, later, with the 5th Division; and the ground was thoroughly mopped up. The battalion had suffered more than a hundred casualties, but had captured 300 prisoners, of better physique and appearance than any previously taken.

The 10th Manchesters had met with equal success on the left. Encountering wire west of the railway, Lance-Corporal Revell rushed forward, and though the wire was still under our own barrage, he cut a gap through which the section passed. A little later, Revell charged a machine-gun post and bayoneted the crew. The railway cutting was a ravine, down the steep banks of which the Oldham men stumbled and rolled in the dark. It was strongly held and deadly machine-gun fire was brought to bear upon them, but they were quickly masters of the situation, and at the scheduled time a green flare signalled that the 10th Manchesters held the railway line. The Green Line was also captured to time. There was much bitter hand-to-hand fighting in the dark, and numerous instances of the rushing and capture of machine-gun posts. So well was the direction kept that the right company found itself exactly on the spot on the Green Line at which it had aimed. The leading companies were now enfiladed by two machine-guns in the sunken road, so Captain J. A. C. Taylor, D.S.O., M.C., took two men forward with a Lewis gun, which, however, he was unable to fire, owing to the mud. He brought up a German machine-gun, but this also jammed. He next went several hundred yards under continuous machine-gun fire to obtain rifle-grenades, which he fired, and then rushed forward, shot two of the enemy with his revolver, and made the rest run. This prompt and courageous action—for which the bar to the M.C. was awarded—cleared up the situation on the Green Line, and ensured a capital starting-point for the 6th Manchesters.

During the early hours of the morning of October 20th, both in the darkness and at dawn, there were numerous instances of daring, resource, and initiative, every one of which is well worth recording if space permitted. A few may be picked out at random, as typical of many others performed by officers and men of all battalions engaged that day. On the left Sergeant S. R. Lees, in command of a platoon of the 10th Manchesters engaged in clearing the railway cutting, worked round to the rear of a crater strongly held by machine-guns, which they attacked and captured. He then pushed on to Solesmes, outside the divisional boundary, mopping up the whole railway triangle, accounting for a number of the enemy on the way and taking their machine-guns, and got into touch with the 62nd Division. This platoon cleared more than 1000 yards of the railway. Corporal W. Martin, with two men of the 10th Manchesters, came upon a body of nearly fifty of the enemy. The three opened fire and shot several Germans, then charged with the bayonet, killed and wounded others, and put the remainder to flight. Sergeant T. O'Connel, leading his men with great dash,

Typical Incidents, October 20

rushed and captured five machine-guns in succession. Captain J. C. S. Rowbotham rushed two machine-gun posts, shooting the crews, taking the guns, and accounting for twenty-four of the enemy. Private J. H. Chapman, No. 1 of a Lewis-gun, when passing through wire was fired at by a machine-gun at close range. He brought his gun into action and killed the crew. Being wounded, he handed his gun to No. 2 and continued the advance to the final objective 1500 yards away, where he bayoneted a number of the enemy, and only had his wounds dressed when the position had been consolidated.

On the right, similar heroism was shown. Sergeant W. Fletcher and two men of the 5th East Lancashires rushed a post containing twenty Germans and two machine-guns, and killed or captured the lot. Lieutenant W. Cookson, with six men, charged a machine-gun nest containing an officer and thirty men, killed eight and took the rest prisoner. Privates Yegliss, M.M., and Chalkley were sent with a message to Battalion H.Q. On the way they encountered three separate armed parties of the enemy, overcame their resistance, and delivered the message and eight unwounded prisoners. A section of the same battalion came under very deadly machine-gun fire which caused a number of casualties. Seeing his comrades hesitate, Private A. Waterhouse called out, "I'm hit, lads, but I'm going on!" Inspired by this example, the survivors of the section promptly followed the lead and captured the post. Another private, W. Kehoe, at a time of confusion due to enfilading machine-gun fire and the obstacle of wire in front, organized a party of platoon strength, including N.C.O.s, and gave them the correct direction towards the final objective, going in advance with a Lewis-gun—though not a Lewis-gunner himself—and checking every twenty-five or thirty yards to fire a few rounds. In all this hand-to-hand fighting Stokes-gunners, machine-gunners and Lewis-gunners took their share and gained decorations. Sterling courage was shown in bringing up the ammunition across ground swept by hostile machine-guns, and also in collecting ammunition from the wounded. The stretcher-bearers were no less heroic, and their devotion saved many lives.

At 7 a.m. the 127th Brigade passed through the 126th, the 5th Manchesters on the right, the 6th on the left, and the 7th in support. At the outset the 5th Manchesters were badly knocked about by enfilading machine-gun fire from the right flank, which caught the advancing waves on the bare high ground, south of Marou and west of Maison Rouge, which had to be crossed. The deadliness of this enfilading fire was due to the fact that very strong enemy counter-attacks had forced the division on the right to withdraw temporarily, so the right flank of the Wigan men was in the air. The enemy was offering a stubborn resistance, infantry and machine-gunners fighting skilfully and well. But the 6th Manchesters on the left overcame all obstacles. At the start the leading company suffered many casualties from machine-guns, which held up the advance for a short time. Lieutenant F. C. Benton successfully organized attacks against these nests, and took fifty prisoners. The Red Line was secured, and the hamlet of Marou cleared with machine-gun, rifle and bayonet. Sergeant W. Tinsley led an attack against a strongly held position. His section had to pass through fierce machine-gun fire and shell fire, but the post was captured, and Tinsley himself killed five men with the bayonet. Private A. Brewer, when his section commander was killed, took charge of a section, and, attacking a machine-gun nest which was holding up the advance, captured twelve prisoners and the gun. The 6th, though anxious to press forward to the final objective, were ordered to remain on the Red Line until the situation on the right had improved.

The 7th Manchesters were now brought up, "D" Company forming a defensive flank on the right of the 5th. The line was advanced, but the enfilading fire was still too destructive to permit the capture of the objective until the division on the right could make good. It was during the hottest of the fighting on this flank that Private Alfred Wilkinson, 5th Manchesters, gained the Victoria Cross by the most noteworthy of many individual acts of heroism on this day. His company was held up in an exposed position by very heavy machine-gun fire from the front and right flank. All other means of communication having failed, four runners were sent out in succession with messages asking for assistance, and all four were killed before many yards had been covered. Though Wilkinson had seen the four shot down, and therefore knew how slight his chance of escape would be, he volunteered to carry the message. The distance was more than 600 yards, but somehow, though scores of bullets only missed him by inches, he got through, and assistance was sent. Throughout the remainder of the day Wilkinson continued to do splendid work. Private J. Bowers, of the same battalion, carried his wounded officer through very heavy shell fire to a place of safety. Though himself twice wounded while doing this, he refused to give in until he had got the officer under cover and had found stretcher-bearers, and undoubtedly saved the officer's life. Great gallantry had been displayed by the 7th Manchesters, under Captain James Baker. The company had lost heavily from enemy shelling and machine-guns, both during the assembly and when attacking, but though its strength had been reduced to thirty-five when Captain Baker formed a defensive flank on the right of the 5th Manchesters, it repelled strong counter-attacks, held on for eight hours, and eventually made the position secure.

Soon after midday the enemy massed for a counter-attack, but the assembly was broken up by the artillery and outstanding work by the machine-guns. About 4 p.m. the 5th Division attacked under a heavy barrage, the 5th and 7th Manchesters, with companies of the 8th which had been brought forward, co-operating. This advance was successful and the Red Line was secured. A machine-gun nest on the right, which had been very troublesome all

R. SELLE FIGHTING. A SUNKEN ROAD. SOLESMES IN THE DISTANCE.

R. SELLE FIGHTING. MAROU.

CAPTURED TANKS NEAR LE QUESNOY.

LC.-CORP. A. WILKINSON, V.C., 1/5 BN. MANCHESTER REGT.

All Objectives Gained

morning, was captured by " C " Company, 7th Manchesters. The 6th Manchesters were now able to resume their attack, which had been postponed, as the artillery had been required to switch the barrage to other objectives; and the final objective, the Brown Line—more than 1000 yards beyond Marou—was captured about 9 p.m., some hundreds of the enemy being driven from the last position, in the sunken cross-roads half-way between Marou and Vertigneul, with heavy loss. Privates H. W. Jarvis, M.M., and M. Fearn, 6th Manchester stretcher-bearers, had displayed great devotion in attending to the wounded and bringing them into safety at a time when the violence of the machine-gun fire made it almost certain death to move about. Throughout the rest of the day and in the evening these two men worked incessantly in constant peril, and saved many more lives.

The enemy artillery had been active since early morning, their fire being especially concentrated upon our guns. Battery D/211 was put out of action gun by gun, until one gun remained, with only Sergeant W. Ritchie and Gunners J. Willis and H. Watts to work it. After a time Ritchie was too badly wounded to be able to give any assistance, but the two gunners continued to fight their gun until at last it was put out of action by a direct hit. All three received the D.C.M.

The night of October 20th closed with all the Division's objectives secured. The Prussians of the " Invincible " 25th Division had plenty to think about—both those in the divisional cage and those still at large. They had been very thoroughly beaten and very roughly handled; and when it had come to " in-fighting " they had been soundly thrashed again and again by half their numbers. They had met two of the East Lancashire brigades to their sorrow, and were soon to experience similar treatment from the third.

The newly-won positions were consolidated next day, October 21st. In the afternoon there was heavy enemy shelling with H.E. and gas; and low-flying aeroplanes were active over the front. The Germans were by no means done for; they meant to resist stubbornly any further advance, and had brought artillery from other sectors into position. During the night of the 21st–22nd the 125th Brigade relieved the 127th, and the enemy shelling continued at intervals during the day and night of the 22nd. It was unusually heavy at midnight, and the assembly of the brigade for the attack was made under most unfavourable conditions, the number of casualties among the Fusiliers being serious.

The advance of the Third Army was resumed in the early hours of the 23rd October, the Fourth and First Armies co-operating. The 42nd Division held the left of the 4th Corps front, with the 5th Division on the right, and the 3rd Division, 6th Corps, on the left. At 3.20 a.m. the Divisional and New Zealand Artillery put down a barrage which lifted at the rate of 100 yards in six minutes. The Division's final objective was, roughly, the line of the River Harpies from the north of Beaurain on the right to

Vertigneul in the centre, and to the outskirts of Romeries, north-east of Vertigneul, on the left. The advance was to be made in three bounds, and the New Zealanders would then pass through the 125th Brigade at 8.40 a.m. and continue the advance, supported by the divisional artillery and two companies of the 42nd M.G. Battalion.

At 3.26 a.m. the Fusilier Brigade, with " C " Company, M.G. Battalion, moved off, the 7th Battalion on the right, the 8th on the left, and the 5th in support. Once again the right flank had the greater difficulty, and the progress of the 7th was slow. They were enfiladed from machine-gun posts on the high ground west of Beaurain, from Beaurain itself, and, later, from the quarries north of Beaurain. These poured destructive fire upon them as they strove gallantly to go forward. A couple of tanks were sent to their assistance, and these eased the situation by destroying the nearer machine-gun nests. But the enemy, holding Beaurain very strongly, had checked the advance of the 5th Division, so the flank of the 7th L.F. was in the air, and its right company had been much weakened by heavy losses. The left company, however, made progress in the centre by the Marou–Beaurain road. There were numerous instances of devotion to duty and disregard of personal safety on the part of all ranks. Lieutenant W. J. O'Bryen gained a second bar to his M.C. by leading his men round by a flank against a machine-gun nest which had held them up at 100 yards' range, and capturing the position; and C.S.M. Thos. Roe, M.M., dealt similarly with another nest. Corporal F. Hesford kept his men together under deadly shell fire, and though knocked down by a shell which killed the man next to him, Hesford worked his section steadily through the fire to the flanks of the machine-guns, and captured all three.

Conditions on the left were much more satisfactory. The 8th L.F. had advanced steadily, and as the 3rd Division was making corresponding progress on the left, their flank was not unduly exposed. Still, they had to fight their way step by step, held up time after time by the numerous machine-gun nests, but always overcoming the resistance, and turning the enemy out of his holes at the bayonet's point. Soon after the start Captain D. G. Bird's company came under fierce fire from machine-gun nests. Led by their officer, the company rushed the posts and bayoneted the entire garrison. Pushing on, Bird led his men to the final objective, north of Beaurain, and held it under very heavy fire. C.S.M. Riley, whose courage and coolness in the assembly had been conspicuous, made personal reconnaissances under heavy fire during the attack, and brought valuable information regarding the situation on the flanks. He was the first man on the final objective. Sergeant C. Carter, seeing that the troops on his right were held up, rushed the enemy post with two men, and captured the gun. He then took nine prisoners from a dug-out close to the post. Lance-Corporal W. Walmsley, though wounded in the side by a bayonet, led his section against a machine-gun nest which had been holding up the advance, and captured it, all

Capture of Vertigneul, October 23

the enemy being killed with the bayonet. Privates C. H. Perkins and F. Peace worked a Lewis-gun under heavy artillery and machine-gun fire, and though Perkins was severely wounded in the knee, the two men continued to fight the gun until they had killed or captured the whole of the opposing machine-gun crew. Privates H. A. Jackson and G. H. Robson attacked a machine-gun nest with a Lewis-gun, killed four men and captured or dispersed the rest. As similar instances of pluck and confidence were being shown in all parts of the fighting area between Marou, Beaurain and Vertigneul, and the trench-mortar crews and machine-gunners fought with rifle, bayonet and revolver; and stretcher-bearers, R.A.M.C. and signallers, though not taking part in hand-to-hand combats with the bayonet, were doing their duty with equal disregard of their own safety, the final objective was reached, at first on the left, where Vertigneul was captured by the 8th L.F., and later on the right flank, where Captain Kirsopp, G.S.O. 3, of the 42nd, gave valuable assistance by a reconnaissance outside the divisional boundary, north-west of Beaurain. Here he came across a company of the Cheshires and led them to their objective, where they linked up with the 7th L.F., and the front was securely established. The 8th L.F. had captured more than 100 prisoners, two field-guns, thirty-four machine-guns, and some trench-mortars. The 7th and 5th had also made good captures.

This attack of the 125th Brigade was as brilliant an exploit as any during the war. The difficulty of assembly in the dark had been augmented by the complicated tactics required by the need to align the barrage to suit divisions on the flanks. An outward wheel on one flank of the Brigade and an inward wheel on the other flank had to be made in pitch darkness, and while in actual conflict with the enemy, before the whole line could advance. The area was saturated with enemy gas, and machine-gun nests abounded. Orders had been frequently changed, and it was only possible to issue final orders to the Brigade at 2 p.m. at Belle Vue Farm. Company commanders then had to crawl considerable distances to attend a hastily summoned conference. This left little time to get the orders down to platoon commanders, and objectives could not be pointed out in daylight. But the Fusiliers went over the top as though on parade and took all objectives. The laurels gained here are worthy of a place beside those won at Minden.

At the scheduled time, 8.40 a.m., the New Zealanders passed through the 125th Brigade, and continued the advance beyond the line of the Harpies, two companies of the 42nd M.G. Battalion going with them. This was the second flying start given them by the Division.

Prisoners taken by the 42nd Division during the operations of October 20-23 numbered 927, and the booty included three field-guns, 102 machine-guns, nine trench-mortars, and twenty-two anti-tank rifles. A number of enemy batteries were put out of action by our artillery. Five hundred and fifteen enemy dead were counted on the battlefield—men of the shattered and demoralized 25th German Division, and to a lesser extent of the 18th Division. The 42nd, which had lost 138 killed and 707 wounded, withdrew west of the Selle, and on October 24 concentrated in Beauvois, a pleasant little town, only slightly damaged by the war, where really good billets were enjoyed for the first time since March. The inhabitants of Beauvois and Caudry had been in German hands for four years, and their delight at having Englishmen as guests, instead of Germans as tyrants, was displayed in a manner rather disconcerting to many lads, who found it embarrassing to be kissed and fussed over, and to be called " deliverers " and " saviours." However, they appreciated the many evidences of kindliness and goodwill, and helped in their own way to cement the friendship and understanding between the nations; and they were truly glad to be once more in an inhabited country. Everything possible was done to make the men happy and comfortable. The canteens were well supplied; massed bands gave enjoyable concerts; and the Divisional Concert Party gave daily performances of *Sweet Fanny Adams* and *April Fools* in a factory that had been converted into a theatre. The enemy had been pressed so hard that they had left, almost intact, an excellent bathing establishment where hot baths could be obtained. The Divisional Reception Camp was moved up to Aulicourt Farm, and, while training was by no means neglected, plenty of opportunity was given for recreation. The Divisional Boxing Tournament was won by the 8th L.F., as was also the Band Contest. Most popular of all was the Football Competition, in the final of which the 7th N.F. (Pioneers) beat the R.A.M.C. by two goals to nil. Ten pleasant days were spent at Beauvois, and on the night of November 3 the Division began its move forward to relieve the N.Z. Division in the Forêt de Mormal.

CHAPTER XIV

FORÊT DE MORMAL AND HAUTMONT

(*November* 3-11, 1918)

An advance along the entire fronts of the Fourth, Third and First Armies, French armies co-operating, had been planned for the 4th November. The attack on the 4th Corps front was to be carried out by the 37th Division on the right and the N.Z. Division on the left; and the 42nd Division was to pass through the New Zealanders, and the 5th Division through the 37th, on the night of November 5-6. As secrecy was essential, movements of troops prior to the opening of the battle had to be made in darkness.

The 126th Brigade marched out of Beauvois soon after darkness fell on November 3, the 127th following, and the 125th bringing up the rear. The roads had been much damaged by heavy traffic and rain, and the going was bad. The 127th Brigade completed its first stage—to Viesley—before midnight, and the 126th Brigade arrived at Solesmes between 2 and 3 a.m. on the 4th, and remained there until the attack of the 4th Corps was launched, at 5.30 a.m. Secrecy being no longer necessary the march was then resumed. By 6 p.m. the New Zealanders reported the capture of Le Quesnoy, with 1000 prisoners, and the 126th and 127th Brigades were now in touch with the situation on the N.Z. Division's front, the former having reached Beaudignies, about 3000 yards south-west of Le Quesnoy.

The 126th Brigade passed through Le Quesnoy to Herbignies on the morning of the 5th November, keeping about 6000 yards in rear of the New Zealanders, and the rear brigade, the 125th, reached Beaudignies. Here D.H.Q. opened during the morning of the 5th, but on account of the situation moved further forward, to Potelle Château. In the afternoon the leading brigade entered the extensive Forêt de Mormal* at a point about half a mile east of Herbignies. Bad as the conditions of the march from Beauvois had been, they now became far worse. Rain had been falling steadily for some days, and the roads and forest tracks—bad at the best of times—

---

* The Forêt de Mormal, covering more than thirty-four square miles, is referred to by Field-Marshal Viscount French, in his book "1914," as a serious obstacle to his retiring army. It was a still greater obstacle to the Advance of November 1918, as by that time the roads had undergone four years' heavy wear, without repairs, and there was no material other than logs and fascines that could be used in the work of making deviations round the huge craters.

were ankle-deep, and in places almost knee-deep in mud and decaying leaves. At the main cross-roads huge craters had been blown, measuring from 60 to 80 feet in diameter, with a depth of 30 feet. One of these was bridged by the sappers, and a corduroy deviation road made round the biggest—just west of Forester's House—a way being cut through the trees for horses and vehicles. Four men in each platoon had been furnished with hatchets and bill-hooks in anticipation of obstacles in the forest, and wood-warfare had formed part of the training given at Beauvois.

Meanwhile the leading brigade pressed forward, leaving its transport behind. Progress was slow, as machine-guns, Lewis-guns, munitions and supplies had to be man-handled. The enemy continued to shell the forest spasmodically, and though casualties were infrequent, the sound of the shells crashing through and tearing off the branches was not exhilarating. The long and arduous passage through the Mormal Forest will long be remembered by all three brigade groups as a drab and depressing episode, unrelieved by the excitement of fighting, or even seeing the enemy.

The weather, the congestion, and the condition of the roads had become worse, and the 127th Brigade, which entered the forest on the following day, had a more wretched experience even than the others. For two days they had had no shelter from the bitterly cold rain, and as they were badly in need of a rest, the 125th Brigade was ordered up from Herbignies, where shelter and rest had been obtained, to become the support brigade, the 127th being moved to billets in Le Carnoy for a couple of days. The central road past Forester's House was the widest and best of the routes, but even here there was barely room for one wagon to pass another. Trees had been blown across it; there were bogs on either side, and its eastern part was shelled continually. If, in making way for motor-traffic, a gun- or wagon-wheel got off the track by so much as a foot, it was at once bogged up to the axle. The Divisional Commander therefore issued an order prohibiting the use of motors beyond a certain point, so Generals and Staff Officers had to proceed on horseback or on foot. It was a necessary but not a popular order, particularly with supply officers, but in spite of all adverse conditions—rain and mud, craters and blown culverts, congestion of men, horses, guns, ammunition and ration vehicles—the transport was most efficiently managed; supplies and ammunition got through, and the troops even received a hot meal from the field-kitchens in the middle of the forest. The Engineers and Pioneers worked magnificently, as always.

On the evening of November 5 the command of the left division sector of the 4th Corps front passed to the G.O.C. 42nd Division, and by 3.30 a.m. on the 6th the relief of the leading N.Z. Brigade by the 126th Brigade had been completed. The relief had been peculiarly difficult, on account of the intense darkness, the uncertainty of the location of the troops to be relieved, and the state of the forest roads. The front taken over ran from a point just beyond

FORESTER'S HOUSE AND CRATERS IN THE FÔRET DE MORMAL.

EASTERN EDGE OF THE FÔRET DE MORMAL.

NOVEMBER 1918. THE ENEMY'S EFFORTS TO DELAY OUR ADVANCE.

FORT EAST OF HAUTMONT, NEAR WHICH THE DIVISION HAD ITS LAST FIGHTING ON NOV. 8, 1918.

HAUTMONT, CAPTURED BY 126TH BRIGADE ON NOV. 8, 1918. THE BRIDGES WERE ERECTED BY THE DIVISIONAL ENGINEERS.

the forest near Petit Bayay on the right and along the extreme eastern fringe a little further north, then bent back through the forest to Les Viviers and La Grande Rue, where the situation was obscure, the right division of the 6th Corps being echeloned some 3000 yards to the rear of the 42nd's front. The 4th Corps front was, as usual, in advance of the Corps to right and left, and once again the 42nd Division formed the spearhead of the 4th Corps offensive, taking this rôle turn and turn about with their New Zealand comrades. To cover the exposed left flank a second M.G. Company was allotted to the 126th Brigade.

At 6.30 a.m. on the 6th—about three hours after the completion of the relief—the advance was resumed, with the 5th E. Lancs. on the right and the 8th Manchesters on the left. There could be little artillery support as the difficulties of movement through the vast expanse of forest had increased with the continuous rain and the heavy traffic over the soft tracks, and though officers and men of the artillery brigades worked like heroes they could not accomplish the impossible. The 5th E. Lancs. gained their objective—the road running south from Les 5 Chemins and Hoisies Farm—after severe fighting and numerous casualties, inflicted mainly by the enemy machine-guns strongly posted in the neighbourhood of Hoisies Farm and, further south, in the orchards and gardens between Petit Bayay and the River Sambre.

On the left the progress of the 8th Manchesters was slower. Their left flank was entirely exposed to intense machine-gun fire, particularly from Hargnies to the north-east and Coutant to the north, and their casualties were serious, one company losing all officers but one. They had to make a way through numerous thick hedges, every gap of which was under direct machine-gun fire, and despite gallant attempts to go forward the battalion was held up on a line between one hundred and two hundred yards east of the forest boundary. Fighting continued until darkness supervened, when the troops lay on the roadside, in ditches, or under hedges, in the cold and rain. The 10th Manchesters, in close support, experienced the same trying conditions.

As the nearest point to which ambulances could be brought was two and a half miles in rear of the fighting, the evacuation of the wounded was a matter of much difficulty. The badness of the roads and tracks and the persistence of enemy shelling and machine-gun fire on all forward roads gave a heavy and dangerous task to the stretcher-bearers. It was largely due to the energy of Lieut.-Colonel Callam, D.S.O., commanding the 1st Field Ambulance, in rearranging and supervising the system of evacuation, that the wounded were successfully cleared. The R.E. and the Pioneer Battalion worked day and night on the road craters and blown culverts in the Mormal Forest, and gradually the routes were opened up.

On the evening of the 6th orders were received that the advance would be continued in the early morning by the divisions on the right and left, and that the 42nd Division would not attempt to push

o

forward until the right division of the 6th Corps, on its left, had made progress. By 8.45 a.m. on the 7th this division had passed through Coutant and come up into line, and the 126th Brigade resumed its forward move. The 10th Manchesters had been brought into the centre of the front line, with the 5th E. Lancs. on the right and the 8th Manchesters on the left. The three battalions advanced steadily, and by 10 a.m. Hoisies Farm, the Five Roads, and the hamlet of Hargnies had been captured. Casualties were now slight, for the enemy, no longer able to enfilade the left flank, gave ground without waiting for our troops to get to close quarters.

At 10.30 a.m. the Divisional Commander rode round the front and ordered the advance to be continued by means of strong patrols, which pushed forward at once to the line Vieux Mesnil–Boussières. By noon the high ground beyond Vieux Mesnil and between that village and Boussières had been occupied. In view of the heavy losses of the previous day the 8th Manchesters had been withdrawn into brigade reserve, and the other battalions continued their advance. Little opposition was encountered at first, but later Vieux Mesnil was heavily shelled, and the left flank, which was again exposed, suffered from machine-gun fire.

On the evening of November 7th the 126th Brigade was given a further objective, the high ground immediately east of the River Sambre, including Hautmont, a small manufacturing town situated on both banks of the river, and the Bois-du-Quesnoy. On the following morning the 125th Brigade would pass through the 126th and advance to the final objective, east of the Maubeuge–Avesnes road, *i.e.* on a line running due south from Maubeuge.

Before daybreak on the 8th the 126th Brigade had seized the Bois d'Hautmont, a large wood west of the Sambre, and had sent patrols into the western outskirts of the town, surprising a small enemy rearguard there. By 10.15 a.m. the parts of the town on the western bank of the Sambre had been secured. All the bridges had been destroyed, but, though the river here is from 40 to 50 yards in width, the leading companies of the 10th Manchesters and 5th E. Lancs. at once set to work to improvise a crossing. The main road had been carried over a lock to an island by a bridge of masonry, and then across the stream by another bridge. The explosions that had dropped these bridges had partially demolished houses on the island and on both banks, so there was ample material on the spot. Assisted enthusiastically by the inhabitants of Hautmont, who dragged doors, beds, and mattresses to the river bank, the Oldham and Burnley men managed to connect with the island, and thence with the further bank. Parties of both battalions then engaged the enemy rearguards, which were holding out with machine-guns in the eastern parts of the town and with field-guns near Fort Hautmont, more than half a mile east of the town. Street fighting continued in the outskirts until the Germans were finally driven from the town, though they still held a position at the cemetery about half a mile east of the river.

Capture of Hautmont, November 8

The reception given to the victorious troops by the delighted inhabitants will never be forgotten. Shells were still crashing into the houses, and machine-gun bullets flew around, but these were utterly disregarded in the exultation of the moment. Women threw their arms round the necks of the soldiers, old men embraced them, girls ran to them with cakes and flowers and wine. The horrors of a long captivity were forgotten in the joy of victory and the impulse to welcome and honour the victors. The enemy artillery made a special target of the Prisoners of War cage and hospital, in which were two English doctors and about thirty British patients, and shelled this quarter vigorously.

Meanwhile, at about 8 a.m., the 125th Brigade had crossed the Sambre near Pont-sur-Sambre, and a little later—the river here forming a loop northwards—had crossed again by a footbridge thrown across by the sappers near Boussières, and had approached Hautmont from the south as the 126th Brigade closed upon it from the west. Enemy shell fire was heavy, his batteries occupying forward positions and remaining in action until the infantry were close upon them. Enemy rearguards held strong positions at Fort Hautmont and Ferme de Forêt (the latter being about 800 yards south-east of the fort), and were well supplied with field artillery. The Fusiliers, however, made good progress, and by 5 p.m. the 5th L.F., on the right, were due south of Fort Hautmont and near to Ferme de Forêt, where much opposition was met from enemy machine-guns. The 7th L.F. on the left were close to the fort, threatening to envelop it from west and north, and patrols were working further north, beyond the cemetery. The 8th L.F., in close support, covered the exits from the town, formed a defensive flank facing north, and drove the Germans from the position they had held on to at the cemetery. At dusk fighting patrols worked forward and succeeded in ejecting the enemy from Fort Hautmont and Ferme de Forêt. This ended the fighting. The Fusilier Brigade had had a stiff march during the morning before coming into contact with the enemy, and their experiences of the previous day in the Mormal Forest had been anything but restful and invigorating; but their work to the south and east of Hautmont showed that "hammering the Hun" was more to their taste than any amount of rest would have been. By capturing the high ground around Hautmont on November 8, the 125th and 126th Brigades had—in the soldiers' phrase—" broken Jerry's heart," and at last he was really " on the run."

The division was now disposed with the 125th Brigade advancing towards the Maubeuge–Avesnes road, the 126th in Hautmont, and the 127th in Hargnies and Vieux Mesnil. D.H.Q. had moved to Haute Rue. At 10.45 p.m. on the 8th all three Fusilier battalions were working forward. Their losses had been comparatively slight, and at 4.40 a.m. on November 9 they occupied the final objective on the entire front.

The division on the left was still echeloned to the rear, and between 6 a.m. and 7 a.m., patrols of the 7th L.F. pushed forward to Louvroil, a suburb of Maubeuge outside the Division's boundary, and found that the enemy had withdrawn. No further infantry advance being intended on this day (November 9) the 3rd Hussars and the 4th Corps Cyclists were sent forward. They got into touch with the German rearguards on the line of the River Thure.

The nearest railhead was at Caudry, more than 30 miles in rear of Maubeuge, and delayed-action mines, cunningly hidden, and timed to explode on different days, continued to blow up the railway line and roads. The Motor Transport Company of the Divisional Train had served the Division well throughout the campaign, but now its heavy vehicles could not get through the narrow, congested, badly damaged tracks of the forest, and had to make a long detour through Bavay. Without transport it was impossible, even for British infantry, to keep up with the rapidly retiring enemy, who had the use of a thoroughly efficient railway system and undamaged roads, all of which were destroyed later by his rearguards. The horse transport of the R.A.S.C. succeeded in bringing up the absolutely essential supplies, and the Sappers and Pioneers made this possible, though they had to work and march both day and night to keep up with the rate of advance. In addition, the bridging equipment of the three field companies and of the N.Z. Engineers had to be brought as close up to the front as possible, and at the same time kept free from any serious risk of damage by shell fire, for there was no bridging park available to replace damaged pontoons. At 10 a.m. on November 9 the Divisional Engineers began to bridge the Sambre, and by 8 p.m. a girder bridge over the lock and a pontoon bridge over the river were open for traffic. While this work was in progress the Pioneer Battalion, assisted by a crowd of willing French civilians, had cleared away all the debris, including a large coal-dump, that had blocked the approaches to the bridges.

In the afternoon the divisional front was taken over by the 7th L.F., with an outpost line 1000 yards east of the Maubeuge–Avesnes road, and the other battalions were withdrawn into billets in Hautmont, where D.H.Q. was now opened. In the evening, patrols of the 7th L.F. entered Ferrière and Les Trieux—nearly two miles beyond the outpost line—and captured three trains full of munitions, a motor-lorry, and machine-guns.

Orders were received on the morning of the 10th for the Division to take over the infantry outpost line on the whole of the Corps front. This was carried out during the day, the 7th L.F. covering the front with two outpost companies and two companies in support; and the pursuit of the enemy on the Third Army's front was taken over by the 6th Corps.

On the morning of November 11, 1918, the order was issued—

> **Hostilities will cease at 11 a.m. to-day. Troops will stand fast on line reached at that hour. Defensive precautions will be maintained. There will be no intercourse of any description with the enemy.**

November 11, 1918

A few hours later the Divisional Commander issued a Special Order of the Day—

"The Armistice proclaimed to-day has brought the operations in which the Division was engaged to a premature conclusion.

"Generally speaking, the recent fighting was not of the violent nature in which you have previously taken part and so greatly excelled. At the commencement of the operation, however, it was sufficiently severe, and the conditions imposed by the Forest of Mormal and the bridgeless River Sambre were such as to call for the highest soldierly qualities.

"After long marches at night in bad weather over boggy forest tracks, although cold and wet, hungry and tired, you attacked and defeated the enemy with your customary indomitableness.

"When the history of the war is written your efforts, commencing in the Forest, then forcing the passage of the bridgeless River Sambre in the face of severe enemy fire, and culminating in the capture of the town of Hautmont, will rank very high among the exploits of soldiers during this great war.

"I consider that the Divisional Motto has once again, probably for the last time, been entirely upheld.

"Officers, N.C.O.s and men of all arms and services in the Division, I am proud to be your Commander and to be able once more to thank you, in the name of our King and Country, for your gallant deeds and your steadfast loyalty."

SPECIAL ORDER OF THE DAY

Charleroi, 18th March, 1919.

DEMOBILIZATION is so rapidly scattering the officers and men of the Division, that the time has arrived when I must take a formal farewell of those who, during the past two years, have served me so well.

On such an occasion, it will not be out of place briefly to review the achievements of the Division throughout the great war.

The first critical days of August, 1914, brought with them the call to the Territorial Force to volunteer for active service abroad. The East Lancashire Division eagerly offered itself, and may well be proud of its unique record of being the first division of the Territorial Force to leave England for service abroad.

In September, 1914, the Division sailed to Egypt. There the work of training was relieved by a share of the garrison duty and defensive operations in Egypt which, in February, 1915, brought the Division its first fighting in the repulse of the Turkish attack on the Suez Canal.

In May, 1915, the Division landed in Gallipoli. There for eight long months it fought a campaign of unceasing danger and privation, punctuated only by fierce and bloody engagements. The Division, and those in East Lancashire who are associated with it, may well be proud of its achievements on June 4th, 5th and 6th, 1915.

Following the evacuation of the Dardanelles, the early months of 1916 saw the Division on another front—Sinai Peninsula. There it took part in the pursuit of the Turkish army to El Arish.

The month of March, 1917, brought the Division into France, and its achievements there are still comparatively fresh in our minds.

After its earliest tours of duty at Epéhy and Havrincourt, it took its part in the operations at Ypres in 1917. Thence it went to Nieuport, where for a spell it held a particularly difficult sector.

The winter of 1917–1918 saw it holding the line astride the Béthune–La Bassée Canal, cheerfully undergoing the trials, dangers and discomforts of a winter of trench life. During its tour here, the Division worked strenuously on a system of defence destined to prove of vital importance in the enemy offensive on the Lys in April, 1918; and its sister Division, the 55th West Lancashires, has paid a generous tribute to the assistance this work rendered them when they won renown in the heroic defence of Givenchy.

The Commander's Farewell Order

In March, 1918, the Division was plunged into the final phase of the war. From rest billets behind Béthune it was hurried in busses to the area north of Bapaume to help in stemming the great enemy offensive. This it effectually did in an epic battle in a manner which has earned for it undying fame. From the 23rd March on, it stubbornly faced a determined enemy flushed with success and far superior in numbers of men and guns. With its flanks often in the air, and no artillery support but what its own gunners could give, it coolly and gallantly covered the disorganization in the rear areas. For seventeen consecutive days it remained in action and held its ground in a manner that cannot be surpassed by the performance of any troops in any period of history.

On the 21st August, 1918, after three months' continuous duty in the line near Hébuterne, and without any preliminary training, the Division took part in the opening stage of the great Allied attack. From that time until the Armistice on November 11th it played a continuous part in the great offensive. We can with reason be proud of the Division's share in that fighting. Its record includes an advance of 64 miles, during which it fought in 12 general actions—each of several days' duration. Its captures include 18 towns and villages, over 4000 prisoners, 37 guns of all calibre, 122 trench mortars, 455 machine guns, and much other valuable booty.

Early in 1918 I set the Division a motto, " Go ONE BETTER," believing the spirit it expressed would always carry them to success. It has invariably acted up to that motto, and it is my pride to be able to say that never has the Division been called upon to undertake an operation in which it did not succeed, and never was it set a task which it did not more than accomplish.

Such honours have not been won without a heavy toll in wounded and in dead. Many a gallant Lancashire lad lies in a soldier's grave in Gallipoli, Sinai, France and Belgium, but the memory of their glorious deeds will live in our hearts for ever.

[For those who remain, I hope before relinquishing my command, to have organized a " 42nd DIVISION OLD MEMBERS ASSOCIATION." Through its agency we will meet again from time to time, and so keep alive old memories and old friendships, and lend a hand to those amongst us who may be in need, in the same spirit of mutual helpfulness which has inspired us during the past.

In bidding farewell to the Division, in command of which I have spent the happiest and proudest moments of my life, I wish to express to all ranks of every arm and department my deep admiration for the noble services they have rendered to their King and Country, and my overwhelming gratitude for the loyal support they have always accorded to me as their Divisional Commander.

GOOD LUCK.
GOD PROSPER YOU.

A. SOLLY-FLOOD, MAJOR-GENERAL,
Commanding 42nd (E.L.) Division.

ROLL OF HONOUR

"Their name liveth for evermore"

Killed, Died of Wounds or Sickness, and Missing

HEADQUARTERS STAFF

Brig.-Gen. Noel Lee, Commanding 127th Infantry Brigade.
Brig.-Gen. V. A. Ormsby, Commanding 127th Infantry Brigade.
Captain L. Gordon, Brigade Major, 126th Infantry Brigade.

'A' SQUADRON, 1/1 DUKE OF LANCASTER'S OWN YEOMANRY

Officers

Bibby, Maj. H. L.
Crook, Lieut. P. J.

Other Ranks

Ashman, Tpr. L.
Berry, Tpr. O.
Birch, Tpr. J. W.
Fox, Tpr. S.
Harris, Cpl. S.S. A.
Harrison, Tpr. J. F.

Hills, Tpr. H.
McKenna, Tpr. R.
Moore, Tpr. G. W.
Nickells, Tpr. W. C.
Siddall, L.-Cpl. T. H.

Smith, Tpr. A.
Stott, Tpr. H.
Turner, S.S. S.
Williams, Tpr. J. H.
Williams, Tpr. T.

42ND (EAST LANCS.) DIVISIONAL R.F.A.

Officers

Boone, Maj. H. G., D.S.O.
Hall, Maj. A. G., M.C.
Dickenson, Capt. W. H. E. de B.
Greenwood, Capt. G. W.
Simon, Capt. H. H.
Appleton, Lieut. A.

Bury, Lieut. J.
Carrick, Lieut.
Garnett, Lieut. J. K.
Hartley, Lieut. C. R.
McPherson, Lieut. W.
Nuttall, Lieut. A.
Pierpont, Lieut.

Bowles, 2nd Lieut. P.W., M.C., M.M.
Butler, 2nd Lieut.
Fry, 2nd Lieut.
Lechertier, 2nd Lieut. J. A.
Wells, 2nd Lieut. M. G.

1ST EAST LANCS. BRIGADE, R.F.A. (T.)

(See also 210th Brigade)

THE BLACKBURN ARTILLERY

Other Ranks

Airey, Dvr. W.
Baldwin, Dvr. H.
Baldwin, Dvr. T.
Ballard, Siglr. H.
Beardwood, Cpl. H.
Bennison, Bdr. J.
Bentley, Gnr. H.
Biltcliffe, Gnr. J. W.
Bonnell, Gnr. G.
Booth, Sgt. H. G.

Bridge, Dvr. H.
Brunskill, Gnr. H.
Brunt, Dvr. F.
Burgis, Dvr. F.
Burnell, Sgt. S.
Cain, Dvr. M.
Carr, Bdr. E.
Chappell, Cpl. T.
Clegg, Gnr. G.
Dewhurst, Gnr. G.

Duckworth, Sgt. J.
Edmundson, Dvr. G.
Fitzmaurice, Dvr. H.
Gibson, Dvr. R.
Groom, Dvr. J.
Haken, Gnr. W.
Hall, Dvr. W. A.
Haseley, Gnr. R.
Heap, Fitter-Cpl. F. C.
Heap, Dvr. R.

Heathcote, Dvr. J.
Henderson, Dvr. J.
Heys, T.
Heyworth, Dvr. J. A.
Hindman, J.
Holden, Gnr. H.
Holden, Gnr. T.
Ingham, Gnr. J.
Isherwood, Gnr. F.
Jeffrey, Sgt. J.
Kelshaw, Bdr. G.
Kenyon, Cpl. W.
Knowles, Dvr. J.
Lee, Cpl. H.
Livesey, Gnr. A.
Livesey, F.

Lucas, Bdr. J.
Lupton, Bdr. L. P.
Norris, Sgt. J. B.
Nuttall, Gnr. F.
Pate, Gnr. W.
Peel, Gnr. R.
Peel, Whlr. H.
Pheasey, A.
Puzzar, Gnr. R.
Read, Bdr. E. A.
Rennard, Gnr. F.
Renwick, Gnr. M. J.
Riley, Gnr. R.
Rushton, Gnr.
Seeney, Bdr. E.
Simpson, Sgt. H. B.

Simpson, Gnr. R.
Smith, Dvr. F.
Smithies, Dvr. A.
Spurr, Dvr. T.
Starkie, Bdr. R.
Thompson, Dvr. T.
Tuck, Cpl. W.
Wakefield, Sgt. J. W.
Walmesley, Gnr. A.
Walmesley, Gnr. R.
Walmsley, Gnr. R.
Waring, Dvr. W.
Wilkinson, Dvr. A.
Woods, Bdr. J.
Wright, Cpl. G.

2ND EAST LANCS. BRIGADE, R.F.A. (T.)
(See also 210th and 211th Brigades)
THE MANCHESTER ARTILLERY
Other Ranks

Ashley, Fitter-Sgt. A.
Ayrton, Cpl. H.
Bebbington, Gnr. H.
Beech, Dvr. F.
Binns, Cpl. G. W.
Boulton, Gnr. J. W.
Brierley, Dvr. J.
Brierley, J. A.
Broadmeadow, Bdr. S. E.
Butler, Gnr. N.
Calverley, Dvr. H.
Dalton, Dvr. T.
Dieterich, Gnr. W.
Dooley, Dvr. R.
Duckworth, Gnr. F.
Edwards, Dvr. T. P.
Fletcher, Dvr. H.
Flint, Gnr. W. E.
Ford, Gnr. J.
Foster, Sgt. J. W.

Fox, Bdr. C.
Gadsby, Sgt. F.
Gartside, Dvr. H.
Gibson, Gnr. W.
Goodier, Gnr. J.
Hall, Gnr. J. P.
Hamlett, Gnr. T.
Hawksworth, Dvr. J.
Henshaw, Gnr. W. H.
Hessner, W.
Howsam, Gnr. G.
Hulme, Gnr. F.
Huxley, Gnr. F.
Ingham, Bdr. F.
Keenan, Gnr. T.
Kelshaw, A/Bdr. A.
Kirkham, Gnr. C.
Mallinson, Cpl. L.
McGuire, Dvr. J.
McLoughland, Dvr. W.

Morgan, Q.M.Sgt. D.
Moss, Gnr. H.
Naylor, Gnr. J.
Palmer, Gnr. J. H.
Price, L/Bdr. E.
Prichard, D.
Radford, J.
Rogers, L/S. A.
Ryan, Gnr. J.
Shaw, Sgt. H.
Spence, Bdr. S.
Taylor, Bdr. G.
Telford, Cpl. W. S.
Tierney, Dvr. J.
Wilkinson, Sgt. E.
Williams, Gnr. A.
Williams, Gnr. G. D.
Wright, Dvr. S.
Wylde, Dvr. O. V.
Yates, Gnr. A.

3RD EAST LANCS. BRIGADE, R.F.A. (T.)
(See also 211th Brigade)
THE BOLTON ARTILLERY
Other Ranks

Alcock, Gnr. G. A.
Bailey, Drv. C.
Bates, Cpl. W. G.
Boon, J.
Brandwood, Cpl. A.
Briggs, Gnr. J.
Brooks, Gnr. W.
Brown, Gnr. J.
Brownlow, Gnr. J. V.
Brownson, Gnr. W.
Cain, Dvr. P.
Carter, Drv. H.
Chadburn, S/S. Cpl. S.
Chadwick, Gnr. J.
Clayton, Bdr. J.
Clegg, Bdr.
Connor, Dvr. H.
Coucill, Gnr. F.
Davies, Gnr. F.
Easey, Drv. H.
Edge, Bdr. F.
Farrer, Gnr. J.
Gallagher, Sgt. J.
Garner, Bdr.
Glover, Dvr. J.
Goodman, Sadlr. E.
Greenhalgh, Dvr. G.
Guffogg, Bdr. S.

Halsall, Gnr. H.
Hardman, Bdr. F.
Helm, Dvr. H. B.
Heywood, Gnr.
Hodgkinson, Bdr. F.
Holdbrook, Dvr. S.
Holliday, Dvr. R.
Howard, Gnr. W.
Husband, Gnr. E. H.
Hutchinson, Sadlr. P.
Johnson, Bdr. A.
Lee, Bdr. G.
Lee, Gnr. H.
Lever, Fitter J.
Lewis, Gnr. J. E.
Lodge, Bdr. H.
Marsh, Gnr. W.
Mather, Gnr. R.
Matthews, Dvr. W.
Martin, Bdr. J.
McGuinness, Dvr. C.
Meek, Dvr. B.
Mulvaney, Dvr. K. H.
Murray, Gnr. H.
Nield, Cpl. C. H.
Olive, Dvr. J.
Parkinson, Gnr. J. D.
Pilkington, Dvr. C.

Pilkington, Bdr. W.
Poppleton, Bdr. F.
Pover, Dvr. J.
Ratcliffe, J.
Roscoe, Dvr. J.
Rowbotham, Gnr. J.
Russell, Dvr. H.
Schofield, Sidlr. P.
Shell, Gnr. P.
Sixsmith, Dvr. J. H.
Smith, Gn. F.
Smith, Dvr. H.
Smith, Gnr. J. M.
Thornley, Gnr. H.
Thornley, Gnr. T.
Tildesley, H.
Warbrick, Fitter W.
Warburton, Sgt. F.
Webster, Gnr. J. E.
Westby, Dvr. H.
Wilkinson, Dvr. R.
Wilson, Gnr. S. C.
Wood, Gnr. J.
Woodcock, Bdr. H.
Worsley, Sadlr. G.
Wrigley, Dvr. J.
Yound, Gnr. J.
Young, Dvr. H.

4TH EAST LANCS. BRIGADE, R.F.A. (T.)
(See also 210th and 211th Brigades)

THE CUMBERLAND ARTILLERY

Other Ranks

Adams, Gnr. H. S.
Armstrong, Gnr. J.
Banks, Cpl. A. R. (R.A.M.C.).
Beeby, Gnr. W.
Belenkin, Cpl. J. N.
Bell, Bdr. J.
Birrell, Gnr. F.
Brophy, Gnr. C.
Brown, Gnr. J.
Brown, Gnr. J.
Bushby, Gnr. E. O.
Campbell, Gnr. J.
Chadwick, Gnr. G. H.
Clark, Gnr. J.
Cleveland, S/S. Cpl. J.
Coulthard, Sgt. W.
Curtis, Bdr. W. J.
Denver, Gnr. B.
Dixon, Dvr. M.
Dovey, Gnr. F.
Edie, B.Q.M.Sgt. R.
Edwards, Gnr. T.
Fell, Bdr. J.
Fish, Gnr. L.

Fowler, Gnr. T.
Fox, Gnr. H.
Fox, Sgt. W.
Frazer, Gnr. S.
Gambles, Bdr. J.
Gilmour, B.Q.M.Sgt. R.
Graham, Bdr. A. B.
Graham, Gnr. W. D.
Halliday, Gnr. A.
Heasman, Cpl. G.
Hodgson, Gnr. F. W.
Homewood, Gnr. N. E.
Howe, Gnr. R.
Hunter, Gnr. N.
Jackson, Sgt. J.
Jeffrey, Dvr. H.
Jenkinson, Gnr. J. T.
Johnstone, Cpl. P.
Lawson, Bdr. T.
Massy, Sgt. A., D.C.M.
McCullough, Sgt. J.
McDowell, Gnr. T.
McKenzie, Sgt. H., M.M.
McLoughlin, Gnr. R.

McMillan, Gnr. J.
Monkhouse, B.Sgt.-Maj. R.
Murphy, Cpl. R.
Murray, Dvr. F. G.
Pritt, Sgt. R.
Reed, Gnr. M.
Roberts, Gnr. C. A.
Robinson, Gnr. T.
Sewell, Dvr. T.
Sibbald, Gnr. G.
Signoratti, Dvr. F.
Sinclair, Gnr. A.
Smith, Sgt. W. M.
Sowerby, Gnr. W.
Stockdale, Gnr. J.
Tetterington, B.Q.M.Sgt. J
Thornburrow, Dvr. J.
Tyson, Dvr. S.
Varty, Gnr. T. B.
Wheatcroft, Dvr. W.
Wilson, Sgt. J.
Wilson, Dvr. J. H.
Wannop, Cpl. I. J.

210TH BRIGADE, R.F.A. (T).

Other Ranks

Adams, Gnr. G.
Airey, Gnr. T.
Alderson, Dvr. G.
Baron, Gnr. F.
Becconsall, Sgt. R.
Bell, Bdr. J. M.
Blackwell, Gnr. N.
Bradford, S/S. F. W. D.
Brooker, Dvr. L.
Brown, Siglr. C.
Bullock, Cpl. R.
Calcutt, Dvr. J. H.
Carr, Gnr. N.
Catlow, Sgt. R.
Chadderton, Gnr. A.
Colburn, Gnr. A.
Colburt, Gnr. A.
Conboy, Bdr. J. W.
Demaine, Tptr. J.
Douglas, Gnr. A. H.
Edwards, Bdr. J.
Fish, Gnr. L.
Fletcher, Cpl. E.
Fritzhugh, Gnr. H. A.
Gallagher, Dvr. T.
Gilbert, Dvr. B.

Graham, Bdr. A.
Gregory, Dvr. A.
Hill, Dvr. A.
Holden, Dvr. W.
Isaacson, Dvr. G. R.
Jones, Gnr. T.
Jones, Dvr. W.
Jowett, Gnr. J.
Jowett, Gnr. J. F.
Lascelles, Dvr. E. M.
Lee, Dvr. J.
Lee, Gnr. J.
Lidlil, Gnr. C.
Lightfoot, Gnr. W.
Liversidge, Gnr. T.
Maguinness, Dvr. F.
Marsden, Gnr. T.
Maxwell, Gnr. J.
McCluskey, Gnr.
McFarlane, Dvr. W.
McKeown, Cpl. J.
Midwinter, Gnr.
Mitchell, Dvr. A.
Moulden, Bdr. H.
Nolan, Cpl. W. A.
Ormrod, Gnr. P.

Parkington, Dvr. J.
Parkinson, Siglr. R.
Peak, Cpl. W.
Pickup, Gnr. E.
Rees, Dvr. G.
Riding, Dvr. T.
Robinson, Cpl. R.
Ryan, Bdr. J.
Sanderson, Bdr. R. H.
Sherlock, Gnr. A.
Slack, Gnr. G.
Smith, Bdr. G. H.
Smith, Bdr. H.
Stock, Dvr. G. F.
Stockdale, Gnr. J.
Stott, Gnr. F.
Tallent, Gnr. W.
Thornburrow, Dvr. J.
Tonkin, Gnr. J.
Turner, Dvr. J.
Tyson, Dvr. S.
Waddington, Dvr. E.
Waldwin, Gnr. W.
Wilson, Dvr. P.
Woodruffe, Dvr. F. E.
Wolsey, Dvr. S.

211TH BRIGADE, R.F.A. (T.)

Other Ranks

Ashworth, Fitter-Cpl. R.
Ashworth, Gnr. S.
Bardsley, Gnr. H.
Baybutt, Cpl. A.
Bewley, Dvr. J.
Blenkin, Cpl. T. J.
Boardman, Gnr. T. H.
Bridge, Gnr. A.
Bush, Gnr. P.
Bushby, Gnr. E.

Chipchase, Gnr. J.
Clayton, Sgt. E.
Connor, Gnr. J. W.
Cook, Sgt. T.
Cook, Dvr. W.
Crickett, Gnr. J.
Cunnane, Gnr. T.
Curtis, Bdr. W.
Dixon, Gnr. R.
Dixon, Dvr. W.

Earnshaw, Dvr.
Edwards, Dvr. A.
Edwards, Gnr. R.
Fell, Bdr. J.
Ford, Gnr. A.
Fox, Sgt. W.
Gambles, Bdr. J.
Gray, Farr.-Sgt. W.
Hallworth, Cpl. T.
Hancock, Siglr. G. A.

Roll of Honour

Hardman, Gnr. E. C.
Hardy, Gnr. H.
Hart, Sgt. T. V.
Heaney, Dvr. W.
Henshall, Gnr. D.
Holliday, Gnr. R.
Holmes, Bdr. W.
Hope, Bdr. L.
Howarth, Dvr. C. J.
Hunter, Gnr. N.
Jeffrey, Dvr. H.
Johnstone, Gnr. H.
Kent, Dvr. S.

Lawson, Bdr. T.
McEvoy, Gnr. R.
McGee, Gnr. A.
Murray, Dvr. F.
Oliver, Dvr. A. E.
O'Neill, Dvr.
Reed, Gnr. M.
Rowbotham, Dvr. S.
Russell, Dvr. N.
Schofield, Gnr. J.
Sharpe, L.-Cpl. J. H.
Shaw, Cpl. T.
Shortland, Dvr. E.

Smith, Sgt. W.
Taft, Gnr. S.
Thompson, Sgt. J.
Threlfall, Gnr. L. H.
Varty, Gnr. T. B.
Waddington, Bdr. R.
Wagstaff, Gnr. S.
Warburton, Bdr. R.
Webster, Gnr. H. L.
Whiteley, Gnr. R.
Whitworth, Gnr. C.
Wilson, Cpl. J. G.
Wood, Gnr. W. H.

42ND DIVISIONAL AMMUNITION COLUMN

Other Ranks

Benson, Dvr. H.
Duerden, Cpl. E.
Harding, Dvr. A.

Holt, Dvr. L.
Pontefract, Dvr. V.
Prattley, Dvr. G. T.

Rolley, Dvr. J.
Whaite, Dvr. A.
Wilson, S/S. J.

ROYAL ENGINEERS
427 FIELD COY., R.E.

Officers

Eastwood, Lieut. R. A.
Mackenzie, Lieut. L. A.

Taunton, Lieut. O., M.C.
Ainley, 2nd Lieut. K. E. D.

Hunter, 2nd Lieut. J. K.
Malcolm, 2nd Lieut. W. N.

Other Ranks

Abrahams, 2nd Cpl. E.
Bailey, Sap. E.
Bancroft, Sap. A.
Barlow, Sap. E.
Bettley, Sap. J. H.
Bird, Drv. C.
Birkenshaw, Sap. F.
Bishop, Sap. T.
Bowker, Sap. A.
Bowker, Drv. T.
Broady, Sap. G. H.
Burke, Sap. F.
Burton, Sap. L.
Catterall, Sap. J.
Cawley, Sap. H.
Coglan, Sap. T.
Conway, Sap. T.
Dixon, Sap. R.
Dwyer, Sap. A.

Eastwood, Sap. H.
Farnworth, Sap. J.
Francis, Sap. F.
Garstang, Sgt. J. E.
Giles, Sap. W. D.
Gloyne, Sap. H.
Greenhalgh, Sap. E. A.
Halliwell, Sap. G. N.
Henderson, L.-Cpl. J. F.
Hopkins, Sap. H. B. J.
Horne, 2nd Drv. W.
Hulme, Sap. J.
Hurring, Sap. W.
Jennings, Sap. A.
Later, Sgt. J. O.
Lee, Sap. H. A.
Lees, Drv. F. B.
Leppard, Sap. P.
Loxley, Sap. E.

Maher, Sap. R.
Melville, Sap. H.
Moss, Sgt. H.
Mottram, Sap. W.
Nolan, Sgt. J. W.
Owen, Sap. H.
Penny, Sap. A.
Perkins, L.-Cpl. F.
Probyn, Sap. H.
Ritchie, Sap. C.
Smith, L.-Cpl. E.
Smith, Sap. H.
Smith, Drv. J.
Sproson, Cpl. G.
Tolson, 2nd Cpl. H.
Wilkinson, Sap. W.
Wright, Drv. W.

428 FIELD COY., R.E.

Officers

Carver, Capt. O. A.
Bull, Lieut. G. J. O.

Angus, 2nd Lieut. R. B.
Saint, 2nd Lieut. J. H.

Woods 2nd Lieut. B. H.

Other Ranks

Atkinson, Sap. M.
Barlow, Sap. W.
Bold, Drv. C. H.
Bradshaw, Sap. A.
Brooks, Trmptr. W.
Brocklesby, L.-Cpl. E.
Butterworth, L.-Cpl. J.
Cooper, Sap. A.
Dunn, Sap. J.
Elliott, Sap. C. K.
Farmer, Drv. H.
Goldstraw, 2nd Cpl. R.
Gore, Sap. A.
Greenhalgh, Sap. H.
Greenwood, Sap. W.
Grimshaw, Sap. G. H.
Hampson, Sap. G.

Harwood, Sap. J.
Hinsley, Sap. T.
Hodge, Sap. W. R.
Jackson, Sap. H.
Kelsall, Sap. J. H.
Kerridge, Cpl. W.
Knott, Sap. W.
Magee, Drv. J.
McLeavy, Cpl. G.
McLeod, Sap. W.
McQuinn, L.-Cpl. O.
Mellor, Sgt. W.
Moor, Sap. H.
Moscrop, Sap. J. A.
Mountfield, Sap. H.
Naylor, Cpl. W.
Nugent, Sap. J.

O'Donnell, Sap. F.
Palmer, Sap. J. E.
Pickston, L.-Cpl. H. V.
Potts, Sap. J.
Robinson, Sap. G.
Saunders, Sap. J.
Scott, Sap. J.
Shaw, Cpl. H.
Shaw, L.-Cpl. T. E.
Staresmere, Sap. W.
Stephenson, Sap. F.
Swift, L.-Cpl. H.
Taylor, Drv. J.
Warburton, Sap. H.
Ward, Sap. T. H.
Waterhouse, Sap. T.
Wielding, 2nd Cpl. T.

The 42nd Division

Chapman, Lieut. D. C.

429 FIELD COY., R.E.

Officers

Other Ranks

Ashton, Sap. A.
Baker, Sap. W. F.
Barraclough, Sap. F.
Bates, Sap. S.
Carter, Sap. J. W.
Cooke, Sap. F.
Deedman, Sap. S. F.
Evan, Sap. J. T.
Flynn, Sap. J.
Galpine, Sap. H.
Hellon, Sap. J. W.
Holland, Sap. J.

Hynes, Cpl. W.
Jones, Drv. B.
Kershaw, Sap. G. B.
Mansfield, Sap. A.
McCannah, Sap. S.
Meckin, L.-Cpl. J.
Mort, Cpl. S. C.
Newton, Sgt. J. L.
Rooney, Sap. J.
Royles, Sap. J. H.
Scott, Sap. W.
Shaw, Sap. T. J.

Staveley, Sap. H.
Tomlinson, Sap. J.
Thompson, Sap. J. C.
Walker, Drv. A. W.
Walker, L.-Cpl. G. H.
Watson, Sap. H. H.
Williams, Sap. C.
Williams, Sap. R. C.
Wilkinson, Sap. W.
Wright, L.-Cpl. D.
Yates, Sap. S.

42ND DIVISION SIGNAL COY., R.E.

Officers

Williamson, Capt. C. H., M.C.   Moore, Lieut. H. T. P., M.C.

Other Ranks

Aitchison, Sap. E.
Ardis, Cpl. J.
Bayley, Drv. T.
Broderick, Sap. J., D.C.M.
Couch, L.-Cpl. H., M.M.
Cox, L.-Cpl. R. S.
Dowd, Sap. H. W.
Edwards, S.S. T.
Fielding, Cpl. J., M.M.
Findlay, Pioneer R.
Garside, Sap. F.
Hall, Pioneer E.

Hartley, Drv. W.
Heap, Sap. C.
Heywood, Sap. A.
Higginbottom, Sap. G.
Humphreys, Sap. C. Y.
Jackson, Sap. F.
Kennedy, Cpl. J.
Latter, Sap. S.
Law, Pioneer J. W.
Ling, Sap. A.
Lorimer, Sap. W. E.

Lowe, Drv. J.
McGuire, Drv. J.
Naylor, Sap. E. C.
Penson, Sap. C. W.
Poole, Sap. A.
Richardson, Pioneer J
Sheppard, Sap. F. W.
Sinclair, Sap. J.
Smith, Sap. J. W.
Sutcliffe, Pioneer N.
Walsh, Sap. J.

125th INFANTRY BRIGADE

1/5 BATTALION LANCASHIRE FUSILIERS

Officers

Clive, Lt.-Col. P. A., D.S.O.
Holberton, Lt.-Col. P.V.
Bentley, Capt. F. M., M.C.
Bridge, Capt. J. K.
Briggs, Lieut. W. L.
Hudson, Capt. A. P.
Jemkins, Capt. E. E., M.C.
Kay, Capt. G. C.
Milnes, Capt. S. H.
Paton, Capt. M. B.
Cameron, Lieut. W. G.

Frizelle, Lieut. E. S.
Fryer, Lieut. W. B.
Grant, Lieut. R. W. G.
Harrison, Lieut. C. H.
Hawksey, Lieut. B. R.
Hinckley, Lieut. A.
Hoyle, Lieut. H. K.
Mashiter, Lieut. T. A. G.
Morgan, Lieut. V. H.
Murphy, Lieut. G.

Page, Lieut. J. K. S.
Renshaw, Lieut. A.
Stafford, Lieut. A. D.
Stott, Lieut. W. E.
Tankard, Lieut. W.
Templeman, Lieut. J. W.
Thompson, Lieut. M. B.
Tristram, Lieut. E. B.
Whittam, Lieut. F.
Yapp, Lieut. W. C.

Other Ranks

Adams, Pte. H.
Alderson, Pte. R. A.
Aldridge, Pte. G.
Allcock, Pte. W.
Allen, Pte. H.
Allen, Pte. W.
Alliban, Pte. H.
Alston, L.-Cpl. H.
Andrews, L.-Cpl. H. H.
Andrews, Pte. J.
Andrews, Pte. R. A.
Ansins, Pte. G.
Antrobus, Pte. W.
Archer, Pte. E. J.
Armstrong, L.-Cpl. W.
Ash, Pte. G. V.
Ashton, Pte. A.
Ashton, Pte. J. H.

Ashton, Pte. R. J.
Ashworth, Pte. H.
Atkinson, Pte. W.
Austin, Pte. J.
Austin, Pte. R.
Bageant, Pte. F.
Bamford, Pte. B. P.
Bamford, Pte. W.
Bamford, Pte. W.
Banks, C.Sgt.-Mjr. W.
Barker, Pte. L.
Barker, Pte. T.
Barker, Cpl. T. H.
Barley, Pte. G.
Barlow, Pte. F.
Barnes, L.-Cpl. C. E.
Barton, Pte. J. A.
Beardsworth, Pte. R.

Beaumont, Pte. J.
Bedford, Pte. C.
Bedford, Pte. C. J.
Bennett, Pte. J.
Bennett, Sgt. J.
Bent, Pte. W.
Berry, Pte. H.
Berry, Pte. J.
Berry, Pte. L.
Bills, Pte. H.
Birch, Pte. H.
Birchall, Pte. F.
Bird, Pte. W. T.
Bishop, Pte. C.
Boardman, Pte. C.
Boardman, Pte. D.
Boon, L.-Cpl. J. J.
Booth, Pte. N.

Booth, Sgt. H.
Booth, Pte. J. W.
Booth, Pte. S.
Boothman, Pte. J.
Bowden, Cpl. C.
Bowker, Cpl. T.
Bradburn, Pte. H.
Bradford, Pte. L.
Bradley, Pte. H.
Bradshaw, Pte. A.
Brand, Sgt. H.
Brennan, Cpl. J.
Brierley, Pte. J. J.
Brocklehurst, Pte. F.
Brooks, Pte. A.
Brooks, Cpl. W.
Brown, Pte. T.
Brown, Pte. G.
Brown, Pte. H.
Buckley, Cpl. E. F.
Buckley, Pte. J.
Bunn, Pte. A.
Bunn, L.-Cpl. J. J.
Burden, Pte. F.
Burke, Pte. J.
Burke, Cpl. P.
Burrows, Pte. C.
Burston, Pte. W.
Butterworth, Pte. A.
Butterworth, Pte. E.
Butterworth, Pte. F.
Butterworth, Pte. G.
Butterworth, Cpl. J.
Butterworth, Pte. J.
Butterworth, Pte. R.
Butterworth, Pte. W.
Butterworth, Cpl. W.
Buxton, Pte. G. V.
Calderbank, Pte. F.
Calverley, L.-Cpl. J. E.
Carless, C.Sgt.-Mjr. W., D.C.M.
Carmichael, Pte. R. F.
Carney, Pte. J.
Carr, Pte. J.
Carroll, Pte. W.
Carruthers, Pte. J. R.
Chadwick, C.Sgt.-Mjr. J.
Chamley, Pte. W.
Chapman, Pte. E.
Charles, Pte. D.
Charman, Pte. A.
Clarke, Pte. G.
Clarke, Pte. W.
Clarke, Cpl. S. E.
Clifford, Pte. M.
Cockcroft, L.-Cpl. E.
Coe, Pte. A.
Collantine, Pte. J.
Collinson, Pte. F.
Compston, Cpl. T. H.
Connell, Pte. W.
Connelly, Pte. J.
Consterdine, Sgt. W.
Cookson, Pte. H.
Cooper, Pte. A.
Cooper, Pte. W. E.
Corlett, Pte. J. A.
Corser, Cpl. F.
Cowley, Pte. J.
Crabtree, Pte. J.
Crabtree, Pte. W.
Crawford, Pte. H.
Crawford, Pte. W.
Crawford, Pte. W.
Crook, Pte. A.
Crossley, Pte. J. H.
Crowther, Pte. W.
Cryer, Pte. F.

Cullen, Pte. J.
Curran, Pte. J.
Curran, Pte. T.
Cutts, Pte. H.
Dakin, Pte. E. B.
Davison, Pte. T.
Dawson, L.-Cpl. W. L.
Dean, Pte. R.
Dearden, Sgt. F.
Dickie, L.-Cpl. D.
Dixon, Pte. C.
Dixon, Pte. F.
Dobson, Pte. T.
Dodd, Pte. T.
Douglas, Pte. J. W.
Duckworth, Pte. R.
Dudley, Pte. H.
Duncan, Pte. W.
Duxbury, Pte. W.
Eatough, Pte. L.
Eccles, Pte. T.
Eckersley, Sgt. E.
Eckersley, Pte. F.
Egerton, Pte. F.
Entwistle, Pte. D.
Evans, Pte. C.
Evans, L.-Cpl. E. R.
Fitzsimmonds, Pte. T.
Fletcher, Pte. G.
Flook, Pte. A.
Ford, Pte. J.
Foxcroft, Pte. A.
Foxcroft, Pte. W.
Fraser, Pte. J.
French, Pte. G.
Frith, Pte. C.
Garland, Pte. A.
Garner, Pte. G. H.
Garner, Pte. W. R.
Garswood, Pte. G.
Gibbons, Pte. C.
Glasgow, Pte. R.
Gledhill, Pte. F.
Goldsmith, Pte. F.
Goodall, Pte. E.
Goodfellow, Pte. J.
Greaves, Pte. F.
Green, Pte. T.
Green, Pte. W.
Greenhalgh, L.-Cpl. F.
Greenwood, Pte. H.
Griffiths, Pte. P.
Grimshaw, Pte. C.
Grimshaw, Pte. R.
Grimston, Pte. R.
Grundy, Pte. J.
Guthrie, Pte. J.
Guy, L.-Cpl. J. W.
Hall, Pte. F.
Hall, Pte. E.
Hall, Pte. H.
Hall, Pte. H.
Hall, Pte. J.
Hall, Pte. R.
Hall, Pte. S.
Hall, Pte. W.
Hallisey, Pte. J.
Hamer, Pte. J.
Hamilton, Sgt. J.
Hardman, Pte. J.
Harling, Pte. J.
Harness, Pte. A.
Harper, Sgt. H.
Harrington, Pte. F.
Harrison, Pte. S.
Hart, Pte. S.
Hartney, Pte. J.
Haslam, Pte. E.

Head, Pte. W. C.
Hearst, Pte. A.
Heaton, Pte. S. J.
Hemmings, Cpl. J.
Heyes, L.-Sgt. W.
Heywood, Pte. R.
Heywood, Pte. W.
Hill, Pte. F.
Hill, Cpl. J.
Hill, Pte. T.
Hines, Pte. W.
Hockey, Pte. E. J.
Hodges, Cpl. L.
Hodgson, Pte. D.
Hodgson, Pte. G.
Holcroft, Pte. P.
Holden, Sgt. A.
Holden, L.-Cpl. J. G.
Holden, Pte. R.
Holden, Pte. W.
Holding, Pte. G.
Holland, Pte. W. H.
Holt, Pte. C.
Holt, Cpl. J.
Holt, Pte. J.
Holt, Pte. J. C.
Holt, Pte. T.
Holt, Pte. W.
Hopkinson, Pte. J.
Hopkinson, Pte. P.
Hopwood, Pte. W. P.
Horgan, Cpl. C.
Horrocks, Pte. S.
Horrocks, Pte. T.
Horsman, Pte. J. E.
Hough, Pte. F.
Houghton, Pte. H.
Houghton, Pte. J.
Howard, Pte. H.
Howard, Pte. J.
Howard, Pte. W. E.
Howarth, Sgt. J.
Howarth, Pte. R.
Howarth, Pte. S.
Howarth, Pte. W.
Howell, Pte. S.
Huddleston, Pte. A.
Hughes, Pte. J.
Hulmes, Pte. H.
Hunt, Pte. T. H. M.
Hurst, Pte. H.
Hurst, Pte. J.
Hutchinson, Pte. H.
Hutchinson, Cpl. R.
Hutton, Pte. W.
Hyland, L. Cpl. M.
Ingham, C.Sgt.-Mjr. A.
Jeffries, Pte. A.
Johnson, C.Q.M.Sgt. H. K.
Jones, Pte. E.
Jones, Pte. H.
Jones, Pte. J.
Jones, Pte. T.
Jones, Pte. W.
Jones, Pte. W.
Kay, Pte. D.
Kay, L.-Cpl. W.
Kean, Pte. F.
Keighley, Pte. J.
Kelly, Pte. J. M.
Kelly, Pte. T.
Kenyon, L.-Cpl. H.
Kershaw, Pte. F.
Kershaw, Pte. J.
Kildare, Pte. R.
Kirk, Pte. J. W.
Kirkman, Sgt. F.
Kirkman, L.-Cpl. M.

Knight, Cpl. A. J.
Knowles, Sgt. E.
Knowles, Pte. R.
Lawless, Pte. J.
Lee, Pte. E.
Lee, Pte. G.
Lee, Cpl. J.
Lee, Pte. P.
Leech, Pte. J.
Lever, Pte. J.
Lewis, Pte. W. H.
Linton, Pte. G.
Livesey, Pte. F.
Livsay, Pte. W.
Lockwood, Pte. R.
Lomas, Pte. S.
Lomax, Pte. F.
Lomax, Pte. S.
Lomax, Pte. S.
Lord, Pte. A.
Lord, Pte. F.
Lord, Pte. J. E.
Low, L.-Cpl. W. A.
Lowe, Pte. F.
Lowe, Pte. P.
Lowe, Pte. R.
Lowe, Pte. S.
Lowery, Pte. J. F.
Lowther, L.-Cpl. W.
Lundregan, Pte. G.
Mahon, Pte. E.
Mahoney, L.-Sgt. P.
Manley, Pte. A. R.
Mapley, Pte. G. F.
Martin, Pte. R.
Martin, Sgt. T.
Mason, L.-Cpl. C.
Mather, Pte. A. H.
Mather, Sgt. F.
Mather, Pte. J.
Matthews, Pte. A. D.
Maughan, Pte. J. J.
May, Pte. J.
May, Pte. J.
Mayall, Pte. J. G.
Mayor, Pte. F.
McLaren, Pte. T.
McLean, Pte. J.
McMahon, Pte. W. H.
McNamara, Pte. A.
Merriman, Pte. T.
Metcalf, Pte. M.
Micklesfield, Sgt. J.
Midgley, Pte. F.
Mighall, Sgt. J.
Milburn, C.Q.M.Sgt. F.
Mitchell, Pte. W.
Monks, Pte. J.
Moore, Pte. G. W.
Morris, Pte. J.
Moult, Pte. J. W.
Murphy, Cpl. S.
Murray, Pte. R.
Nabb, Pte. W.
Nadin, Pte. S. H.
Naylor, Pte. F.
Nesbitt, Pte. R. W.
Newbury, Pte. W.
Newton, Pte. W. B.
Noble, Pte. G.
Nolan, Pte. W.
Nuttall, Pte. H.
Nuttall, Cpl. J.
Nuttall, Pte. N.
Nuttall, Sgt. W.
Nuttall, Pte. W.
O'Brien, Pte. J. W.
O'Connell, Pte. W.

Ogden, Pte. H.
Ogden, Pte. W.
Oliver, Sgt. J. A.
Orrell, Sgt. J.
Orrell, Pte. W.
Park, Pte. A.
Park, Pte. J.
Parker, Pte. F. M.
Parker, Pte. J. H.
Parker, Pte. T.
Parks, Pte. J.
Partington, Pte. F.
Partington, L.-Cpl. H.
Partridge, Pte. L.
Pearson, L.-Cpl. C.
Pearson, Pte. J.
Petrie, Pte. G.
Phillips, Pte. H. C.
Pitcher, Pte. P. H.
Pitt-Pladdy, Cpl. J. K.
Pollitt, Pte. J.
Pollitt, Pte. T.
Poole, Pte. C. A.
Pooley, Pte. J.
Porter, Pte. F. M.
Porter, Pte. P.
Porter, Sgt. R. W.
Preston, Pte. H. A.
Price, L.-Sgt. F.
Radcliffe, Pte. E.
Ramsbotton, Pte. J.
Ratcliffe, Pte. H.
Rawcliffe, Pte. J. R.
Reed, Pte. C. R.
Regan, Pte. F. A.
Richardson, L.-Cpl. S.
Rigby, Pte. F.
Rigby, L.-Cpl. J.
Rigby, L.-Cpl. J.
Riley, Pte. F.
Riley, Cpl. R.
Riley, Pte. W.
Roach, Pte. H.
Robinson, Pte. C. R.
Robinson, L.-Cpl. L.
Robinson, Pte. R.
Rogers, Pte. B.
Rowbotham, Pte. F.
Rowe, Pte. A.
Rowlstone, Pte. E.
Rudd, Pte. F.
Rumins, Pte. G.
Sagar, Pte. A.
Sale, Pte. H.
Sampler, Pte. A.
Savage, Pte. J. J.
Scaife, Pte. W.
Schofield, L.-Cpl. J.
Schofield, Pte. W.
Scholes, Pte. N.
Scorey, Pte. L. H.
Scotson, Pte. J.
Scotting, Pte. W. H.
Scowcroft, Pte. J.
Sculley, Pte. W.
Seal, Pte. W.
Sedgwick, Sgt. F.
Sharples, Pte. L.
Shaw, Pte. F.
Shaw, Pte. W.
Sheldon, Pte. G.
Shepherd, Pte. B.
Shepherd, Pte. F.
Shepherd, Pte. W.
Shillingford, Pte. A.
Sillifant, Pte. R. S.
Simson, Pte. J.
Skeen, Pte. J. T.

Slinger, Pte. R.
Smethurst, Pte. A.
Smethurst, Pte. R.
Smith, Pte. A. W.
Smith, L.-Cpl. C. F.
Smith, Pte. F.
Smith, Pte. G.
Smith, Pte. H.
Smith, Pte. H.
Smith, Sgt. J.
Smith, Pte. J. G.
Smith, Pte. T.
Smith, Sgt. W.
Spencer, Pte. G.
Spinks, Pte. W.
Stanley, Pte. H.
Starling, Pte. M.
Steele, Pte. A. A.
Stockdale, Pte. E.
Storey, Sgt. J. E.
Stott, Pte. W.
Street, Pte. A.
Stringfellow, Pte. A.
Stroud, Pte. W. J.
Studholme, Pte. W.
Sumpter, Pte. A.
Sutcliffe, Pte. A.
Sutcliffe, Pte. C.
Sykes, Sgt. N.
Taylor, Pte. A.
Taylor, Pte. D. W.
Taylor, Pte. E.
Taylor, Pte. H.
Taylor, Pte. G.
Taylor, Pte. J. W.
Taylor, Pte. W.
Taylor, L.-Cpl. W. H.
Tedford, Pte. G.
Tennant, Pte. F.
Tennant, L.-Cpl. J. H.
Tetlow, Pte. L. H.
Thomas, Pte. W.
Thompson, Pte. F.
Thompson, Pte. J. A.
Thompson, Pte. W.
Thompson, Pte. W.
Thornton, Pte. S.
Todd, Pte. W. F.
Tootall, Pte. T.
Toothill, Pte. T.
Travis, Pte. H.
Treloar, L.-Cpl. H.
Turner, Pte. F.
Tweedale, Pte. W.
Tyrer, Pte. J.
Unsworth, Pte. F.
Upham, Pte. H.
Vardon, Pte. R.
Viggers, L.-Cpl. H.
Wagstaff, L.-Cpl. H.
Wakes, Pte. G.
Walker, Pte. C.
Walker, Pte. J.
Wall, Pte. T.
Waller, Pte. F.
Walling, Pte. J.
Walmsley, Pte. H.
Walmsley, Pte. H. A.
Walsh, Pte. R.
Walton, L.-Cpl. H. A.
Walton, Pte. T.
Watson, Pte. A.
Watts, Pte. T.
Webb, Pte. W.
Whalley, Pte. J.
Whalley, Pte. S.
Wharton, Pte. H.
Whatmough, Pte. R.

Whitehead, Pte. J.
Whitehead, L.-Cpl. S.
Whiteley, Pte. F.
Whittaker, Pte. J.
Whittam, Sgt. J.
Whittingham, L.-Cpl. H.
Wickstead, Pte. J.
Wild, Pte. F.
Wilding, Pte. W.
Wiles, Pte. G.
Wilkinson, Pte. A.

Wilkinson, Pte. D.
Wilkinson, Pte. J.
Wilkinson, Pte. J.
Wilkinson, Pte. M.
Williams, Pte. A. E.
Williams, Pte. G. W.
Williamson, Pte. J.
Wilson, Pte. A.
Wilson, Pte. E.
Wood, Pte. H.
Wood, Pte. H.

Wood, Pte. J.
Wood, Sgt. J.
Woods, Pte. J.
Woodward, Pte. A.
Wright, Pte. W.
Wroe, Pte. V.
Yates, Pte. H.
Yates, C.Sgt.-Mjr. J. H.
Yates, Pte. T. F.
Yates, Pte. W.
Young, Pte. W.

1/6 BATTALION LANCASHIRE FUSILIERS

Officers

Blake, Capt. G. S.
Clegg, Capt. A. V.
Griffiths, Capt. and Q.M. W. H.
Spafford, Capt. and Adjt. A. L.
Griffiths, A.-Capt. J. F. U.
Harvey, Lieut. F. W.

Holden, Lieut. N. V.
Leake, Lieut.
O'Neill, Lieut. S.
Smith, Lieut. J. H.
Aitken, 2nd Lieut. J. F.
Duckworth, 2nd Lieut. E.

Isherwood, 2nd Lieut. N.
Noxon, 2nd Lieut. F. C.
Taylor, 2nd Lieut. T. R.
Thompson, 2nd Lieut. G. C.
Wyatt, 2nd Lieut. J. L.

Other Ranks

Ackroyd, Pte. B.
Acton, Pte. J. W.
Adams, Cpl. G.
Adshead, Pte. L.
Allsopp, Cpl. A.
Anderson, Pte. A.
Appleton, Sgt. H.
Armstrong, Pte. J. W.
Armstrong, Pte. J. W.
Armstrong, Pte. W.
Ashton, Pte. E.
Ashurst, Pte. I.
Ashworth, Pte. F.
Ashworth, Pte. G.
Ashworth, Pte. J.
Ashworth, Pte. N.
Atkinson, Pte. F.
Atkinson, Pte. G.
Bailey, Cpl. W.
Ball, Cpl. F.
Bamford, Pte. W.
Barker, Pte. F. A.
Barlow, Pte. O.
Barnes, Pte. J. T.
Beaman, Pte. P.
Beere, Pte. R. E.
Benbow, Sgt. J. E.
Berry, Pte. F. W.
Birbeck, Pte. J.
Black, Pte. T.
Boardman, Cpl. J.
Boocock, Pte. F.
Boocock, Pte. T.
Boothman, Sgt. W.
Bowker, Pte. A.
Boyes, Pte. J.
Boyes, Pte. J.
Brereton, L.-Sgt. T.
Bridge, Pte. H.
Bridge, Pte. T.
Brierley, Pte. J. W.
Britton, L.-Cpl. F.
Broadbent, Sgt. S.
Brookes, Pte. J.
Brown, Pte. W.
Broxton, Pte. E.
Burgess, Sgt. J.
Burrows, Pte. J.
Butterworth, Pte. F.
Butterworth, Pte. W.
Callow, Pte. J. W.
Carpenter, Pte. W. H.

Carr, Sgt. P.
Chadwick, Pte. C. H.
Chadwick, Pte. H.
Chadwick, Pte. W.
Cheadle, Pte. A. P.
Child, Pte. J. W.
Clark, Pte. H.
Clarke, Pte. E.
Clarke, Pte. W.
Clegg, Pte. A.
Cockerill, Pte. W.
Connolley, Pte. F.
Connolly, Pte. J.
Conoley, Pte. T.
Consterdine, Pte. F.
Cook, Pte. C.
Cook, L.-Sgt. R.
Copeland, Pte. G.
Cotton, Pte. E.
Crossley, A.-Sgt. G.
Crossley, Pte. N.
Crosswell, Pte. H.
Crowther, Pte. H.
Cryer, Pte. E.
Cryer, Cpl. J.
Curran, Pte. P.
Daniels, C.Sgt.-Maj. S.
Davies, Pte. C.
Dawson, Pte. W.
Dean, Pte. A.
Dean, Sgt. J.
Dearden, Pte. E.
Dix, Pte. C. H.
Donegani, Pte. T.
Doswell, Pte. H.
Dougherty, Pte. J.
Drouthwaite, Pte. W.
Emerson, Pte. W.
English, Pte. P.
Entwistle, Pte. H.
Etcalfe, Pte. C.
Evans, Pte. G. E.
Farnworth, Pte. E. A.
Farrar, Pte. J. W.
Farrar, Pte. W.
Fielder, Pte. F.
Firth, Pte. F.
Firth, Pte. F.
Fitton, Pte. A.
Fitton, Pte. J. A.
Fitton, Cpl. W.
Fitton, Sgt. W.

Fores, Pte. A.
Foulds, Pte. W.
Foulger, Pte. H.
Foxall, Pte. J.
Foxhall, Pte. J.
Freestone, Pte. J. W.
Fretwell, Pte. G. H.
Fretwell, Pte. J.
Gallagher, Pte. J. T.
Gannon, Pte. T.
Garlick, Pte. H.
Garlick, Pte. H.
Geldard, A.-Cpl. G.
Gibbons, Pte. F.
Gibbs, Pte. J.
Gibson, Sgt. T.
Gledhill, Pte. A. W.
Gorden, Pte. F.
Gordon, Pte. F.
Gosling, Pte. C.
Gosling, Pte. J.
Grant, Pte. C.
Gregory, Pte. T.
Greenwood, Pte. F.
Greenwood, Pte. H.
Greenwood, Pte. H.
Greenwood, L.-Cpl. W.
Greenwood, Pte. W.
Greenwood, Pte. W. A.
Grime, Sgt. A.
Grimshaw, Pte. J.
Gruchy, Cpl. J.
Guthrie, Sgt. T.
Hadley, Pte. J. R.
Halliwell, Pte. A.
Hamer, Pte. H.
Hamer, Pte. W. H.
Hammond, Pte. R.
Hammond, Pte. R.
Haney, Pte. J.
Hannel, Pte. W. A.
Hardiker, Pte. H.
Hargreaves, Pte. H.
Harrison, Pte. T.
Haselgrave, Pte. H.
Hassall, Pte. S.
Hayes, Pte. E.
Heanon, L.-Cpl. T.
Heap, Pte. E.
Heap, Pte. W.
Heap, Pte. W.
Henderson, Pte. E.

208   The 42nd Division

Hesketh, Pte. W.
Heveron, Pte. E.
Heywood, Pte. O.
Hilton, Pte. H. C.
Holbrook, Pte. J.
Holden, Pte. B.
Holden, Cpl. E.
Holding, Pte. P.
Holding, Pte. P.
Hollows, Pte. B.
Holt, Pte. F.
Holt, Pte. F.
Hopkins, Pte. A.
Hopkinson, Pte. J.
Hosker, L.-Sgt. W.
Howard, Pte. E.
Howard, Cpl. P.
Howarth, Pte. F. B.
Howarth, Pte. F. B.
Howarth, L.-Cpl. O.
Howarth, Pte. S.
Hoyle, Pte. J.
Humphreys, Pte. F.
Hunt, Pte. A.
Hunt, Pte. J.
Hyland, L.-Cpl. E.
Hyland, Cpl. J.
Ingham, Pte. W.
Irving, Pte. J.
Izatt, Sgt. J.
Jackson, A.-Sgt. E.
Jackson, Pte. H.
Jackson, Pte. H.
Jackson, Pte. H.
Jackson, Pte. S.
Jackson, Pte. W.
Jacques, Pte. R.
James, Sgt. S.
Jamieson, Pte. A.
Jeffreys, Pte. R.
Jewel, Pte. T.
Jolly, A.-Cpl. J.
Jones, Pte. W.
Keary, Pte. T.
Kelly, Pte. T.
Kennedy, Pte. S.
Kinna, Pte. T. V.
Kirkby, Cpl. C.
Knight, Pte. H.
Knott, Pte. J.
Lamb, Pte. J.
Langdale, Pte. J.
Langley, Pte. J. W.
Lawrence, Pte. J.
Lawton, Pte. J.
Lees, Pte. H.
Lewis, Pte. F.
Liddle, Pte. A.
Livesey, Pte. J.
Livesey, Pte. R.
Longbottom, Pte. D.
Lord, C.Sgt.-Maj. J.
Lord, Pte. S. R.
Lovatt, Pte. H.
Maddock, Pte. A.
Marsden, L.-Cpl. J.
Marshall, Pte. F.
Marshall, Pte. F.
Mason, C.Sgt.-Maj. J.
McCann, Pte. J.
McDermott, Pte. G.

McDonald, Pte. G.
Mellor, Pte. F.
Mellor, Sgt. J.
Mellor, Pte. S.
Metcalfe, Pte. C.
Middleton, Pte. R.
Mills, Pte. F.
Mills, Pte. F.
Mills, Pte. H.
Milne, Pte. H.
Mitchell, Pte. A.
Mitchell, Pte. G.
Mitchell, Pte. G.
Morris, Pte. A.
Morris, Pte. T.
Morris, Pte. T.
Morrow, L.-Sgt. A.
Murphy, Pte. A.
Naylor, Pte. T.
Newton, Pte. J.
Nightingale, Pte. J.
Nuttall, Pte. A.
O'Donnell, Pte. P.
Ogden, Sgt. J.
Ogden, Pte. R.
Oldfield, Cpl. J.
Oliver, Pte. L.
Osbaldston, Pte. G.
Owen, Pte. J. H.
Palfreyman, Cpl. H.
Parry, Pte. E.
Parry, Pte. W.
Partington, Pte. J.
Parton, Pte. E.
Parton, Pte. E.
Paskell, Pte. E. C.
Pearson, Pte. H. J.
Pickersgill, Pte. C.
Pickles, Pte. E.
Pickles, Pte. F.
Pilkington, Pte. E. L.
Pilling, Pte. H.
Pollitt, Pte. J.
Potter, Pte. G. R.
Potter, Pte. G. R.
Powell, Pte. G.
Prince, Pte. S. J.
Ratcliffe, Pte. F.
Ratcliffe, Pte. T.
Rawle, Pte. P.
Reed, C.Sgt.-Mjr. W.
Richards, Pte. E.
Richardson, Pte. H.
Richardson, Pte. W.
Riley, Pte. F.
Riley, Pte. J. T.
Risby, Pte. R.
Roberts, Pte. H. W.
Robinson, L.-Cpl. W. H.
Robinson, Pte. W. H.
Rogers, Cpl. D.
Rostern, Pte. W.
Rushton, Pte. J. R.
Russell, Pte. F.
Russell, Pte. G.
Ryle, Pte. W.
Sanderson, Pte. J.
Saville, Pte. R.
Schofield, Pte. F.
Scholes, Pte. W.
Scott, Pte. W.

Seal, Sgt. A.
Seal, L.-Cpl. H.
Senior, Pte. H.
Seville, Pte. T.
Seville, Pte. T.
Sharpe, Pte. N.
Sheard, Pte. J.
Shepherd, Pte. A.
Shepherd, A.-Sgt. W.
Sherriff, Pte. W.
Simpson, Pte. J.
Simpson, L.-Cpl. W.
Simpson, Pte. W.
Simpson, Cpl. W. H.
Skyes, Pte. N.
Smith, L.-Cpl. A. W.
Smith, Pte. J.
Smith, Pte. W.
Spencer, Cpl.
Spencer, L.-Cpl. J. W.
Stafford, L.-Cpl. J.
Stansfield Pte. R. H.
Stansfield, L.-Cpl. T.
Stock, Pte. A.
Stockport, Pte. J.
Stockton, Pte. J. W.
Stott, Pte. F.
Stott, Pte. J.
Stringer, Pte. N.
Styles, Pte. G. E.
Sutcliffe, Pte. F.
Sutcliffe, Pte. F.
Sutcliffe, Pte. W.
Taylor, Pte. H.
Taylor, A.-Cpl. I.
Taylor, Pte. J.
Taylor, Pte. R. R.
Thompson, Cpl. E. J.
Tillitson, Pte. J.
Timms, Pte. J.
Travis, Pte. W.
Turles, Pte. H.
Turner, Pte. C. E.
Turner, Pte. E.
Turner, Pte. F.
Turner, Pte. J.
Turner, Pte. W.
Turner, Pte. W.
Wacey, Pte. W.
Walsh, Pte. J.
Walters, L.-Cpl. R.
Walton, Pte. G.
Walton, Pte. J. A.
Walton, Pte. S.
Walton, Pte. W.
Weaver, Pte. W.
Webster, Pte. A.
Wedge, Pte. J.
Wellens, Pte. W.
Wheelan, Pte. A.
Whittaker, Pte. T.
Whittaker, Pte. W.
Whittaker, Pte. W.
Whitworth, Pte. H.
Whitworth, Pte. J.
Wilcock, Cpl. H.
Wild, Cpl. G.
Wild, Pte. G.
Wild, Pte. J.
Wilde, Sgt. J.
Worsley, Pte. T.

1/7 BATTALION LANCASHIRE FUSILIERS

Officers

Cade, Maj. R. H.
Law, Maj. W. J.
Blease, Capt. H.
Humphreys, Capt. A. C.
Murgatroyd, Capt. H. L., M.C.
   (Leicester Regt.)
Waterhouse, Capt. R.
Morrison, Act.-Capt. L. (Lt.
   Liverpool Regt.)
Austin, Lieut. S.
Burleigh, Lieut. B.

Ripperger, Lieut. H. T. A., M.C.
   (4th Gloucester Regt.)
Roberts, Lieut. E. W.
Spink, Lieut. E. W.
Tennant, Lieut. A. S.
Andrews, 2nd Lieut. H. G.
Battye, 2nd Lieut. R.
Beecroft, 2nd Lieut. W. H.
   (6th Gloucesters)
Carter, 2nd Lieut. H. J.
Downham, 2nd Lieut. H.
Hartley, 2nd Lieut. W. R.

Heaton, 2nd Lieut. H. W.
Kerr, 2nd Lieut. R. C., R.F.A.
   (S.R.)
Lakeman, 2nd Lieut. H. L.,
   R.A.S.C.
Steele, 2nd Lieut. W.
Thompson, 2nd Lieut. J. S.
   (West Riding)
Usher, 2nd Lieut. R. W. A.
Weyman, 2nd Lieut. P.
Williams, 2nd Lieut. T. J.

Other Ranks

Aden, Pte. C.
Agnew, Pte. J.
Aldons, Cpl. G.
Anslow, Pte. T.
Appleton, Sgt. J. M. M.
Appleton, Pte. R.
Arkustell, L.-Cpl. A. T.
Arkwright, Pte. T.
Arnold, Pte. T.
Armstrong, Pte. J.
Ashcroft, L.-Cpl. J.
Ashley, Pte. J.
Ashton, Pte. W.
Ashworth, Pte. E.
Atkinson, Pte. W.
Backhouse, Pte. A.
Bagg, Pte. S.
Bailey, Pte. J. W.
Baker, Sgt. D.
Baker, Pte. H.
Baker, Pte. R. W.
Baldestone, Pte. J. H.
Bamford, Pte. J.
Barber, Pte. J. J.
Bardsley, Pte. F.
Bardsley, Pte. G.
Barker, Pte. C. W. R.
Barlow, Pte. J.
Barlow, Pte. W.
Barrowclogh, Pte. C. E.
Beale, Pte. J. A.
Beamish, Pte. W.
Beardmore, Pte. J. B.
Beaumont, Pte. R.
Berry, Pte. J.
Bird, Pte. E.
Bishop, Pte. B. V.
Bishop, Sgt. J.
Bishop, Pte. L.
Blakely, Pte. J.
Blakeway, Pte. T. I.
Blekeley, Pte. W. H.
Bond, Pte. J.
Bouston, Pte. S. J.
Bower, Sgt. W.
Boyer, Sgt. W.
Bradbury, Pte. A.
Braddock, Pte. G. W.
Bradley, L.-Cpl. W.
Bradshaw, Pte. E.
Brearley, Pte. H.
Brock, Cpl. A. D.
Brooks, Pte. A.
Brooks, Pte. E.
Brough, L.-Cpl. J.
Brown, Pte. T.
Brown, C.Q.M.Sgt. W
Bowen, Pte. T.
Bull, Pte. B.

Bullock, Pte. S.
Bunting, Pte. S.
Burfoot, Pte. A.
Burfoot, Pte. C.
Burgess, Pte. S.
Burgoyne, Pte. W.
Burke, Pte. R.
Bush, Pte. S. L. A.
Cameron, Pte. C.
Carey, Pte. E. P.
Carr, Pte. J. F.
Carr, Pte. G.
Carter, L.-Cpl. F. J.
Carter, Pte. W.
Cartwright, Pte. S.
Cathaside, Pte. J.
Catlin, Pte. A.
Caulfield, Pte. J.
Chadderton, Pte. A.
Chadwick, Pte. E.
Chadwick, Pte. R.
Chadwick, Pte. R.
Chantry, Pte. H.
Chapman, Pte. S.
Cheetham, Sgt. R. C.
Chetwood, Pte. J. W.
Chilcutt, Pte. W.
Chorlton, Pte. J.
Chorlton, Pte. J. E.
Christian, Pte. J.
Clarke, Pte. A.
Clarke, Pte. F.
Clarke, Pte. J.
Clayton, Pte. H.
Clewlow, Pte. S.
Coackley, Pte. F.
Coates, Pte. R. E.
Cockrane, Pte. D.
Collins, Pte. A. F.
Colling, L.-Cpl. R. M.
Conlan, Pte. J.
Conner, Pte. J.
Cooke, Pte. D.
Cordner, Pte. J.
Cotton, Pte. J.
Courtney, Sgt. F.
Cowborn, Pte. J.
Crane, Pte. D.
Critchley, Pte. T.
Cronshaw, Pte. H.
Crotch, Pte. A.
Cullen, Pte. J.
Cunningham, Pte. T.
Curzon, Pte. L.
Dalling, Cpl G.
Daly, Pte. M.
Damson, Pte. F. H.
Davenport, Pte. H.
Davenport, Sgt. W. H.

Davidson, Pte. G. J.
Dawe, Pte. H.
Deavall, Pte. J.
Devine, Pte. B. W.
Devine, Pte. T. B.
Dickenson, Pte. G. A.
Dickson, Pte. J.
Dilworth, Sgt. J. T. T.
Dodd, Pte. E.
Dolby, Pte. F.
Donelly, Pte. F.
Dorber, Pte. W.
Downes, Pte. A.
Downton, L.-Cpl. W.
Dudd, Pte. J. S.
Duffy, Pte. P.
Duffy, Pte. W.
Dunham, Pte. W. F.
Dunthorne, Pte. W.
Durnford, Pte. T. E.
Dutton, Pte. J.
Dutton, L.-Cpl. R.
Earnshaw, Pte. J.
Easthan, Cpl. W.
Eckersall, Pte. S.
Eckersley, Pte. E.
Edge, Pte. W.
Ellison, Pte. F.
Evans, Pte. E.
Evans, Pte. F.
Evans, Pte. W.
Everall, Pte. T.
Farquharson, Pte. J.
Farrar, Pte. J. R.
Fender, Pte. J.
Ferrier, Pte. J. R.
Fisher, Pte. J.
Flynn, L.-Cpl. E.
Foulkes, Cpl. J. H.
Franklin, Cpl. T.
Freer, Cpl. T.
Friary, Pte. J.
Gainan, Pte. F.
Gandy, Pte. H.
Gaskell, Pte. W.
Gee, Pte. D.
Gee, Pte. J. W.
Gee, Pte. R.
Gelder, Pte. A. E.
Gerard, Pte. F.
Giblin, Pte. C. T.
Gibson, Pte. C.
Gillespy, Pte. A.
Gillings, Pte. A.
Gillow, Pte. J.
Goddard, Pte. J. C.
Goodhall, Pte. H.
Gorman, Pte. H. T.
Gorton, Pte. J.

P

Graham, Pte. F.
Grant, Pte. A.
Green, Pte. J.
Green, Pte. J. R.
Green, Pte. P.
Gregory, Pte. H.
Gregory, L.-Cpl. R. C.
Gregory, Pte. S.
Grice, Pte. A.
Griffin, Pte. F.
Griffiths, Pte. E. V.
Grimshaw, Pte. J.
Grimsley, Pte. A.
Hack, Pte. A.
Hackney, L.-Cpl. A.
Hacking, Pte. W.
Hall, Pte. B. R.
Hall, Pte. C.
Hall, Pte. E.
Hall, Pte. G.
Hall, Pte. H.
Hall, Pte. S.
Hanley, Pte. J.
Haigh, Pte. G.
Hardman, Pte. G.
Hardman, Pte. R.
Hardy, Pte. J. H.
Harley, Pte. E.
Harries, Pte. S. J.
Hart, Cpl. T.
Hartley, Pte. J.
Harvey, L.-Cpl. A.
Hasey, Pte. F.
Hassall, Pte. H.
Hawthorn, Pte. T.
Hayward, Pte. J.
Hayes, Pte. T.
Hayes, Pte. W.
Heardley, Pte. G., D.C.M., M.M.
Hearne, L.-Cpl. H.
Heath, Pte. H. H.
Henderson, Pte. E.
Henshaw, Pte. J.
Higgins, Pte. G.
Higgins, L.-Cpl. J. R.
Higson, Pte. W.
Hinde, Pte. C.
Hitch, Pte. H.
Hodges, Pte. W.
Hodgson, Cpl. H. B.
Holden, Pte. G. T.
Holder, Pte. E. E.
Holliday, Pte. A. B.
Hollinsead, Pte. A.
Holman, Cpl. F. J.
Holman, L.-Cpl. H. G.
Holmes, Pte. A.
Holmes, Pte. F.
Holroyd, Pte. E.
Holt, Pte. C. A.
Holt, Pte. W.
Hopton, L.-Cpl. T.
Hosler, Pte. G.
Houghton, Pte. J.
Houghton, Pte. W.
Howard, Pte. J.
Howard, Pte. J. L.
Howarth, Pte. J.
Howell, Pte. J. H.
Hughes, Pte. A.
Hughes, L.-Cpl. E.
Hughes, Pte. F.
Hughes, Pte. J.
Hughes, Pte. R.
Hughes, Pte. W.
Hunt, Pte. F.
Hunt, Pte. T.
Hurine, Pte. B.
Irvin, Sgt. W.

Jackson, Pte. H. E.
Jackson, Pte. J. M.
Jackson, Drummer J. T.
James, Pte. J.
Jarvey, Pte. G.
Jeffries, Pte.
Jenkins, Pte. J.
Jennings, Pte. J. W.
Jepson, Pte. E.
Jepson, Pte. H.
Jepson, Pte. H.
Jerrum, Pte. F. G.
Johnson, Pte. J. E.
Johnson, Pte. W.
Johnson, Cpl. W. J.
Johnstone, Pte. W.
Jones, Pte. P.
Jones, Pte. R.
Jones, Pte. W.
Joynson, Pte. J. W.
Kay, Pte. A.
Kay, Pte. T.
Kearnes, Pte. J. A.
Keeley, Pte. E.
Kellett, Pte. H.
Kendall, Pte. T.
Kenyon, Pte. A.
Kershaw, Pte. J.
Kershaw, Cpl. J.
Kershaw, Cpl. S.
Kilroy, Pte. A.
Knowles, Pte. A.
Lamb, Pte. H.
Lamming, L.-Cpl. H.
Larkin, Pte. J. A.
Laudy, Pte. J.
Lavery, Pte. J. H.
Lazenby, Pte.
Lee, Pte. C.
Lee, Pte. W.
Lees, Pte. T.
Lester, Pte. J.
Lettle, Pte. N.
Lewis, L.-Cpl. J.
Lindley, Pte. W.
Lindon, C.Sgt.-Maj. J.
Loftwood, Pte. A.
Long, Pte. S.
Lord, Pte. G.
Macdonald, L.-Cpl. J.
Mackey, Pte. N.
Maddock, Pte. A.
Maddocks, Pte. H.
Maguire, Pte. T.
Mallandaine, Pte. W.
Manning, Pte. G.
Marchant, Pte. C. F.
Marland, Pte. W. T.
Marshall, Pte. W. R.
Massey, Sgt. A.
Matthews, Cpl. E. J.
Matthews, Cpl. F.
Matthews, Pte. G.
Matthewson, Pte.-Bglr. W. A.
McCarthy, Pte. J.
McDonald, Pte. C.
McDonald, Pte. H.
McMurdo, L.-Cpl. T.
McIver, Pte. J.
McLean, Pte. I.
Mellor, Pte. C. B.
Millington, Pte. J.
Millington, Pte. W. H.
Mills, Pte. F.
Millward, Pte. H. L.
Mitchell, Cpl. J.
Mitchell, Pte. M.
Mitchell, Pte. T. A.
Mogerley, Pte. F.

Molloy, Pte. J.
Monksfield, Pte. J. W.
Mooney, L.-Cpl. L. P.
Morgan, Pte. F. R.
Morrell, Pte. J.
Morris, Pte. J. H.
Morrison, Pte. W. J.
Muir, Pte. A.
Mulholland, Pte. F.
Neale, Sgt.
Nesbitt, Pte. A.
Newberry, Pte. W.
Newlove, Pte. J. W.
Nicholls, Pte. E. A.
Nicholls, Pte. J.
Noakes, Pte. F.
O'Connor, Pte. J. F.
O'Connor, Pte. T.
O'Gorman, Pte. H. J.
Olive, Pte. A.
O'Neill, Pte. W.
Ong, L.-Cpl. G. A.
Openshaw, Pte. J. H.
Ormerod, Cpl. H.
Osborne, Pte. A.
Owen, Cpl. A.
Owen, Pte. T.
Owen, Pte. W.
Oxborough, Pte. A. B.
Palmer, Pte. G.
Palmer, Pte. H.
Parkes, Pte. J.
Parry, Pte. L.
Partington, Pte. N.
Patten, Pte. W.
Pendlebury, Pte. A.
Pendlebury, Pte. V.
Penkethman, Pte. H.
Peppin, Pte. J. E.
Perry, Pte. R.
Petrie, Pte. W.
Pickering, Pte. G.
Pickersgill, Pte. W. S.
Pieri, Pte. W. L.
Pilling, Pte. E.
Pinder, Pte. T. H.
Platt, Pte. A.
Pollard, Cpl. E.
Pollitt, Pte. J. E.
Pomfret, Pte. T.
Pooley, Pte. J.
Post, Pte. J.
Potter, Pte. J.
Powell, L.-Cpl. J.
Powell, Pte. J.
Pratt, Pte. R. R.
Preston, Pte. J.
Price, Pte. A.
Price, Pte. J.
Priddle, Pte. H. J.
Pyne, Pte. J. H.
Quigley, Pte. W.
Rae, Pte. A.
Rawlings, Pte. E. L.
Raynor, L.-Cpl. C.
Reynolds, Pte. J.
Reynolds, Pte. W.
Rhodes, Pte. J.
Richards, Pte. A.
Richards, Pte. G. L. W.
Richardson, Pte. J.
Ridgway, L.-Cpl. T.
Riding, Pte. G.
Ringrose, L.-Cpl. C. R.
Rivers, Pte. W.
Robb, Pte. W.
Roberts, L.-Cpl. A.
Roberts, Cpl. T.
Robinson, Pte. J.

Roll of Honour

Robson, Pte. J.
Rowe, Pte. F.
Rowlands, Pte. W.
Rowley, C.Sgt.-Mjr. A.
Royle, Pte. J.
Ruddings, Pte. C.
Rutherford, Pte. J.
Ryan, Pte. L.
Sankey, Pte. T.
Searle, Pte. W.
Seed, C.Sgt.-Mjr. W., M.M.
Schofield, Pte. A.
Schofield, Pte. E.
Schofield, Pte. T.
Scriven, L.-Sgt. A. E.
Sharp, Cpl. W.
Shaw, Pte. F.
Shaw, Pte. H.
Shaw, Pte. T. H.
Sheldon, Sgt. H.
Shepherd, Pte. H.
Simpson, Pte. J.
Skerratt, Pte. H.
Skidmore, Pte. E.
Slater, Pte. G. H.
Slater, Pte. L. E.
Smith, Pte. B. J.
Smith, Pte. C.
Smith, Pte. H.
Smith, Pte. H. J.
Smith, Pte. J.
Smith, Pte. J.
Smith, Sgt. J. A.
Smith, Pte. T.
Sommerville, Pte. J.
Spencer, Pte. W.
Stacey, Pte. G.
Stafford, Pte. H.
Stanley, Pte. F.
Stanley, Pte. W.
Starkey, Sgt. R.
Stephenson, Pte. R.
Stocker, L.-Cpl. J. T.
Stockton, Cpl. A.
Stockton, Cpl. H.
Stoll, Pte. D.
Sumner, Pte. E.
Sumner, Sgt. H.
Sutton, Pte. H.
Swindles, Pte. F.
Tarren, Pte. H.
Tate, Pte. J.
Taylor, Pte. A.
Taylor, Pte. G. D.
Taylor, Pte. J.
Thompson, Pte. R.
Thompson, L.-Cpl. S.
Thorley, Pte. H.
Thornton, Pte. W.
Thorpe, Pte. T. T.
Throupe, Pte. G. F.
Tomkins, Pte. N.
Tomlinson, Pte. C.
Toms, Pte. L.
Tonge, Pte. R.
Treharnes, Pte. W. S.
Truman, Pte. A. C.
Turner, Pte. J.
Turner, Pte. W.
Tyson, Pte. H.
Tweed, Pte. J.
Unsworth, Pte. J.
Vagg, Pte. C.
Varley, Pte. B. R.
Vaughan, Sgt. R.
Vickers, Pte. F.
Vickers, Pte. L.
Vickers, Pte. P.
Walker, Cpl. J. E.
Walker, Pte. H.
Walker, Pte. W.
Walkins, Pte. W.
Walsh, Pte. J. S.
Walsh, Pte. M.
Warburton, Pte. J. J.
Ward, L.-Cpl. A.
Ward, L.-Cpl. A.
Wardman, Pte. J. T.
Warner, Pte. E.
Warren, Pte. A.
Watts, Pte. G.
Webb, Pte. A. G.
Wedgewood, Pte. G.
Weir, Sgt. J.
Whatmough, L.-Cpl. P.
Whealing, Pte. J. H.
White, Pte. H.
Whiting, Pte. G. S.
Whittall, Sgt. A. E.
Whyatt, Pte. W.
Wilkins, Pte. H.
Wilkinson, Pte. H.
Wilkinson, Pte. H.
Wilkinson, L.-Cpl. W.
Williams, Cpl. J. H.
Williams, Pte. L.
Willington, Pte. W.
Wills, Pte. J.
Wilson, L.-Cpl. J.
Wilson, Pte. L. A.
Winder, Cpl. E. B.
Winn, Sgt. R.
Withers, Pte. J.
Wood, L.-Cpl. A.
Wood, L.-Cpl. F.
Wood, Pte. S.
Wooton, L.-Cpl. W. R.
Worrall, Pte. H.
Worsley, Cr.-Sgt. T.
Wray, Pte. J.
Wright, Pte. J.
Yates, Pte. S.
Yeoman, Pte. E.
Young, Pte. L.

1/8 BATTALION LANCASHIRE FUSILIERS

Officers

Davies, Lt.-Col. O. St. L. (1/6 Manchester Regt. attd.).
Fallows, Lt.-Col. J. A.
Hope, Lt.-Col. G. E., M.C.
Waterhouse, Lt.-Col. R. D.
Baddeley, Mjr. E. L.
Alderson, Capt. R., M.C.
Fisher, Capt. J. D. (10th North Staffs. attd.).
Frankland, Capt. R. C. (3rd North Staffs. attd.).
Goodfellow, Capt. A. J.
Humphrey, Capt. E. S.
McCulloch, Capt. J. A.
Parke, Capt. A., M.C.
Radford, Capt. A. L. (9th K.L.R. attd.).
Bailey, Lieut. F.
Horner, Lieut. B.
Ingleton, Lieut. H. J.
Littler, Lieut. J. T.
Sturt, Lieut. H. M.
Tayleur, Lieut. (10th North Staffs. attd.).
Battye, 2nd Lieut. C. (4th West Riding Regt. attd.).
Boydell, 2nd Lieut. W. V.
Clay, 2nd Lieut. L. J.
Deacon, 2nd Lieut. R. E. (10th North Staffs. attd.).
Lodge, 2nd Lieut.
Mason, 2nd Lieut. G. J.
Middleton, 2nd Lieut. A. C.
Morris, 2nd Lieut. I. R. C. (Herts. Yeomanry attd.).
Phillips, 2nd Lieut. G. (Gloucester Regt. attd.).
Proctor, 2nd Lieut. G. H. V.
Rose, 2nd Lieut. E. W.
Tucker, 2nd Lieut. C. H. (10th North Staffs. attd.).

Other Ranks

Ackroyd, Pte. H.
Adams, Pte. A. C.
Adams, Pte. W.
Allcock, Pte. B.
Allwood, Pte. A.
Ambler, Pte. E.
Amers, Pte. R.
Andrews, Sgt. H.
Ansell, Pte. S.
Appleton, L.-Sgt. T. E.
Archer, Pte. A. E.
Armstrong, Pte. G. (attd. 125 T.M.B.)
Armstrong, Pte. W. J.
Arnold, Pte. J.
Arnold, Pte. W. A.
Ashcroft, Pte. E.
Ashton, Pte. J. W.
Ashworth, Pte. H.
Aspinall, Pte. S. G.
Atherton, Pte. W.
Atkinson, L.-Sgt. J.
Bailey, L.-Cpl. H. J.
Barber, Cpl. F.
Barber, Pte. W. H.
Barlow, Pte. E.
Barlow, Pte. J.
Barlow, Pte. W.
Barnett, Pte. H.
Barron, L.-Cpl. H. B.
Barron, Sgt. A.
Baugh, Pte. M.
Baxter, Pte. F.
Baxter, Pte. W.
Beale, Pte. E.
Bembridge, Pte. T.
Berrington, Pte. G.
Berry, Pte. L.
Beswick, Pte. W.

Birchall, Pte. J.
Bishop, Pte. J.
Black, Pte. F.
Blake, Pte. P. G.
Blakeney, Pte. A. E.
Boardman, Pte. J.
Bolland, Pte. A.
Booth, Pte. A.
Bowden, L.-Sgt. F.
Boyer, Sgt. R.
Brady, Pte. F.
Bramble, Pte. J.
Brett, Pte. A.
Brierley, C.Q.M.Sgt. T.
Britton, Pte. H.
Brooks, L.-Cpl. C. R.
Brooks, Pte. A.
Brookes, Pte. J.
Brown, Pte. D.
Brown, Pte. J.
Brown, Pte. J.
Brown, Pte. J.
Brown, Pte. T.
Brunning, Pte. S.
Burgess, Pte. L.
Burgess, Pte. W.
Burton, Sgt. W. E.
Bush, Pte. H.
Caldicott, Sgt. H.
Caley, Pte. A.
Campbell, Pte. J.
Caplan, Pte. H.
Carlisle, Pte. T.
Carney, Pte. A.
Carr, Pte. A.
Carr, Pte. J.
Carter, Sgt. H. J.
Chadwick, Sgt. J. W.
Chadwick, Pte. T.
Chapman, Pte. J.
Chase, Pte. S. J.
Cheatle, Pte. J.
Chilton, Pte. A.
Choularton, Pte. G.
Clamp, Cpl. G. W.
Clark, Pte. A.
Clarke, Pte. P.
Clayton, Pte. J.
Clowes, Pte. P.
Coates, Sgt. A.
Coffey, Pte. A. E.
Colbridge, Pte. A.
Collett, Pte. S. J.
Conlon, Pte. P.
Conquest, Pte. A.
Constable, Pte. E. E.
Cooper, Pte. J. T.
Cook, Pte. C. H.
Cooke, Pte. A. G.
Corlett, Pte. J.
Corrigan, L.-Sgt. M.
Covell, Pte. J.
Cowell, Cpl. R., D.C.M.
Cowell, Pte. W.
Crawford, Pte. H.
Creasey, Pte. F.
Crompton, Pte. J.
Crompton, Pte. R.
Crosby, L.-Cpl. A. S.
Crossley, Pte. W. E.
Crowe, Pte. L.
Cryer, Pte. S.
Cryer, Pte. T.
Cummings, Pte. P.
Curley, Pte. P.
Curran, Pte. A.
Curtis, Pte. F. G.
Curtis, Pte. J.
Cuthbert, Pte. P.

Daly, Pte. J.
Davenport, Pte. R.
Davies, Pte. H.
Dawson, Pte. W.
Denman, Cpl. P.
Dennison, Pte. T.
Dimbleby, Pte. F.
Dodds, Pte. W.
Dodman, Pte. A.
Dolan, Cpl. J., D.C.M.
Drage, Cpl. T. H., M.M.
Draper, Pte. R.
Dryden, Pte. J. H.
Dunn, Pte. J.
Dutson, Pte. J.
Dutton, Pte. E.
Dyson, Cpl. G.
Eagling, Pte. G.
Eden, Pte. J. H.
Edgar, Pte. R. F.
Edgar, Pte. T.
Edwards, Pte. J.
Ellis, Dmr. A.
Ellis, L.-Cpl. F.
Ellison, Pte. F.
Ellison, Pte. T.
Ellwand, Pte. R. H.
Elwell, Pte. J. H.
Emery, Pte. T.
Entwistle, Pte. J.
Evans, Cpl. J.
Evans, Pte. W.
Fairclough, Pte. F.
Farmer, Pte. J.
Farnworth, Pte. A., D.C.M.
Farnworth, Pte. W.
Farrand, Pte. J.
Faulkner, Pte. E.
Fawcett, L.-Cpl. E.
Fawcett, Pte. J. A.
Finch, Cpl. E.
Fisher, Pte. E.
Fletcher, Pte. F. A.
Fletcher, Pte. J. W.
Fletcher, Pte. T.
Foxwell, Pte. C.
Frost, Sgt. J.
Fryer, Pte. J.
Fyfield, Cpl. W. R.
Gandy, Pte. F.
Ganley, Pte. B.
Garbutt, Pte. T.
Garnett, Pte. R.
Garrett, Pte. J. F.
Gawthorpe, Pte. W.
Gee, Pte. R.
Gibbons, Pte. C. H.
Gibbs, Cpl. J.
Gill, Pte. W.
Glasper, Pte. G.
Glaulin, Pte. W.
Glendinning, Pte. A.
Glossop, Pte. B.
Graham, Pte. W.
Greenwood, Dmr. E.
Greenwood, Pte. T.
Greenwood, Pte. W.
Grey, Pte. R.
Grime, Pte. J.
Grimshaw, Pte. W.
Goodall, Pte. J. H.
Goodman, Pte. A.
Goodman, Pte. C. E.
Gordon, Pte. H.
Gough, Pte. H.
Guckion, Pte. M.
Hale, Pte. W.
Hallsworth, Pte. R.
Hambleton, Pte. W. E.

Hamilton, Pte. R. J.
Hamnett, Cpl. E.
Hampson, Pte. J.
Hand, Pte. G.
Hand, Pte. O. C.
Hankinson, Pte. E.
Hanson, Pte. H.
Hardcastle, Pte. W.
Hardie, Cpl. H.
Hardy, Pte. J.
Harper, Pte. W.
Harridine, Pte. F.
Harris, Pte. J.
Harrison, Pte. J.
Harrison, L.-Sgt. W.
Harrop, Pte. J.
Harwood, Pte. W.
Hatton, L.-Cpl. W.
Hayhurst, Pte. A.
Hayton, Cpl. W.
Heron, Pte. W.
Heywood, Pte. E.
Hibbert, Pte. P.
Hickson, Cpl. W.
Higginson, Pte. G. F.
Hiles, Pte. G.
Hill, Pte. H.
Hill, Pte. J. W.
Hill, Pte. W. R.
Hillier, L.-Cpl. C.
Hilton, Pte. C.
Hodgson, Pte. T.
Holland, Pte. C.
Holmes, Sgt. J. E.
Holt, Pte. J. T.
Hook, L.-Cpl. J.
Hopton, Pte. J. A.
Houghton, Pte. C.
Howard, Pte. H.
Howlett, L.-Cpl. W.
Howley, Pte. A.
Howson, Pte. J.
Hughes, Pte. F.
Hughes, Pte. J.
Hunter, L.-Cpl. W.
Hurine, Pte. J.
Hussey, Pte. J.
Isherwood, Pte. W. R.
Jackson, Pte. C.
Jackson, Pte. J.
Jackson, Pte. N.
James, Pte. G.
Jones, Pte. C.
Jones, Pte. E.
Jones, Pte. H.
Jones, Pte. T.
Jones, Pte. W.
Jones, Pte. W. H.
Jenkins, Pte. W.
Kay, Pte. J. H.
Kelly, Pte. J.
Kelly, Pte. S.
Kennedy, Sgt. J.
Kent, Pte. R. T.
Kenyon, Pte. H.
Kerfoot, Pte. H.
Kerry, L.-Cpl. J.
Kerry, Pte. C.
Keyte, Pte. W. E.
Kilroy, Pte. J.
King, L.-Sgt. H.
King, Pte. H. J.
King, Pte. W.
Kirk, Pte. G. T.
Kirk, Pte. J. R. (attd. 125 T.M.B.)
Knight, Pte. J. W.
Knowles, Pte. R.
Langton, Pte. W.

Lawlor, Pte. W.
Lawson, Pte. J.
Lawson, Pte. W.
Lear, Pte. E.
Lee, Pte. M.
Lee, Pte. W. M.
Leicester, Cpl. W.
Leigh, Pte. C.
Leigh, Pte. F.
Leonard, Pte. R.
Lever, Pte. G.
Lightfoot, L.-Cpl. J. (attd. 9th K.L.R.).
Limmage, Pte. J.
Lomax, Sgt. F.
Long, Pte. W. F. F.
Longson, Pte. R.
Lyons, Pte. L.
Maben, Pte. G.
Mackay, Pte. A.
Maddocks, Pte. G. J.
Makin, Pte. J.
Manley, Pte. F.
Marsh, Pte. E.
Martin, Pte. G.
Mason, Pte. J.
Mason, Pte. R. E. I.
Mason, Pte. R. H.
Mason, Pte. W.
Massey, Cpl. R.
Mathews, Pte. A.
Mathison, Pte. J.
Mayne, Pte. W. B.
Mayor, Pte. F.
McBurney, Pte. T.
McClurg, Pte. R.
McCracken, Pte. H.
McDonald, Pte. J.
McFarlane, Pte. G.
McFarland, Pte. J. H.
McGarry, Pte. J.
McGuire, Pte. W.
McLaine, Pte. A. H.
McLoughlin, Pte. T.
McManus, Dmr. F.
Middleton, Pte. J.
Midgeley, Pte. H.
Miller, Pte. J.
Miller, Cpl. P.
Millett, Pte. E.
Mills, Pte. A. W.
Mills, Pte. E.
Mills, Pte. W.
Milner, Pte. G. H.
Mitchell, Pte. J.
Mitchell, Pte. M.
Mitchell, Pte. W.
Moffett, Pte. E. H.
Molloy, Pte. T.
Moore, Pte. W.
Moore, Pte. W.
Moran, Pte. J.
Morgan, Pte. G.
Morphet, Pte. T. H.
Morriss, Pte. S.
Morris, Pte. T. H.
Moss, Dmr. J.
Moss, Pte. S.
Moss, Pte. T.
Murphy, L.-Cpl. W.
Murphy, Pte. F.
Murphy, Pte. H.
Muskett, Pte. H.
Mycock, Pte. T.
Nesbitt, Pte. G.
Nesbitt, Pte. J.
Newell, Pte. G.
Newman, L.-Cpl. G. E.
Newman, L.-Sgt. J. R., M.M.

Newton, Pte. F.
Oddie, Pte. T.
Ogden, Pte. G.
O'Keefe, Cpl. F. P.
O'Mara, Pte. J.
Ong, C.Q.M.Sgt. W.
O'Niell, Pte. P.
Orman, Pte. P.
Orme, Pte. J.
Orrell, Pte. J.
Outram, Pte. A.
Owen, Pte. J.
Paiton, Pte. A.
Parker, Pte. J.
Parker, Pte. S.
Parkinson, Pte. W.
Pearce, L.-Cpl. P.
Pearson, Pte. J. E.
Pearson, Pte. S.
Peel, Pte. E.
Pemberthy, Pte. W.
Pemberton, Pte. D. J.
Pendlebury, L.-Cpl. C.
Perry, Pte. H.
Petchey, Pte. G.
Plumb, Pte. E.
Potter, Pte. C. S.
Potts, Cpl. J.
Powell, Pte. J.
Powell, Pte. J.
Proctor, Pte. W.
Pulman, Pte. F.
Purkiss, C.Sgt.-Mjr. A.
Pyper, Pte. F.
Quinn, Cpl. J.
Read, C.Q.M.Sgt. P.
Rees, Pte. W. D.
Reid, Pte. J.
Revington, Pte. A.
Ridler, Pte. W.
Riley, Pte. W.
Roach, Pte. A.
Roberts, Pte. F.
Roberts, Pte. G.
Roberts, Pte. H.
Roberts, Pte. T.
Robinson, Pte. C.
Robinson, Pte. F., M.M.
Robinson, Pte. J.
Robinson, Pte. J.
Robson, Pte. H. S.
Rogerson, Pte. R.
Rollings, Pte. H.
Rosevere, Pte. H.
Ross, Pte. J.
Royle, Pte. J.
Ryan, Pte. M.
Sagar, Cpl. F.
Saunders, L.-Cpl. A.
Scanlon, Pte. T. E.
Schofield, Cpl. A.
Schofield, Sgt. H. (Instr. K.O.R.L. attd.).
Scott, Pte. C. F. D. S.
Seaton, Pte. P.
Setchell, Pte. G. T.
Sharpe, Pte. G.
Sharples, Pte. N.
Shaw, Pte. H.
Shaw, C.Sgt.-Mjr. R., D.C.M.
Shaw, Pte. W.
Sheeran, Pte. J. J.
Shepherd, Pte. A. H.
Shepherd, Pte. E. W.
Shepherd, Pte. W.
Sherman, Pte. H.
Shippam, Pte. J.
Shorrocks, Cpl. F.
Slater, Pte. W.

Slater, Pte. W.
Smart, Pte. A.
Smart, Pte. J.
Smedley, Pte. W. H.
Smethurst, Pte. F. C.
Smith, Pte. A. L.
Smith, Pte. D. H.
Smith, Pte. F.
Smith, Pte. F.
Smith, Pte. G. W.
Smith, Pte. J.
Smith, Pte. O. N.
Smith, Pte. T.
Smith, L.-Cpl. W.
Smith, Pte. W.
South, Pte. R.
Southern, Pte. E.
Southern, Pte. J. E.
Stansfield, Pte. A. E.
Steele, Pte. R.
Stoddart, L.-Cpl. T.
Stone, Pte. W. H.
Stones, Pte. C.
Stott, Pte. E.
Stott, L.-Cpl. J.
Straw, Pte. F. W.
Sumner, Pte. T.
Sutcliffe, Pte. W.
Swale, Pte. J.
Swift, Pte. W.
Tait, Pte. A. J.
Tamblin, Pte. A.
Taylor, L.-Cpl. H.
Taylor, Sgt. J.
Taylor, Pte. J.
Taylor, Pte. L.
Teasdale, Pte. T. H.
Tennant, Pte. S.
Tetlow, L.-Cpl. F.
Tetlow, Pte. H.
Tetzloff, Sgt. P. H.
Thomas, Pte. H.
Thomason, Pte. R.
Thompson, Pte. J.
Thornton, Pte. S. G.
Todd, Pte. H.
Todd, Pte. H.
Tomlinson, Pte. C.
Tonge, Pte. J. E.
Toole, Pte. J.
Towle, Pte. T.
Travis, Pte. J.
Varley, Pte. A.
Vaughan, Sgt. H.
Vickers, Pte. G.
Vickers, Pte. W. H.
Vickerstaff, Pte. C.
Waddington, L.-Cpl. R.
Wagstaffe, Pte. R.
Walden, L.-Cpl. H. T.
Walker, Pte. C.
Walker, Sgt. E. G.
Wallace, Pte. A. R.
Wallwork, Pte. H.
Warner, Pte. G.
Warner, Pte. T.
Warrington, Pte. F.
Waterson, Pte. F. E.
Webster, Pte. R.
Welch, Pte. J.
Wheatley, Pte. C.
White, Pte. S.
Whitehead, Pte. J. W.
Whittingham, Cpl. A.
Wilde, Pte. J. A.
Wilkinson, Pte. F.
Wilkinson, Pte. H.
Williams, Pte. D.
Williams, Pte. O. W.

214 The 42nd Division

Williams, Pte. T.
Williams, Pte. T.
Williams, Pte. T. R.
Williams, Pte. W. T.
Willoughby, Pte. F.
Wilson, Pte. J.
Wolfendale, Pte. J.

Wolfendale, Pte. J. A.
Womersley, Pte. F.
Wood, Pte. C.
Wood, Pte. G.
Woodward, Pte. W.
Worsiey, Pte. E.
Worsley, Pte. R.

Wright, Pte. E.
Wright, Pte. L.
Yardley, Pte. H.
Yates, Pte. E.
Yates, Pte. S.
Young, Pte. G.
Young, Pte. T. W.

126th INFANTRY BRIGADE
1/4 BATTALION EAST LANCASHIRE REGIMENT

Officers

Smith, Maj. J. T.
Papprill, Capt. F. E.
Dewhurst. Lieut. J. M.
Jackson, Lieut. G.
Sames, Lieut. W. F.
Thwaites, Lieut. R.
Whalley, Lieut. H. W.

Wolf, Lieut. P.
Woods, Lieut. E.
Ashton, 2nd Lieut. J. R. W.
Coles, 2nd Lieut. C.
Fyldes, 2nd Lieut. A. W.
Heywood, 2nd Lieut. T. A.
Hornby, 2nd Lieut. W. R.

de Pennington, 2nd Lieut. A.
Sykes, 2nd Lieut. J.
Taylor, 2nd Lieut. J. B.
Wilding, 2nd Lieut. J.
Woodhouse, 2nd Lieut. E.

Other Ranks

Adams, L.-Cpl. L.
Ainsworth, Pte. A.
Ainsworth, Pte. A.
Ainsworth, Cpl. H.
Ainsworth, Pte. H.
Airey, Pte. W.
Alston, Sgt. R. B.
Ardis, Cpl. J.
Ashworth, Pte. P.
Aspden, Sgt. W.
Atherton, Pte. W.
Austin, L.-Cpl. J.
Barker, Pte. F.
Barrett, Cpl. G.
Barrett, Pte. W.
Bartlett, Pte. R. J.
Bassett, Pte. J.
Battle, Pte. J.
Bell, L.-Cpl. C. W.
Bentley, Pte. H.
Blackburn, Co.Sgt-Mjr. A. W.
Bleasdale, Pte. J.
Boswell. L.-Cpl. T.
Bousfield, Pte. H.
Bousfield, Pte. P.
Brandwood, Pte. A.
Brayshaw, Pte. H.
Brightmore, Pte. W.
Brown, Pte. A. I.
Brown, Pte. D.
Brown, Pte. W.
Burke, Pte. H.
Callum, L.-Cpl. M.
Carney, Pte. F.
Carr, Pte. J.
Carter, Pte. M.
Casey, Pte. G.
Cawson, Pte. W.
Charnley, Pte. F.
Chesworth, Pte. J.
Chew, Pte. W.
Chiney, Pte. C.
Clarke, Pte. G. W.
Clarkson, Pte. R.
Clarkson, Pte. T.
Clough, Pte. W.
Cook, Pte. R.
Coote, Pte. J.
Cornwall, Pte. J.
Cotton, Pte. A.
Cowell, Pte. E.
Cox, Cpl. F. N.
Crawford, L.-Cpl. J.

Croasdale, Pte. W.
Crowther, Pte. B.
Culshaw, L.-Cpl. H.
Culshaw, Pte. J.
Cuthbert, Pte. A.
Davies, Pte. J. S.
Davies, Pte. J. T.
Davis, Pte. J.
Dawson, Pte. H.
Dawson, Pte. W.
Dean, Pte. R.
Decaux, Sgt. J.
Dennett, L.-Cpl. W.
Denny, Cpl. T. H.
Devaney, Pte. M.
Dewhurst, Pte. R.
Dickenson, Pte. H. (L.-Cpl.).
Dickinson, Pte. C.
Dougherty, Pte. B.
Dougherty, Pte. W.
Douglas, Pte. E.
Downham, Pte. J. J.
Duckworth, Pte. J.
Duckworth, Pte. W.
Duerden, Pte. J.
Dunn, Pte. A.
Durham, Pte. J.
Duxbury, Pte. F.
Eastham, Pte. A. (L.-Cpl.).
Eccles, Pte. F. W.
Eccles, Pte. J.
Edwards, Pte. J.
Entwistle, Pte. A.
Entwistle, Pte. W. E.
Evans, Pte. A.
Evans, Pte. A. E.
Fallon, Pte. J.
Fay, Pte. J.
Fay, Pte. R.
Fielding, Pte. A.
Fielding, Pte. T. A.
Fineberg, Pte. F.
Firth, Cpl. J.
Fish, Pte. J.
Flatt, Pte. J.
Fleming, Pte. J.
Forrest, Pte. J. R.
Fowler, Pte. E.
Fynn, Pte. J.
Gale, Pte. J.
Garner, Pte. H.
Gillibrand, Pte. C.
Gillibrand, Pte. W.

Gleave, Pte. T.
Goodier, Pte. T.
Greenwood, Sgt. S.
Grogan, Pte. A.
Hadfield, Pte. J.
Hall, Pte. R.
Hall, Pte. T.
Halliwell, Pte. J. R.
Hampson, Pte. J.
Harbour, Pte. J. W.
Hargreaves, Pte. C. V.
Hargreaves, L.-Cpl. R.
Hargreaves, Pte. R.
Harrison, Pte. H.
Hartley, Pte. L.
Harwood. Pte. E.
Harwood, Pte. H. C.
Haslam, Pte. J.
Haslewood, Cpl. D. N.
Haworth, Pte. A.
Haworth, Cpl. J.
Haworth, Pte. J.
Haworth, Pte. W.
Heap, Sgt. W. H. J.
Heaps, Cpl. J.
Heaps, Pte. R.
Heron, Sgt. H.
Heywood, Pte. W.
Higginson, Pte. R.
Hilton, Pte. W.
Hindle, Pte. A.
Hogg, Pte. J. R.
Holden, Pte. B. P.
Holden, Pte. E.
Holden, Pte. J.
Holden, Pte. J.
Holden, Pte. J.
Holden, Pte. J.
Holden, L.-Cpl. W.
Hollinghurst, Pte. H. R. R.
Hope, Pte. G.
Houghton, Pte. T.
Howson, Pte. W.
Hoyle, Pte. J.
Hulme, Pte. J.
Hulton, Pte. F.
Hurst, Pte. H.
Hustwaite, Pte. W.
Huxley, Pte. F.
Hyde, Pte. F. S.
Ince, Pte. E.

Roll of Honour 215

Ingham, Pte. A.
Ingham, Pte. J.
Irwin, Pte. A.
Isherwood, Pte. W.
Jackson, Cpl. R.
Jennings, Pte. T.
Jepson, Pte. J. R.
Johnson, Pte. M.
Johnson, Pte. T.
Jones, Pte. A. E.
Jones, Pte. G.
Joyner, Pte. C.
Jubb, Pte. G.
Kay, Pte. J.
Kay, Pte. J.
Kelsall, Pte. A.
Kirk, Pte. A.
Knights, Cpl. J.
Knowles, Pte. L.
Knowles, Pte. W.
Lamb, Pte. J. C.
Law, L.-Cpl. E.
Lawrence, Pte. A.
Lawson, Pte. C. T.
Lawson, Pte. E.
Lee, Pte. J.
Lee, Pte. R.
Leeming, Pte. H.
Leonard, Pte. J. J.
Lightbown, Pte. T. H.
Lomas, Cpl. J.
Lowe, Pte. L.
Lowe, Pte. R.
Lyons, L.-Cpl. P.
Marsden, Pte. J.
Marsden, Pte. N.
Marsh, Pte. G. H.
Marshall, Sgt. E.
Martin, Pte. A. E.
Mashiter, Pte. G.
May, Cpl. H.
McDairmid, Pte. J.
McLaren, Pte. J.
McLoughlin, Pte. W.
McNamara, Pte. T.
McNulty, Pte. P.
Mellor, Pte. F.
Mercer, Pte. C.
Moore, L.-Cpl. H.
Moran, L.-Cpl. W.
Morley, Pte. J.
Myers, Pte. H.

Neville, Pte. J.
Noble, Pte. J.
Noblett, Pte. H.
Noon, Pte. A.
Noon, Pte. M.
Norse, Pte. T.
Ormerod, L.-Cpl. H. A.
Parkinson, Pte. R.
Parsonage, Pte. T.
Pemberton, Sgt. W.
Pendergast, Pte. T.
Perry, Pte. H.
Phillips, Cpl. W.
Pickervance, Pte. H.
Pickup, Pte. A.
Pilkington, L.-Cpl. M.
Pinder, L.-Cpl. B.
Pinder, Pte. J.
Place, Pte. T.
Pollard, Pte. L. (L.-Cpl.).
Powell, Pte. W.
Preston, Pte. J. B.
Preston, Pte. C.
Proctor, Dmr. F.
Proctor, Pte. W.
Pym, Pte. A.
Rawlinson, Pte. E. P.
Rawlinson, Pte. T. C.
Readett, Pte. S.
Remington, Pte. T.
Reynolds, Pte. A.
Richmond, Pte. J.
Roberts, Pte. J.
Rogers, Pte. J. W.
Rothwell, Pte. S.
Sandham, Pte. W.
Scott, Pte. C.
Scowcroft, Cpl. W.
Seed, Pte. L. F.
Shackleton, Sgt. J. C.
Shaw, Pte. F.
Shaw, Pte. R. W.
Shuttleworth, Sgt. D.
Shuttleworth, Pte. J.
Simms, Pte. J.
Sipson, Pte. E. B.
Slater, Pte. J.
Slater, Pte. J.
Slater, Pte. R.
Slater, Pte. R.
Slinger, Pte. F.
Smart, Pte. D. D.

Smith, Pte. A.
Smith, Pte. G. T.
Smith, Pte. J.
Smith, Pte. J. J.
Smith, Pte. J. R.
Smith, Pte. T.
Smith, Pte. T. R.
Snape, L.-Cpl. B. S.
Sprague, Sgt. B.
Starkie, Pte. J.
Stewart, Pte. H.
Stoddart, Pte. J.
Sutcliffe, Pte. A. F.
Sweeney, Pte. J.
Taylor, Pte. A.
Taylor, Pte. J.
Taylor, Pte. W.
Taylor, Pte. W. F.
Thomas, Sgt. J. R. H.
Thompson, Pte. J. J.
Thompson, Pte. M.
Townsend, Dmr. J.
Townsend, Pte. J.
Tucker, Pte. A.
Turbutt, Sgt. J.
Valentine, Pte. A.
Wallace, Sgt. E.
Walmsley, Pte. T.
Walsh, Cpl. F.
Waring, Pte. J.
Watson, Cpl. J. K.
Whittaker, Pte. J. H.
Whittingham, Pte. J.
Whittle, Pte. J.
Widdop, Pte. R.
Wilcock, Pte. R.
Wilcock, L.-Cpl. W.
Wild, Sgt. T.
Wilde, Pte. R.
Wignall, Pte. H.
Williams, Pte. G.
Williams, Pte. J.
Wilson, Pte. M.
Windle, Pte. A.
Woodburn, Pte. W.
Woods, Pte. A.
Worsley, Pte. H.
Wright, Pte. W.
Yates, Pte. E.
Young, Pte. L.
Younger, Pte. D.

1/5 BATTALION EAST LANCASHIRE REGIMENT

Officers

Bolton, Capt. H. H.
Brewis, Capt. A. P.
Molke, Capt. E.
Robinson, Capt. J. C. C. H.
Walmsley, Capt. S. H.
Barker, Lieut. J. H. J.
Dyson, Lieut. C. B.
Sprake, Lieut. G. E.

Bolton, 2nd Lieut. J.
Brash, 2nd Lieut. J. Jnr.
Davenport, 2nd Lieut. R.
Edwards, 2nd Lieut. H. W.
Farmer, 2nd Lieut. G. B.
Hart, 2nd Lieut. J. S.
Hunwick, 2nd Lieut. E. N.
Kippax, 2nd Lieut. J. E.

Pickup, 2nd Lieut. W.
Rodgers, 2nd Lieut. A. E.
Sachs, 2nd Lieut. R. D.
Smith, 2nd Lieut. A. V., V.C.
Stansfield, 2nd Lieut. F.
Thomas, 2nd Lieut. W.
Walkden, 2nd Lieut. A. C.
Webber, 2nd Lieut. A. F. A.

Other Ranks

Allcock, Pte. J. M.
Allen, Pte. A.
Alston, Pte. B.
Anyon, Pte. J.
Armstrong, Pte. P.
Arrandale, Pte. J.
Ash, Pte. S.
Ashton, Pte. G.
Ashworth, Pte. F.

Ashworth, Pte. F. F.
Ashworth, L.-Sgt. J. W.
Atkinson, Pte. C.
Austin, Pte. A.
Balderson, Pte. J.
Baldwin, L.-Cpl. E.
Bamber, Sgt. J.
Bamford, Pte. D.
Banham, Pte. R. A.

Barber, Pte. R.
Barker, Cpl. E.
Barlow, Cpl. T. B.
Barnes, Pte. W. H.
Barrett, Sgt. A. E.
Barrow, Pte. G.
Bentham, Pte. R.
Berry, Pte. H.
Bilsborough, Pte. J.

Black, Pte. G. E.
Blackledge, Pte. A.
Blakey, Pte. F.
Boley, Pte. W. M.
Booth, Cpl. H.
Bordley, Pte. A. J.
Borick, Pte. P.
Bowden, L.-Cpl. J.
Bowler, Pte. H.
Boyes, Cpl. B.
Bradley, Pte. G.
Brambles, Pte. J.
Bray, Pte. H.
Briggs, Sgt. R. H.
Brindle, Pte. T.
Brown, Pte. C. A.
Brown, Pte. J. W.
Brown, Pte. W.
Buckle, Pte. F. E.
Bullock, Pte. J.
Burgess, Pte. F.
Burrell, L.-Cpl. C.
Burrows, Pte. J. R.
Burton, Pte. O.
Bury, Pte. R.
Butterworth, Pte. H.
Butterworth, L.-Cpl. J.
Butterworth, Cpl. W.
Calverley, Pte. W.
Calvert, L.-Sgt. T.
Campion, L.-Cpl. W. E.
Carter, Pte. A.
Cawtherley, Pte. J. R.
Chadwick, Pte. R.
Chadwick, Pte. T.
Chapman, Pte. J. W.
Cheeseborough, Pte. A.
Christian, Pte. A.
Clinch, Pte. W.
Clough, Pte. F.
Clough, Pte. J.
Cocker, Pte. J.
Colenso, Pte. F.
Collinge, Pte. A.
Conway, Pte. F.
Cook, Pte. A.
Cook, Pte. R.
Coombes, Pte. E.
Cooper, L.-Cpl. H.
Cosgrove, Pte. T.
Cottam, Pte. J.
Cottam, Pte. L.
Cowgill, Pte. R. R.
Crabtree, C.Sgt.-Mjr. G. E.
Crabtree, L.-Cpl. M.
Cropper, L.-Cpl. J. W.
Crowther, Sgt. J.
Crowther, Pte. W. B.
Crummett, Pte. E. W.
Cryer, L.-Cpl. C.
Culpan, Pte. E.
Dand, Pte. J. G.
Davies, Pte. W.
Davis, Pte. J. J.
Davis, Pte. S.
Dawkes, Pte. A.
Dean, Pte. J.
Dearden, Pte. L.
Devey, Pte. A.
Dickenson, Pte. J.
Dickenson, Sgt. W.
Drake, Pte. H. O.
Drewery, Pte. H.
Driver, Pte. L.
Duckett, L.-Cpl. J.
Duckworth, Pte. T.
Dunlavey, Pte. T.
Durkin, Pte. J.
Duxbury, Pte. W.

Eastwood, L.-Sgt. E.
Eccleston, Pte. A.
Eckersley, Pte. J.
Eddleston, Pte. R.
Edmonson, Pte. A.
Ellis, Pte. C.
Emmett, Pte. H.
Entwistle, Pte. H.
Evans, Pte. F.
Evans, Pte. H.
Fay, Pte. P.
Fenn, Pte. P.
Fish, Pte. J.
Fletcher, Cpl. A.
Ford, Pte. E.
Forshaw, Pte. R.
Forster, Pte. F.
Freear, Pte. A.
Furber, Pte. C. H.
Gardner, Pte. S.
Gavin, Pte. T. H.
Gelding, Pte. G. H.
Gillett, Pte. J.
Gorton, L.-Cpl. A. E.
Gotthardt, Pte. F.
Gould, Pte. F.
Graham, L.-Cpl. R.
Graham, Pte. T. A.
Green, Pte. J.
Green, L.-Cpl. J. W.
Greenwood, Pte. H.
Greenwood, Pte. R.
Greenwood, L.-Cpl. W.
Greenwood, Pte. W.
Gregory, Pte. O. B.
Grogan, Pte. P.
Grundy, C.Sgt.Mjr. G.
Grunshaw, Pte. A.
Hacking, Pte. P.
Hale, Sgt. W.
Hall, Pte. F.
Hall, Pte. W.
Hallet, Pte. A. S.
Halstead, L.-Cpl. A. C.
Halstead, Pte. J. H.
Halstead, Pte. T.
Halton, Pte. D.
Handley, Pte. J. H.
Hardacre, Pte. G.
Hardcastle, Pte. J.
Hargreaves, Pte. T.
Harker, Pte. G. A.
Harris, Pte. G. E.
Harris, Pte. S. E.
Hartley, Pte. C. E.
Hartley, Pte. J.
Hartley, Pte. J. N.
Hartley, Pte. R.
Hartley, Pte. W.
Harwood, Pte. S.
Haydock, Sgt. G.
Hayes, Pte. J. L.
Hayles, Pte. W. J.
Healey, L.-Cpl. W.
Hedderman, Pte. J.
Hepworth, Pte. J.
Hetherington, Pte S.
Hewitt, Sgt. N.
Heys, Pte. R. H.
Heyworth, Pte. J.
Higham, L.-Cpl. B. J. W.
Hilton, Pte. H.
Hindle, Pte. A.
Hodgkinson, Pte. J. C.
Hodgson, Pte. D. T.
Hodson, Pte. W.
Holden, Pte. J.
Holden, Pte. S. H.
Holdworth, Pte. N.

Holgate, Pte. T.
Holland, Pte. E. P.
Holland, Pte. J.
Holt, Pte. G.
Holt, Pte. H.
Hook, Sgt. A.
Hoolahan, Pte. J. H.
Horrocks, Pte. W.
Horsfield, Pte. W.
Houghton, Pte. R. C.
Howarth, Pte. J. C.
Howarth, Pte. J. E.
Howarth, Pte. R.
Howarth, Pte. R.
Howarth, Pte. W.
Howorth, Pte. O.
Hughes, Pte. H.
Hunter, Pte. W.
Hutchings, Pte. W.
Ingham, Pte. J. H.
Jackson, Pte. R. W.
Johnson, L.-Sgt. G.
Johnston, Pte. J. W.
Jones, L.-Sgt. H.
Kay, Pte. H.
Kay, L.-Sgt. W.
Kennerley, L.-Cpl. W.
Kent, L.-Sgt. G.
Kenyon, L.-Sgt. G.
Keown, Pte. C.
Kershaw, Pte. W.
Key, Pte. W.
Killean, Pte. J.
Killean, Pte. J.
Kirkman, Sgt. S.
Lane, Pte. C.
Law, Pte. G.
Lawless, Pte. F. G.
Laycock, Pte. E.
Leatherbarrow, Pte. E.
Leaver, Pte. A.
Lee, Pte. H.
Lee, Pte. T. W.
Leonard, Pte. G.
Leyland, Pte. F.
Lightbown, Pte. J.
Livesey, C.Sgt.-Mjr. P.
Lockett, Pte. H.
Lockett, Pte. T. W.
Lord, Pte. E.
Lord, C.Q.M.Sgt. G. H.
Lowe, Pte. C.
Lowe, Pte. R. J.
Lucas, Pte. J.
Lynch, Pte. M.
Magnall, Sgt. J.
Maloney, Pte. J.
Marsden, Pte. J.
Marsland, Pte. H.
Maschiter, Pte. R.
Maslin, Pte. W.
Masterson, Pte. J.
Mather, Pte. W.
Maymond, Pte. F.
McClelland, Pte. J. H.
McDonald, Pte. M.
McGrath, Pte. G. H.
McHugh, Sgt. P.
Messenger, Pte. J.
Metcalf, Pte. W.
Mills, Pte. D. H.
Milner, Pte. J. H.
Mitchell, Pte. O. J.
Molloy, Dmr. W.
Moore, Pte. G.
Moore, Pte. G.
Moore, Pte. T.
Moore, Pte. W.
Moran, Pte. W.
Morgan, Pte. H.

Morton, Sgt. J.
Murgatroyd, Pte. F.
Murphy, Pte. J.
Murphy, Pte. W.
Murray, Pte. G.
Nightingale, Pte. M.
Ninness, Pte. J.
Nuttall, Pte. H.
Nutter, Pte. W.
O'Brien, Pte. D.
Orr, Pte. J.
Owen, Pte. H.
Parkin, Pte. G. R.
Parkinson, Pte. T.
Parkinson, Pte. T.
Parkinson, Pte. W. F.
Payne, Sgt. R.
Peach, Pte. J.
Pearce, Pte. C.
Pearson, Pte. J. E.
Pedley, Pte. W.
Pennington, Pte. C.
Pettifer, Pte. W. S.
Pickles, Pte. A.
Pickup, Pte. J. J.
Pickup, Pte. R.
Piercy, Pte. H. A.
Pilkington, Pte. A. V.
Pinder, Pte. J. E.
Pinder, Pte. R.
Powell, Pte. T.
Pratt, Cpl. W.
Procter, Pte. E.
Proctor, Pte. H.
Proctor, Pte. J. H.
Pyle, Pte. G. S.
Quinn, Pte. S.
Ralston, Cpl. P.
Rawstron, Pte. F.
Redman, Pte. H.
Reed, Pte. J.
Richardson, Pte. C.
Rickard, Pte. H.
Riley, Pte. E.
Riley, Pte. J. H.
Riley, Pte. W.

Riley, Pte. W.
Robertshaw, Pte. R.
Robinson, L.-Cpl. J.
Robinson, Pte. J.
Robinson, Pte. R.
Robinson, Pte. W.
Rothwell, Pte. R. H.
Rowley, Pte. H.
Rushton, Sgt. F. W.
Rushton, Pte. H.
Sargeant, Pte. C. W.
Saunders, Pte. A.
Savage, Pte. J.
Scales, Pte. W. T.
Scott, Pte. A.
Scott, Pte. H.
Sellings, Pte. E. V.
Shapcott, Pte. A.
Shapcott, Dmr. W.
Sharples, Pte. J.
Simpson, Pte. J.
Sisson, Pte. J.
Slater, Pte. L.
Smallshaw, Pte. W. T.
Smith, Pte. E.
Smith, Pte. H.
Smith, Pte. R.
Smithies, Pte. R.
Snape, Pte. J. H.
Sockett, L.-Cpl. J.
Spencer, Pte. J. S.
Stanton, Pte. M.
Starkie, Pte. H.
Starmer, Pte. H.
Steele, Pte. A.
Stride, Pte. G. H.
Stott, Pte. J. T.
Sugden, C.Sgt.-Mjr. J. W.
Sutcliffe, Cpl. H.
Sykes, Pte. D.
Tattersall, Pte. T. A.
Tattersall, Pte. W.
Taylor, Pte. H.
Taylor, Cpl. F. J.
Taylor, Pte. J.
Teasdale, L.-Sgt. J. F.

Thompson, Pte. C. F.
Thornber, Pte. B.
Thornber, L.-Cpl. W.
Thornton, Pte. T.
Thorpe, Pte. T.
Thwaites, Pte. T.
Tillotson, Pte. W.
Tomlinson, Pte. J.
Towers, Pte. H.
Towler, Pte. E.
Townsend, Pte. A.
Truman, Pte. F.
Turner, Sgt. S.
Usher, Pte. J.
Wadsworth, C.Q.M.Sgt. A.
Wall, Pte. G.
Walker, Pte. J.
Walker, Pte. W.
Walmsley, Pte. J.
Walton, Pte. J. E.
Walton, Pte. R.
Ward, Sgt. A.
Ward, Pte. F.
Ward, Pte. W.
Watson, Pte. J.
Watson, Pte. O.
Weston, Pte. J. E.
Whipp, Pte. J.
Whisker, Pte. H.
Whitehead, Pte. A.
Whitehead, Pte. J.
Whitehead, Pte. J. W.
Whittaker, Pte. F.
Wilkinson, Sgt. J., D.C.M.
Williamson, Pte. J.
Wilson, Pte. P.
Wilson, Pte. R.
Winder, Pte. R.
Wollett, Pte. G.
Wolstenholme, Sgt. H.
Woodhead, Pte. L.
Wormwell, Pte. J.
Worsfold, Pte. W. C.
Wright, Pte. E.
Yates, Pte. G.

1/9 BATTALION MANCHESTER REGIMENT

Officers

Anderson, Mjr. W. J.
Archbutt, Mjr. W. H.
Hilton, Mjr. A.
Hamer, Capt. F.
Sugden, Capt. H.
Cooke, Lieut. C. E., M.C.

Marsden, Lieut. P. S.
Porter, Lieut. S.
Wade, Lieut. J. M.
Dearnaley, 2nd Lieut. I.
Dixon, 2nd Lieut. H. F.
Freedman, 2nd Lieut. B.

Hudson, 2nd Lieut. A. H.
Jones, 2nd Lieut. F.
Robson, 2nd Lieut. J. M.
Stringer, 2nd Lieut. A. E.
Woodhouse, 2nd Lieut. P. A.

Other Ranks

Adshead, Pte. W.
Andrew, Pte. J. W.
Appleby, Cpl. J. E.
Ashcroft, L.-Cpl. T.
Atkin, Pte. B.
Bailey, Pte. M.
Ballagher, Pte. J.
Ballard, Pte. F.
Bardsley, Pte. C.
Barker, Pte. J.
Barker, Pte. M.
Barker, Pte. W.
Barrett, L.-Cpl. H.
Bates, Pte. J.
Bell, Pte. G.
Bell, Pte. J.
Bennett, Pte. H.

Bennett, Pte. J.
Bertenshaw, L.-Cpl. J.
Birchall, C.Sgt.-Mjr. W.
Blaize, Pte. T.
Blandford, L.-Cpl. J.
Bolter, Cpl. H.
Booth, Pte. A.
Booth, Pte. C.
Booth, Pte. C.
Bourne, Pte. W.
Bowker, Pte. E.
Bown, Pte. F.
Bradbury, Pte. H.
Bradbury, Pte. W.
Brady, Pte. J.
Braithwaite, Sgt. N. D.
Brammall, Pte. W.

Bridge, Pte.
Broadbent, Pte. J.
Brough, Pte. J.
Brown, Pte. J. H.
Buckley, Pte. S.
Burgess, L.-Cpl. A.
Burgess, Pte. R.
Burke, L.-Cpl. W.
Butler, Pte. T.
Cain, Pte. G. F.
Campbell, Pte. R.
Carr, Pte. T. A.
Chadderton, Pte. E.
Chadwick, Pte. H.
Chapman, Pte. J.
Christian, Pte. H.
Clarkson, Pte. F.

Clegg, Pte. H.
Clegg, Pte. W.
Coffey, Pte. J.
Connolly, Pte. J. H.
Cooke, Dmr. H.
Cooper, Pte. J. H.
Crane, Pte. J.
Crompton, L.-Cpl. J.
Cuppello, Cpl. J.
Cusick, Pte. B.
Daley, Pte. J.
Daley, Pte. J. W.
Doran, Pte. T.
Downs, Pte. J.
Dyson, Pte. F.
Earle, Sgt. H.
Earnshaw, L.-Cpl. E.
Elliott, Pte. H.
Evans, Pte. T.
Eyre, Sgt. G.
Farnley, Pte. J.
Favier, Pte. F.
Fielding, Pte. T.
Finiucane, Pte.
Finnigan, Pte. J.
Foden, Pte. W. S.
Forrester, Pte. W.B.
Foster, Pte. R.
Garside, Pte. E.
Garside, Pte. H.
Garside, Pte. S.
Gaskell, Pte. T.
Gee, Pte. A.
Gee, Pte. J.
Gibson, Cpl. C.
Gibson, Cpl. H.
Gibson, L.-Cpl. H.
Gibson, Cpl. R.
Godding, Pte. A. V.
Gorman, Pte. T.
Green, Pte. A.
Green, Pte. E.
Green, Pte. H.
Green, L.-Cpl. S.
Gregory, Pte. H.
Gunnell, Pte. F.
Hague, Pte. A.
Hague, Pte. J.
Hall, Pte. T.
Hall, Pte. T.
Hamer, Pte. W. H.
Handley, Cpl. R.
Hanley, Pte. W.
Hanson, Pte. F.
Hardman, Pte. T.
Hare, Pte. A.
Harling, Pte. A. G.
Harrison, Pte. H.
Harrison, Pte. T.
Haughton, Pte. G.
Heinemann, Pte. E.
Heginbottom, Pte. J.
Herod, L.-Cpl. G.
Hibbert, Pte. E.
Higgins, Pte. C.
Higham, L.-Sgt. T.
Hodgkiss, Pte. E.
Hollingworth, L.-Cpl. J.
Hopkins, Pte. H.
Howard, Pte. J.
Hudson, Pte. G. W.
Hughes, Cpl. J.
Hughes, Pte. T.
Humphreys, Pte. C. H.
Illingworth, Sgt. H.
Jackson, Pte. F.
Jenkinson, Pte. J.
Jenneys, Pte. J. W.
Jevons, Pte. J. W.
Jones, Pte. A.
Jones, Pte. E.
Jones, Pte. F.
Jones, Pte. J.
Jones, Pte. O.
Jubb, Pte. J.
Kellett, Pte. S.
Kelly, Pte. E.
Kenyon, Pte. H.
Kerr, Pte. J.
Kerrick, Pte. H. H.
Lawton, Sgt. J.
Lawton, Pte. J.
Lee, Pte. F.
Lee, Sgt. T. H.
Leech, Pte. W.
Leech, Pte. W.
Lewis, Pte. A.
Lilley, Pte. W.
Lindley, Pte. J.
Lomas, Sgt. T.
Lord, Pte. H.
Lord, Pte. S.
Love, Pte. J.
Lunn, Pte. H.
Margreave, Pte. E.
Markham, Pte. J.
Marland, Dmr. A.
Martin, Pte. J.
Martyn, Pte. E.
Mason, L.-Cpl. W.
Massey, L.-Cpl. G.
Mather, Pte. S.
Mather, Pte. W.
Matthews, Cpl. H.
McClusky, Pte. R.
McDonald, Pte. J.
McDonnell, Pte. F.
Metcalfe, Pte. A.
Millar, Pte. L. S.
Mitcheson, Cpl. W.
Molyneaux, Pte. A.
Morris, Pte. J. H.
Moss, Pte. T.
Mycock, Pte. F.
Nally, Pte. W.
Newton, Pte. E.
Newton, Pte. H.
Nicholson, Pte. P.
Noonan, Pte. G.
Norman, Pte. T.
Nuttall, Pte. W.
O'Connor, Pte. J. J.
Ogden, Pte. H.
Ogden, Pte. S.
Oldfield, L.-Cpl. F.
Pearson, Pte. S.
Penny, Pte. T.
Portington, Pte. T.
Postle, Pte. W.
Potter, Pte. H.
Potts, Pte. W.
Poulston, Pte. P.
Pridham, Pte. W.
Rawlings, Pte. B.
Redfern, Pte. M.
Reyner, Pte. J.
Ridings, Pte. P.
Robinson, Pte. E.
Robson, Pte. G.
Rogan, Pte. M.
Rowbottom, Pte. J.
Ryder, Pte. J.
Ryding, Pte. H.
Schofield, Pte. R.
Sellers, Pte. J.
Sellers, Pte. J. E.
Shatwell, Pte. B.
Shepherd, Pte. F.
Sheridan, Pte. A.
Shuttleworth, Pte. W.
Sidebottom, Pte. H.
Sinclair, Pte. W.
Skirvin, Pte. E.
Smith, Pte. A.
Smith, Pte. C.
Smith, Pte. E.
Smith, Pte. F.
Smith, Pte. F.
Smith, Pte. I.
Smith, Pte. J.
Smith, Pte. J. W.
Smith, Pte. T.
Smith, Cpl. W.
Snape, Pte. A.
Speddings, Pte. J.
Spurrett, Cpl. A.
Stelfox, Pte. S.
Stevens, Pte. S.
Stones, Pte. P.
Stott, Pte. R.
Strutt, Pte. S.
Summersgill, Pte. J.
Swain, Pte. J. E.
Travis, Pte. J.
Taylor, Sgt. J.
Taylor, Pte. P.
Tetlow, Pte. J.
Thomas, Pte. R. A. L.
Thompson, Pte. B.
Thompson, Pte. H.
Thompson, Ptc. J.
Tilbury, Pte. F.
Tindall, Pte. J.
Townley, Pte. W.
Turner, Pte. C.
Varey, Pte. R.
Walker, Pte. G. H.
Walker, Pte. G. H.
Walker, Pte. J.
Walker, Pte. J.
Walley, Pte. S.
Watson, Pte. P.
Watson, Pte. S.
Welford, Pte. C. J.
Wilde, Cpl. J.
Wilde, Pte. J.
Williamson, Pte. E.
Wilshaw, Pte. I.
Wood, Pte. H.
Worsley, Pte. G.
Wrigley, Pte. A.
Wyatt, Dmr. F.

1/10 BATTALION MANCHESTER REGIMENT

Officers

Lewis, Lt.-Col. R. P.
Baird, Capt. L. B.
Owen, Capt. G. W.
Speelman, Capt. H. L. I.
Cook, Lieut. F. E.
Cooper, Lieut. C. M.
Clegg, Lieut. J.
Clegg, Lieut. J. H.
Griffiths, Lieut. F. N. G.
Norris, Lieut. W. J.
Shaw, Lieut. W. D.
Thorley, Lieut. G.
Ashcroft, 2nd Lieut. R. G. L.
Elliott, 2nd Lieut. F. P.
Emmott, 2nd. Lieut. J. B.
Gregory, 2nd Lieut. S.
Kirk, 2nd Lieut. T.
Nevinson, 2nd Lieut. H. K. B.
Stott, 2nd Lieut. J.
Wilson, 2nd Lieut. T. L.

Other Ranks

Adams, L.-Cpl. R.
Addyman, Dmr. W.
Allen, Pte. H. S.
Alty, Pte. H.
Ambrose, Pte. G. G.
Anderson, Pte. H.
Anderton, Pte. J. C.
Andrew, Pte. S.
Arundale, Pte. J.
Ashton, Pte. P.
Ashton, Pte. W.
Aspen, Pte. A.
Aspin, L.-Cpl. J.
Bailey, Pte. A.
Bailey, Pte. H.
Bailey, Pte. H.
Bailey, L.-Cpl. J.
Bairstow, Pte. S.
Bakewell, Pte. H.
Bamford, Pte. J.
Bannister, Pte. C.
Bannister, Pte. H. S.
Bardsley, Pte. J.
Bardsley, Pte. J.
Barker, Pte. A.
Barker, L.-Cpl. C.
Barlow, Pte. J.
Barnes, Pte. J.
Barratt, Pte. S.
Bates, Pte. E.
Bates, Pte. J.
Bayley, Pte. G.
Beaumont, L.-Cpl. T. E.
Beever, Pte. B.
Belshaw, Pte. J.
Belshaw, Pte. W. H.
Bennett, Pte. A. E.
Berry, Pte. J. L.
Betterley, Pte. G.
Biram, L.-Cpl. H.
Black, Dmr. T.
Blains, L. Cpl. T.
Blamey, Pte. D.
Bliss, L.-Cpl. J.
Bocking, Pte. W.
Booth, Pte. S.
Bould, Pte. J.
Bowden, Sgt. F.
Bowman, Pte. J.
Boxwell, L.-Cpl. J. D.
Boyd, Pte. W.
Boyle, Cpl. J.
Bradley, Pte. H.
Brennan, Pte. F.
Brierley, Pte. J.
Briggs, Pte. H.
Brooks, Pte. W. G.
Brown, Pte. E.
Brown, Pte. E.
Brown, Pte. G.
Brownbill, Pte. R.
Buckley, Cpl. J. N.
Buckley, Pte. W.
Burke, Pte. J. C.
Burgess, Pte. J.
Burgess, Pte. R.
Bushell, Pte. C.
Byrne, Pte. J.
Cadman, Pte. J.
Calvert, Pte. H.
Carrington, Pte. E.
Carter, Pte. W.
Cartledge, Pte. G.
Chadwick, Pte. M.
Chappell, Pte. J.
Chandley, Pte. G.
Charleswood, Pte. J.
Charnley, Pte. J. E.
Cheetham, Pte. T.
Chester, Pte. H.
Claber, L.-Cpl. T.
Claber, Pte. H.
Clark, Pte. H.
Claney, Pte. J.
Clarkson, Pte. J.
Clegg, Pte. H.
Clegg, Pte. P.
Clegg, Pte. P.
Clutton, Sgt. H.
Coates, Pte. J.
Coleman, Cpl. J.
Coles, L.-Cpl. C. E. J.
Collinge, Pte. H.
Connolly, Pte. A.
Cook, Pte. W.
Cook, Pte. G. H.
Cookes, Pte. C. C.
Cooper, Pte. J.
Coppins, Pte. F. J.
Cotterell, Pte. R. L.
Coyne, Pte. R.
Crawshaw, Pte. G.
Creek, Pte. L.
Crewe, L.-Cpl. T. H.
Crompton, Pte. R.
Crossley, Pte. F.
Culshaw, Pte. R.
Currie, Pte. J.
Currie, Pte. W.
Dalton, Pte. A.
Daly, Pte. J.
Darlington, Pte. E.
Davies, Pte. M. H. J.
Dawes, Pte. J. W.
Dean, Dmr. C.
Dinkwater, Sgt. E.
Dobson, Pte. W.
Dodgson, Pte. F.
Doran, Pte. J.
Drabble, Pte. F.
Drayton, Pte. G.
Dunkerley, C.Sgt. Mjr. F.
Dyson, Pte. T.
Dyson, Pte. W.
Eastwood, Pte. H.
Edwards, Pte. R.
Ellery, Pte. A.
Elson, Pte. E.
Elson, Pte. T.
Etchells, Pte. F.
Etchells, Pte. J.
Evans, L.-Cpl. J.
Ewers, Pte. G.
Exley, Pte. H.
Fallows, L.-Cpl. S.
Fannon, Pte. T.
Finlan, Pte. H. A.
Finney, Pte. A.
Fitton, Pte. E.
Fitton, Pte. J.
Fitzgerald, Pte. G.
Fizzard, Pte. A.
Fleetham, Cpl. G.
Fletcher, Pte. A.
Fletcher, Pte. J. E.
Fletcher, Pte. J. W.
Fletcher, Pte. L.
Foden, Pte. S. B.
Ford, Pte. J.
Francis, Cpl. F.
Frost, L.-Cpl. W.
Gales, L.-Cpl. M. H.
Gardiner, Sgt. J.
Gibson, Pte. W.
Gledhill, Pte. H. C.
Goldsby, Pte. J.
Goodier, Pte. J.
Goodier, Pte. W.
Gorbett, L.-Cpl. F.
Grady, L.-Cpl. A.
Greaves, Pte. A.
Greaves, Pte. L.
Greaves, Pte. W.
Green, Pte. J. A.
Greenwood, Pte. F.
Greenwood, Cpl. J.
Greenwood, Pte. W.
Gregson, L.-Cpl. J. H.
Grundy, Pte. H. B.
Hadfield, Cpl. F.
Hadfield, Pte. J. W.
Hadfield, Pte. J. A.
Hadfield, Pte. W.
Hague, Pte. A.
Hague, Pte. G.
Hague, Pte. T.
Hall, Pte. J.
Hallam, Pte. J.
Hardman, L.-Cpl. S.
Hargreaves, Pte. A.
Hargreaves, Pte. F.
Harrison, Pte. J.
Harrison, L.-Cpl. S. H.
Harrop, L.-Cpl. J.
Hayes, Pte. G.
Healey, Pte. D.
Henthorn, Pte. H.
Hewitt, Pte. W.
Heywood, Pte. R. W.
Highton, Pte. H.
Hilton, Cpl. J.
Hinchcliffe, Sgt. H.

Hinchcliffe, Sgt. H.
Hitchen, Pte. A.
Holden, Pte. J.
Holden, Pte. S.
Holland, Pte. H.
Holmes, Pte. E.
Holmes, Pte. J. E.
Holt, Pte. W.
Holt, Pte. G.
Hornby, Pte. W.
Horton, L.-Cpl. E. M.
Howard, Pte. C.
Howard, Pte. O.
Hoyle, Pte. F.
Hufton, Sgt. W.
Humphreys, Pte. J. C. R.
Hutchins, Pte. E.
Huxley, Pte. H.
Isherwood, Pte. J.
Jackson, Pte. H.
Jackson, Pte. J.
Jackson, Pte. J.
Jackson, Pte. J. W.
Johnson, Sgt. E.
Johnson, Pte. J. J.
Jones, L.-Cpl. E.
Jones, Pte. E.
Jones, Pte. F.
Jones, Cpl. G. A.
Jones, Pte. J.
Jones, Pte. T.
Jowett, Pte. C.
Kealey, Pte. T.
Kelly, Pte. J.
Kent, L.-Sgt. F.
Kenworthy, Pte. H.
Kenyon, Pte. E.
Kershaw, Pte. A.
Kidd, Cpl. W.
Kirkman, Cpl. H.
Kite, Pte. N.
Kitson, Sgt. F.
Knott, Pte. H.
Knott, Pte. T. H.
Lane, Pte. R.
Langley, Sgt. C.
Lawson, Pte. W.
Lawton, Pte. F.
Leach, Pte. L.
Lees, Pte. J. W.
Lewis, L.-Cpl. H.
Little, Pte. T.
Littlewood, Pte. W.
Lloyd, Pte. F. A.
Lomas, Pte. J.
Lowe, Pte. F.
Lycett, Pte. E.
Lynn, Pte. J.
Mason, Cpl. W.
Mason, Pte. J. T.
Massey, Pte. J. H. T.
Massey, Pte. S.
Maxwell, Pte. J.
McConnell, Pte. T.
McNulty, Pte. J.
Mead, Pte. J.
Melia, Pte. T.
Mellor, Pte. A.
Mellor, Pte. F.
Mellor, Pte. S.
Mewitt, Pte. J. E.
Miller, Pte. G. R.
Miller, Pte. J.
Milner, Sgt. J.
Mills, Pte. H.
Mills, Pte. W.
Mills, Pte. W.
Molyneux, Pte. T. W.
Monks, Pte. G.

Moorcroft, Pte. W.
Moran, Pte. F.
Morgan, Pte. H.
Morgan, Pte. J. E.
Morgan, Pte. T.
Morgan, Pte. W.
Morris, Pte. J. L.
Murphy, Pte. J.
Nanson, Sgt. W.
Needham, L.-Sgt. J.
Needham, Pte. J.
Nelson, Pte. G.
Neville, Pte. M.
Newman, Pte. E.
Newton, Pte. H.
Nicholas, Pte. D. J.
Nicholls, Pte. F.
Norcross, Pte. H.
Norman, Pte. A.
Ogden, Pte. A.
Ogden, Pte. E.
Ogden, Pte. H.
Ogden, Pte. J.
Olive, Pte. E.
Openshaw, Pte. J.
Owen, Pte. T.
Owens, Pte. R.
Palmer, Pte. R. H.
Patchett, Pte. W.
Percy, Pte. C. N.
Pickering, Pte. J.
Pickering, Pte. T.
Pickles, Pte. W.
Pinder, Pte. J.
Platt, Pte. E.
Platt, Pte. J.
Platts, Pte. H.
Pollitt, Pte. J.
Pool, Pte. T.
Powall, Pte. H.
Powell, Pte. J. D.
Powell, Pte. R.
Prescott, Pte. G.
Pritchard, Pte. W.
Ramsden, Pte. J.
Ratcliffe, L.-Cpl. J.
Rayment, Pte. T.
Rees, Pte. G. J.
Redford, Pte. W.
Regan, Pte. J.
Renshaw, Pte. E.
Richardson, Pte. J.
Riley, Pte. J.
Rinnie, Pte. J.
Robertson, L.-Cpl. J.
Robinson, Pte. E.
Robinson, L.-Cpl. F.
Robinson, Pte. F.
Robinson, Pte. S.
Robinson, Pte. T. E.
Roscoe, Pte. R.
Rose, Cpl. P. J.
Ross, Pte. H.
Rothwell, Pte. W. H.
Rourke, Pte. G.
Royle, Pte. H.
Ryatt, Pte. G. B.
Saint, Pte. H.
Saunders, Pte. R.
Saville, Pte. G.
Schofield, Pte. B. G.
Schofield, Pte. H.
Schofield, Pte. H.
Scholes, Pte. F.
Scholes, Pte. F.
Scott, Pte. W.
Seville, Sgt. H.
Seville, Pte. W.
Shaw, Pte. G.

Shaw, Pte. J.
Shepherd, Pte. C.
Shepherd, Pte. L. J.
Shires, Pte. H.
Shirley, Pte. J.
Skitt, Pte. J.
Slinger, Pte. H.
Smalley, Pte. E. R.
Smedley, Pte. S.
Smith, Pte. F.
Smith, Pte. H.
Smith, Pte. J.
Smith, Pte. J. T.
Smith, Sgt. R.
Snare, L.-Cpl. A. A.
Snore, Pte. A.
Stafford, Pte. C.
Stansfield, L.-Cpl. F.
Stansfield, Pte. J.
Stanton, Pte. T. W.
Stephenson, Pte. J.
Stockton, Pte. A.
Stott, Pte. C.
Stott, Pte. E.
Stott, Pte. F. H.
Stott, Pte. J.
Stott, Pte. J. S.
Strachen, L.-Cpl. T. H.
Stubbs, Pte. W. H.
Styles, Pte. H.
Sutcliffe, Pte. W.
Sutton, Pte. C. V.
Sutton, Pte. J.
Sykes, Pte. F.
Taulbutt, Pte. G.
Taylor, Pte. G.
Taylor, Pte. J.
Taylor, Pte. J. L.
Taylor, Pte. J. W.
Taylor, Pte. S.
Taylor, Pte. W.
Taylor, Pte. W.
Thomas, Pte. D. J.
Thorpe, Pte. J. R.
Titley, Pte. J.
Tomlinson, Pte. J.
Travis, Pte. G.
Travis, Pte. J.
Turner, Cpl. A.
Turner, L.-Cpl. E.
Turner, L.-Cpl. J.
Turner, Pte. W.
Turnock, Pte. W
Twiggs, Pte. F.
Tyson, Pte. J. E.
Viner, Pte. A. W.
Wales, Pte. J.
Walker, Pte. E.
Walker, Pte. J.
Walker, Sgt. T.
Walmsley, Pte. R.
Walsh, Cpl. P. J.
Wandrey, Pte. J.
Ward, Pte. T.
Wardle, Pte. P.
Warrener, Pte. E.
Watson, Pte. H.
Whewell, L.-Cpl. T.
Whitehead, Pte. J. W.
Whitmore, Cpl. R.
Whittaker, Pte. R.
Whittaker, Pte. R.
Whitworth, Pte. J. E.
Wilde, Pte. E.
Wilkinson, Pte. W.
Wilson, Pte. E. R.
Wilson, Pte. L.
Wolstencroft, Sgt. S.
Wood, Pte. A.

Roll of Honour

Wood, Sgt. J. W.
Wood, Pte. J. W.
Worthington, Pte. J. W.
Wright, L.-Cpl. A.
Wright, Pte. H.
Wrinson, Pte. R.
Wyatt, Pte. F.
Wyke, Sgt. W.

127th INFANTRY BRIGADE
1/5 BATTALION MANCHESTER REGIMENT

Officers

Ainscough, Capt. C.
Brown, Capt. F. S.
Dickson, Capt. L. E., M.C.
Hindley-Smith, Capt. E. H.
James, Capt. F. A.
Johnson, Capt. W. G. E.
Jowett, Capt. J. S.
Leech, Capt. A. C.
Rogers, Capt. H. M.
Winterbottom, Capt. D. D.
Box, Lieut. P. J.
Cowan, Lieut. B. T. R.
Dicksey, Lieut. R. G. A.
Foster, Lieut. L. T. L.
Iveson, Lieut. F. T.
James, Lieut. G. S.
Johnson, Lieut. H. N.
Lamb, Lieut. E. R.
Skipworth, Lieut. P. J.
Arnold, 2nd Lieut. J.
Batten, 2nd Lieut. P. W.
Brook, 2nd Lieut. A. C.
Byron, 2nd Lieut. H.
Davis, 2nd Lieut. L. E.
Harman, 2nd Lieut. A. G.
James, 2nd Lieut. R. F.
Mather, 2nd Lieut. D.
McGeorge, 2nd Lieut. T. L.
Pagett, 2nd Lieut. L. H.
Penton, 2nd Lieut. H.
Porter, 2nd Lieut. H. J.
Scott, 2nd Lieut. F. G., M.M.
Smith, 2nd Lieut. W. C.
Walker, 2nd Lieut. T. C.

Other Ranks

Acton, Cpl. C.
Aldred, Pte. J.
Allcock, Pte. W.
Allen, Cpl. F.
Arden, L.-Cpl. F.
Arstall, Pte. B. C. S.
Ashcroft, Pte. J.
Askey, Pte. W.
Atkins, Pte. J. B.
Austin, Pte. J.
Bainbridge, Pte. G.
Baldwin, Pte. T.
Bampkin, Pte. T.
Banks, Pte. A.
Banks, Cpl. J.
Banks, Pte. T.
Bann, Pte. A.
Bardsley, Pte. F.
Bargery, Pte. A.
Barker, Pte. E.
Barlow, Pte. W.
Barlow, Pte. W. H.
Barnes, Pte. A.
Barnes, Pte. J.
Barnfield, Pte. H.
Barnish, Pte. S.
Baron, Cpl. E.
Barrett, Pte. J. F.
Barrett, Pte. W. J.
Barrow, Pte. T.
Barton, Pte. S.
Bate, L.-Cpl. F.
Bates, L.-Cpl. G.
Bates, L.-Cpl. T.
Battersby, Pte. J.
Baxendale, Sgt. R.
Bayley, Pte. J.
Beaumont, Pte. H.
Beaver, Pte. A. E.
Beeley, L.-Cpl. J. W.
Bendale, Pte. J.
Bennett, Pte. W.
Bennison, Sgt. W.
Bentham, Pte. E.
Beresford, Pte. W.
Bickley, Cpl. G.
Birchall, Pte. A. H.
Blackledge, Pte. J.
Bloor, L.-Cpl. S.
Boardman, Pte. J.
Boardman, Pte. R.
Bolton, Pte. J.
Bolton, Pte. J.
Booth, Pte. J.
Bowden, Pte. C.
Boyle, Sgt. A. McN.
Braithwaite, Pte. J.
Bramall, Pte. V.
Brennand, Pte. J. W.
Bridge, Sgt. J.
Bridgwater, Pte. W. J.
Brindle, Dmr. W.
Brittain, Pte. L.
Britton, Pte. E., M.M.
Brown, L.-Cpl. E.
Brown, Pte. J.
Brown, Pte. P.
Brown, Pte. W. L.
Buckley, Pte. J.
Burke, Pte. J.
Burns, Pte. J.
Buzza, Pte. A.
Byrne, Pte. W.
Calderbank, Pte. J.
Calderbank, Pte. T.
Callaghan, Pte. A.
Campsall, Pte. W. L.
Carey, Pte. T.
Carney, Pte. T.
Carr, Pte. G.
Carter, Pte. A.
Cartmer, Pte. J.
Case, Pte. J. T.
Catterall, Pte. H.
Causey, Pte. R.
Chadwick, Cpl. F., D.C.M.
Chadwick, Pte. E.
Chadwick, Pte. F.
Chapman, Pte. W.
Cheetham, L.-Cpl. A.
Clarke, L.-Cpl. J.
Clarkson, Pte. J.
Claxton, Pte.
Clay, L.-Cpl. F.
Clements, Pte. C.
Clitheroe, Pte. J.
Cole, Pte. J. L.
Collinge, Pte. R.
Collins, L.-Cpl. B.
Conway, Pte. T.
Cooke, Pte. S.
Cooper, Pte. C.
Cordingly, Pte. J.
Cosgrove, Pte. J.
Cottam, Pte. G.
Coulthard, Pte. G. W.
Cox, Pte. S. W.
Cragg, Pte. C.
Critchley, Pte. C.
Crofts, Pte. W.
Crooks, Pte. J.
Crossland, Pte. W.
Cullen, Pte. T.
Cush, C.Sgt.-Mjr. J. A.
Dainteth, Pte. J.
Dakin, Pte. G. A.
Daniels, Pte. J.
Danson, Pte. W.
Darlison, Pte. G.
Davenport, Pte. J.
Davenport, L.-Cpl. W.
Davies, Pte. J.
Davies, Pte. W. P.
Dawson, Pte. J.
Dawson, Pte. L.
Dean, Pte. J.
Dean, Pte. J. W.
Dean, Pte. T.
Dempsey, Sgt. P.
Dennerley, Pte. L.
Dent, Pte. J.
Devereaux, Pte. C. E.
Ditchfield, Pte. O.
Doherty, Pte. J. P.
Doughty, Pte. J.
Dowd, Pte. J.
Downham, Pte. R.
Downing, Pte. T.
Duckworth, Pte. R.
Duddle, Pte. W.
Duddy, Pte. J.
Duggan, Pte. H.
Dutton, Pte. T.
Eccles, Pte. P.
Eckersley, Pte. R.
Edge, Pte. G. E.
Fallas, Pte. J.
Farrell, Pte. P.
Fergusson, Dmr. J.
Fisher, Pte. F.
Flannagan, Pte. J. W.
Fleming, Pte. F. W.
Fletcher, Pte. J.
Foster, Cpl. C.
Foulkes, Pte. J.
Fowler, Sgt. W.

Fox, Pte. J.
Fox, Pte. J. T.
France, Pte. J.
Garswood, Pte. E.
Garswood, Pte. T.
Gaskell, Pte. J.
Giblin, Pte. J.
Gillow, Pte. J. A.
Glover, C.Sgt.-Mjr. J., M.M.
Glover, Pte. R.
Goodwin, Pte. F.
Graham, Pte. A.
Grayless, Pte. T.
Green, Pte. W.
Greenacre, Pte. C. A.
Griffiths, L.-Cpl. C.
Grimshaw, Pte. J. T.
Gregory, Pte. J.
Gregory, Pte. J.
Gregson, Pte. J.
Hall, Pte. S. R.
Hallam, Pte. H.
Halliwell, Pte. G.
Halliwell, Pte. T.
Hardman, Pte. W.
Harrison, Pte. A.
Harrison, Pte. P.
Harrison, Pte. T.
Harrison, Pte. W.
Harron, Pte. H.
Harwood, Pte. W.
Hawkins, Pte. G.
Heaton, Pte. C.
Heaton, Pte. J.
Henderson, Pte. J.
Henley, Pte. J.
Henshall, L.-Cpl. J. H.
Hersnip, Pte. J.
Hesford, Pte. R.
Hessey, Pte. H.
Hetherington, Cpl. J.
Heyes, Pte. J.
Heywood, Pte. A.
Hicks, Pte. H.
Higgins, Pte. T. E.
Highton, Pte. W.
Hill, Pte. F. S.
Hilton, Sgt. A., D.C.M.
Hilton, Pte. H.
Hilton, Pte. H. A.
Hilton, L.-Cpl. J.
Hilton, Pte. R.
Hocking, Pte. R. J.
Holdgate, L.-Cpl. G.
Holland, Pte. E.
Holland, Pte. T. R.
Holland, Pte. W.
Hollingsworth, Pte. W.
Hollins, Pte. F.
Holmes, Pte. J.
Hopper, Cpl. A.
Horrocks, Pte. J.
Horrocks, Sgt. J.
Horrocks, Pte. T.
Horsfield, Sgt. E.
Houghton, Pte. A.
Houghton, Pte. J.
Houghton, Pte. R.
Houghton, Pte. R.
Howard, Sgt. J.
Howard, Pte. W.
Hudson, Pte. W.
Hughes, Pte. F.
Humphreys, Pte. R.
Hunt, Pte. A.
Huntley, Pte. T. E.
Huthart, Pte. T.
Iddon, Pte. P.
Jackson, Pte. J.

Jacobs, Cpl. J. W.
Jarvis, Pte. W.
Jenkinson, Pte. S.
Jennings, Pte. J.
Jepson, Pte. H.
Johns, Pte. A.
Johnson, Pte. C. P.
Johnson, Pte. H.
Jones, Pte. A.
Jones, Pte. G.
Jones, Pte. G.
Jones, Pte. G. H.
Jones, Pte. H.
Jones, Pte. J.
Jones, Pte. J.
Jones, Pte. P.
Jones, Pte. R.
Jones, Pte. W. B.
Kay, Pte. S.
Kay, Pte. W.
Keefe, Pte. H.
Keegan, Pte. J.
Kelly, Pte. E.
Kelly, Pte. T.
Kenderdine, Pte. C. S.
Kershaw, Pte. J.
Kinder, Pte. W.
Kirk, Pte. J.
Knott, Pte. H.
Labiff, Pte. T.
Lacey, L.-Cpl. J.
Lambert, Pte. G.
Lambert, Pte. G. A.
Lancaster, Pte. C.
Lawton, Pte. S.
Leadbetter, Pte. F. N.
Lee, Pte. F., M.M.
Lee, Pte. J.
Lee, Pte. J. J.
Lees, Pte. H.
Lewis, Pte. J.
Lewis, Pte. N.
Lightfoot, Pte. R.
Lindsay, Pte. J. T.
Liptrot, Cpl. S. H.
Little, Pte. R.
Livesey, L.-Sgt. C. E.
Longson, Pte. A.
Loughlin, Pte. E.
Lowe, Cpl. J.
Loynd, Sgt. A.
Macdonald, Pte. W.
Madden, Pte. E.
Mahon, Pte. J.
Mainey, Pte. J.
Marlor, Pte. E.
Marsh, Pte. J.
Martin, Pte. T.
Martindale, Pte. J.
Martland, Pte. J.
Mason, Pte. H.
Mather, Pte. H. T.
McCallum, Pte. W.
McCombes, Pte. J.
McGann, Pte. J.
McGregor, Pte. J.
McNamara, Pte. T.
Mee, Pte. J.
Middlehurst, Pte. T.
Millington, Cpl. W.
Milner, L.-Cpl. R. H.
Moore, Pte. A.
Moores, Pte. J.
Morres, Pte. G.
Morris, Pte. R. W.
Mortimer, Pte. S.
Moss, Pte. T.
Moss, Pte. W.
Mullarkey, Pte. J.

Mulrooney, Cpl. J.
Mulvehill, Pte. J.
Murphy, L.-Cpl. W.
Murphy, Pte. L.
Myers, Pte. W.
Naish, Pte. H.
Naylor, Pte. J.
New, Pte. I.
Newcombe, Pte. C. W., M.M.
Newton, Pte. J.
Ode, Pte. J.
Ogden, Pte. H.
Oldfield, Pte. B. S.
Oliver, Pte. J. A.
Otter, Pte. J. H.
Parkes, Pte. W.
Parr, Pte. H.
Parry, Pte. W. H.
Peake, Pte. J.
Pendlebury, Pte. J. J.
Pennington, Pte. H.
People, Pte. T. A.
Pickles, Sgt. J.
Pickvance, Pte. S.
Pilkington, Pte. S.
Pollard, Pte. E.
Potter, Pte. W.
Prescott, Pte. F.
Preston, Pte. T.
Priestley, Pte. R. T.
Pritchard, Pte. A.
Raddcliffe, Pte. W., M.M.
Ramsdale, Dmr. J.
Rathbone, Pte. J.
Rawlinson, Pte. C.
Ready, Pte. J.
Regan, Pte. A. E.
Rhodes, Pte. J. W.
Riley, Cpl. E. W.
Rocks, Pte. J.
Roberts, Pte. T.
Robinson, Pte. C.
Roden, Pte. T.
Rogers, Pte. J.
Rogers, L.-Sgt. P.
Rooney, Pte.
Rostron, Pte. W.
Rothwell, Pte. A.
Rowe, Pte. A., M.M.
Rowlands, Pte. W.
Rowlandson, L.-Cpl. F.
Rudd, Cpl. H.
Ruorke, Pte. J.
Rushworth, Pte. W.
Rylands, Sgt. A. H.
Sanderson, C.Q.M.Sgt. A.
Sargent, Pte. C.
Seddon, Pte. J.
Shaw, Pte. J.
Shaw, Pte. T.
Sharples, L.-Cpl. G.
Shepherd, Pte. G.
Shone, Pte. H.
Shore Pte. R.
Shufflebottom, Cpl. A. S.
Shuttleworth, Pte. W.
Simms, Pte. T.
Simpkin, Pte. J.
Sissons, Pte. G. W.
Slater, L.-Cpl. J.
Smallman, Pte. A.
Smith, Pte. G.
Smith, Sgt. G. W.
Smith, Pte. H.
Smith, Sgt. J., D.C.M.
Smith, Pte. J.
Smith, Pte. J. S.
Smith, Pte. R.
Smith, Pte. R.

Smith, Pte. W.
Southern, Pte. C.
Southern, Pte. E.
Spencer, C.Sgt.-Mjr. W.
Stanley, Pte. J.
Stattar, Sgt. C.
Statter, Cpl. W.
Stockton, Cpl. S., D.C.M.
Stott, L.-Cpl. J., D.C.M.
Strike, Pte. E.
Stuart, Sgt. T., M.M.
Summers, Pte. A. H.
Sumner, Pte. J. W.
Sumner, Pte. R. K.
Swanson, Pte. S.
Sweeney, Pte. T.
Talbot, Pte. W.
Talbot, Sgt. W.
Tapp, Pte. F. T.
Tate, Pte. J.
Taylor, Pte. R.
Telford, L.-Cpl. J.
Telford, L.-Cpl. J. G.
Telford, Pte. R.
Thomas, Pte. E. A.

Thomas, Pte. H.
Thompson, Pte. A.
Thompson, Pte. G.
Thompson, Pte. J.
Thompson, L.-Cpl. W.
Tickle, C.Q.M.S. J. M.
Tighe, Cpl. J.
Tither, Pte. R. T.
Tomlinson, Pte. B. J.
Topping, Sgt. J.
Trotman, Pte. G. H.
Trousdale, Cpl. F., D.C.M.
Turner, Pte. A. M.
Turner, Pte. J.
Turner, Pte. P.
Unsworth, Pte. F.
Wadsworth, Pte. J. H.
Walker, Pte. E.
Wallace, Pte. G. F.
Warren, Pte. H.
Warren, Pte. W. F.
Waterworth, Pte. A.
Watts, L.-Cpl. H. P.
Webb, Pte. A.
Wedlock, Pte. W. C.

Westhead, Pte. T.
White, Pte. W. O.
Whittle, Sgt. S. W.
Wilkinson, Pte. J.
Wilkinson, Pte. J.
Williams, Pte. B.
Williams, Pte. F.
Williams, Sgt. J.
Wilson, Pte. E.
Wimpenny, Pte. H.
Winnard, Pte. J.
Winstanley, Pte. W.
Wood, L.-Cpl. D.
Wood, Pte. P.
Wood, Pte. W.
Woodhall, Pte. R.
Woodward, Pte. A.
Worsley, Pte. J.
Worthington, Pte. J.
Worthington, Pte. J.
Wright, Pte. J.
Wright, Pte. W.
Yates, Pte. A.
Yorke, Cpl. A.
Young, Pte. A.

1/6 BATTALION MANCHESTER REGIMENT

Officers

Holberton, Lt.-Col. P. V.
Worthington, Lt.-Col. C. S., D.S.O.
Davies, Lt.-Col. O. St. L.
Heywood, Maj. A. G. P.
Bazley, Capt. W. N.
Bedford, Capt. R. H.
Bridgford, Capt. S. L.
Brierley, Capt. H. C.
Cawley, Capt. H. T.
Edgar, Capt. G.
Holt, Capt. J.
Hunter, Capt. A. D.
Jackson, Capt. S. F.
Kessler, Capt. E.

Pilkington, Capt. H. B.
Reiss, Capt. W. E.
Waine, Capt. W. H.
Walker, Capt. A. J.
Brook Taylor, Lieut. A. C.
Donald, Lieut. A. J.
Knight, Lieut. H. H.
McDougall, Lieut. S.
Mills, Lieut. T. R.
Thorburn, Lieut. E. F.
Young, Lieut. E. T.
Barber, 2nd Lieut. L. H.
Bennett, 2nd Lieut. J.
Brooks, 2nd Lieut. A. C.
Collier, 2nd Lieut. S., M.C.

Compton Smith, 2nd Lieut. R.
Farrington, 2nd Lieut. W. B.
Greenhough, 2nd Lieut. J. W., D.C.M.
Hankinson, 2nd Lieut. R. H.
Jackson, 2nd Lieut. M. R.
Killick, 2nd Lieut. R. D.
Love, 2nd Lieut. J. R.
Milne, 2nd Lieut. A. H.
Pearson, 2nd Lieut. F. W.
Rainbow, 2nd Lieut. J.
Sitford, 2nd Lieut. L. J.
Vipond, 2nd Lieut. H.
Worthington, 2nd Lieut. T. R.

Other Ranks

Ainsworth, Pte. W.
Alderman, Pte. H.
Alexander, Pte. J.
Allen, Pte. F. E.
Anderson, Pte. A. E.
Anderson, Pte. R. E.
Apperley, Pte. A.
Arnold, Pte. E. W.
Ashley, Pte. C. S.
Ashton, Pte. W.
Aspinwall, Pte. R. A.
Atherton, Pte. J.
Atkinson, Pte. R.
Atkinson, Pte. S.
Austin, Pte. H. E.
Bailey, Pte. H.
Bailey, Pte. T.
Baker, Pte. J. E.
Ballantine, Pte. G.
Ballingall, L.-Cpl. A. S.
Bamford, Pte. M.
Banks, Pte. S. E.
Barber, Pte. G.
Bardsley, Pte. M.
Barker, Pte. W. R.
Barlow, Pte. C. H.
Barlow, Pte. G.
Barlow, Pte. H.
Barne, L.-Cpl. V.

Barnes, Pte. H.
Barratt, Pte. A.
Bates, L.-Cpl. C. B.
Bateson, Pte. E.
Battye, Pte. W. T.
Bebbington, Pte. J.
Booston, Pte. F.
Bell, Pte. A.
Bell, Pte. E. F.
Bell, Pte. F. A.
Belshaw, Pte. A.
Bennett, Sgt. J.
Benson, Pte. J. W.
Berry, L.-Sgt. A. J.
Berry, Pte. S. C.
Bickerton, Pte. M.
Binns, Pte. C. F.
Birch, Pte. G. R.
Blacklock, Pte. J.
Blades, Pte. A.
Blaikie, Pte. M.
Bleakley, Pte. E. D.
Bleakley, Pte. W.
Blears, Pte. H.
Blease, Pte. F. S.
Booth, Pte. W. H.
Bordson, L.-Cpl. L.
Boswell, Sgt. P. W.
Boyd, Sgt. L. D.

Boyes Varley, Sgt. C. T.
Bradbury, Sgt. G. S.
Brierley, Pte. H.
Brimblecombe, Pte. T. L.
Brittain, Pte. L. A.
Broadhent, Pte. F.
Dromhead, L.-Cpl. T.
Brooklebank, Pte. T.
Brooks, Pte. W. H.
Broome, Pte. G. E.
Brown, Pte. S. O.
Browne, Pte. W. E.
Browne, Pte. W. H.
Bryan, Pte. C. T.
Buckley, Pte. A.
Buckley, Pte. B. C.
Buckley, Pte. I.
Buckley, Sgt. R. M.
Buerdsell, Pte. A.
Burgess, Pte. A.
Burgess, Pte. F.
Bullock, Pte. A.
Butterfield, Pte. S.
Butterworth, Cpl. E. C.
Buzza, Pte. J.
Byron, Pte. G.
Cadman, Pte. V.
Cain, Pte. J.
Carhart, Pte. C. S.

Carter, Pte. F.
Carter, Pte. W.
Causer, Cpl. A. B.
Chilton, Pte. T.
Clarke, L.-Sgt. J. H. A.
Clarke, Pte. F. M.
Clarke, Sgt. J.
Clarke, Pte. S.
Clarke, Pte. V. E.
Clarke, Pte. W. J.
Clayton, Pte. A. B.
Clayton, Pte. S. C.
Clegg, Sgt. J.
Cliff, Pte. A.
Clifton, Pte. R. H.
Clind, Cpl. H. P.
Cloy, C.Sgt.-Mjr. H.
Collard, Pte. E.
Collinge, Pte. A.
Collins, Pte. G. H.
Compton, Pte. R. S.
Const, Pte. W.
Cooney, Pte. J. D.
Cooper, Pte. C. H.
Cooper, Pte. R. H. M.
Cooper, Pte. W.
Coops, Pte. H.
Coppack, Pte. W.
Corbishley, Pte. R.
Corbitt, Cpl. H.
Cordt, Pte. T. H.
Corless, Pte. J.
Cornes, Pte. H. W.
Cornwell, Pte. J.
Cory, L.-Sgt. B. C.
Cottrill, Pte. G. H.
Courtman, Pte. P.
Cowell, Pte. H.
Coxhill, Pte. O. R.
Craddock, Pte. E. L.
Craven, Pte. T. R.
Craythorne, Pte. J.
Cressy, Pte. R. P.
Crewe, Pte. P.
Crompton, Pte. W.
Crompton, Sgt. W.
Crook, Pte. J.
Cross, Pte. G. A.
Crowder, Cpl. C. E.
Cummock, Pte. A.
Cumpsty, Pte. S. H.
Cundall, L.-Cpl. W. L.
Daarden, Pte. F.
Daber, Pte. A.
D'Arcy, Pte. J.
Darlington, Pte. H. C.
Davies, Pte. A. L.
Davies, Pte. R.
Davies, Pte. W. W.
Davy, Pte. A.
Dawson, Pte. J.
Dearden, Pte. J.
Denham, Pte. J. D.
Dennett, Pte. W.
Derry, Pte. W.
Dibman, Pte. W.
Dick, Pte. H.
Dobson, Pte. L.
Dodd, Pte. W. N.
Doig, Pte. A. M.
Duggins, Pte. M.
Duke, Pte. W.
Dunbar, Pte. H.
Dunkerley, Pte. J.
Dyer, Pte. J.
Dyson, Pte. C.
Earle, Pte. J.
Eckersley, Pte. T.
Edwards, L.-Cpl. F.

Edwards, Pte. J. G.
Egerton, Pte. J. W.
Ellis, Sgt. W.
Elton, Pte. J. F.
Evans, Pte. G.
Evans, Pte. L.
Evans, Pte. W.
Evanson, Pte. W.
Fagan, Sgt. T.
Fairy, Pte. W.
Fancourt, Pte. L. C.
Felton, Pte. N.
Ferguson, Pte. A.
Ferguson, Pte. D.
Few, Cpl. H. A.
Fields, Pte. S. J.
Finningley, Pte. A.
Fitton, Pte. L.
Fleming, Sgt. A. J
Fletcher, Pte. R.
Foley, Pte. J. C.
Forbes, Pte. S. H.
Fox, L.-Cpl. W. H.
Fox, Pte. W.
Freeman, Pte. H.
French, Pte. A. R.
Fry, Pte. A. H.
Gant, Pte. A.
Galley, Pte. G.
Garner, Pte. T. H.
Garside, Pte. C.
Gaskell, Pte. F.
Gaskell, Pte. T.
German, Pte. A.
Gerrard, Pte. N. W.
Gilbert, Pte. J.
Gill, Pte. E. G.
Gilland, Pte. T.
Gond, Pte. F.
Goodall, Pte. C.
Goodall, Pte. E. L.
Goodier, Pte. G.
Gradisky, Pte. F.
Graham, Pte. F.
Gray, Pte. D.
Green-Goddard, Pte.
Griffith, Pte. G.
Griffiths, Cpl. R. F.
Griffiths, Pte. H.
Grimes, Pte. C. R.
Grimshaw, Pte. E. M
Grimshaw, Pte. W.
Grogan, Pte. T.
Groomes, Pte. S. J.
Grove, Pte. D.
Gunn, Pte. R.
Hackett, Pte. J.
Hadfield, Pte. E.
Hadfield, Sgt. F.
Hahn, L.-Cpl. W. F.
Haig, Pte. E.
Hall, Pte. J.
Halliday, Pte. F. H.
Hambleton, Pte. W.
Hammond, Pte. J. L.
Hanley, Pte. C. A.
Harrison, Pte. B.
Harrison, L.-Cpl. T.
Harrop, Pte. J.
Harwood, Pte. J.
Hawthorn, Pte.
Hayes, Sgt. A.
Hayes, Pte. W.
Haynes, Pte. H.
Hayward, Pte. F. C.
Hayward, Pte. J. H.
Hayward, Pte. T. B.
Heap, Pte. E. A.
Heard, Cpl. R. L.

Heath, Pte. H.
Heeley, Pte. A. E.
Hewitt, Pte. J.
Heydon, L.-Cpl. S.
Heyes, Pte. W.
Heywood, Pte. A.
Heywood, Pte. W.
Hickman, Pte. F. P.
Hickson, Pte. J. F.
Higgins, Pte. H. W.
Hill, Pte. G. A.
Hind, Pte. R. B.
Hindley, Pte. H.
Hobday, Pte. A. M.
Hocknell, Pte. T.
Hodgson, Pte. F.
Holden, Pte. G. A.
Holland, Pte. T.
Holland, Pte. T. A.
Holme, Pte. N. Z.
Holme, Pte. T.
Holt, Pte. W. N.
Holyoake, L.-Cpl. F.
Honniball, Pte. W.
Hornbrook, Pte. H.
Horne, Pte. J. L.
Horrocks, Pte. W. T.
Hough, Pte. J. H.
Houghton, Pte. A.
Houghton, Pte. T.
Houldsworth, Pte. H. S.
Howarth, Pte. A.
Howarth, Pte. F.
Howarth, C.Sgt.-Mjr. J.
Howarth, Pte. N. D.
Howell, Pte. A. H.
Huddleston, Pte. L. F.
Huff, Pte. L.
Hulse, L.-Cpl. A.
Humphreys, Pte. J. L.
Hurst, L.-Cpl. H. G.
Hyman, Pte. H.
Ismay, Pte. T.
Jackson, Pte. A.
Jackson, Pte. W.
Jagger, Pte. J. A.
Jarratt, Pte. H.
Jefferies, Pte. F.
Johnson, Pte. E. A.
Johnson, Pte. L. A.
Johnson, Pte. S. R.
Jones, Pte. E.
Jones, Pte. H.
Jones, Pte. H.
Jones, Pte. J.
Jones, Pte. P.
Jones, Pte. R. E.
Kay, Pte. H.
Kelly, Pte. C. L.
Kelsey, Pte. J.
Kent, Sgt. G.
Kenyon, Pte. S.
Kershaw, Sgt. F.
Kershaw, Pte. R.
Kershaw, Pte. S.
Kerwin, Pte. J.
King, Pte. E.
Kitchen, Pte. C. F.
Kitson, Pte. F.
Knight, Pte. A.
Knight, Sgt. T.
Laimbeer, Pte. H. N.
Lamb, Pte. J.
Lancaster, Pte. D. G.
Langford, Pte. G.
Lawson, L.-Cpl. W. F. B.
Leach, Pte. H. A.
Lee, Pte. J.
Lee, Pte. S.

Roll of Honour 225

Leese, Pte. J. S.
Leigh, L.-Cpl. W.
Leighton, Pte. W.
Lilley, Pte. L.
Lister, Pte. J. B.
Livesley, Cpl. A.
Livingstone, Pte. J.
Llewellyn, Pte. F.
Lloyd, Pte. N. V.
Loughland, Pte. H. V.
Loughlin, Pte. W.
Lowe, L.-Sgt. W. A.
Lown, Pte. S.
Mackenzie, Pte. W.
Magee, Pte. H. H.
Maguire, Pte. J.
Mahony, Pte. F.
Maloney, C.Sgt.-Mjr. H.
Mantle, Pte. J.
Marsden, Pte. F. C.
Marsden, Pte. T. F.
Marsh, L.-Cpl. A.
Martin, Pte. J.
Martin, C.Sgt.-Mjr. J. R.
Martin, L.-Cpl. R. J.
Mason, Pte. F.
Massey, Pte. T.
Mather, Pte. A. S.
Mathews, Pte. J.
Mathews, Pte. S.
Mathewson, Pte. T. A.
Mayall, Pte. W.
McIntyre, Sgt. P. S.
McMillian, L.-Cpl. S.
McNab, Pte. G.
McNaughton, Sgt. W. M.
McNulty, Pte. E.
McSpiret, Pte. G. P.
Mellor, Pte. C. L.
Mercer, Pte. W.
Merron, Pte. E.
Metcalf, Pte. H. G.
Metcalfe, Pte. J.
Metcalfe, Pte. W.
Millar, Cpl. C. W.
Mills, Pte. F. T.
Mills, Pte. R.
Mitchell, Pte. F.
Molyneaux, Pte.
Moores, Pte. S.
Moorhouse, Pte. W. C.
Moreton, L.-Cpl. B. W.
Morris, Pte. D.
Morris, Pte. W. T.
Mortimer, Pte. H.
Morton, Pte. C. L.
Moss, Pte. F. B.
Moss, Pte. H.
Moss, Pte. S.
Mould, Cpl. H.
Mullins, Cpl. P.
Murphy, Pte. F.
Musgrave, Pte. W.
Neaves, Pte. C. A.
Needham, Pte. F.
Neill, Pte. T.
Newlove, L.-Cpl. G.
Nicholson, Pte. S.
Nightingale, Pte. F.
Nightingale, Pte. R.
Nobbs, Pte. B. J.
Norton, Sgt. E.
Oarton, Pte. W.
Ogden, Pte. A.
Ollerenshaw, Pte. J.
Orme, Sgt. J.
Owens, Pte. T.
Palmer, Pte. T. E.
Parker, Pte. G.

Parker, Pte. G. C.
Parker, Pte. J. N.
Partt, Pte. E.
Payne, Pte. A. R.
Peat, Pte. C.
Peel, Pte. S.
Penn, Pte. H.
Penny, Pte. T. H.
Peover, Pte. J. W.
Percival, Pte. A.
Phillips, Sgt. D.
Pickup, Pte. J. B.
Pierpoint, Pte. H. W.
Pilling, Pte. H.
Pilling, Pte. J. G. C.
Pilling, Pte. S. B.
Pinders, Cpl. C.
Place, Pte. W. A.
Plant, L.-Cpl. H. M.
Plevin, Pte. H.
Pollack, Pte. F.
Pollard, Pte. J.
Porter, Pte. T. C.
Pounder, Pte. W. H.
Prescott, Pte. N.
Price, Cpl. H.
Prince, Pte. C.
Pugh, Pte. J.
Pyggot, Sgt. T.
Rae, Pte. C. W.
Ralphs, Pte. F.
Ralphs, Pte. H.
Rankin, Pte. W. M.
Reade, Pte. N. E.
Rebbitt, Pte. H. R.
Redfern, Pte. R. L.
Redhead, Pte. J. F.
Reid, Pte. W.
Renwick, Pte. T.
Reynolds, Pte. C.
Rhodes, Pte. B. C.
Richards, L.-Cpl. A. G.
Richards, Sgt. G. A.
Richardson, Pte. A. V.
Richardson, Pte. S. C.
Roberts, L.-Cpl. B.
Roberts, L.-Cpl. W.
Roberts, Pte. C.
Roberts, Pte. G. A.
Robinson, Pte. E. J.
Robinson, Pte. J.
Robinson, Pte. W. R.
Robinson, Pte. W. T.
Rogers, Pte. S.
Rogerson, Pte. E.
Romington, Pte. C.
Roscoe, Pte. F. N.
Rothwell, Pte. J.
Rowland, Pte. F.
Rowlinson, Pte. J. G.
Rutherford, Pte. W. L.
Rutter, Cpl. C. A. G.
Ryder, Pte. A. D.
Ryder, Pte. W.
Salomon, Pte. S.
Scholes, Pte.
Scotchford, Pte. G.
Scott, Pte. J.
Seames, Pte. F.
Senior, L.-Cpl. J. K.
Sharples, Pte. A.
Shawcross, Sgt. J.
Shenton, Pte. R.
Shepherd, Pte. L.
Sidebottom, Pte. E.
Sides, Pte. W.
Simm, Pte. A.
Sinclair, Pte. D. C.
Slater, Pte. E. C. H.

Slater, Pte. G. H.
Smith, Cpl. A. B.
Smith, Cpl. D.
Smith, Pte. G.
Smith, Pte. G. S.
Smith, Pte. H.
Smith, Cpl. H. M.
Smith, Cpl. M.
Smith, Pte. W.
Smith, Pte. W. F.
Smith, Pte. W. N.
Snape, Pte. W.
Sorton, Sgt. E.
Southam, Pte. P.
Spring, Pte. W. H.
Stables, Pte. G.
Stacey, Pte. J.
Stead, Pte. J. R.
Stear, Pte. R.
Steward, Pte. P.
Stones, Pte. H.
Stott, Sgt. R.
Summers, Pte. G.
Sutton, Pte. F.
Sykes, Pte. E.
Tabb, Pte. P.
Taglforth, Sgt. W.
Talbot, Pte. E.
Tatlow, Pte. H.
Tattersall, Pte. G.
Taylor, Pte. A.
Taylor, Pte. O. H.
Taylor, Pte. F.
Taylor, Pte. G. E.
Taylor, Pte. P. E.
Taylor, Pte. T.
Taylor, Pte. T. H.
Taylor, Pte. W.
Taylor, Pte. W. H.
Tease, Sgt. T. A.
Thirlwall, Cpl. G. H.
Thompson, Pte. A.
Thompson, L.-Cpl. F.
Thompson, Pte. G. S.
Tollett, Pte. W.
Tomlin, Pte. E.
Torkington, Pte. R.
Tozer, Pte. N. S. F.
Troacher, Pte. W.
Trueman, Pte. S.
Tulk, Pte. A. L.
Turner, Pte. R. W.
Turton, Pte. C. G.
Tyldesley, Pte. T. H.
Utley, Pte. C.
Valentine, L.-Sgt. C. K.
Veitch, Cpl. A. P. P.
Wade, Pte. G.
Walker, Pte. F. G.
Walker, Pte. F. J.
Wallace, Pte. F.
Walley, L.-Cpl. A.
Walley, Pte. F.
Walters, Pte. A. J.
Walters, Sgt. W.
Walton, Pte. C.
Walton, Pte. G.
Ward, Pte. W. E.
Wardley, Pte. C. S.
Warrington, Pte. P.
Warwick, Pte. R.
Waterland, Pte. F.
Waters, Pte. G. E.
Webster, Pte. L.
Webster, Pte. T.
Whitbread, Pte. L. G.
Whitehead, Pte. S. L.
Whitla, Pte. C. M.
Whittaker, Pte. A. D.

Q

226 The 42nd Division

Whittaker, Pte. G.
Wilcox, Cpl. F.
Wild, Pte. C. P.
Wild, L.-Cpl. E.
Wild, Pte. J. W.
Wilkinson, Pte. W.
Williams, Pte. E.
Williams, Pte. E.
Williams, Pte. E.
Williams, Pte. F. N.
Williams, Pte. H.

Williams, Pte. H.
Williams, Pte. H.
Wilson, Pte. C.
Wilson, Pte. H.
Wilson, L.-Cpl. J.
Wilson, Pte. J.
Wilson, C.Q.M.Sgt. W.
Wood, Pte. E.
Wood, Pte. E.
Woodhead, Cpl. C. S.
Worthington, Sgt. T. R.

Wright, Cpl. A. E.
Wright, Pte. R.
Wright, Pte. T. H.
Yardley, Sgt. H.
Yates, C.Sgt.-Mjr. A.
Yates, Pte. A. C.
Yates, Pte. R. F.
Yates, Sgt. R.
Yates, Pte. W. C.
Young, Pte. J.

1/7 BATTALION MANCHESTER REGIMENT

Officers

Staveacre, Maj. J. W.
Allen, Capt. C. R., M.C.
Philp, Capt., R.A.M.C.
Rylands, Capt. R. E.
Savatard, Capt. T. W.
Sivewright, Capt. W. J.
Tinker, Capt. A. H.
Williamson, Capt. C. H., M.C.
Bacon, Lieut. A. H.

Brown, Lieut. T. F.
Carley, Lieut.
Cooper, Lieut. C. M.
Dudley, Lieut. C. L.
Freemantle. Lieut. W. G.
Granger, Lieut. H. M.
Grant, Lieut. R. W. G.
Kay, Lieut. H. N.
Lomas, Lieut. F.

Ludlam, Lieut. E. W.
McLaine, Lieut. D.
Pearson, Lieut. H.
Ray, Lieut. H. M.
Thewliss, Lieut. H. G.
Thorpe, Lieut. W. T.
Tyrer, Lieut. J. R.
Ward, Lieut. G. H.
Wood, Lieut. A. S.

Other Ranks

Abercrombie, Pte. E.
Adamson, Pte. C.
Adderley, Pte. E.
Alman, Pte. T.
Anderson, Cpl. R.
Anderton, Pte. F.
Ashton, Pte. C. B.
Ayres, Pte. W. A.
Bailey, Pte. W.
Bain, Pte. T. P.
Baker, Pte. H.
Balf, Pte. C.
Balon, Pte. E.
Bamber, Pte. M.
Bancroft, Pte. J. W.
Banks, Pte. A.
Bannan, Pte.
Barber, Pte. S.
Barks, Pte. F. C.
Barnes, Pte. J. H.
Barnett, Pte. I.
Barratt, Pte. R.
Barrow, L.-Cpl. T. E.
Barry, Pte. R. J.
Barton, Pte. T.
Beckett, Pte. J.
Beckett, Pte. R.
Bedford, Pte. F. A.
Bell, Pte. A.
Bennet, Cpl. C.
Bennett, Pte. R.
Bent, Pte. W.
Berry, Cpl. J.
Berry, Pte. J.
Beswick, Pte. R.
Billington, Pte. H.
Bincliffe, Pte. A.
Blackledge, Pte.
Bland, Pte. H. W.
Bleasdale, Pte. W
Boaley, Pte. A.
Boardman, Pte. A. H.
Boden, Pte. G. C.
Bouchier, Pte. G. C.
Bowe, Pte. G.
Bowling, Pte. T.
Boyd, Cpl. H.
Bracegirdle, Pte. L.
Brewer, Pte. M. C.
Bridge, Pte. E.

Bridson, Pte. R.
Bright, Pte. W.
Bromley, L.-Cpl. E.
Brookes, Pte. A.
Brookes, Pte. J.
Broughton, Pte. V.
Brown, Pte. E.
Brown, Pte. G.
Brown, Sgt. H.
Brown, Pte. J. W.
Bruce, Pte. W.
Byrne, Pte. T.
Buckley, Pte. L.
Buckley, Pte. W.
Burgess, Pte. A.
Burgess, Pte. A.
Burgess, Pte. J.
Burns, Pte. R.
Burr, Pte. C.
Butcher, Pte. H.
Calardine, L.-Cpl. J.
Callaghan, Pte. H.
Callon, Pte. J. W.
Carpenter, Pte. C.
Carr, Pte. A. E.
Carroll, Sgt. J.
Castrey, Pte. E.
Cavanagh, Pte. F.
Cavanagh, Pte. J.
Cawley, Pte. B.
Chadwick, Pte. C.
Chadwick, Pte. W.
Chantler, Pte. J.
Chappell, Cpl. J. H.
Chappell, Pte. L.
Clare, Pte. H.
Clarke, Pte. E. E.
Clegg, Pte. H.
Cliffe, Pte. G.
Clime, Pte. J.
Colley, Pte. W. J.
Collier, L.-Cpl. C.
Collins, Pte. R. C.
Collins, Pte. W.
Connell, Pte. A.
Connor, Pte. J.
Cookson, Sgt. S. R.
Cookson, Pte. W.
Cott, Pte. T.
Couper, Pte. G.

Cousell, Pte. J.
Cox, Pte. J.
Croughan, Cpl. C.
Cunnington, Pte. R.
Dale, Pte. H.
Daley, Pte. A.
Darbyshire, Pte. H.
Davidson, Pte. S.
Davies, Pte. C.
Davies, Pte. G.
Davies, Pte. G.
Davies, Pte. H.
Davies, Pte. T. A.
Dawson, Pte. T. B.
Day, Pte. H. G.
Dean, Pte. H.
Dillon, Pte. H.
Dingle, Pte. W. H.
Dodd, Pte. J.
Dodds, Pte. J. E.
Doherty, Pte. T.
Doolen, Pte. R. J.
Downey, Pte. O.
Draper, Pte. J. E.
Driver, Pte. R.
Duffy, Pte.
Dyehouse, L.-Cpl. W. H.
Dyke, Pte. F. G.
Eardley, Pte. G.
Earnshaw, Pte. N.
Ebourne, Pte. W.
Edgerton, Pte. G. J. A.
Edwards, Pte. J.
Elphinstone, Pte. R. J.
England, Pte. E.
England, Pte. W.
Evans, Pte. G.
Fairhurst, Pte. F.
Farrar, Pte. A.
Farrington, Pte. A.
Fawdrey, Pte. G.
Finch, Pte. H B. L.
Finch, Pte. S.
Fisher, Pte. B.
Fisher, Pte. J.
Fitchett, Pte. F.
Fitzsimmons, Pte. J.
Fletcher, Pte. E. H.
Foden, Sgt. W.
Forbes, Pte. W.

Roll of Honour 227

Ford, Pte. P.
Ford, Pte. R.
Forester, Pte. J. H.
Franklin, Pte. L.
Gamble, Pte.
Gardener, Pte. W.
Garratt, Pte. J.
Garrett, Pte. A.
Gibbons, Pte. J.
Gibson, Pte. F.
Gibson, Pte. J.
Gilbert, Pte. R.
Gillibrand, Pte. A.
Goddard, Pte. T.
Golton, Pte. J.
Goulding, Pte. P.
Graham, Pte. J. A.
Graham, Pte. W. H.
Grainger, Pte. H. M.
Green, Pte. J. D.
Greenhalgh, Pte. J.
Gregory, Pte. J.
Gresty, Pte. F.
Hall, Pte. C.
Hall, Pte. H.
Hallam, Pte. F.
Hamilton, Pte. G.
Hammersley, Pte. J.
Hampson, Pte. J.
Hardy, L.-Sgt. A.
Hargreaves, Pte. H.
Harling, Pte. J.
Harrison, Pte. E.
Harrison, Pte. H. N.
Harrison, Pte. T. S.
Harrison, Pte. W.
Harrop, Pte. W.
Hartnett, R.S.M.
Haselwood, Pte. T.
Haydock, Pte. J.
Hazeltine, Pte. J. R.
Heath, Sgt. F.
Heath, Pte. G.
Hewitt, Pte. W.
Heyward, Pte. S.
Higham, Pte. T.
Hilditch, Pte. H.
Hills, L.-Cpl. G. G.
Hilton, Pte. W.
Hinchcliffe, Pte. W.
Hind, Pte. W.
Hindly, Pte. J. B.
Hobbs, Pte. T.
Hodgkins, Pte. W.
Hodkinson, Pte. J. D.
Hodson, Pte. F.
Holcroft, Pte.
Holdcroft, Pte. F.
Holland, Pte. J. H.
Hollingworth, Pte. D.
Holmes, Pte. S.
Holmes, Pte. S.
Holt, Pte. J.
Hope, Pte. J. W.
Horrocks, Pte. W. E.
Horrox, Pte. W.
Hunt, Pte. E.
Hunt, Pte. H.
Hunt, Pte. S. A.
Hunt, Pte. W.
Ikin, Pte. J. W.
Ingram, Pte. H.
Jackson, L.-Cpl. E.
Jackson, L.-Cpl. J.
Jackson, Pte. J.
Jackson, Pte. J. S.
Jacques, Pte. G.
Jennings, Pte. W. G.
Jepson, Pte. W.

Johnson, Pte. A.
Johnson, Pte. J. H.
Johnson, Pte. R.
Johnson, Pte. W. A.
Jones, Pte. H.
Jones, Pte. J.
Jones, Pte. J.
Judge, Pte. M.
Kaufmann, Pte. S.
Kay, Pte. R.
Kearney, Pte. A. D.
Keeber, Pte. H.
Keeble, Pte. F.
Keegan, Pte. G.
Kellett, Pte. W.
Kelly, Pte. H.
Kelly, Pte. J.
Kenyon, Pte. A.
Kenyon, Pte. F.
Keogh, Pte. F.
Kerfoot, Pte. F.
Kershaw, Pte. J. H.
Kirby, Pte. H.
Kidd, Pte. T.
Krell, Pte. J.
Lamb, Pte. R.
Laver, Pte. H.
Lawton, Sgt. C. H.
Leach, Pte. R.
Lee, Pte. J. M.
Lee, Pte. W. H.
Lees, Pte. W.
Leigh, Pte. L.
Leigh, Pte. W.
Livesey, Pte. W.
Lockett, Cpl. S. E.
Lomas, Pte. F.
Lomas, Pte. G. A.
Longshaw, Pte. R.
Lowerson, Pte. H.
Lowry, Pte. H.
Lyons, Pte. J.
Lyons, Pte. T.
Lythe, Pte. F.
Makin, Pte. A. W.
Maley, Pte. E.
Mallis, Pte. G. W.
Manley, Pte. J. N.
Marshall, Pte. R.
Martin, Pte. W. H.
Marvin, Pte. G.
Mason, Pte. J.
Master, Pte. E. H.
Mates, Cpl. J.
McCartney, L.-Cpl. H. S.
McCleod, Pte. A.
McClure, Pte. E.
McHugh, Pte. H.
McKeown, Pte. E.
McKie, Pte. W. K.
McVey, Pte. J.
McWilliam, Pte. R.
Mellor, Pte. G.
Merriman, Cpl. R.
Midgeley, Pte. F.
Milligan, Pte. A.
Milligan, Pte. A. J.
Milligan, Pte. J.
Millington, Pte. P.
Milward, Pte. K.
Minns, Sgt. W.
Minshall, Pte. F.
Mitchell, Pte. H.
Mitchell, Pte. H.
Moisey, Pte. J.
Molyneaux, Pte. H. S.
Moore, Pte. G.
Moran, Pte. J.
Morrell, Pte. J.

Morris, Pte. A.
Morris, Pte. E.
Morris, Pte. H.
Munday, Sgt. F.
Myers, Pte. R.
Nevin, Pte. J. S.
Newbold, Pte. S.
Newman, Pte. G. E.
Norman, Pte. E.
Norton, Pte. J.
Nuttall, Pte. H. W.
Oarkinson, Pte. A. C.
Oates, Pte. L.
O'Brien, Pte. A.
Oldfield, Pte. W. F.
Oldham, Pte. W.
Ormerod, Pte. A. E.
Page, Pte. A.
Pannell, Pte. T.
Pardoe, Pte. P.
Parsonage, Pte. A. F.
Parsons, Cpl. F. M.
Passant, Pte. R.
Peacock, Pte. W. H.
Pearce, Pte. F.
Pearson, Pte. G.
Pease, Pte. W. F.
Pender, Pte. W.
Percival, Pte. J
Phillips, Pte. J. P.
Pickles, Pte. W.
Platt, Pte. R.
Platt, Pte. W. C.
Pollitt, Pte. E.
Pope, Pte. W.
Powell, Pte. A. E.
Prendergast, Pte.
Raper, Pte. A. E.
Rawlings, Pte. H.
Rawlinson, Pte. W. R.
Rawson, Pte. W.
Redford, Pte. S. F.
Reid, Pte. J.
Rhodes, Pte. J. W.
Rideal, L.-Cpl. J. H.
Riley, Sgt. R.
Roberts, Pte. A.
Roberts, Pte. J.
Robertson, Pte. G.
Rogers, Pte. S.
Rogerson, Pte. W. H.
Rosewell, L.-Sgt. A.
Ross, Pte. C.
Royle, Pte. F. E. H.
Russell, Pte. W. H.
Salt, Pte. G.
Salter, Pte. H.
Sanderson, Pte. A.
Scraton, Pte. C.
Shaw, Pte. B.
Shearere, Pte. G.
Shepherd, Pte. J. E.
Shipley, Pte. J. R.
Sidebottom, Pte. H.
Skelmerdine, Pte. G.
Slowe, Pte. J. W.
Smith, Pte. H.
Smith, Pte. M.
Smith, Pte. R. S.
Smith, Pte. W. H.
Smith, Pte. W. H.
Sowden, Pte. W. P.
Sparling, L.-Cpl. P.
Stahler, Pte. J.
Stanton, Cpl. W.
Starkie, Pte. C.
Steel, Pte. R.
Stocks, Pte. T.
Stoddart, Pte. L.

Stott, Pte. A.
Super, Pte. C.
Sweeney, Pte. J.
Tanner, Sgt. A.
Tanner, Sgt. E.
Taylor, Pte. H.
Taylor, Pte. J.
Taylor, Pte. J. H.
Taylor, Pte. J. W.
Taylor, Pte. S.
Thomas, Pte. E.
Thomas, Pte. J. A.
Thompson, Pte. S. E.
Thompson, Pte. T.
Thornily, Pte. B.
Timothy, Pte. E.
Titterington, Cpl. F.
Tracey, Pte.
Treadway, Pte. T.
Twigg, Pte. F. A.
Vardon, Pte. C.
Verity, L.-Cpl. J.
Vickers, Pte. J. H.
Vipond, Pte. A.
Wakefield, Pte. A.

Wakefield, Pte. G.
Walker, Pte. J. W.
Walker, Pte. R.
Walker, Pte. S.
Wallace, Pte. G.
Walley, Pte. H.
Wallis, L.-Cpl. E.
Walsh, Pte. M.
Wanstall, Pte. H.
Ward, Pte. A.
Ward, Pte. J.
Ward, Pte. J.
Watmough, Pte. A.
Watmough, Pte. W.
Webb, Pte. S.
Webster, Sgt. H.
Welsh, Pte. R.
Whelan, Pte. J.
White, Pte. R.
Whiteley, Pte. J. B.
Whittaker, Pte. A. T.
Wilbraham, Pte. T.
Wild, Pte. G.
Wilde, Pte. H. J. R
Wilde, Pte. J. V.

Williams, Pte. A.
Williams, Pte. F.
Williams, Pte. H.
Williams, Pte. J.
Williams, Pte. R.
Williams, Pte. S.
Williams, Pte. W. V.
Wilson, Pte. L.
Winter, Pte. D.
Winterbottom, L.-Cpl. G.
Wiskin, Pte. A.
Wittle, Pte. G.
Wolstencroft, Pte. R. K.
Wood, Pte. A.
Wood, Pte. E.
Woodward, Pte. H.
Wookey, Pte. A. J.
Worrall, Pte. J. R.
Worrall, Pte. S.
Wrigley, Pte. J.
Yearsley, Pte. A.
Young, Pte. G.
Young, L.-Cpl. H.

1/8 BATTALION MANCHESTER REGIMENT

Officers

Heyes, Lt.-Col. W. G., T.D.
Forbes, Capt. A.
Hall, Capt. B. C.
Hepburn, Capt. A. J.
Oldfield, Capt. E. G. W.
Rose, Capt. H. J.
Standring, Capt. D. H.
Thody, Capt. C. J.
Whitworth, Capt. H.
Davies, Lieut. C. J.

Deakin, Lieut. C. K.
Evans, Lieut. J. E. M.
Eller, Lieut. C. R.
Hall, Lieut. S.
Heywood, Lieut. S.
Ingram, Lieut. W. H.
Marsden, Lieut. R.
Womersley, Lieut. J. W.
Bowen, 2nd Lieut. A.

Davie, 2nd Lieut. S. J.
Helm, 2nd Lieut. F.
Johnson, 2nd Lieut. P. C.
McLauchlan, 2nd Lieut. A.
Moran, 2nd Lieut. J.
Scott, 2nd Lieut. W. J. de V.
Tuson, 2nd Lieut. W.
Westbrook, 2nd Lieut. E. W.
Wilkinson, 2nd Lieut. J. Y.

Other Ranks

Abbott, Pte. G. A.
Abbott, Pte. W.
Allen, Pte. A.
Allen, Pte. E.
Allen, Pte. J. W.
Almond, Pte. W.
Anderson, Pte. W.
Antill, Pte. C. S.
Antrobus, Pte. A.
Arnold, Pte. J.
Ashby, Pte. J. H.
Ashcroft, Pte. G.
Banham, Pte. D. J. K.
Bardsley, Pte. T. H.
Barker, Pte. H.
Barlow, L.-Cpl. W.
Bartle, Pte. J. W.
Batkin, Pte. W. H.
Bayliss, Pte. A.
Beamish, Pte. C.
Beddows, Pte. L.
Bell, Pte. G. T.
Bellen, L.-Cpl. T.
Bennett, L.-Cpl. G. A.
Benson, Pte. R.
Bent, Pte. A.
Blackshaw, Sgt. F.
Blades, Pte. A.
Blakey, Pte. P.
Boddis, Cpl. T.
Booth, Pte. A.
Borrell, Pte. W.
Bottomley, Pte. J.
Boughton, Pte. A. W.
Bowers, Pte. S. L.
Bowes, Pte. S.

Bowker, Pte. J.
Boyle, Pte. M.
Bracegirdle, Pte. J.
Bray, Pte. J.
Breakey, Pte. H.
Bridge, Pte. A.
Bridgewood, Pte. T.
Briggs, Pte. L.
Broadbent, Pte. J.
Brown, Pte. B.
Brown, Cpl. E.
Brown, Pte. J.
Brown, Pte. T.
Bryan, Pte. T.
Bryan, Pte. W.
Buckley, Pte. E.
Bullock, Pte. J.
Burke, Pte. L.
Burrows, Pte. H.
Bury, Pte. S. W.
Butler, Pte. W.
Buzza, Pte. H.
Cadmore, Sgt. A.
Campbell, Pte. A.
Cannon, Pte. T.
Carden, Pte. S.
Carruthers, Cpl. C.
Carswell, Pte. J. L.
Cartledge, Pte. F.
Caton, Co. Sgt.-Mjr. J.
Certmar, Pte. W.
Chamberlain, Pte. W.
Chambers, Pte. J. W.
Chambers, Sgt. T. A.
Chapman, Pte. S.
Charlesworth, Pte. R.

Charlton, Pte. F.
Chelmick, Pte. C.
Chester, Pte. G.
Chorlton, Pte. J. W.
Clarence, Pte. C. B.
Clarke, Pte. A.
Clarke, Pte. J.
Clarkson, Pte. J. W.
Clayton, Pte. A. T.
Clements, Pte. H. J.
Clemson, Dmr. J. W.
Coach, Pte. J.
Cockrane, Pte. A.
Coffey, Pte. J.
Collinson, Pte. J.
Collinwood, Pte. R. W.
Concoran, Pte. J.
Connell, Pte. A.
Connell, Pte. J. E.
Connor, Pte. H.
Connor, Pte. W.
Cook, Pte. A.
Cooke, Pte. J. J.
Cooper, Pte. G. H.
Cooper, Pte. W.
Coote, Pte. F.
Corlett, Pte. C. H.
Corlett, Pte. W.
Cowden, Pte. H.
Cowzens, Pte. H.
Cox, Pte. H.
Cranshaw, Pte. G.
Craven, Pte. J.
Creighton, L.-Cpl. A.
Crilley, Pte. A.
Crompton, Pte. J.

Roll of Honour

Crumbleholme, Pte. J.
Dandy, Sgt. H.
Davidson, Cpl. J.
Davies, Pte. A.
Davies, Pte. H.
Davies, Pte. R.
Davies, Pte. W.
Dickinson, Pte. G.
Dollery, Pte. L.
Dorset, Pte. F.
Downes, Pte. A.
Draper, Pte. B. G.
Dudley, Pte. R.
Dyson, Pte. S.
Eardley, Pte. H.
Edwards, Pte. F.
Edwards, Pte. F.
Edwards, Pte. L.
Edwards, Pte. T.
Ellis, Pte. J. A. C.
Entwistle, Pte. J. R.
Evans, Pte. J.
Evans, Pte. W.
Fairclough, Pte. A.
Farrell, Pte. B.
Farrell, Pte. J.
Featherstone, Pte. H.
Finn, Pte. G.
Fitton, Pte. R.
Flattery, Pte. J. E.
Flynn, Pte. T. E.
Foran, Pte. W.
Ford, Pte. J.
Ford, Pte. H.
Forrestor, Pte. F. M.
Foster, Pte. C.
Foster, Pte. G.
Foulds, Pte. W.
Fraser, Pte. A.
Fullen, Pte. H.
Furey, Pte. F.
Gallaway, Pte. J.
Gannon, Pte. J.
Garchan, Pte. D.
Gardner, Pte. J.
Garner, Pte. J.
Garside, C.Q.M.Sgt. E.
Gibbons, Pte. C.
Gibson, Pte. H.
Giddley, Pte. T. E.
Gill, Pte. N.
Glasby, Pte. A.
Gleaves, Pte. H.
Glynn, Cpl. J.
Goacher, Pte. E.
Goodfellow, Pte. A.
Goodman, Pte. W. H.
Goodyear, Pte. J. W.
Graeves, Pte. A.
Grange, L.-Cpl. A.
Graves, Pte. W. E.
Greatorex, Pte. E. B.
Greatorix, Pte. J. W.
Green, Pte. H.
Green, Pte. W.
Greenwood, Pte. J.
Gregory, Pte. H.
Gregory, Pte. J.
Gregory, Pte. W.
Gregson, L.-Cpl. G.
Gribbin, Pte. J.
Griffiths, Pte. T.
Grindrod, Pte. H.
Gunshon, Pte. J.
Hampson, Pte. S.
Hanman, Pte. W. P.
Hardman, Pte. W. R.
Harling, Pte. C. E.
Harper, Pte. J.

Harris, Pte. G. T.
Harris, Pte. W.
Harrison, Pte. E.
Harrison, Pte. S.
Harrop, Bdsm. W.
Harry, Pte. C.
Hart, Pte. D.
Hartley, Pte. J. H.
Hassell, Pte. C.
Heap, Pte. J.
Heathcote, Pte. J.
Herbert, Pte. H.
Hetherington, Pte. H.
Hevison, Pte. T.
Hilton, Pte. S. L.
Hindle, Pte. W.
Hobson, Pte. W. H.
Hodgson, Pte. A. E.
Holdsworth, C.-Sgt. W. H.
Holmes, Pte. C.
Holtam, Pte. J.
Horn, Pte. H.
Horsefield, Pte. T. G.
Hough, Pte. W. B.
Howard, Pte. J.
Huband, Pte. A.
Hudson, Pte. A.
Hughes, Pte. W.
Hull, Pte. H. J.
Hulme, Pte. J.
Hulse, Pte. J.
Humphreys, Pte. J.
Hunt, Pte. H.
Hurst, Pte. R.
Illidge, Pte. E.
Irlan, Pte. J.
Irons, Pte. R.
Irvine, Pte. F. R.
Irving, Pte. G.
Jackson, Pte. J.
Jackson, Pte. R.
Johnson, Pte. H.
Johnson, Pte. R.
Johnson, Pte. W.
Jones, Pte. B.
Jones, Pte. E. S.
Jones, Pte. F.
Jones, Pte. G. G.
Jones, Pte. L. H.
Keeley, Pte. A.
Keeling, Sgt. H.
Keeling, Pte. T.
Keenan, Pte. M.
Kellett, Pte. C.
Kellett, Pte. F.
Kelly, Co. Sgt.-Mjr. A.
Kelly, Pte. E.
Kelly, Pte. J.
Kemp, Pte. G.
Kerridge, Pte. W. E.
Kershaw, Sgt. E.
Kight, Pte. G.
Kilroy, Pte. W.
King, Pte. L.
Kirwin, Pte. J.
Kitts, Pte. J.
Knott, R. Sgt.Mjr. J.
Laing, Pte. D. C.
Lamb, Pte. R.
Langley, Pte. G.
Lavner, Pte. W.
Laycock, Pte. J.
Leake, Sgt. R. F.
Lee, Pte. C. J.
Lee, Pte. R.
Leeming, Pte. E.
Leigh, Pte. C.
Leigh, Pte. T.
Lewis, Pte. W. S.

Limb, Pte. J.
Lloyd, Pte. T.
Logan, Pte. W.
Lomax, Pte. J.
Low, Pte. J. P.
Lowe, L.-Cpl. N. E.
Lucas, Pte. W.
Lupton, Pte. C.
Lynch, Pte. J.
Maddocks, Pte. W. H.
Madeley, Pte. C. H.
Mann, Pte. J.
Mansley, Pte. J.
Manwaring, Sgt. F.
Mapleton, Pte. W.
Markwell, Pte. F. G.
Marsden, Pte. J.
Marsland, Pte. J.
Massey, Sgt. J.
Mather, Pte. A. H.
Matthews, Pte. J.
Maxwell, L.-Cpl. H.
Mayoh, Pte. F. L.
McCartney, L.-Cpl. G.
McCovey, Pte. J. S.
McCullough, Pte. R.
McDermott, Pte. P.
McGee, Pte. F. G.
McGee, Pte. S. T.
McMaster, Pte. K. S.
McPhee, Pte. J.
Mellor, Cpl. J.
Mellor, Pte. J.
Merrick, Pte. A.
Millington, Pte. J.
Mills, Pte. F.
Mitcham, Pte. H.
Mitchell, Sgt. J.
Moores, Pte. J.
Moreton, L.-Cpl. A.
Morgan, Pte. W.
Morgan, Pte. W. J.
Moron, Pte. J. F.
Morris, Pte. A.
Morris, Pte. H. A.
Mott, Pte. J.
Mottram, Pte. G.
Mottram, Pte. H. J.
Muckley, Pte. T.
Muir, Pte. H. F.
Mullins, Pte. J.
Murphy, Pte. P.
Murray, Pte. E.
Murthwaite, Pte. H.
Muscroft, Sgt. J.
Needham, Pte. G
Neild, Pte. D.
Nelson, Pte. W.
Nelson, Pte. W. C.
Newbiggin, Pte. R.
Newman, Cpl. H.
Newton, Pte. A.
Nicholson, Pte. J. W.
Nield, L.-Cpl. J.
Noble, Pte. D.
Norcross, Pte. F.
O'Brien, Pte. J.
O'Brien, Pte. R. C. J.
O'Connor, Pte. P.
O'Neill, Pte. T.
Osbourne, L.-Cpl. J
Osbourne, Pte. J.
Overend, Pte. W
Owen, Pte. J. G.
Parton, Pte. C. H.
Pass, Pte. J.
Patten, Pte. C.
Paul, Pte. J.
Pearson, Pte. A.

Peduzzi, Sgt. J.
Peers, Pte. T. E.
Pennington, Pte. E.
Percy, Pte. C. N.
Perry, Pte. A. R.
Phillips, Pte. J.
Pigot, Pte. F. W.
Pitman, Pte. S.
Poke, Pte. J.
Potts, Pte. T.
Pover, L.-Cpl. D.
Powell, Pte. W.
Poyner, Pte. H.
Prestwich, Pte. C.
Price, Pte. A. E.
Price, Pte. J.
Price, Pte. J. W.
Proctor, Pte. R. W.
Proudlove, Cpl. J.
Pry, Pte. A. E.
Pulford, L.-Sgt. N. N.
Quinn, Pte. J.
Ramsbottom, Pte. E.
Ramsden, Pte. E.
Ramsden, Cpl. H.
Reardon, Pte. A.
Redford, Pte. J. J.
Reeder, Pte. G. A.
Reid, Pte. W. R.
Richardson, Pte. C. C.
Ridgard, Pte. R.
Riley, Pte. E.
Riley, Pte. G. F.
Roberts, Pte. S.
Robinson, Pte. C. E.
Robinson, Pte. J.
Robinson, Pte. W.
Rofe, Pte. H. H.
Ross, L.-Cpl. A.
Routledge, Pte. H.
Rowbottom, Pte. S. W.
Rowsone, Pte. G.
Royle, Pte. I.
Royle, Pte. J.
Royle, Pte. T. E.
Rutledge, Pte. A.
Rylott, Pte. H.
Satchwell, Pte. F.
Scott, Cpl. T.
Scrivener, Pte. W. G.
Shaw, Pte. A.
Shaw, Pte. F.
Shaw, Pte. S.

Shaw, Pte. T.
Sheilds, Pte. J.
Shepley, Pte. T.
Shepstone, Pte. A. G.
Shields, L.-Cpl. J.
Shields, Pte. T.
Simms, Pte. J.
Simpson, Pte. G.
Slattery, Pte. P. W. E.
Sloane, Pte. J.
Smethurst, Pte. T. F.
Smethurst, Sgt. W.
Smith, Pte. A.
Smith, Pte. E.
Smith, Cpl. F.
Smith, Sgt. G. E.
Smith, Pte. R.
Spencer, Sgt. R.
Spencer, Pte. W.
Splaine, Pte. J.
Staley, Pte. H.
Stanley, Pte. E.
Stanway, Pte. T.
Steeles, Cpl. H.
Steen, Pte. W. H.
Stenning, Pte. C. S.
Stockdale, Pte. H.
Stone, Pte. J.
Stone, Pte. J.
Stone, Sgt. J.
Stott, Pte. C.
Sutcliffe, Pte. T.
Sutton, Pte. G.
Sutton, Sgt. J. H.
Swift, Pte. J. H.
Swindells, Pte. J.
Sykes, Pte. W.
Tabbener, Pte. A. E.
Taberner, Pte. J.
Tate, Pte. R.
Taylor, Pte. H. J.
Taylor, Pte. N.
Taylor, Sgt. W. H.
Tew, Pte. J. H.
Thatcher, Pte. J.
Thomas, Pte. S. B.
Thompson, Pte. W.
Thorneycroft, Pte. D.
Tierney, Pte. T.
Tingle, Pte. A. H.
Titley, Pte. T. H.
Tollitt, Pte. T.
Tomlinson, Pte. W. G.

Towler, Pte. W.
Tudbury, Pte. A.
Turner, Sgt. C.
Tyrrell, Pte. G. H.
Tytler, Co. Sgt.-Mjr. D. H.
Uden, Pte. A.
Upton, Pte. A.
Vernon, Pte. A.
Vernon, Pte. H. H.
Wade, L.-Cpl. T.
Wagwell, Pte. A.
Walker, Pte. S. N.
Walley, L.-Cpl. W.
Walmesley, Pte. J. W.
Walton, Pte. A.
Ward, Pte. F.
Wareham, Pte. E.
Warner, Pte. J. C. G.
Warrington, Pte. G.
Waterhouse, Sgt. J.
Waters, Pte. E.
Watson, Pte. B.
Watson, Pte. J.
Webb, Pte. F. H. M.
Welfare, Pte. J. E.
Westcombe, Pte. W.
Westover, Pte. G. O.
Wheeler, Pte. E.
White, Pte. T.
Whittaker, Sgt. C.
Wilcock, Pte. W.
Wild, Pte. G.
Wilde, Pte. J.
Wilkinson, Pte. H. B.
Wilkinson, Pte. J.
Williams, Pte. A.
Williams, Pte. H.
Williams, L.-Cpl. J. W.
Williams, Pte. R.
Williams, Pte. S.
Williamson, Pte. J.
Wilson, Pte. C.
Wilson, Pte. T. C.
Winkle, Pte. S.
Winstanley, Dmr. A.
Withers, Pte. F.
Wood, Pte. C. E.
Wood, Pte. J.
Wood, Pte. R.
Woodbine, Pte. T.
Worthington, Pte. G.
Worthington, Pte. P.
Yeoman, Pte. H. N.

7 BATTALION NORTHUMBERLAND FUSILIERS
(PIONEER BATTALION)

Officers

Davis, Lieut. G. C.

Merivale, Lieut. F.

Stiles, Lieut. E. W.

Other Ranks

Allsopp, Pte. B. H.
Armstrong, Pte. T. H.
Bennison, Pte. R.
Clark, Pte. J.
Crawford, Pte. W.
Cutts, Pte. L. R.
Dobby, Pte. F. W.
Dyson, Pte. H.
Evans, L.-Cpl. F.
Fisher, Pte. J.
Foster, L.-Sgt. J. W.
Gowens, Cpl. E.

Graham, Pte. T. W.
Greenwood, Pte. F. J.
Heron, Pte. F.
Hood, Pte. C.
Humphreys, Pte. P.
Hurst, L.-Cpl. W.
Martin, Pte. C.
McPherson, Pte. J.
Mills, Pte. W.
Monoghan, Cpl. O.
Pizer, Pte. L.

Playford, Pte. W. A.
Probert, Pte. B.
Robinson, L.-Cpl. R. E.
Skelly, Pte. W.
Stephens, Pte. C.
Thain, Pte. J.
Watson, Pte. E.
Wilkinson, Pte. I.
Williamson, Pte. W.
Wilson, Pte. W.
Young, L.-Sgt. A.

1/1 EAST LANCASHIRE FIELD AMBULANCE

Other Ranks

Adams, Pte. F. E.
Bennett, Pte. E.
Bridge, Pte. A. J.
Greenhalgh, Pte. G. A.

Hartley, Pte. H.
Hubbard, Sgt. S. S.
Newall, Cpl. H.
Rathbone, Pte. A.

Shiers, Pte. A. W.
Tough, Pte. G.
Wharmby, Pte. A.

It is regretted that it has been impossible to obtain complete casualty lists of the Divisional Artillery, 42nd Machine Gun Battalion, the 2nd and 3rd Field Ambulances and some of the smaller formations of the Division.

HONOURS AND AWARDS

It is regretted that it has been impossible to obtain complete lists of Honours and Awards of the Divisional Artillery, the 42nd Machine Gun Battalion, the 2nd and 3rd Field Ambulances and some of the smaller formations of the Division.

DIVISIONAL AND BRIGADE HEADQUARTERS

OFFICERS. *See pages 242-246.*

WARRANT OFFICERS AND NON-COMMISSIONED OFFICERS.

Conductor G. Hardy, M.S.M.
Staff-Sergt. M. Brooks, M.S.M.
C.Q.M.S. J. W. Mann, M.S.M.
S.Q.M.S. S. C. Clark, M.S.M.
C.S.M. H. Turner, M.S.M.
Sergt. T. P. Pickering, M.S.M.
Staff-Sergt. F. J. Mathers, M.S.M.
Sergt. J. Armstrong, M.S.M.

C.S.M. A. Warburton, M.S.M.
Staff-Sergt. C. V. Lewis, D.C.M.
Sergt. H. De Boller, M.S.M.
S.Q.M.S. A. H. Bowden, M.S.M.
L.-Corp. W. Seddon, M.S.M.
C.S.M. Leayd, M.S.M.
Staff-Sergt. L. McLean, M.S.M.
C.S.M. T. E. Ransom, M.S.M.

Pte. A. Fletcher, M.S.M.

'A' SQUADRON, 1/1 DUKE OF LANCASTER'S OWN YEOMANRY

Officers

Bates, Capt. D. H., M.C.
Paramor, Lieut. A. L., M.C.
Clark, Lieut. C. F. (F.).

Other Ranks

Hindle, Sgt. T. B., D.C.M.
Meredith, Sgt. J. S., D.C.M.
Abbot, Tpr. P. H., M.M.
Jackson, Sgt. E. W., M.M.
Jarvis, Sgt. A. L., M.M.
Sullivan, Sgt. W. (F.).
Hinde, Sgt. T. B. (F.).

42ND (EAST LANCS.) DIVISIONAL R.F.A.

Officers

Birtwistle, Brig-Gen. A., C.B., C.M.G., D.S.O.
Inches, Lt.-Col. E. J., C.M.G., D.S.O.
Burnyeat, Maj. R. W., D.S.O, (Bar)
Walker, Col. C. E., D.S.O.
Mason, Lt.-Col. D. J., D.S.O.
Bickerdike, Maj. R. B., D.S.O.
Birtwistle, Maj. W., D.S.O.
Boone, Maj. H. G., D.S.O.
Brown, Maj. D., D.S.O.
Browning, Maj. J. G., D.S.O.
Nall, Maj. J., D.S.O.

Collin, Capt. G., M.C. (Bar)
Adamson, Maj. J., M.C.
Hall, Maj. A. G., M.C.
Highet, Maj. W. T., M.C.
Barclay, Capt. H. B., M.C.
Best, Capt. (Chaplain), M.C.
Carsus, Capt. F. X. S., M.C.
Duff, Capt. C. G., M.C.
Hartley, Capt. G., M.C.
Hartley, Capt. R., M.C.
Jackson, Capt. F. J. G., M.C.
Knowles, Capt. F., M.C. (F.).
Mack, Capt. L. D., M.C.
Trench, Capt. (Chaplain), M.C.

Bowles, Lieut. P.W., M.C., M.M.
Birtwistle, Lieut. A. E., M.C.
Cooke, Lieut. R., M.C.
Horner, Lieut. H. B., M.C.
McIvor, Lieut., M.C.
Middleton, Lieut. J. A., M.C.
Malcolm, Lieut. G. D., M.C.
Moore, Lieut., M.C.
O'Smaston, Lieut., M.C.
Rees, Lieut. C. C., M.C.
Shelley, Lieut., M.C.
Topping, Lieut. H., M.C.
Blackborough, 2nd Lieut., M.C.
Kearns, Capt. H. W. L. (F.).

Honours and Awards

ROYAL ENGINEERS

Officers

Mousley, Lt.-Col. J. H., D.S.O.
Riddick, Lt.-Col. J. G., D.S.O.
Wells, Lt.-Col. L. F., D.S.O.
Johnson, Maj. S. G., D.S.O.
Roberts, Capt. A., M.C. and Bar.
Entwistle, Maj. J., M.C.
Bateman, Capt. W. H., M.C.
Broad, Capt. G. L., O.B.E., M.C.
Horner, Capt. H., M.C.
Jones, Capt. C. E. T., M.C.

Newton, Capt. R. S., M.C.
Williamson, Capt. C. H., M.C.
Bogle, Lieut. J. M. L., M.C.
Brown, Lieut. H. G., M.C.
Cameron, Lieut. A., M.C.
Echlin, Lieut. J. P., M.C.
Ellis, Lieut. A. J., M.C.
Fletcher, Lieut. P. C., M.C.
Mellor, Lieut. W. L., M.C.
Moore, Lieut. H. T. P., M.C.

Osmaston, Lieut. G. H., M.C.
Taunton, Lieut. O., M.C.
Nicolson, 2nd Lieut. J. F. H., M.C.
Lawford, Lt.-Col. A. N. (F.).
Riddick, Maj. J. G. (F.).
Wells, Maj. L. F. (F.).
Allard, Capt. W. (F.).
Gracey, Capt. R. L. (F.).
Roberts, Capt. A. (F.).

Other Ranks

Broderick, Sap. J., D.C.M.
Cliffe, Cpl. L., D.C.M.
Davies, Co. Sgt.-Mjr. H. M., D.C.M.
Eachus, Sap. W., D.C.M.
Gourlay, Sap. A., D.C.M.
Gray, Pioneer A. S., D.C.M.
Gray, Co. Sgt.-Mjr. W., D.C.M.
Hahn, Sgt. A., D.C.M.
Jones, Sap. A., D.C.M.
Kirkpatrick, Cpl. D., D.C.M.
Mallalieu, Sgt. J., D.C.M.
Moores, Cpl. H. J., D.C.M.
Needham, Sgt. A., D.C.M.
Pinder, Sgt. H., D.C.M.
Pollitt, Sap. G., D.C.M.
Sowray, Reg.-Sgt.-Mjr. F. J., D.C.M., M.S.M.
Smith, Sap. H., D.C.M.
Vick, Sap. E. H., D.C.M.
Waterworth, Co. Sgt.-Mjr. W., D.C.M.
Wilcock, Co. Sgt.-Mjr. H., D.C.M.
Williams, C.Q.M.S. C., D.C.M.
Williams, 2nd Cpl. W., D.C.M.
Baldwin, Cpl. A. O., M.M. and Bar.
Ashworth, L.-Cpl. R., M.M.
Bennett, Sap. J., M.M.
Brightmore, Cpl. R., M.M.
Butler, L.-Cpl. W. H., M.M.
Collins, L.-Cpl. W., M.M.

Duffy, 2nd Cpl. J., M.M.
Fielding, Cpl. J., M.M.
Flaws, Cpl. L. R., M.M.
Gregson, Cpl. W., M.M.
Hart, 2nd Cpl. M., M.M.
Jackson, Sap. R. C., M.M.
Jenkinson, Cpl. W., M.M.
Johnson, Sap. T. H., M.M.
Jones, 2nd Cpl. J., M.M.
Kinley, Sgt. J., M.M.
Kirkman, Pioneer J., M.M.
McEwan, L.-Cpl. F., M.M.
Mullaney, L.-Cpl. J., M.M.
Phillips, Pioneer H. H., M.M.
Pike, Cpl. W., M.M.
Pinder, Sgt. H., M.M.
Reeder, Pioneer R. H., M.M.
Rhodes, Cpl. T., M.M.
Riding, Cpl. T. E., M.M.
Roscoe, Cpl. E., M.M.
Rylance, Sap. J., M.M.
Taylor, Cpl. T. E., M.M.
Templeton, Sgt. B., M.M.
Thompson, 2nd Cpl. J., M.M.
Tudor, Sap. W. G., M.M.
Walsh, Sap. J., M.M.
Williamson, Sap. J., M.M.
Eccles, Cpl. S., M.S.M.
Folwell, 2nd Cpl. A. T., M.S.M.
Garnett, Co. Sgt.-Mjr. J. H., M.S.M.
Gilt, C.Q.M.S. H., M.S.M.
Higgins, Sgt. W., M.S.M.

McGrath, Sap. J., M.S.M.
Rowlands, Sap. A., M.S.M.
Shimmin, Sgt. W. H., M.S.M.
Taylor, Sap. H. V., M.S.M.
Whitehead, Cpl. R. V., M.S.M.
Young, C.Q.M.S. A. J., M.S.M.
Boyes, Cpl. B. (F.).
Broderick, Sap. J. (F.).
Buckle, Dvr. H. N. (F.).
Cottriall, Sap. J. (F.).
Cowsill, Co. Sgt.-Mjr. J. H. (F.).
Ellwood, Sgt. J. (F.).
Garnett, Sgt. J. H. (F.).
Hall, Sap. E. V. (F.).
Hardman, L.-Cpl. W. H. (F.).
Harrison, Sgt. R. (F.).
Hughes, Sap. A. (F.).
Johnson, Sgt. G. H. (F.).
Mills, Cpl. J. (F.).
Redfern, Sap. G. (F.).
Robinson, L.-Cpl. J. (F.).
Robinson, Sgt. W. O. (F.).
Rowlands, Sap. L. (F.).
Scanlon, L.-Cpl. G. (F.).
Scott, Cpl. J. M. (F.).
Sowray, Sgt.-Instr. F. J. (F.)
Spaven, Sap. R. J. (F.).
Waterworth, Sgt. W. (F.).
Watters, Sap. W. (F.).
West, 2nd Cpl. F. (F.).
Wood, Sgt. T. (F.).

125th INFANTRY BRIGADE

1/5 BATTALION LANCASHIRE FUSILIERS

V.C. Smith, Sgt. E., D.C.M.

Officers

Isherwood, Lt.-Col. J., V.D., C.B.
Wood, Capt. and Adjt. G. B. G., D.S.O.
Tickler, Capt. W. M., M.C. and Bar.

Horridge, Capt. W., M.C.
Jenkins, Capt. E. E., M.C.
Johnson, Capt. A. M., M.C.
North, Capt. S., M.C.
Butcher, Lieut. R. W., M.C.

Page, Lieut. J. K. S., M.C.
Sackett, Lieut. A. B., M.C.
Waugh, Lieut. H. R., M.C.
Clarke, Lieut. C. (F.).

Other Ranks

Barnes, Sgt. G. H., D.C.M.
Bateson, Pte. R., D.C.M.
Calvert, Co. Sgt.-Mjr. F. W., D.C.M.
Carney, Pte. J., D.C.M.
Fletcher, C.Q.M.S. W., D.C.M.
Fisher, Co. Sgt.-Mjr. J., D.C.M.
Hughes, Sgt. W., D.C.M.
Leeming, Sgt. T., D.C.M.

Lord, Pte. E., D.C.M.
Morris, Sgt. E., D.C.M.
Newsham, L.-Cpl. J., D.C.M.
Ogden, Pte. T., D.C.M.
Rowan, Sgt. J., D.C.M.
Standring, L.-Sgt. C., D.C.M.
Stewart, Pte. G., D.C.M.
Taylor, Sgt. J., D.C.M.
Watson, Co. Sgt. Mjr. H. R. W., D.C.M.

Wild, Sgt. S., D.C.M.
Acton, C.Q.M.S. T. E., M.M.
Blackburn, L.-Cpl. H., M.M.
Clarke, Pte. J., M.M.
Cottam, Pte. E., M.M.
Dimmock, Pte. J., M.M.
Dolan, Pte. J., M.M.
Feerick, Pte. T., M.M.
Hall, Pte. H., M.M.
Heywood, Dvr. J., M.M.

234 *The 42nd Division*

Holt, Pte. J. E., M.M.
Hopwood, Dvr. T., M.M.
Howarth, Cpl. C., M.M.
Kirkby, Sgt. E., M.M.
Lindsey, Pte. L., M.M.
McDonald, Pte. H., M.M.
McMurdo, L.-Cpl. J., M.M.
Morris, Pte. A., M.M.
Ogden, Pte. W. H., M.M.

Powell, Pte. T., M.M.
Rothwell, Sgt. H., M.M.
Smethurst, Cpl. F., M.M.
Squires, Pte. W., M.M.
Taylor, Pte. H. W., M.M.
Tomney, L.-Cpl. S., M.M.
Walliss, Pte. W., M.M.
Bell, C.Q.M.S. E. R., M.S.M.
Berry, Sgt. W., M.S.M.

Dickinson, Cpl. E. D., M.S.M.
Earnshaw, R.Q.M.S. J., M.S.M.
Rogers, R. Sgt.-Mjr. J., M.S.M.
Smith, Co. Sgt.-Mjr. W. L., M.S.M.
Lea, Sgt. J. (F.).
Robinson, R. Sgt.-Mjr. J. (F.)..

1/6 BATTALION LANCASHIRE FUSILIERS

Officers

Lees, Maj. R. L., D.S.O., O.B.E.
Woolmer, Capt. E., D.S.O., M.C.
Scott, Capt. G., D.S.O.
Herridge, Capt. A. L., M.C. and Bar.
Newton, Capt. R. S., M.C.

Robinson, Lieut. and Adjt. A. M., M.C.
Barker, Lieut. J. S., M.C.
Brentnall, Lieut. C. G. (R.A.M.C. attd.), M.C.
Candy, 2nd Lieut. K. E., M.C.

Hornby, 2nd Lieut. R. P., M.C.
Skeene, 2nd Lieut. J., M.C.
Scott, Maj. G. (F.)
Woolmer, Maj. E. (F.)

Other Ranks

Allen, Pte. R., D.C.M.
Allister, Co. Sgt.-Mjr. B., D.C.M.
Butterworth, L.-Cpl. H., D.C.M.
Childs, Pte. J. W., D.C.M.
Cryer, Pte. J., D.C.M.
Durrans, Sgt. O., D.C.M.
Hamer, Sgt. A., D.C.M.
Watkins, R. Sgt.-Mjr. W., D.C.M.

Bamford, Pte. J. H., M.M.
Brown, L.-Cpl. S., M.M.
Carter, Pte. J., M.M.
Greenwood, Pte. T., M.M.
McConville, Pte. J., M.M.
Mitchell, Pte. R., M.M.
Rigby, Pte. J., M.M.
Saunders, Pte. A., M.M.

Schofield, Pte. J., M.M.
Stock, Pte. R., M.M.
Taylor, L.-Cpl. E., M.M.
Tregay, L.-Cpl. E., M.M.
Ward, Sgt. G., M.M.
Durrans, Sgt. O. (F.).
Hartley, Pte. E. (F.).

1/7 BATTALION LANCASHIRE FUSILIERS

Officers

Brewis, Lt.-Col. G. S., D.S.O. and Bar.
Alexander, Lt.-Col. C. T., D.S.O.
Elliott, 2nd Lieut. A., D.S.O., M.C. and Bar.
O'Bryen, Capt. W. J., M.C. and 2 Bars.
Debenham, Maj. A. M. G., M.C.
Gillies, Maj. F. A., M.C.
Gledhill, Maj. M. P., M.C.

Scott, Maj. W. S., M.C.
Boyd, Capt. A. W., M.C.
Brewis, Capt. R. R., M.C.
Fitzgerald, Capt. C. C., M.C.
Mainprice, Capt. F. H., M.C.
Morrison, Capt. L., M.C.
Murgatroyd, Capt. H. L., M.C.
Shelmerdine, Capt. B., M.C.
Webb, Capt. F. B., M.C.
Gould, Lieut. H. M., M.C.
Kershaw, Lieut. C., M.C.
McCready, Lieut. J., M.C.

Ripperger, Lieut. H. T. A., M.C.
Worden, Lieut. A. F., M.C.
Ashworth, 2nd Lieut. J. E., M.C.
Garbutt, 2nd Lieut. J. R., M.C.
Pearson, 2nd Lieut. C. M., M.C.
Wood, 2nd Lieut. F., M.C.
Walker, 2nd Lieut. F., M.C.
Law, Maj. W. J. (F.).
Saunders, Capt. C. E. E. H. H. (F.).

Other Ranks

Bann, Co. Sgt.-Mjr. T. W., D.C.M.
Bent, Sgt., D.C.M.
Blacklock, Sgt., D.C.M.
Boardman, L.-Cpl. H., D.C.M.
Bradbury, Sgt. G., D.C.M.
Casey, Pte., D.C.M.
Clarke, Pte., D.C.M.
Downton, Cpl., D.C.M.
Dulhanty, Cpl. F., D.C.M.
Ellis, Sgt. J., D.C.M.
Evans, Pte. T. F., D.C.M.
Field, Sgt., D.C.M.
Framstone, L.-Cpl. E., D.C.M.
Gresty, Sgt., D.C.M.
Hall, Co. Sgt.-Mjr. C. W., D.C.M.
Harvey, Sgt., D.C.M.
Heardley, Pte. J., D.C.M.
Hesford, Cpl. F., D.C.M.
Hopkins, L.-Cpl., D.C.M.
Lindon, Co. Sgt.-Mjr. J., D.C.M.
Mottershead, Pte., D.C.M.
Petrie, Pte. T., D.C.M.
Pinder, Sgt. M., D.C.M.
Prince, Pte. T., D.C.M.
Prince, Pte. W., D.C.M.
Smith, Sgt. J. A., D.C.M.
Tempest, Pte. J., D.C.M.
Waller, R. Sgt.-Mjr. A. E., D.C.M.

Gerrard, Sgt. T., M.M. and Bar.
Phipps, Sgt. J., M.M. and Bar.
Taylor, Sgt. B., M.M. and Bar.
Appleton, Sgt. J., M.M.
Ball, Pte. F., M.M.
Ball, Pte. J. H., M.M.
Benedicty, Pte., M.M.
Berry, Pte. J., M.M.
Bloomley, Pte. J., M.M.
Brierley, L.-Cpl. S., M.M.
Broe, Co. Sgt.-Mjr. T., M.M.
Dulhanty, Pte. F., M.M.
Eddey, Pte. F., M.M.
Edmunds, Pte. F., M.M.
Finn, C.Q.M.S. W., M.M.
Garlick, Sgt. A., M.M.
Glynn, Pte. J., M.M.
Halman, Pte. H., M.M.
Hampson, Pte. G., M.M.
Hampton, Sgt., M.M.
Heardley, Pte. G., M.M.
Hucher, Pte. F., M.M.
Hull, Pte. G., M.M.
Johnson, Pte. M., M.M.
Johnstone, Sgt. R. C., M.M.
Lewis, Cpl. F., M.M.
Littler, Pte. A., M.M.
Mann, L.-Cpl. J. W., M.M.
Marsh, Sgt. G., M.M.

Marshall, Pte. R., M.M.
Moore, Pte. J., M.M.
Myerscough, L.-Cpl. J., M.M.
Newbury, Pte., M.M.
Pickerill, Pte. J., M.M.
Pickup, Sgt. J., M.M.
Rogers, Pte. J., M.M.
Rylands, Pte. E., M.M.
Sims, Pte. C., M.M.
Smith, Pte. J., M.M.
Stokes, Pte. C. W., M.M.
Stretch, L.-Sgt. A., M.M.
Tempest, Pte., M.M.
Watson, L.-Cpl. E., M.M.
Welden, Pte. H., M.M.
Whitham, Pte. A. E., M.M.
Wild, Pte., M.M.
Wilding, Sgt., M.M.
Ashton, C.Q.M.S. H., M.S.M.
Fairclough, Sgt., M.S.M.
Fremstone, C.E., M.S.M.
Galley, Sgt. G., M.S.M.
Balland, Co. Sgt.-Mjr. H. (F.).
Field, Sgt., (F.)
Waller, R. Sgt.-Mjr. A. E. (F.).
Waller, R. Sgt.-Mjr. A. E., Long Service and Good Conduct Medal.
Whittaker, L.-Cpl. W. (F.).

Honours and Awards 235

1/8 BATTALION LANCASHIRE FUSILIERS

Officers

Macleod, Lt.-Col. J., D.S.O.
Bird, Maj. M. G., D.S.O.
Shaw, Maj. A. Ll. B., D.S.O.
Kirkby, Capt. and Adjt. H. A., D.S.O.
Sutton, Capt. G. W., D.S.O.
Fairhurst, Capt. and Adjt. E., M.C. and Bar.

Cumming, Capt. H. D., M.C. and Bar.
Bedale, Capt. F. S., R.A.M.C. (T.) att., M.C.
Bird, Capt. D. G., M.C.
Thorpe, Capt. T. E., M.C.
Ivers, Lieut. H. B., M.C.
Alderson, 2nd Lieut. R., M.C.

Charnock, 2nd Lieut. W., M.C.
Gibbons, 2nd Lieut. A. C., M.C.
Rose, 2nd Lieut. E. W., M.C.
Sumner, 2nd Lieut. C. W., M.C.
Topham, 2nd Lieut. F. H., M.C.
Smith, Rev. C. (Army Chaplain att. C. of E.), M.C.
Zimmern, Capt. N. H., M.C.

Other Ranks

Baldwin, Cpl. J. W., D.C.M.
Carter, L.-Sgt. C., D.C.M.
Cowell, Cpl. R., D.C.M.
Dolan, Cpl. J., D.C.M.
Farnworth, Pte. A., D.C.M.
Finney, Sgt. H., D.C.M.
Fletcher, Co. Sgt.-Mjr. W., D.C.M., M.S.M.
Girling, R. Sgt.-Mjr. W. A., D.C.M.
Kilgour, Pte. J., D.C.M.
Kneale, Sgt. J. L., D.C.M.
Lever, Sgt. J., D.C.M.
Nickson, Sgt. J. J., D.C.M.
Partington, L.-Sgt. S., D.C.M.
Ridyard, Sgt. G., D.C.M.
Shackleton, Co. Sgt.-Mjr. J., D.C.M.
Shaw, Co. Sgt.-Mjr. R., D.C.M.
Taylor, Sgt. F., D.C.M.
Walmesley, L.-Cpl. W., D.C.M.
West, Pte. F., D.C.M.
Wilde, Sgt. L. R., D.C.M.
Lewis, L.-Cpl. H., M.M. and Bar.

Spedding, Pte. W., M.M. and Bar.
Allcock, Pte. E., M.M.
Ashworth, L.-Sgt. W., M.M.
Axon, Cpl. C., M.M.
Barker, Pte. H., M.M.
Barlow, Pte. E., M.M.
Birmingham, Sgt. J., M.M.
Black, Pte. T., M.M.
Carter, Pte. T., M.M.
Connor, Pte. R., M.M.
Davies, Cpl. W., M.M.
Drage, Cpl. T. H., M.M.
Drinkwater, L.-Cpl. H., M.M.
Dyson, Pte. H., M.M.
Eachus, Pte. H., M.M.
Emmett, Pte. J., M.M.
Falconer, Pte. J., M.M.
Green, Pte. H., M.M.
Griffiths, Pte. W. J., M.M.
Grindrod, Sgt. J., M.M.
Haigh, Pte. F., M.M.
Hargreaves, Pte. J. H., M.M.
Jackson, Pte. E., M.M.
Jackson, Pte. H. A., M.M.

Lockett, Pte. J., M.M.
Lockley, L.-Sgt. T., M.M.
Massey, Sgt. W., M.M.
Morris, Sgt. W., M.M.
Nance, Sgt. F., M.M.
Newton, Pte. H., M.M.
Oliver, L.-Cpl. T., M.M.
Orchard, Pte. L., M.M.
Peace, Pte. F., M.M.
Pease, Cpl. A., M.M.
Peover, Pte. A., M.M.
Perkins, Pte. C. H., M.M.
Richmond, Sgt. J., M.M.
Riley, Co. Sgt.-Mjr. J., M.M.
Robinson, Pte. F., M.M.
Robson, Pte. G. H., M.M.
Rule, Co. Sgt.-Mjr. W., M.M.
Thornton, Sgt. T., M.M.
Vigar, Pte. J. W., M.M.
Wood, Pte. J. W., M.M.
Evans, Sgt. T., M.S.M.
Kellett, Sgt. F., M.S.M.
Sloan, R.Q.M.S. R., M.S.M.
Kelsey, R.Q.M.S. C. (F.).
Morris, Sgt. W., M.M. (F.).
Robinson, L.-Cpl. J. (F.).

126th INFANTRY BRIGADE

1/4 BATTALION EAST LANCASHIRE REGIMENT

Officers

Battye, Lt.-Col. C. W., D.S.O., to be Brevet Lt.-Col.
Bolton, Capt. M. B., M.C.
Green, Capt. L., M.C.

Bennett, Lieut. and Q.M. G., M.C.
Robinson, Lieut. A. J. D., M.C.
Davenport, 2nd Lieut. A. A. O., M.C.

Burrows, Maj. H. M., I.A. (F.).
Mellowes, Capt. and Adjt. H. A., (F.).

Other Ranks

Gertson, Cpl. F., D.C.M.
Murphy, Co. Sgt.-Mjr. J. (A. R.S.M.), D.C.M.
Potts, Co. Sgt.-Mjr. A., D.C.M.
Smith, Pte. T., D.C.M.
Wilkinson, Pte. T., D.C.M.
Bury, Pte. J., M.M.
Driver, Sgt. R., M.M.

Graham, Sgt. R., M.M.
Jennings, Pte. M., M.M.
Kay, Pte. F., M.M.
Kay, Pte. G., M.M.
Middlehurst, Pte. J., M.M.
Atkinson, R.Q.M.S. J., M.S.M.
Clarke, R. Sgt.-Mjr. F. J., M.S.M.

Lonsdale, Pte. A., M.S.M.
Cooper, L.-Cpl. L. (F.).
Dean, Cpl. J. S. (F.).
Wearing, L.-Cpl J. D. (F.).
Dugdale, Sgt. W. R., to be C.-Sgt.

1/5 BATTALION EAST LANCASHIRE REGIMENT

Officers

V.C. Smith, 2nd Lieut. A. V.
Clare, Lt.-Col. O. C., D.S.O. and Bar, M.C.
Hodge, Capt. A., D.S.O., M.C.
Murray-White, Lt.-Col R. S., D.S.O.
Acton, Maj. W. M., D.S.O.
Dick, Capt. W. H., D.S.O.
Reed, J., M.C. and Bar.
Wintle, M.C. and Bar.

Worswick, Capt. H. B., M.C. and Bar.
Hoxey, Lt.-Col. J. P., M.C.
Baxter, Capt. W. H., M.C.
Britcliffe, Capt. F., M.C.
Curl, Capt. C., M.C.
Kay, Capt. G. B., M.C.
Rawcliffe, Capt. J. M., M.C.
Bolton, Lieut. G. G. H., M.C.
Cooke, Lieut. S. D., M.C.
Dunkerley, Lieut. W., M.C.

Dunlop, Lieut. G. H., M.C.
Elliott, Lieut. A. C., M.C.
Lancaster, Lieut. P. G., M.C.
Little, Lieut. W. B., M.C.
Cookson, 2nd Lieut. W., M.C.
Gledhill, 2nd Lieut. A., M.C.
Holdsworth, 2nd Lieut. H., M.C.
Pacey, 2nd Lieut. S. W., M.C.
Smith, 2nd Lieut. A. V. (F.).

Houston, Co. Sgt.-Mjr. D., D.C.M. and Bar.
Birkett, Co. Sgt.-Mjr. J., D.C.M.
Cooke, Pte. J. L., D.C.M.
Entwistle, Sgt. J., D.C.M.
Evans, Sgt. H. E., D.C.M.
Gowers, Sgt. G. W., D.C.M.
Greenhalgh, Cpl. W., D.C.M.
Hargreaves, Cpl. T., D.C.M.
Harrison, Pte. J., D.C.M.
Harrison, Co. Sgt.-Mjr. J. H., D.C.M.
Haslam, R. Sgt.-Mjr. J., D.C.M.
Jolly, Cpl. J., D.C.M.
Jones, Pte. E., D.C.M.
Keohoe, Pte. W. H., D.C.M.
Kinsella, Sgt. W., D.C.M.
Marshall, Sgt. J., D.C.M.
Pratt, Co. Sgt.-Mjr. W. H., D.C.M.
Spiers, Sgt. J., D.C.M.
Steele, Co. Sgt.-Mjr. R. J., D.C.M.
Stezaker, Co. Sgt.-Mjr. A., D.C.M.
Swarbrick, Cpl. W., D.C.M.
Waterworth, Pte. A., D.C.M.
Whitehead, L.-Cpl. G., D.C.M.
Whittaker, Pte. F., D.C.M.
Wilkinson, Sgt. J., D.C.M.
Littlewood, Sgt. R., M.M. and Bar.

Other Ranks

Airey, Pte. G. F., M.M.
Baldwin, Pte. E., M.M.
Bannister, Pte. H., M.M.
Baxter, Co. Sgt.-Mjr. E., M.M.
Berry, L.-Cpl. H., M.M.
Brierley, Pte. E., M.M.
Brindle, Sgt. T., M.M.
Brotherton, Pte. T., M.M.
Burnett, Pte. W., M.M.
Cain, Pte. M. H., M.M.
Chadwick, Pte. E., M.M.
Clarke, Pte. J. T., M.M.
Cole, Pte. R., M.M.
Connolly, Pte. J., M.M.
Cooper, Pte. G., M.M.
Cox, Pte. H., M.M.
Farrell, Pte. J. A., M.M.
Gillibrand, Pte. G., M.M.
Gorse, Pte. E., M.M.
Green, Pte. J., M.M.
Greenhalgh, L.-Cpl. A., M.M.
Gregson, Sgt. G., M.M.
Haffner, Sgt. G. C. A., M.M.
Hardman, Pte. G., M.M.
Hargreaves, Pte. D. E., M.M.
Hargreaves, Sgt. W., M.S.M., M.M.
Hartley, Pte. W., M.M.
Higgins, Pte. J., M.M.
Horne, Pte. H., M.M.
Hurley, Sgt. J., M.M.
Kneale, Pte. J. W., M.M.
Lewis, Pte. A., M.M.
Livesey, L.-Cpl. O., M.M.
Longworth, Pte. H., M.M.
Maloney, Pte. J., M.M.
McGlynn, L.-Cpl. T., M.M.
Moden, Sgt. A. W., M.M.
Partington, Pte. J., M.M.
Patefield, Pte. W., M.M.
Potter, Pte. H. G., M.M.
Sarginson, Pte. H., M.M.
Singleton, Pte. J. H., M.M.
Smith, Pte. G., M.M.
Steele, Sgt. R. J., M.M.
Sullivan, Pte. J., M.M.
Ward, L.-Cpl. C., M.M.
Whittaker, Sgt. A., M.M,
Wilson, Pte. J., M.M.
Yegliss, Pte. H., M.M.
Yoxall, Pte. W., M.M.
Hudson, Co. Sgt.-Mjr. H., M.S.M.
Oliver, Sgt. W. J., M.S.M.
Stezaker, R.Q.M.S. W., M.S.M.
Haffner, C.Q.M.S. G. C. A. (F.).
Hargreaves, Cpl. T. (F.).
Harrison, Co. Sgt.-Mjr. J. M., D.C.M. (F.).
Jones, Pte. A. H. (F.).
Marshall, Pte. F. (F.).

1/9 BATTALION MANCHESTER REGIMENT

Officers

V.C. Forshaw, Lieut. W. T.
Lloyd, Lt.-Col E. C., D.S.O. and Bar.
Connery, Q.M. and Hon. Maj. M. H., M.C.

Stephenson, Capt. D. B., M.C.
Wood, Lieut. R. G., M.C. (F.)
Cooke, 2nd Lieut. C. E., M.C.
Hunt, 2nd Lieut. C., M.C.

Sutton, 2nd Lieut. O. J., M.C.
Howorth, Maj. T. E. (F.).
Nowell, Maj. R. B. (F.).
Welbon, Capt. F. W. (C.F.), M.C.

Other Ranks

Bayley, Cpl. S., D.C.M.
Christie, R. Sgt.-Mjr. J. C., D.C.M.
Davies, L.-Cpl. A., D.C.M.
Grantham, Sgt. H., D.C.M.
Greenhalgh, Sgt. J., D.C.M.
Hibbert, Pte. J., D.C.M.
Horsfield, Sgt. J., D.C.M., M.M.
Latham, Pte. A., D.C.M.
Littleford, Pte. S., D.C.M.
May, Cpl. R., D.C.M.
Moss, Cpl. J., D.C.M.
Pearson, L.-Cpl. S., D.C.M.
Pickford, Pte. T., D.C.M.
Sylvester, L.-Cpl. G. J., D.C.M.
Thickett, Sgt. F., D.C.M.
Holden, Pte. J., M.M. and Bar.

Adshead, Pte. A., M.M.
Allen, Sgt. G., M.M.
Atherton, Sgt. J., M.M.
Byrom, Pte. T. H., M.M.
Chadderton, Pte. H., M.M.
Chadderton, Pte. W., M.M.
Eastwood, Cpl. A., M.M.
Garside, Pte. H., M.M.
Gorman, Pte. F., M.M.
Hall, Cpl. R., M.M.
Horton, Pte. A., M.M.
Howard, Pte. T. M., M.M.
Kinsella, Pte. J., M.M.
Longson, Pte. J., M.M.
Metcalfe, Sgt. H., M.M.
O'Donnell, Cpl. R., M.M.

Pemberton, Pte. F., M.M.
Price, L.-Cpl. R., M.M.
Radcliffe, L.-Cpl. F. D., M.M.
Ratcliffe, Pte. F. E., M.M.
Roberts, L.-Sgt. H., M.M.
Shelmerdine, Pte. J., M.M.
Simister, Pte. N., M.M.
Tipton, L.-Sgt. T., M.M.
Vause, Pte. J., M.M.
White, Pte. F., M.M.
Howard, Cpl. J., M.S.M.
Andrew, L.-Cpl. R. (F.).
Christie, R. Sgt.-Mjr. J. A., D.C.M. (F.).
Horsfield, Sgt. J., D.C.M. (F.).
Sheekey, Pte. W. (F.).

1/10 BATTALION MANCHESTER REGIMENT

V.C. Mills, Pte. W.

Officers

Robinson, Brig.-Gen.G.W., C.B.
Peel, Lt.-Col. W. R., 2 Bars to D.S.O.
Wilde, Maj. L. C., D.S.O.
Taylor, Capt. J. A. C., D.S.O., M.C. and Bar.

Bletcher, Capt. T., M.C.
Butterworth, Capt. A., M.C.
Hampson, Capt. H. J., M.C.
Hardman, Capt. F., M.C.
Cook, Lieut. F. E., M.C.
Howarth, Lieut. F., M.C.

Shaw, Lieut. W. D., M.C.
Hassall, 2nd Lieut. H., M.C.
Whitehead, 2nd Lieut. J. B., M.C.
Williams, 2nd Lieut. W., M.C.

Honours and Awards

Toogood, Co. Sgt.-Mjr. K., D.C.M. and Bar.
Ayre, L.-Cpl. C., D.C.M.
Baddeley, L.-Cpl. F., D.C.M.
Brown, Sgt. D., D.C.M.
Darby, Pte. E., D.C.M.
Haskey, Sgt. M., D.C.M.
Langley, Sgt. O., D.C.M.
Lees, Sgt. S. R., D.C.M., M.M.
Leigh, Cpl. R., D.C.M.
Lloyd, Cpl. O., D.C.M.
Owen, L.-Cpl. E., D.C.M.
Revell, L.-Cpl. W., D.C.M.
Rigby, Cpl. R., D.C.M.
Schofield, Pte. F., D.C.M.
Seddon, L.-Cpl. J., D.C.M.
Spedding, Cpl., D.C.M.
Sugden, Sgt. J., D.C.M.
Taylor, Pte. T., D.C.M.
McNamara, Pte. W., M.M. and Bar.
Ashurst, Pte. W., M.M.
Bradbury, Sgt. M. R., M.M.
Bradshaw, L.-Cpl. J., M.M.
Bridge, Pte. J., M.M.

Other Ranks

Brimelow, Pte. J. L., M.M.
Brookes, Cpl. H., M.M.
Butterworth, Sgt. E., M.M.
Carroll, Cpl. H., M.M.
Clutton, Sgt. T. H., M.M.
Cooke, Pte. H., M.M.
Creswell, Sgt. F., M.M.
Critchley, Pte. F., M.M.
Davies, Pte. J., M.M.
Dukenson, Pte. G. R., M.M.
Fisher, Cpl. A., M.M.
Hancock, Pte. A., M.M.
Hayes, Pte. J., M.M.
Hayes, Pte. J. R., M.M.
Heslop, Pte. R. W., M.M.
Hulme, Pte. S., M.M.
Hutchins, Pte. E., M.M.
Matthews, Pte. F., M.M.
Milner, Sgt. J., M.M.
Newton, Sgt. H., M.M.
Nicholson, Pte. W., M.M.
Parker, L.-Cpl. W., M.M.
Radcliffe, Pte. W., M.M.
Robinson, Cpl. B. B., M.M.
Silverwood, Pte. T., M.M.

Smith, Pte. G. A., M.M.
Smith, Sgt. R. S., M.M.
Spink, Pte. E., M.M.
Squires, Sgt. W., M.M.
Stockton, Cpl. E., M.M.
Storey, Pte. J., M.M.
Sugden, Sgt. J., M.M.
Ward, Pte. R. B., M.M.
Weston, Pte. T., M.M.
Whittaker, Pte. H., M.M.
Dransfield, Cpl. J., M.S.M.
Gartside, Sgt. J., M.S.M.
Hollingsworth, Sgt. J. E., M.S.M.
Keighley, Cpl. J. H., M.S.M.
Robinson, L.-Cpl. B. B., M.S.M.
Scholes, Cpl. J., M.S.M.
Trevitt, R.Q.M.S. J. P., M.S.M.
Coulson, Pte. J. (F.).
Hammond, Pte. J. (F.).
Haslam, Sgt. S., (F.).
McHugh, Sgt. M. (F.).
Whitehead, L.-Cpl. R. (F.).
Wilde, Pte. S. (F.).

127th INFANTRY BRIGADE
1/5 BATTALION MANCHESTER REGIMENT

V.C. Wilkinson, L.-Cpl. A.

Officers

Darlington, Lt.-Col. H. C., C.M.G.
Cronshaw, Lt.-Col. A. E., D.S.O.
Woods, Capt. W. T., D.S.O.
Welsh, Lieut. R. H., D.S.O.
Simpson, Lt.-Col. A. W. W., O.B.E.
Frost, 2nd Lieut. C. E., M.C. and Bar.
Bryan, Maj. J. L., M.C.
Bryham, Maj. A. L., M.C.
Fletcher, Maj. B. L., M. C.

Burrows, Capt. E. J., M.C.
Burrows, Capt. M. K., M.C.
Clayton, Capt. P. C., M.C.
Dickson, Capt. S., M.C.
Douglas, Capt. R. A., M.C. (U.S.A.)
Ellis, Capt. R. R., M.C.
Frost, Capt. M., M.C.
Greer, Capt. J. M., M.C.
Just, Capt. L. W., M.C.
Sanders, Capt. J. M. B., M.C.
Woods, Capt. W. T., M .C.
Fletcher, Lieut. P. C., M.C.

Fox, Lieut. J., M.C.
Taylor, Lieut. S., M.C.
Barker, 2nd Lieut. J. P., M.C.
Bootland, 2nd Lieut. F. R., M.C.
Lockyer, 2nd Lieut. H. R., M.C.
Rourke, 2nd Lieut. T., M.C.
Cronshaw, Lt.-Col. A. E. (F.).
Darlington, Lt.-Col. H. C. (F.).
Simpson, Lt.-Col. A. W. W. (F.).

Other Ranks

McCartney, Sgt. J., D.C.M. and Bar.
Andrews, Pte. F., D.C.M.
Barnes, Sgt. C., D.C.M.
Bent, Pte. R., D.C.M.
Blythe, Co. Sgt.-Mjr. G., D.C.M.
Casey, Cpl. A. E., D.C.M.
Chadwick, Cpl. F., D.C.M.
Christy, R.Q.M.S. W. H., D.C.M.
Davies, Pte. A., D.C.M.
Greensmith, Sgt. W., D.C.M.
Gregory, Cpl. R., D.C.M.
Grimshaw, L.-Cpl. J., D.C.M.
Hibbert, Pte. J., D.C.M.
Hills, Pte. S. L., D.C.M.
Hilton, Pte. A., D.C.M.
Lever, C.Q.M.S. J., D.C.M.
McCarty, Co.Sgt.Mjr. T., D.C.M.
Moore, Pte. W., D.C.M.
Morrisin, R. Sgt.-Mjr. J., D.C.M.
Oldham, Cpl. A., D.C.M.
Seddon, Pte. T., D.C.M.
Smith, Sgt. J., D.C.M.
Stockton, Cpl. S., D.C.M.
Stott, L.-Cpl. J., D.C.M.

Stridgeon, Co. Sgt.-Mjr. J., D.C.M.
Trousdale, L.-Cpl. F., D.C.M.
Ward, Pte. R. W., D.C.M.
Cunningham, L.-Sgt. J., M.M. and Bar.
Abrahams, Pte. J. W., M.M.
Atherton, Sgt. J., M.M.
Barker, Cpl. J., M.M.
Barker, Cpl. J., M.M.
Bevan, L.-Sgt. J., M.M.
Bowers, Pte. S., M.M.
Brennan, Pte. E., M.M.
Britton, Pte. E., M.M.
Carroll, Pte. J., M.M.
Carter, Pte. W., M.M.
Chadwick, Pte. A., M.M.
Coogan, Pte. E., M.M.
Creed, Pte. J., M.M.
Drouthwaite, Sgt. T., M.M.
Flavill, Cpl. H., M.M.
Florendine, Cpl. J., M.M.
Hamer, Sgt. J., M.M.
Hayes, L.-Cpl. H., M.M.
Hewitt, Pte. J., M.M.
Hooley, Pte. H., M.M.

Hosler, Pte. T., M.M.
Kane, Pte. R., M.M., M.S.M.
Lee, Pte. F., M.M.
Lee, L.-Cpl. J. E., M.M.
Lomas, Pte. W., M.M.
Lowe, Pte. T., M.M.
Melling, Cpl. J., M.M.
Millward, Pte. H. S., M.M.
Molyneux, Pte. C., M.M.
Morgan, Pte. G., M.M.
Newcombe, Pte. C., M.M.
Parrott, Pte. W., M.M.
Pattison, Pte. C., M.M.
Penkethman, Cpl. H., M.M.
Poole, Pte. H., M.M.
Radcliffe, Pte. W., M.M.
Ralphs, Pte. T., M.M.
Reynolds, Pte. J., M.M.
Roberts, L.-Sgt. H., M.M.
Rooke, Pte. J., M.M.
Rowe, Pte. A., M.M.
Smith, Cpl. J., M.M.
Stamper, C.Q.M.S. P. A., M.M.
Stuart, Sgt. T., M.M.
Teague, Pte. A. E., M.M.
Turner, Pte. J. H., M.M.

Valentine, Pte. H., M.M.
Walsh, L.-Sgt. S., M.M.
Webb, Pte. J., M.M.
Whitehead, Pte. J., M.M.
Whittle, Pte. W., M.M.
Wilde, Pte. W., M.M.

Hyde, Pte. T., M.S.M.
Jones, Cpl. R., M.S.M.
Leake, Sgt. G., M.S.M.
Owen, Co. Sgt.-Mjr. J., M.S.M.
Seddon, Cpl. W., M.S.M.
Stone, Sgt. H., M.S.M.

Taylor, C.Q.M.S. F., M.S.M.
Gill, Co. Sgt.-Mjr. G. (F.).
Grimes, Pte. J. (F.).
Dandy, Pte. H. (F.).
Lomas, Pte. W. (F.).

1/6 BATTALION MANCHESTER REGIMENT

Officers

Pilkington, Lt.-Col. C. R., C.M.G.
Holberton, Capt. and Adjt. P. V., to be Brevet Major.
Worthington, Lt.-Col. C. S., D.S.O. and Bar.
Blatherwick, Lt.-Col. T., D.S.O.
Wedgwood, Lt.-Col. G. H., D.S.O.
Benton, Capt. F. C., M.C.

Blatherwick, Capt. T., M.C.
Kershaw, Capt. G. G., M.C.
Kershaw, Capt. G. V., M.C.
Molesworth, Capt. W. N., M.C.
Norris, Capt. A. H., R.A.M.C., M.C.
Till, Capt. G. F.. M.C.
Wilson, Capt. H., R.A.M.C., M.C.
Wood, Capt. J., M.C.

Collier, Lieut. S., M.C.
Crossley, Lieut. F., M.C.
Hammick, Lieut. H. A., M.C.
Maule, Lieut. R., M.C.
Warburton, Lt.-Qr. Mr. W. R. M.C.
Heyhoe, 2nd Lieut S. G., M.C.
Martin, 2nd Lieut. H. R., M.C.
Lane, 2nd Lieut. W. J., M.C.
Holberton, Maj. P. V. (F.).

Other Ranks

Roberts, Sgt. W., D.C.M. and Bar.
Ashley, Pte. E., D.C.M.
Cutter, Pte. G. R., D.C.M.
Davies, Pte. T. J., D.C.M.
Dennerly, L.-Sgt. R., D.C.M.
Doig, Pte. A. M., D.C.M.
Farthing, R.Sgt.Mjr. J., D.C.M.
Gill, Sgt. R. W., D.C.M.
Hartshorn, Cpl. E. P., D.C.M.
Hashim, Pte. R., D.C.M.
Hay, Co. Sgt.-Mjr. F., D.C.M.
Holden, Sgt. H., D.C.M.
Hurdley, Co. Sgt.-Mjr. J., D.C.M.
Ingham, Pte. J. R., D.C.M.
Kent, R.Sgt.-Mjr. W. A., D.C.M.
Martin, Co. Sgt.-Mjr. J. R., D.C.M.
McDonald, L.-Sgt. A., D.C.M.
McDowell, Sgt. A., D.C.M.
Moores, Pte. S., D.C.M.
Murphy, Pte. J., D.C.M.
Roberts, Co. Sgt.-Mjr. W., D.C.M.
Senior, L.-Cpl. W. A., D.C.M.
Sturgess, Sgt. S., D.C.M.
Whitford, Co. Sgt.-Mjr. H. D., D.C.M.
Wignall, Sgt. A., D.C.M.
Wilson, Co. Sgt.-Mjr. S. H., D.C.M.
Wood, Sgt. G. H., D.C.M.
Jarvis, Pte. H. W., M.M. and Bar.
Shea, Cpl. M., M.M. and Bar.

Stubbs, Pte. B., M.M. and Bar.
Aldridge, Pte. J., M.M.
Allen, Pte. G., M.M.
Atherton, L.-Cpl. E. A., M.M
Baker, Cpl. W., M.M.
Barker, Pte. W., M.M.
Beresford, Pte. T., M.M.
Berry, Sgt. A. J., M.M.
Brooks, Pte. A., M.M.
Butterworth, Pte. S., M.M.
Clarke, Pte. J., M.M.
Crowther, Pte. J. C., M.M.
Dugdale, L.-Cpl. F., M.M.
Dutton, Pte. G., M.M.
Farrand, Pte. W., M.M.
Farrell, Pte. J., M.M.
Fearn, Pte. M., M.M.
Fletcher, Pte. W. S., M.M.
Foster, Cpl. J. M., M.M.
Fox, L.-Cpl. W. H., M.M.
Gibbons, Sgt. W. G., M.M.
Gorman, L.-Sgt. D. W., M.M.
Griffiths, Pte. W. H., M.M.
Hadfield, Pte. E. G., M.M.
Hallworth, Pte. W., M.M.
Halstead, Pte. G., M.M.
Hancock, Pte. H., M.M.
Houghton, Pte. W. S., M.M.
Irwin, Pte. S., M.M.
James, L.-Cpl. W. H., M.M.
Johnson, Sgt. R., M.M.
Jones, Pte. J. N., M.M.
Kennedy, Pte. P. J., M.M.
Kent, Sgt. G., M.M.
Lockett, Sgt. P., M.M.
Maskell, Sgt. C. H., M.M.

McCarthy, Pte. D., M.M.
McDermott, Pte. J., M.M.
Mitton, Cpl. S. H., M.M.
Mullins, Cpl. P., M.M.
Parkinson, Pte. G. V., M.M.
Parry, L.-Sgt. E. E., R.A.M.C., M.M.
Potts, Cpl. A. V., M.M.
Pounder, Pte. W., M.M.
Ralphs, Pte. T., M.M.
Richardson, Pte. N., M.M.
Saxon, Pte. C., M.M.
Sellers, Pte. J., M.M.
Senior, Pte. W., M.M.
Sidebottom, L.-Cpl. W. J. H., M.M.
Smith, Pte. N. S., M.M.
Smith, Pte. W. E., M.M.
Tomkinson, Pte. W., M.M.
Tomlinson, Pte. S., M.M.
Warburton, Pte. H., M.M.
Whitehead, Pte. E., M.M.
Whittaker, L.-Cpl. O., M.M.
Williams, L.-Cpl. R. D., M.M.
Chadwick, C.Q.M.S. A. R., M.S.M.
Dale, C.Q.M.S. T. R., M.S.M.
Lee, R.Q.M.S. S., M.S.M.
Taylor, Sgt. V., M.S.M.
White, R.Q.M.S. J., M.S.M.
Wills, L.-Sgt. N. T., M.S.M.
Featherstone, Sgt. (F.).
Foster, Cpl. J. M. (F.).
Hurdley, Co. Sgt.-Mjr. J. (F.).
McDowell, Sgt. A. (F.).

1/7 BATTALION MANCHESTER REGIMENT

Officers

Canning, Lt.-Col. A., C.M.G.
Fawcus, Lt.-Col. A. E. F., D.S.O., M.C.
Hodge, Lt.-Col. A., D.S.O., M.C.
Carr, Lt.-Col. H. A., D.S.O., to be Brevet Lt.-Col.
Cronshaw, Lt.-Col. A. E., D.S.O.
Brown, Maj. J. N., D.S.O.
Creagh, Maj. P. H., D.S.O.

Rae, Maj. G. B. L., D.S.O.
Welch, Lieut., D.S.O.
Scott, Maj. and Q.M. J., O.B.E.
Nasmith, Capt. G. W., O.B.E.
Thorpe, Capt. J. H., O.B.E.
Gresty, Lieut. W., M.C. and Bar.
Burn, Maj. F. G., M.C.
Whitley, Maj. N. H. P., M.C.
Allen, Capt. C. R. M.C.

Baker, Capt. J., M.C.
Farrow, Capt. J., R.A.M.C., M.C.
Hayes, Capt. F., M.C.
Hoskyns, Capt. E. C. (C.F.), M.C.
Kirby, Capt. E. T., M.A. (C.F.), M.C.
Nidd, Capt. H. H., M.C.
Williamson, Capt. C. H., M.C.

Honours and Awards 239

Bagshaw, Lieut. K., M.C.
Douglas, Lieut. C. B., M.C.
Edge, Lieut. N., M.C.
Franklin, Lieut. H. C., M.C.
Goodall, Lieut. J. C., M.C.
Goodier, Lieut. A., M.C.
Gorst, Lieut. H., M.C.
Harris, Lieut. L. G., M.C.
Siddall, Lieut. J. R., M.C.

Wilson, Lieut. S. J., M.C.
Harland, 2nd Lieut. J. A., M.C.
Milne, 2nd Lieut., M.C.
Thrutchley, 2nd Lieut. F. D., M.C.
Cronshaw, Lt.-Col. A. E. (F.).
Fawcus, Lt.-Col. A. E. F. (F.).
Brown, Maj. J. N. (4th Class), (F.).

Whitley, Maj. N. H. P. (F.).
Whitley, Maj. N. H. P. (F.).
Brown, Maj. J. N. (F.).
Chadwick, Capt. G. (F.).
Manger, Lt.-Col. E. V., to be Brevet Lt.-Col.
Brown, Maj. J. N., Brevet Majority.

Other Ranks

Bamber, Sgt. F., D.C.M.,M.S.M.
Fleetwood, Sgt. A., D.C.M.
Green, Sgt. J. W., D.C.M., M.M.
Hand, Sgt. A., D.C.M.
Heasman, L.-Cpl. A., D.C.M.
Holbrook, Sgt. J., D.C.M.
Horsfield, Sgt. J., D.C.M., M.M.
King, Cpl. A. W., D.C.M.
Lockett, Cpl. S., D.C.M.
Mather, Sgt., D.C.M.
McHugh, Co. Sgt.-Mjr., D.C.M.
Mort, L.-Sgt. W., D.C.M.
Quinn, Pte. J., D.C.M.
Richardson, Pte. M., D.C.M.
Tabbron, Co. Sgt.-Mjr., D.C.M., M.M.
White, Cpl. F., D.C.M.
Wood, Cpl. T., D.C.M.
Greer, Pte. A., M.M. and Bar
Heath, Sgt. F., M.M. and Bar.
McHugh, Co. Sgt.Mjr., M.M. and Bar.
Twist, L.-Cpl. T., M.M. and Bar.
Aldred, L.-Sgt. J., M.M.
Bailey, Pte. S., M.M.
Banahan, Sgt. J., M.M.
Booker, L.-Cpl. F. W., M.M.
Botham, Pte. W. E., M.M.
Bowman, Pte. J., M.M.
Boydell, Pte. J., M.M.
Bradshaw, Pte. W., M.M.

Braithwaite, Pte. T., M.M.
Broughton, Cpl. A., M.M.
Coffey, Sgt. W., M.M.
Collinge, Pte. H., M.M.
Conrey, Pte. R. E., M.M.
Craven, L.-Cpl. A., M.M.
Daley, Sgt. W., M.M.
Davies, Pte. W. T., M.M.
Dearden, Pte. R., M.M.
Downs, Pte. A., M.M.
Eastwood, Cpl. W., M.M.
Edwards, Pte. R., M.M.
Fidler, Sgt. W., M.M.
Gammond, Sgt. T. A., M.M.
Gregory, Cpl. B., M.M.
Hadfield, Sgt. A., M.M.
Halfhide, Pte. C., M.M.
Hayhurst, Pte., M.M.
Hyde, L.-Cpl. L., M.M.
Jackson, L.-Cpl. E., M.M.
Jennions, Pte. H., M.M.
Jolly, Sgt. J., M.M.
Joyce, Co. Sgt.-Mjr., M.M.
Latham, Pte. H., M.M.
Livesley, Sgt. J. L., M.M.
Lynn, Sgt. H., M.M.
Lyons, Pte. C., M.M.
Maguire, Cpl. A., M.M.
McClean, Pte. T., M.M.
Moore, Pte. T. C., M.M.
Morris, L.-Cpl. G., M.M.
Mottram, L.-Sgt. G., M.M.

Mullin, Pte. C., M.M.
Parker, Sgt. G., M.M.
Parkin, Pte. I., M.M.
Pickering, Pte. W., M.M.
Reeves, Pte. E., M.M.
Riley, Pte. J. G., M.M.
Riley, Sgt. R., M.M.
Rotham, Pte. T., M.M.
Rourke, Pte. A., M.M.
Sanderson, Pte. G., M.M.
Shaughnessy, Pte., M.M.
Standring, Cpl. W., M.M.
Stubbard, Pte. R., M.M.
Thorpe, Sgt. H., M.M.
Titchener, Pte. E., M.M.
Titterington, L.-Sgt. H. L., M.M.
Walsh, Pte. J., M.M.
Walton, Pte. F. G., M.M.
Warrington, Pte. W., M.M.
Whiskin, Pte. A., M.M.
Wilkinson, Pte. H., M.M.
Wilkinson, Pte. J., M.M.
Willmer, Pte. R., M.M.
Anlezark, R. Sgt.-Mjr. W., M.S.M.
Clavering, Sgt. H., M.S.M.
Ogden, R.Q.M.S., M.S.M.
Shields, Co. Sgt.-Mjr. J., M.S.M.
Horsfield, Sgt. J. (F.).
Joyce, Co. Sgt.-Mjr. (F.).

1/8 BATTALION MANCHESTER REGIMENT

Officers

McCarthy Morrogh, Lt.-Col. D. F., C.M.G.
Cross, Lt.-Col. E. G. K., D.S.O.
Bluhm, Maj. Q. M., D.S.O.
Lings, Maj. H. C., D.S.O.

Stewart, Capt. W. H., O.B.E.
Horsfall, Maj. E., M.C.
Moore, Maj. C. G., M.C. (F.)
Barlow, Capt. A. E., M.C.
Norman, Capt. H. I., M.C.

Ross, Capt. E. A., M.C.
Holdaway, Lieut. N. A., M.C.
McGuffie, Lieut. T., M.C.
Parsons, 2nd Lieut. H., M.C.
Stephenson, Lt.-Col. H. M. (F.).

Other Ranks

Code, R.Q.M.S. J. H., D.C.M.
Evans, Cpl. G., D.C.M.
Harrison, Sgt. H., D.C.M., M.M.
Hennessey, Pte. T., D.C.M.
Knott, Co. Sgt.-Mjr. J., D.C.M.
O'Connell, Pte. J., D.C.M.
Simpson, Co. Sgt.-Mjr. H., D.C.M.
Stenton, L.-Cpl. W., D.C.M.
Tasker, Pte. G., D.C.M.
Waterhouse, Sgt. J., D.C.M.
Wood, Pte. H. T., D.C.M.
Boardman, Sgt. E., M.M.
Bogie, Cpl. H. S., M.M.
Bradshaw, Cpl. G., M.M.
Derrig, Sgt. T. H., M.M.
Forrest, Pte. J., M.M.
Halliwell, Pte. J., M.M.
Harris, Pte. W. S., M.M.

Hewitt, Cpl. C., M.M.
Holmes, Pte. C., M.M.
Hooper, Pte. H., M.M.
Jones, L.-Cpl. H., M.M.
Jones, Pte. T., M.M.
Kelly, Cpl. J. C., M.M.
Kirwin, Pte. T., M.M.
Layton, Pte. T., M.M.
McCormick, Pte. J., M.M.
McMullon, Pte., M.M.
Monks, Pte. J., M.M.
Poke, Cpl. J., M.M.
Quinn, L.-Cpl. F. P., M.M.
Rigly, Pte. T., M.M.
Rimmer, Pte. W., M.M.
Russell, Cpl. R. E., M.M.
Slowe, Pte. E., M.M.
Taylor, Pte. W., M.M.

Taylor, R.Q.M.S. W., M.M.
Walker, Cpl. A., M.M.
White, Sgt. W., M.M.
Wood, Pte. F., M.M.
Young, Co. Sgt.-Mjr. W. H., M.M.
Brookshaw, Co. Sgt.-Mjr. W. H., M.S.M.
Clifford, Co. Sgt.-Mjr. T., M.S.M.
Hursthouse, Co. Sgt.-Mjr. J. E., M.S.M.
Rogers, C.Q.M.S. J., M.S.M.
Summerfield, C.Q.M.S. J., M.S.M.
Garside, Cpl. J. (F.).
Owen, Pte. W. P. (F.).
Pollitt, Pte. T. (F.).
Taylor, Cpl. J. (F.).

7 BATTALION NORTHUMBERLAND FUSILIERS
(Pioneer Battalion)

Officers

Liddell, Lt.-Col. H., D.S.O., M.C.

Merivale, Capt. V., M.C. and Bar.

Booth, Lieut. S. P., M.C.
Dodds, 2nd Lieut. J., M.C.

Other Ranks

Allen, Sgt. H. J., D.C.M.
Draper, Co. Sgt.-Mjr. A. V., D.C.M.
Richardson, Co. Sgt.-Mjr. J. R., D.C.M., M.S.M.
Bell, Pte. J., M.M.

Bolton, Sgt. J., M.M.
Bradshaw, Sgt. J., M.M.
Healy, Pte. L., M.M.
King, Pte. J., M.M.
Mann, Pte. H., M.M.

Nesbitt, Sgt. J. W., M.M.
Cairns, Sgt. J., M.S.M.
Lamb, L.-Sgt. W. R., M.S.M.
Pearson, Sgt. G., M.S.M.
Rial, C.Q.M.S. H., M.S.M.

ROYAL ARMY SERVICE CORPS

Officers

England, Lt.-Col. A., C.M.G., D.S.O.
Coulson, Lt.-Col. J., D.S.O.
Needham, Lt.-Col. J. G., D.S.O., O.B.E.
Gillibrand, Maj. A., D.S.O.
Halliwell, Maj. W. A., O.B.E.

Reynolds, Maj. W. P. K., O.B.E.
Russell, Maj. Gordon, O.B.E.
Sykes, Maj. G. A., O.B.E.
Aris, Capt. A. F., O.B.E.
Reynolds, Capt. H. J. B., O.B.E.

Scholtz, Capt. E. K., O.B.E.
Ball, Maj. F., M.C.
Brocklehurst, Capt. J. G., M.C.
Fenner, Capt. A., M.C.
Walsh, Capt. L. E., M.C.
Latham, Lieut. R., M.C.

Other Ranks

Boyer, Staff Sgt.-Mjr. W., D.C.M.
Dyer, Staff Sgt.-Mjr. C., D.C.M.
Johnson, Sgt.-Mjr. W. H., D.C.M.

Gully, Cpl. P., M.M.
Johnson, Sgt.-Mjr. W. H., M.M.
Bowden, S.Q.M.S. A. H., M.S.M.
Brooks, Staff Sgt. M., M.S.M.

Mathers, Staff Sgt. F. J., M.S.M.
McLean, Staff Sgt. L., M.S.M.
Pickering, Sgt. T. P., M.S.M.
Ransome, Co. Sgt.-Mjr. T. E., M.S.M.

1/1 EAST LANCASHIRE FIELD AMBULANCE

Officers

Callam, Lt.-Col. A., D.S.O.
Brentnall, Maj. C. P., M.C.

Douglas, Capt. W. R., M.C.
Fort, Capt. C. W., M.C.

Morley, Capt. J. (F.).

Other Ranks

Hughes, Cpl. W., D.C.M.
Jarman, Sgt.-Mjr. W., D.C.M.
Poole, L.-Cpl. A., D.C.M.
Walton, Cpl. G. A., D.C.M.
Ashworth, Sgt. N., M.M., M.S.M.
Chesney Pte. H., M.M.
Clarke, Pte. C. M. S., M.M.

Clarke, Sgt. G., M.M.
Fenna, Sgt A., M.M.
Freeman, Pte. R., M.M.
Hamilton, Sgt. A., M.M.
Ibbotson, Pte. G., M.M.
Jenkinson, Pte. S. A., M.M.
Lisett, Pte. W. B., M.M.
Levie, Pte. G. S., M.M.

Parry, Cpl. E., M.M.
Wreaks, Pte. A. E., M.M.
Dutson, S. Sgt.-Mjr. F. E., M.S.M.
Marsden, Pte. J. B., M.S.M.
Bolwell, Pte. H. J. (F.).
Quayle, Q.M.S. T. K. (F.).

ROYAL ARMY VETERINARY CORPS

Capt. H. H. Lord, M.C.

42 BATTALION MACHINE GUN CORPS

Officers

Tillie, Lt.-Col. W. K., D.S.O., M.C.
Flavell, Maj. E. W. C., M.C. and 2 Bars.
Dickson, Maj. W. E., M.C. and Bar.
Sale, Maj. H. A., M.C. and Bar.
Herridge, Lieut. A. L., M.C. and Bar.

Mitchell, Lieut. J. K., M.C. and Bar.
Royce, Maj. G. N., M.C.
Bryan, Capt. J. L., M.C.
Rose, Capt. C. C., M.C.
Briedfjord, Lieut. M. A. S., M.C.
Gale, Lieut. R. N., M.C.
Hatch, Lieut. F. S., M.C.
Hobourn, Lieut. P. L., M.C.

Wigelsworth, Lieut. C. E., M.C.
Dibben, 2nd Lieut. H. T. L., M.C.
Fisher, 2nd Lieut. K. L., M.C.
Hough, 2nd Lieut. R., M.C.
Strawson, 2nd Lieut. W. N., M.C.
Taylor, 2nd Lieut. W., M.C.
Royce, Lieut. (T.-Major) G. N., M.C., to be Brevet Major.

Honours and Awards 241

Aylmore, Sgt. G. H., D.C.M.
Barrett, Cpl. J. G., D.C.M.
Benjamin, Sgt. W. G., D.C.M.
Channing, Cpl. W. C., D.C.M.
Cheetham, Cpl. W., D.C.M., M.M.
Delmege, Pte. W., D.C.M.
Dewhurst, Cpl. A., D.C.M.
Griffiths, Sgt. J. L., D.C.M., M.M.
Gresty, Co. Sgt.-Mjr. D., D.C.M.
Lane, Pte. B., D.C.M.
Vincent, Sgt. A. E., D.C.M.
Heywood, Cpl. S., M.M. and Bar.
Smith, Cpl. R. C., M.M. and Bar.
Akers, L.-Cpl. P., M.M.
Bennett, Sgt. E., M.M.
Blake, L.-Cpl. H. C., M.M.
Boon, Pte. C. C., M.M.
Boss, Sgt. J. W., M.M.
Broadhurst, L.-Cpl. A., M.M.

Other Ranks

Burrows, Sgt. H., M.M.
Cornford, Sgt. A. A., M.M.
Cullins, Pte. T. J., M.M.
Davies, L.-Cpl. C., M.M., M.S.M.
Dixon, Sgt. A., M.M.
Ellor, Sgt. G., M.M.
Emmett, Pte. J., M.M.
Fagan, Pte. J., M.M.
Faulkiner, Pte. J., M.M.
Ferguson, Cpl. J., M.M.
Gates, Cpl. B., M.M.
Gavin, Pte. J. G., M.M.
Gilligan, Cpl. F., M.M.
Groves, Pte. G. T., M.M.
Heathcote, Pte. C., M.M.
Henrys, Cpl. W., M.M.
Heron, Sgt. A. G., M.M.
Heys, Pte. R.. M.M.
Hopkins, Pte. A., M.M.
Jukes, Cpl. W. G., M.M.
Kendall, Cpl. J. L., M.M.
Kennedy, Pte. W. B., M.M.
Machray, Pte. G., M.M.

Matley, Pte. W., M.M.
Miles, Pte. E., M.M.
Milne, Pte. E., M.M.
Palmer, Sgt. A. E., M.M.
Parkes, Sgt. G., M.M.
Plant, L.-Cpl. A., M.M.
Richardson, Sgt. G., M.M.
Roberts, Pte. F. S., M.M.
Robinson, L.-Cpl. J. G., M.M.
Rowland, Pte. J. W., M.M.
Rowley, Pte. J., M.M.
Seddon, L.-Cpl. J. A., M.M.
Simmons, Pte. H. H., M.M.
Summers, Sgt. R., M.M.
Taylor, Pte. J., M.M.
Uren, L.-Cpl., M.M.
Vevers, L.-Cpl. J., M.M.
Walker, Sgt. R., M.M.
Ward, Cpl. H., M.M.
Williams, L.-Cpl. T., M.M.
Gerrard, C.Q.M.S. R., M.S.M.
Wheelton, R.Q.M.S. S., M.S.M.

R

HEADQUARTERS STAFF AND COMMANDING OFFICERS, 1914–1919

COMMANDER
Major-Gen. Sir Wm. Douglas, K.C.M.G., C.B., D.S.O.
Major-Gen. B. R. Mitford, C.B., C.M.G., D.S.O.
Major-Gen. A. Solly-Flood, C.B., C.M.G., D.S.O.

A.D.C. 1.
Captain H. T. Cawley, M.P.   Captain R. P. Hornby, M.C.
Lieut. Hon. A. Douglas Pennant.   Lieut. Hon. J. St. J. B. Saumarez.
                Captain J. Cator.

A.D.C. 2.
Lieut. J. W. L. Fry.   Lieut. G. Lewis.
Captain J. Marshall.   Captain J. R. Tylden.
                Major R. Stirling.

G.S.O. 1.
Lt.-Col. A. W. Tufnell, C.M.G.   Major B. C. Battye, D.S.O.
Lt.-Col. A. Crookenden, D.S.O.   Lt.-Col. B. J. Curling, D.S.O.
            Lt.-Col. R. F. Guy, C.M.G., D.S.O.

G.S.O. 2.
Lt.-Col. F. A. Earle.   Major A. E. Pery-Knox-Gore, O.B.E.
Captain R. S. Allen, D.S.O.   Major Hon. E. C. Pery, D.S.O.
Captain W. H. Diggle, D.S.O., M.C. Major J. G. W. Clark, M.C.
            Major G. E. Tallents, D.S.O.

G.S.O. 3.
Captain S. H. Kershaw, D.S.O.   Captain Hon. E. C. Pery, D.S.O.
Captain J. I. Benson, M.C.   Captain E. C. B. Kirsopp, M.C.

INTELLIGENCE OFFICER.
Lieut. G. F. Doble, M.C.

A.A. AND Q.M.G.
Col. W. H. Cummings.   Lt.-Col. H. F. L. Grant, D.S.O.
Lt.-Col. E. S. Herbert, C.M.G., C.B.E. Lt.-Col. R. J. Slaughter, C.M.G., D.S.O.

D.A.A. AND Q.M.G. (LATER D.A.A.G.)
Captain R. S. Allen, D.S.O.   Major E. B. Powell, D.S.O.
Lt.-Col. F. A. Earle.   Major V. R. Burkhardt, D.S.O.
            Major C. R. Maude, O.B.E., M.C.

D.A.Q.M.G.
Major G. F. T. Leather.   Major T. R. P. Warren, C.B.E.
Major R. J. Slaughter, C.M.G., D.S.O.   Captain M. F. Hammond Smith, M.C.
            Major J. M. Young, D.S.O.

LEFT TO RIGHT: BRIG.-GEN. F. W. H. WALSHE, C.M.G., D.S.O., C.R.A.; MAJOR-GEN. A. SOLLY-FLOOD, C.B., C.M.G., D.S.O., COMMANDING 42ND DIVISION; BRIG.-GEN. H. FARGUS, C.B., C.M.G., D.S.O.; BRIG.-GEN. THE HON. A. M. HENLEY, C.M.G., D.S.O.

Commanding Officers

A.D.M.S.
Col. J. Bentley Mann, T.D.
Col. T. P. Jones, C.B., C.M.G.
Col. W. R. Matthews, D.S.O., T.D.

D.A.D.M.S.
Lt.-Col. G. T. Rawnsley, C.B., C.M.G.
Major C. M. Drew.
Major G. Dalziel, M.C.

Senior Chaplain.
C. of E. Rev. D. Fletcher.
Non C. of E. Rev. S. Jones.

A.P.M. (later D.A.P.M.).
Captain T. B. Forwood.
Captain T. C. Robinson, D.S.O., T.D.
Captain Henderson-Cleland, M.C.

D.A.D.V.S.
Lt.-Col. T. Marriott. Major G. W. Godwin.
Major J. Gillies. Major J. A. Connell, T.D.

D.A.D.O.S.
Major O. R. E. Milman, D.S.O.
Captain H. W. S. Whitehouse.
Major F. T. Potter, O.B.E., M.C.

COMMANDING OFFICERS

DUKE OF LANCASTER'S OWN YEOMANRY ("A" SQUADRON)
Major H. L. Bibby.
Major D. H. Bates, M.C.

ROYAL ARTILLERY

Commander.
Brig.-Gen. A. D'A. King, C.B., C.M.G., D.S.O.
Brig.-Gen. F. W. H. Walshe, C.M.G., D.S.O., A.D.C.

Brigade Major.
Major L. W. La T. Cockraft, D.S.O.
Major P. R. Mitchell, D.S.O.
Captain F. E. Morgan.

Staff Captain.
Captain W. T. Highet, M.C.
Captain E. Nuttall.

210th BRIGADE
Lt.-Col. T. Frankish, T.D.
Lt.-Col. A. Birtwistle, C.B., C.M.G., D.S.O., T.D.
Lt.-Col. D. J. Mason, D.S.O., T.D.

211th BRIGADE
Col. C. E. Walker, D.S.O., T.D.
Lt.-Col. E. J. Inches, D.S.O., T.D.
Lt.-Col. F. G. Crompton.

ROYAL ENGINEERS
Commander.
Lt.-Col. C. E. Newton.
Lt.-Col. S. L. Tennant, T.D.
Lt.-Col. E. N. Mozley, D.S.O.
Lt.-Col. D. S. MacInnes, C.M.G., D.S.O.
Lt.-Col. R. E. B. Pratt, D.S.O.
Lt.-Col. A. T. Shakespear, D.S.O.
Lt.-Col. J. G. Riddick, D.S.O.

125TH INFANTRY BRIGADE
Commander.
Brig.-Gen. H. C. Frith, C.B.
Brig.-Gen. H. Fargus, C.B., C.M.G., D.S.O.

Brigade Major.
Major A. J. Allardyce.
Captain I. M. Smith, D.S.O., M.C.
Captain A. E. Lawrence, M.C.
Captain Barton.
Captain P. B. B. Nichols, M.C.

Staff Captain.
Captain J. Kenyon.
Captain I. C. Grant, D.S.O.
Captain E. Woolmer, D.S.O., M.C.
Captain A. O. Needham, O.B.E., M.C.
Captain Bassett.
Captain J. Marshall.

1/5TH BATTALION LANCS. FUSILIERS.
Lt.-Col. J. Isherwood, C.B., V.D.
Lt.-Col. G. Wood, D.S.O.
Lt.-Col. F. A. Woodcock, T.D.
Major W. Webb.
Lt.-Col. P. V. Holberton.
Lt.-Col. Clive, M.P.
Lt.-Col. G. S. Castle, M.C.

1/6TH BATTALION LANCS. FUSILIERS.
Col. Lord Rochdale.
Lt.-Col. R. L. Lees, D.S.O., V.D.
Lt.-Col. R. H. Barker.
Lt.-Col. M. F. Hammond Smith, M.C.
Lt.-Col. E. I. de S. Thorpe, D.S.O.
Lt.-Col. C. H. de S. P. Bunbury.

1/7TH BATTALION LANCS. FUSILIERS.
Lt.-Col. A. F. Maclure, T.D.
Lt.-Col. C. T. Alexander, D.S.O.
Major W. J. Law.
Major M. R. P. W. Gledhill, M.C.
Lt.-Col. H. C. Woodcock.
Major E. W. Lennard.
Lt.-Col. W. E. Maskell.
Lt.-Col. G. S. Brewis, D.S.O.
Lt.-Col. T. J. Kelly, D.S.O., M.C.

1/8TH BATTALION LANCS. FUSILIERS.
Lt.-Col. J. A. Fallows, T.D.
Lt.-Col. J. M. Rogers, D.S.O.
Major J. O. Hardicker.
Lt.-Col. O. St. Leger Davies.
Major G. E. Hope, M.C.
Lt.-Col. A. L. B. Shaw, D.S.O., T.D.
Lt.-Col. R. D. Waterhouse.
Major H. A. Kirkby, D.S.O.
Lt.-Col. H. P. Cochrane.
Major G. S. Castle, M.C.
Lt.-Col. G. S. MacLeod, D.S.O.

126TH INFANTRY BRIGADE
Commander.
Brig.-Gen. D. G. Prendergast, C.M.G.
Brig.-Gen. Visct. Hampden, C.B., C.M.G.
Brig.-Gen. A. W. Tufnell, C.M.G.
Brig.-Gen. A. C. Johnston, D.S.O., M.C.
Brig.-Gen. W. W. Seymour.
Brig.-Gen. G. H. Wedgwood, D.S.O.
Brig.-Gen. T. H. S. Marchant, D.S.O.

Commanding Officers

BRIGADE MAJOR.

Major C. J. Hickie, C.M.G.
Captain L. Gordon.
Major P. V. Holberton.

Captain A. P. Garnier, M.C., M.B.E.
Captain B. Sanderson, M.C.
Captain R. R. Shawcross.
Captain H. Parker, D.S.O.

STAFF CAPTAIN.

Captain T. Robinson, D.S.O., T.D.
Captain C. L. Wauchope.
Captain Porter.

Captain L. St. G. Wilkinson, M.C.
Captain W. M. Tucker, M.C.
Captain D. V. Porteous.

1/9TH BATTALION MANCHESTER REGT.

Lt.-Col. D. H. Wade.
Major R. B. Nowell.
Lt.-Col. R. W. Falcon.

Major Anderson.
Major A. H. Roberts.
Lt.-Col. E. C. Lloyd.

Lt.-Col. J. L. Heselton, D.S.O., M.C.

1/10TH BATTALION MANCHESTER REGT.

Lt.-Col. J. B. Rye, V.D.
Lt.-Col. W. G. Robinson, C.B.

Lt.-Col. R. P. Lewis.
Lt.-Col. W. R. Peel, D.S.O.

1/4TH BATTALION EAST LANCS. REGT.

Lt.-Col. F. D. Robinson, V.D.
Lt.-Col. G. W. G. Lindesay, D.S.O.
Major H. R. Coningsby.

Lt.-Col. C. W. Battye, D.S.O.
Lt.-Col. A. H. S. Hart-Synott, C.M.G., D.S.O.
Lt.-Col. A. L. Wrenford.

1/5TH BATTALION EAST LANCS. REGT.

Lt.-Col. J. Craven Hoyle, T.D.
Lt.-Col. W. E. Sharples, T.D.
Lt.-Col. G. Whitehead.
Lt.-Col. W. M. Acton, D.S.O.

Lt.-Col. R. W. Murray-White, D.S.O.
Lt.-Col. E. W. Lennard.
Lt.-Col. O. C. Clare, D.S.O., M.C.
Lt.-Col. J. P. Hoxey, M.C.

127TH INFANTRY BRIGADE

COMMANDER.

Brig-Gen. Noel Lee, V.D.
Brig-Gen. Hon. H. A. Lawrence, K.C.M.G.
Brig.-Gen. G. S. McD. Elliot, C.B.E.
Brig.-Gen. V. A. Ormsby.
Brig.-Gen. Hon. A. M. Henley, C.M.G., D.S.O.

BRIGADE MAJOR.

Major H. L. Knight, C.M.G., D.S.O.
Captain P. L. Leared.

Captain A. G. Stone, O.B.E.
Captain E. G. T. Tuite-Dalton, M.C.
Captain De V. Stacpoole, M.C.

STAFF CAPTAIN.

Captain T. N. C. Nevill.
Captain W. T. Woods, D.S.O., M.C.
Captain W. G. Orrell.

1/5TH BATTALION MANCHESTER REGT.

Colonel W. S. France, V.D.
Lt.-Col. H. C. Darlington, C.M.G., T.D.
Major J. H. Allen.

Lt.-Col. T. Blatherwick, D.S.O., M.C.
Lt.-Col. W. F. Panton.
Lt.-Col. W. M. Tickler, M.C.

1/6TH BATTALION MANCHESTER REGT.

Lt.-Col. G. G. P. Heywood.
Lt.-Col. C. R. Pilkington, C.M.G.

Lt.-Col. C. S. Worthington, D.S.O., T.D.
Lt.-Col. G. H. Wedgwood, D.S.O.

Lt.-Col. T. Blatherwick, D.S.O., M.C.

1/7TH BATTALION MANCHESTER REGT.

Lt.-Col. H. E. Gresham, T.D.
Major J. Staveacre.
Major P. H. Creagh, D.S.O.
Lt.-Col. A. Canning, C.M.G.
Lt.-Col. A. E. Cronshaw, D.S.O., T.D.
Bt. Lt.-Col. H. A. Carr, D.S.O.
Bt. Lt.-Col. W. T. Bromfield.
Bt. Lt.-Col. E. V. Manger.

1/8TH BATTALION MANCHESTER REGT.

Lt.-Col. W. G. Heys, T.D.
Lt.-Col. F. I. Bentley, T.D.
Lt.-Col. A. E. F. Fawcus, D.S.O., M.C.
Lt.-Col. D. F. McCarthy Morrogh, C.M.G.
Lt.-Col. J. H. Allen.
Lt.-Col. H. M. Stephenson, T.D.
Lt.-Col. C. S. Worthington, D.S.O., T.D.
Lt.-Col. H. T. Dobbin, D.S.O.
Lt.-Col. E. G. K. Cross, D.S.O.
Lt.-Col. H. S. Bowen.
Lt.-Col. A. V. Michaelis.
Lt.-Col. W. F. Panton.
Lt.-Col. F. E. Tetley, D.S.O.
Lt.-Col. A. Hodge, D.S.O., M.C.

1/7TH BATTALION NORTHUMBERLAND FUSILIERS (PIONEER BATTALION).

Lt.-Col. H. Liddell, D.S.O., M.C.

ROYAL ARMY SERVICE CORPS

Lt.-Col. J. G. Needham, D.S.O.
Lt.-Col. J. Coulson, D.S.O.

ROYAL ARMY MEDICAL CORPS

1/1ST FIELD AMBULANCE.

Lt.-Col. H. G. Parker.
Lt.-Col. W. L. Bentley.
Lt.-Col. A. Callam, D.S.O.

1/2ND FIELD AMBULANCE.

Lt.-Col. W. B. Pritchard.
Lt.-Col. W. L. Bentley.
Lt.-Col. W. R. Matthews, D.S.O.
Lt.-Col. W. F. Munro, M.C.

1/3RD FIELD AMBULANCE.

Lt.-Col. W. Howorth.
Lt.-Col. E. H. Cox, D.S.O.
Lt.-Col. H. H. B. Cunningham.

www.ingramcontent.com/pod-product-compliance
Ingram Content Group UK Ltd.
Pitfield, Milton Keynes, MK11 3LW, UK
UKHW020247240426
12048UKWH00027B/1651